MASS VIOLENCE IN
NAZI-OCCUPIED EUROPE

MASS VIOLENCE IN NAZI-OCCUPIED EUROPE

Alex J. Kay and David Stahel

Indiana University Press

This book is a publication of

Indiana University Press
Office of Scholarly Publishing
Herman B Wells Library 350
1320 East 10th Street
Bloomington, Indiana 47405 USA

iupress.indiana.edu

© 2018 by Indiana University Press
All rights reserved

No part of this book may be reproduced or utilized in any form or by any means, electronic or mechanical, including photocopying and recording, or by any information storage and retrieval system, without permission in writing from the publisher.

The paper used in this publication meets the minimum requirements of the American National Standard for Information Sciences—Permanence of Paper for Printed Library Materials, ANSI Z39.48-1992.

Manufactured in the United States of America

Library of Congress Cataloging-in-Publication Data

Names: Kay, Alex J., editor. | Stahel, David, editor.
Title: Mass violence in Nazi-occupied Europe / Alex J. Kay and David Stahel.
Description: Bloomington : Indiana University Press, [2018] | Includes bibliographical references and index.
Identifiers: LCCN 2018015120 (print) | LCCN 2018019404 (ebook) | ISBN 9780253036841 (e-book) | ISBN 9780253036803 (hardback : alk. paper) | ISBN 9780253036810 (pbk. : alk. paper)
Subjects: LCSH: World War, 1939–1945—Atrocities. | Violence—Europe—History—20th century. | Europe—History—20th century.
Classification: LCC D804.G4 (ebook) | LCC D804.G4 M354 2018 (print) | DDC 940.53/37—dc23
LC record available at https://lccn.loc.gov/2018015120

1 2 3 4 5   22 21 20 19 18

Contents

Introduction: Understanding Nazi Mass Violence   1
Alex J. Kay and David Stahel

Part I. Holocaust   15

1. Hitler's Generals in the East and the Holocaust   17
Johannes Hürter

2. Jews Sent into the Occupied Soviet Territories for Labor Deployment, 1942–1943   41
Martin Dean

3. Were the Jews of North Africa Included in the Practical Planning for the "Final Solution of the Jewish Question"?   59
Dan Michman

Part II. Sinti and Roma   79

4. "The Definitive Solution to the Gypsy Question": The Pan-European Genocide of the European Roma   81
Wolfgang Wippermann

5. Deadly Odyssey: East Prussian Sinti in Białystok, Brest-Litovsk and Auschwitz-Birkenau   94
Martin Holler

Part III. "Useless Eaters"   121

6. Soviet Prisoners of War in SS Concentration Camps: Current Knowledge and Research Desiderata   123
Reinhard Otto and Rolf Keller

7. The Murder of Psychiatric Patients by the SS and the Wehrmacht in Poland and the Soviet Union, Especially in Mogilev, 1939–1945   147
Ulrike Winkler and Gerrit Hohendorf

Part IV. Wehrmacht 171

8 Reconceiving Criminality in the German Army on the
   Eastern Front, 1941–1942 173
   Alex J. Kay and David Stahel

9 Bodily Conquest: Sexual Violence in the Nazi East
   Waitman Wade Beorn 195

Part V. Memorialization 217

10 The Holocaust in the Occupied USSR and Its Memorialization
    in Contemporary Russia 219
    Il'ya Al'tman

11 The Baltic Movement to Obfuscate the Holocaust 235
    Dovid Katz

Part VI. History as Comparison 263

12 Comparing Soviet and Nazi Mass Crimes 265
    Hans-Heinrich Nolte

   Selected Bibliography 293
   Index 301

MASS VIOLENCE IN NAZI-OCCUPIED EUROPE

Introduction: Understanding Nazi Mass Violence

Alex J. Kay and David Stahel

AFTER MORE THAN seventy years since the collapse of the Nazi regime in Germany and the end of World War II in Europe, debates continue to rage, both in scholarly and more popular forums, regarding the extent, scope, context, and uniqueness of Nazi mass violence. Important and innovative recent works have taken a closer look at the relationship between the German conduct of the war in the years 1939 to 1945 and the unleashing of extreme mass violence by the National Socialist regime during this period, especially the key role played by food policy, supply, and shortages.[1] However, research on the most systematic and comprehensive of the Nazi murder campaigns, the Holocaust, continues to be carried out in isolation from research on the other strands of Nazi mass killing. The genocide of European Jewry was indeed unique in many ways, but it was nonetheless one part of a larger whole in the context of the war. A comprehensive, integrative history of Nazi mass killing, addressing not only the Holocaust but also the murder of psychiatric patients, the elimination of the Polish intelligentsia, the starvation of captured Red Army soldiers and the Soviet urban population, the genocide of the Roma, and the brutal antipartisan operations, however, is yet to be written.[2] This volume is not designed to fill that gap, but rather to provide an impetus for future research.

A recent trend among scholars is the use of the concept of "mass violence," rather than "genocide," "ethnic cleansing," or "mass crimes," as an approach that is independent of legal or political implications.[3] The term "mass violence" also allows for the analytical inclusion of acts that extend beyond the actual killing of a single victim group. In line with this thinking, the present volume also encourages a broader and more inclusive approach to addressing Nazi atrocities by focusing on widespread phenomena such as sexual violence, food depravation, or forced labor alongside examples of direct mass killing. It presents new research and analysis by scholars from Germany, Russia, Israel, the United States, the United Kingdom, and Australia. This research and analysis is broken down into four areas of mass violence in German-occupied Europe: the Holocaust, the persecution of the Sinti and Roma, the eradication of so-called "useless eaters," and the crimes of the Wehrmacht. Complementing these thematic units are two further segments focusing on the memorialization of the German occupation in Eastern Europe and on the usefulness of a comparative approach in analyzing Nazi mass killing, respectively.

Within this framework, individual chapters in the volume address not only instances of direct, mass killing but also widen the focus to include acts such as forced labor, deportations, imprisonment in camps, systematic plunder, or sexual enslavement, all of which constituted forms of mass violence in German-occupied Europe. The majority of the chapters focus on events in Eastern Europe, above all the occupied Soviet territories, because it was first and foremost here that German rule was saturated in violence, causing horrendous suffering on an unprecedented scale.[4] According to the American historian Peter Fritzsche, in the first six months of Operation Barbarossa, the invasion of the Soviet Union, German forces wiped out one in every five hundred people on the planet.[5] All components of the Nazi complex of mass violence were present in the occupied Soviet territories. Even away from the front line, in cities such as Minsk or Kiev, the everyday violence of German rule soon established itself around a daily routine—a normalization—in which almost nothing was questioned, even as Nazi policy descended into open genocide.[6]

* * *

The last thirty years have seen the Holocaust—the topic of the first thematic unit of this volume, comprising three chapters—become established not only as a subject of research within scholarship on Nazi Germany but also within the wider field of genocide studies.[7] The sixteen-volume source edition *Die Verfolgung und Ermordung der europäischen Juden durch das nationalsozialistische Deutschland 1933–1945* (VEJ) and its English-language pendant *The Persecution and Murder of the European Jews by Nazi Germany, 1933–1945* (PMJ) is—incredibly for an enterprise aimed only at compilation and dissemination rather than analysis and (re)interpretation[8]—the largest single project in the humanities to be funded by the German Research Foundation (*Deutsche Forschungsgemeinschaft*, or DFG), itself Europe's largest research-sponsoring organization. Eleven of the German-language volumes have so far been published and the first three English-language volumes are in production.[9]

Of course, even such large-scale source collections by no means constitute an end to the study of the Holocaust. Indeed, the provision of documents is ongoing and not yet complete. As recently as 2013, the diary of Alfred Rosenberg, the Reich Minister for the Occupied Eastern Territories between 1941 and 1944, was discovered in upstate New York,[10] while in August 2015, some 6,300 documents relating to the Holocaust in Hungary were found behind a wall in an apartment in Budapest.[11] The most important recent discovery, however, was Heinrich Himmler's appointments diary for the years 1938, 1943, and 1944. Unearthed in 2013 at the Central Archives of the Russian Ministry of Defense in Podolsk, near Moscow, it contains over a thousand pages detailing Himmler's daily movements, appointments, and even personal commentaries.[12] Nor was this the only recent discovery from the head of the *Schutzstaffel* (SS). A year later, a collection of Himmler's private letters, along with personal documents and previously unknown photographs were acquired and authenticated from a private citizen and Holocaust survivor in Israel.[13]

The continued discovery of important primary material allows us to enhance the already advanced study of the Holocaust and fill in some of the extant gaps in our knowledge. In light of how sophisticated and differentiated Holocaust research has become, it may come as a surprise that, in contrast to Poland, the Netherlands, or the United States, a professorship for the study of the Holocaust has only very recently been set up for the first time at a German university. The country's first ever professorship for Holocaust studies was inaugurated at Frankfurt's Goethe University in May 2017. While the country has multiple academic programs and researchers focusing on the Nazi genocide of the Jewish people, the new chair is the first long-term professorship with a specific focus on the repercussions that have followed the Holocaust through to the present day.[14]

An illustration of both the depths of Nazi criminality and the infancy of research even seventy years after the war is provided by the findings of the United States Holocaust Memorial Museum's ongoing project to document centers of Nazi persecution across Europe. At the time of writing, just three of the projected seven volumes (planned for completion by 2025) have appeared,[15] but the scale of their findings is shocking. An estimated fifteen to twenty million people died or were imprisoned in these sites, which included ghettos, slave labor enterprises, transit camps, concentration camps, and purpose-built killing centers like Auschwitz-Birkenau. When the research began in 2000, the research team, headed by Geoffrey P. Megargee, expected to locate and document some 7,000 sites based on postwar estimates. Yet, as the research continued, this number grew first to 11,500, then 20,000, then 30,000, and finally surpassed 40,000 to reach the current total of 42,500 sites. As coresearcher Martin Dean has observed, the findings leave no doubt that ordinary German citizens, who after the war maintained their ignorance about Nazi centers of persecution, must have known of their existence. As Dean told *The New York Times*: "You literally could not go anywhere in Germany without running into forced labor camps, POW camps, concentration camps. They were everywhere."[16]

Within this unprecedented network of sites for exploitation and murder, the fate of Central and Eastern European Jews sent as forced laborers further to the East and the relationship between their exploitation as a labor force and their subsequent annihilation is an aspect of the Holocaust that remains thoroughly underresearched, and it is the subject of the chapter written by Martin Dean (chap. 2). The same applies to the Nazi regime's plans for Jews in North Africa and the Middle East, although the latter ultimately remained out of reach for German troops. This topic is addressed by Dan Michman (chap. 3) in his contribution to the volume.

Another central aspect of the Holocaust requiring further research is the part played by the Wehrmacht in the persecution and murder of the European Jews. As British historian Sir Ian Kershaw rightly pointed out many years ago, the Holocaust would not have been possible without the military victories and stubborn resistance of the Wehrmacht. This, however, is only half the story. In fact, it has long been known that numerous regular German Army units actively participated in the mass shootings against Jews in the Soviet Union and in Serbia, either by providing shooters to the SS commandos or by carrying out massacres on their own initiative.[17] This is the subject of Johannes Hürter's chapter in this volume (chap. 1). In spite of this, no historian has yet assumed the task of producing a comprehensive study in German or English focusing specifically on the role of the Wehrmacht in the Holocaust. Only two of the more than sixty contributions to the volume *Die Wehrmacht: Mythos und Realität*, published in 1999, nominally addressed the genocide of Europe's Jews, and even one of those was not actually about the Wehrmacht.[18] The volume was commissioned by the Military History Research Office of the Bundeswehr, the German armed forces, which took a more balanced approach to the Holocaust in its own monumental thirteen-volume work *Das Deutsche Reich und der Zweite Weltkrieg*, a military history of Germany during World War II published between 1979 and 2008.[19]

* * *

What of the non-Jewish victims of Nazi mass violence? The second thematic unit in this volume comprises two chapters on the genocide of Europe's Sinti and Roma. Recognition of the persecution and murder for ethnic reasons of the European Sinti and Roma and the granting of compensation are still awaited by the survivors of this genocide and their descendants. To this day, German authorities refuse to sign a restitution agreement with the Sinti and Roma. In terms of historical research on the subject, several overviews and detailed case studies have appeared in the last few years,[20] but there is still much work to be done. Wolfgang Wippermann (chap. 4) demonstrates in his contribution to the volume that the genocide of the Sinti and Roma—not unlike the Holocaust—was a project that took place across the length and breadth of Europe with considerable assistance provided by the administrations of those states occupied by and allied with Nazi Germany. In his chapter, Martin Holler (chap. 5) provides a case study of the fate of the deported East Prussian Sinti in Białystok, Brest-Litovsk, and Auschwitz-Birkenau.

The volume's third thematic block addresses victims of German occupation policies who were classified in Nazi terminology as "useless eaters" (*unnütze Esser*): Soviet prisoners of war (POWs) and psychiatric patients in Central and

Eastern Europe. Recent English-language studies have once again demonstrated how central extreme violence on a mass scale was to that most symbolic of Nazi institutions of terror and persecution: the concentration camp.[21] As the German historian Nikolaus Wachsmann notes: "SS men saw violence as their birthright.... At the center of their lives stood violence."[22] Not unlike the setting of the concentration camps, Soviet POWs and psychiatric patients found themselves completely and utterly at the mercy of their captors: the one group behind barbed wire, the other within the walls of mental asylums. After the European Jews, the Soviet POWs constituted the largest group of victims of Nazi Germany. It took a long, long time, but in May 2015, seventy years after the end of the war in Europe, the Bundestag, the German parliament, resolved to pay a total of ten million euros in compensation to an estimated 4,000 surviving former Soviet POWs for their suffering at the hands of Nazi Germany. Each survivor is due to receive the largely symbolic sum of 2,500 euros.[23]

In his expert report to the Bundestag, the doyen of research into the treatment of Red Army soldiers in German captivity, Christian Streit, rightly likened the fate of Soviet POWs to Jewish concentration camp inmates: "The fate of the Soviet prisoners of war differs fundamentally from that of all other prisoners of war. It exhibits decisively more similarities to that of the concentration camp inmates, and here also more to that of the Jewish than that of the other concentration camp inmates."[24] The similarity between the fate and treatment of the Soviet POWs and that of the Jewish concentration camp inmates goes even further, however. As Reinhard Otto and Rolf Keller (chap. 6) demonstrate in their chapter, more than one hundred thousand Soviet POWs spent time in German concentration camps. In spite of this, the release of Soviet POWs to the Gestapo and the SS and their transfer to concentration camps remain one of the most neglected aspects of this topic.

Like the genocide of Europe's Sinti and Roma, the systematic murder in the first two years of the war of over 70,000 mentally and physically disabled people on the territory of the German Reich and the expansion of this killing program to the psychiatric institutions of the occupied regions of Eastern Europe remains an oft-overlooked topic of study. The different strands of this murder campaign spanned the entire period of the war and the total number of victims is put at around three hundred thousand.[25] In their contribution to the volume, Ulrike Winkler and Gerrit Hohendorf (chap. 7) provide an overview of the murder of psychiatric patients by the SS and Wehrmacht in Poland and the Soviet Union, with particular emphasis on the eastern Belarusian city of Mogilev.

* * *

The two chapters comprising the fourth main thematic block in this volume focus on less commonly addressed Wehrmacht atrocities. Despite the fact that it has been over twenty years since the Hamburg Institute of Social Research (*Hamburger Institut für Sozialforschung*) produced its groundbreaking and controversial exhibition on the Wehrmacht, a consensus has yet to be reached on the extent of complicity in Nazi crimes among the mass of the regular German soldiers, with prominent and respected historians on both sides of the debate.[26] This ongoing controversy is in large part down to the fact that the Wehrmacht as an institution constituted a cross section of the German male population. Thus, a criminalization of the Wehrmacht would amount to a criminalization of German society at the time, or at least its male members, in its entirety. Of the up to eighteen million men who served in the Wehrmacht during World War II, ten million were deployed at one time or another between 1941 and 1944 in the conflict against the Soviet Union, a theater of widespread and sustained mass violence.[27] In order to answer the question as to how extensive this complicity was, it is necessary first of all to define what constitutes a criminal undertaking. The sheer brutality of the German conduct of war and occupation in the Soviet Union has overshadowed many activities that would otherwise be (rightly) held up as criminal acts, as Alex J. Kay and David Stahel (chap. 8) argue in their chapter.

One important development of recent years is the publication of research on the involvement of the Wehrmacht and other occupation forces in sexual crimes against the occupied peoples, which has long been an overlooked topic in both the mass media and scholarly research, and is the subject of Waitman Wade Beorn's contribution (chap. 9). This applies not only to the rape, torture, and sexual enslavement of Soviet women by regular German troops and members of the SS,[28] which were widespread phenomena, but also the perpetration of sexual assaults on male members of the civilian population and the prosecution of such acts, or lack thereof, by the German authorities.[29]

* * *

The four thematic units are followed by two chapters about the remembrance and commemoration of the German occupation of the former Soviet Union. The way in which the Nazi (and Soviet) past is not only commemorated but also perceived in Eastern Europe, the site of most of the mass killing in the years 1939 to 1945, is very different to the view from Western Europe. The exploitation of recent history for the purposes of nation-building and the construction of a cohesive national identity not only in Russia, Ukraine, Belarus, and the Baltics, but also further west in Germany itself, demonstrates that the Nazi past remains very present, and hotly contested, throughout Europe. Here one sees a worrying trend toward obfuscating criminality and appropriating history for political gain. It was only in 2015 that the Ministry of Education in the Yekaterinburg region of Russia ordered the withdrawal of Antony Beevor's books from schools and colleges. The British author was accused of "promoting stereotypes formed during the Third

Reich" and advancing the "propaganda myth" of Joseph Goebbels that Red Army soldiers committed mass rapes of German women.[30] Government attempts to deny past criminality are nothing new, as the case of Turkey's Armenian genocide attests. Yet Russia's new law to criminalize anybody who defames the Red Army in World War II, which the Minister of Defense, Sergei Shoigu, calls "tantamount to Holocaust denial," has been backed with penalties of up to five years' imprisonment.[31] This kind of authoritarian, state-approved regulation of the World War II narrative does not allow for debate or opposition, which not only evades the topic of Soviet criminality, but, in seeking to avoid evidence of widespread Soviet collaboration, ironically hinders investigation into Nazi criminality as well. This is the subject of the contribution by Il'ya Al'tman (chap. 10) to the present volume.

Nor is it Russia alone. The new Ukrainian government has likewise sought to appropriate history for the purpose of a new national ideology and in doing so has, at the stroke of a pen, erased criminality from the national record. One of its laws condemns "the Communist and Nazi totalitarian regimes in Ukraine and bans propaganda of their symbols." In reality, however, the law focuses on the Soviet era. As German historian Jochen Hellbeck has observed, "All that it [the Ukrainian law] has to say about Nazism is that its racial theories drove certain groups out of their professions. It makes no mention of the mass murder of Jews, let alone the participation of Ukrainians in these atrocities."[32] Clearly, national narratives of twentieth-century history in individual Eastern European nations are very different to the dominant Western European story, but it is the nature of that difference that is most worrying. Reconceiving what constitutes criminality is clearly as much a tool of the past as it is of the present, and given that Nazi criminality pervaded most of the countries of Europe with its own local collaborators and perpetrators, the East-West divide in accepting those realities makes it much more than simply German history. In many ways, therefore, Eastern Europe's struggle with its own criminal past (both Nazi and Soviet) is best summed up as a battle for history in which truth is malleable.

Germany's far right-wing PEGIDA (*Patriotische Europäer gegen die Islamisierung des Abendlandes*) movement,[33] on the other hand, as well as innumerable past Western European political movements such as those of Jörg Haider in Austria and Jean-Marie Le Pen in France, would suggest that the danger of obfuscating criminality, albeit much less successfully, exists on both sides of the continent. The devastation, shock, and horror resulting from Hitler's short-lived regime is still frequently misunderstood and even misappropriated for nefarious motives. In 2015 and 2016, the Nazi-era terms *Lügenpresse* (lying press) and *Volksverräter* (traitor of the people) were named nonwords of the year by German linguists.[34] Such expressions have reemerged into the public discourse thanks to the growing support for the anti-immigrant rallies run by PEGIDA. More serious, however, is the popular embrace of rhetoric evoking a distinct call for a close-knit, ethnically, and nationally homogenous *Volksgemeinschaft* (ethnic community) that, as PEGIDA slogans extol, retains "Germany for the Germans!" The parallels with Germany's National Socialist past are not lost on either side of the political divide, but it is PEGIDA's appropriation of Nazi history without reference to, or concern for, its ubiquitous criminality that should concern us.

It is precisely this flagrant and unscrupulous twisting of the Nazi legacy that has made the 2016 expiry of copyright on Adolf Hitler's *Mein Kampf* a source of great concern to the German historical community and has led to the Institute of Contemporary History in Munich issuing a new "critical" edition.[35] This exhaustively annotated, almost two-thousand-page book seeks to counter the numerous fabrications, inaccuracies, and outright falsehoods of the original text. Clearly, as British historian Neil Gregor has concluded: "*Mein Kampf* still provokes fear. That fear is shaped by memories that define German political culture, and what it means to move through the world as a German, to this day." For that reason, however, and especially in such a politically volatile climate, Gregor is right to observe that *Mein Kampf* must be treated "not only as an intervention in the politics of its own time, but as a potential intervention in ours," too.[36] Uniting Hitler's legacy and the National Socialist state with its criminal past is at the heart of this work, not simply for historical posterity but to counter the troubling manipulation of this past for newfound political purposes.

The challenges facing the European Union's goal of a common foreign policy and a sense of European identity and values cannot therefore be separated from this battle for history. Poland's new hard-line Eurosceptic government freely evokes Nazi imagery to portray a tyrannical German-dominated EU seeking to "occupy" Poland yet again because the EU challenges Polish attempts to control the state's own constitutional court, civil service, and public radio and television.[37] The current Hungarian government is no better, with its own scandalous forays into neo-Nazi rhetoric.[38] Even the more moderate governments of the Baltic States, seemingly among the most pro-Western members of the EU and NATO's experiments in eastern expansion, are proving incapable, or unwilling, to deal with their criminal Nazi past, as demonstrated by Dovid Katz (chap. 11) in his contribution to the volume. Thus, while European integration in a commercial, financial, and to some extent political respect may have progressed at a rapid pace over the last two decades or so, not least with the accession to the European Union and NATO of former Eastern Bloc states such as Estonia, Latvia, Lithuania, Poland, and Romania, the very different historical experiences and memories mean that a common sense of European identity remains out of reach.[39]

While Eastern European governments struggle with their Nazi past, the recent upsurge of populism in the West has seen remarkable levels of support for patently misrepresented concepts of Nazism. A month before Britain's 2016 vote in favor of leaving the European Union, Boris Johnson, who helped head the "leave" campaign, compared the EU to Hitler's drive for European hegemony and even claimed: "The EU is an attempt to do this by different methods."[40] In the 2017 French Presidential race, Jean-François Jalkh, the replacement for Marine Le Pen as acting leader of the Front National, stepped down after evidence suggested that he had called into question Nazi Germany's use of gas chambers in the Holocaust. In the first weeks of US President Donald Trump's administration, a scandal erupted over why the White House omitted any explicit mention of "Jews" from a State Department brief commemorating victims of the Holocaust.[41] Less overt, but no less sinister, the social media platform Facebook has been shown to have avoided removing Holocaust denial material in most of the countries where it is illegal. A leaked company document stated that it did "not welcome local law that stands as an obstacle to an open and connected world," meaning that moderators would only block Holocaust denial material if "we face the risk of getting blocked in a country or a legal risk."[42] Clearly, Eastern Europeans are not the only ones struggling to place Hitler and the Holocaust into an appropriate historical context, but it is the high political level at which these scandals are taking place that is different from past decades and the increasing acceptability of alt-right "alternative historical narratives."

When Vladimir Putin lectures Russian historians before the media, rhetorically asking them why the Nazi-Soviet Pact of August 1939 is condemned, before brazenly suggesting it was in fact an indication of the Soviet state's desire for peace, the lines drawn in the battle for history are clearly a chasm apart.[43] It was into this emergent East-West breach that the American historian Timothy Snyder injected his elegant synthesis of scholarly investigation entitled *Bloodlands: Europe between Stalin and Hitler*, which has contributed with extraordinary impact to reigniting the debate over the legitimacy and value of comparing Nazi and Soviet mass violence.[44] While some historical events and processes might indeed be unique, comparison remains one of the historian's most helpful tools of analysis, as argued by Hans-Heinrich Nolte in chapter 12, which bookends the volume.

Now, more than ever, over seventy years after the end of World War II and in view of the imminent passing of the last of the survivor generation, the new (and old) debates, as well as the intensification of discord over conflicting national narratives, necessitate an integrative, comprehensive history of mass violence and mass killing in Nazi-occupied Europe.

ALEX J. KAY is Visiting Lecturer at the University of Potsdam and Fellow of the Royal Historical Society. From 2014 to 2016, he was Senior Academic Project Coordinator at the Institute of Contemporary History Munich–Berlin. He is the author of *Exploitation, Resettlement, Mass Murder: Political and Economic Planning for German Occupation Policy in the Soviet Union, 1940–1941* (2006) and

The Making of an SS Killer: The Life of Colonel Alfred Filbert, 1905–1990 (2016, German ed. 2017), and co-editor of *Nazi Policy on the Eastern Front, 1941: Total War, Genocide, and Radicalization* (2012).

DAVID STAHEL is Senior Lecturer at the University of New South Wales, Canberra, Australia. His publications include *Operation Barbarossa and Germany's Defeat in the East* (2009), *Kiev 1941* (2012), *Operation Typhoon* (2013), and *The Battle for Moscow* (2015). His most recent book was shortlisted for the British Army Military Book of the Year (2016).

Notes

1. See Christoph Dieckmann and Babette Quinkert, eds., *Kriegführung und Hunger 1939–1945. Zum Verhältnis von militärischen, wirtschaftlichen und politischen Interessen* (Göttingen: Wallstein, 2015), especially the introduction: Christoph Dieckmann and Babette Quinkert, "'Kriegsnotwendigkeiten' und die Eskalation der deutschen Massengewalt im totalen Krieg. Einführende Bemerkungen," 9–32.

2. A comparatively short overview in German is provided by Dieter Pohl, *Verfolgung und Massenmord in der NS-Zeit 1933–1945*, 3rd rev. ed. (Darmstadt: Wissenschaftliche Buchgesellschaft, [2003] 2010). Christian Gerlach, *The Extermination of the European Jews* (Cambridge: Cambridge University Press, 2016) places the Holocaust within the broader context of Nazi violence against other victim groups. Alex J. Kay is under contract with Yale University Press to write a history of Nazi mass killing.

3. See Christian Gerlach, *Extremely Violent Societies: Mass Violence in the Twentieth-Century World* (Cambridge: Cambridge University Press, 2010), esp. 1–9; Dieckmann and Quinkert, eds., "'Kriegsnotwendigkeiten'," 9; Tobias Hof, ed., *Empire, Ideology, Mass Violence: The Long 20th Century in Comparative Perspective* (Munich: Herbert Utz, 2016).

4. See especially Alex J. Kay, Jeff Rutherford, and David Stahel, eds., *Nazi Policy on the Eastern Front, 1941: Total War, Genocide, and Radicalization* (Rochester, NY: University of Rochester Press, 2012); Dieter Pohl, *Die Herrschaft der Wehrmacht. Deutsche Militärbesatzung und einheimische Bevölkerung in der Sowjetunion 1941–1944* (Munich: Oldenbourg, 2008).

5. Peter Fritzsche, *Life and Death in the Third Reich* (Cambridge, MA: Harvard University Press, 2008), p. 186.

6. Stephan Lehnstaedt, "The Minsk Experience: German Occupiers and Everyday Life in the Capital of Belarus," in *Nazi Policy on the Eastern Front, 1941: Total War, Genocide, and Radicalization*, ed. Alex J. Kay, Jeff Rutherford, and David Stahel (Rochester, NY: University of Rochester Press, 2012), 240–266; Alexander Prusin, "A Community of Violence: The SiPo/SD and its Role in the Nazi Terror System in Generalbezirk Kiew," *Holocaust and Genocide Studies* 21, no. 1 (spring 2007): 1–30.

7. See, for example, the international peer-reviewed journal *Holocaust and Genocide Studies*, published since 1987 in association with the United States Holocaust Memorial Museum.

8. Dieter Pohl, "Die Verfolgung und Ermordung der europäischen Juden durch das nationalsozialistische Deutschland 1933–1945. Ein neues Editionsprojekt," *Vierteljahrshefte für Zeitgeschichte* 53, no. 4 (October 2005): 651–659, here 653–654; Wolf Gruner, *Die Verfolgung und Ermordung der europäischen Juden durch das nationalsozialistische Deutschland 1933–1945*, vol. 1: *Deutsches Reich 1933–1937* (Munich: Oldenbourg, 2008), 6–7.

9. See Pohl, "Die Verfolgung und Ermordung"; Moshe Zimmermann, "Stationen kumulativer Radikalisierung. Das Editionsprojekt 'Die Verfolgung und Ermordung der europäischen Juden durch das nationalsozialistische Deutschland'," *Neue Politische Literatur* 59 (2014): 10–22.

10. Jürgen Matthäus and Frank Bajohr, eds., *Alfred Rosenberg: Die Tagebücher von 1934 bis 1944* (Munich: S. Fisher, 2015). On the discovery of the diary see: "The Alfred Rosenberg Diary," http://www.ushmm.org/information/exhibitions/online-features/special-focus/the-alfred-rosenberg-diary (last accessed on August 10, 2016).

11. "Nazi Holocaust Documents Found: 6,300 Files Discovered behind Wall of Budapest Apartment," *The Telegraph*, November 21, 2015.

12. Heike Mund, "Reiseziel KZ—Himmlers Dienstkalender veröffentlicht," *Deutsche Welle*, August 6, 2016, http://www.dw.com/de/reiseziel-kz-himmlers-dienstkalender-ver%C3%B6ffentlicht/a-19447590 (last accessed on September 1, 2016); David Carter, "The Lost Diaries of Heinrich Himmler Record Banality and Evil," *The Australian*, August 2, 2016.

13. "Insight into the Orderly World of a Mass Murderer," *WeltN24*, January 25, 2014, http://www.welt.de/geschichte/himmler/article124223862/Insight-into-the-orderly-world-of-a-mass-murderer.html (last accessed on August 10, 2016).

14. "Goethe-Universität Frankfurt: Eine Professorin nur für Holocaust-Forschung," *Der Tagesspiegel*, May 17, 2017; "Germany to Establish Its First Professorship Dedicated to Holocaust Study," *Haaretz*, July 25, 2015.

15. Geoffrey P. Megargee, ed., *The United States Holocaust Memorial Museum Encyclopedia of Camps and Ghettos, 1933–1945*, vol. I: *Early Camps, Youth Camps, and Concentration Camps and Subcamps under the SS-Business Administration Main Office (WVHA)* (Bloomington: Indiana University Press, 2009); Geoffrey P. Megargee and Martin Dean, eds., *The United States Holocaust Memorial Museum Encyclopedia of Camps and Ghettos, 1933–1945*, vol. II: *Ghettos in German-Occupied Eastern Europe* (Bloomington: Indiana University Press, 2012).

16. Eric Lichtblau, "The Holocaust Just Got More Shocking," *New York Times*, Sunday Review, March 1, 2013.

17. Pohl, *Die Herrschaft der Wehrmacht*, 265, 340, and 342; Jörn Hasenclever, *Wehrmacht und Besatzungspolitik. Die Befehlshaber der rückwärtigen Heeresgebiete 1941–1943* (Paderborn: Schöningh, 2010), 496–497, 501–502, 506–507, 519, and 553–554; Walter Manoschek, *"Serbien ist judenfrei": Militärische Besatzungspolitik und Judenvernichtung in Serbien 1941/42* (Munich: Oldenbourg, 1993).

18. Rolf-Dieter Müller and Hans-Erich Volkmann, eds., *Die Wehrmacht: Mythos und Realität* (Munich: Oldenbourg, 1999). The two chapters in question are written by Jürgen Förster and Peter Klein, respectively.

19. Militärgeschichtliches Forschungsamt, ed., *Das Deutsche Reich und der Zweite Weltkrieg*, 13 vols. (Stuttgart: Deutsche Verlags-Anstalt, 1979–2008); published in English translation as *Germany and the Second World War*, 13 vols. (Oxford: Clarendon Press, 1990).

20. Martin Luchterhand, *Der Weg nach Birkenau. Entstehung und Verlauf der nationalsozialistischen Verfolgung der "Zigeuner"* (Lübeck: Schmidt-Römhild, 2000); Martin Holler, *Der nationalsozialistische Völkermord an den Roma in der besetzten Sowjetunion (1941–1944)* (Heidelberg: Dokumentations- und Kulturzentrum Deutscher Sinti und Roma, 2009).

21. Nikolaus Wachsmann, *KL: A History of the Nazi Concentration Camps* (New York: Farrar, Straus & Giroux, 2015); Christopher Dillon, *Dachau and the SS: A Schooling in Violence* (Oxford: Oxford University Press, 2015).

22. Wachsmann, *KL*, 107 and 113.

23. "Sowjetische Kriegsgefangene erhalten Entschädigung," *Süddeutsche Zeitung*, May 20, 2015.

24. "Dr. Christian Streit, Stellungnahme zum Antrag BT-Drucksache 18/2694," https://www.bundestag.de/blob/374866/5143ffd463b882a99a97531ca44cbc33/dr--christian-streit-data.pdf (last accessed on August 10, 2016): *"Das Schicksal der sowjetischen Gefangenen unterscheidet sich fundamental von dem aller anderen Kriegsgefangenen. Es weist entschieden mehr Gemeinsamkeiten mit dem der KZ-Häftlinge auf, und auch da mehr mit dem der jüdischen als mit dem der anderen KZ-Häftlinge."*

25. Frank Schneider, "Psychiatrie im Nationalsozialismus: Gedenken und Verantwortung," in *erfasst, verfolgt, vernichtet. Kranke und behinderte Menschen im Nationalsozialismus / registered, persecuted, annihilated: The Sick and the Disabled under National Socialism*, ed. Frank Schneider and Petra Lutz (Berlin: Springer, 2014), 203–212, here 204.

26. For a recent example of scholars reaching strikingly different conclusions on the basis of largely the same source material see Felix Römer, *Kameraden. Die Wehrmacht von innen* (Munich: Piper, 2012); Sönke Neitzel and Harald Welzer, *Soldaten. Protokolle vom Kämpfen, Töten und Sterben* (Frankfurt am Main: S. Fischer, 2011).

27. Christian Hartmann, *Wehrmacht im Ostkrieg. Front und militärisches Hinterland 1941/42* (Munich: Oldenbourg, 2009), 12–13 and 16, fn. 29.

28. See especially Regina Mühlhäuser, *Eroberungen: Sexuelle Gewalttaten und intime Beziehungen deutscher Soldaten in der Sowjetunion 1941–1945* (Hamburg: Hamburger Edition, 2010); Birgit Beck, *Wehrmacht und sexuelle Gewalt. Sexualverbrechen vor deutschen Militärgerichten 1939–1945* (Paderborn: Fedinand Schöningh, 2004). In English see David Raub Snyder, *Sex Crimes under the Wehrmacht* (Lincoln: University of Nebraska Press, 2007); Regina Mühlhäuser, "Between 'Racial Awareness' and Fantasies of Potency: Nazi Sexual Politics in the Occupied Territories of the Soviet Union, 1942–1945," in *Brutality and Desire: War and Sexuality in Europe's Twentieth Century*, ed. Dagmar Herzog (London: Palgrave, 2009), 197–220; Birgit Beck, "Sexual Violence and its Prosecution by Courts Martial of the Wehrmacht," in *A World at Total War: Global Conflict and the Politics of Destruction, 1937–1945*, ed. Roger Chickering, Stig Förster, and Bernd Greiner (Cambridge: Cambridge University Press, 2005), 317–331.

29. See especially Michael Schwartz, ed., *Homosexuelle im Nationalsozialismus: Neue Forschungsperspektiven zu Lebenssituationen von lesbischen, schwulen, bi, trans und intersexuellen Menschen* (Munich: Oldenbourg, 2014); Burkhard Jellonek and Rüdiger Lautmann, eds., *Nationalsozialistischer Terror gegen Homosexuelle: Verdrängt und ungesühnt* (Paderborn: Fedinand Schöningh, 2002). In English see Günter Grau and Claudia Shoppmann, *The Hidden Holocaust? Gay and Lesbian Persecution in Germany 1933–1945* (New York: Routledge, 2012). Geoffrey J. Giles is preparing for publication a study on

homosexual behavior among the German occupation forces and the perpetration of homosexual violence against the Soviet civilian population.

30. Antony Beevor, "By Banning My Book, Russia is Deluding Itself about Its Past," *The Guardian*, August 6, 2015. The book in question is Antony Beevor, *Berlin: The Downfall 1945* (London: Viking, 2002).

31. Beevor, "By Banning My Book."

32. Jochen Hellbeck, "Ukraine Makes Amnesia the Law of the Land: Poroshenko Wants His Nation to Forget Its Role in Nazi atrocities," *The New Republic*, May 22, 2015.

33. Translated into English as the "Patriotic Europeans against the Islamisation of the West." PEGIDA was founded in Dresden in October 2014.

34. "Lying Press: Anti-Islam PEGIDA Slogan Chosen Nonword of the Year," *RT*, January 14, 2015, https://www.rt.com/news/222543-germany-pegida-slogan-nonword/ (last accessed on September 15, 2016); Shehab Khan, "Germany Chooses Nazi-linked Term as the Country's Non-word of 2016," *The Independent*, January 11, 2017.

35. Christian Hartmann, Othmar Plöckinger, Roman Töppel, and Thomas Vordermayer, eds., *Hitler, Mein Kampf: Eine kritische Edition* (Munich: Institut für Zeitgeschichte, 2016).

36. Neil Gregor, "*Mein Kampf: Eine Kritische Edition* Review—Taking the Sting out of Hitler's Hateful Book," *The Guardian*, August 10, 2016. Neil Gregor is the author of *How to Read Hitler* (Granta Books: London, 2014).

37. Jon Henley, "Polish Press Invokes Nazi Imagery as War of Words with EU Heats Up," *The Guardian*, January 13, 2016.

38. Cas Mudde, "The Hungary PM Made a 'Rivers of Blood' Speech … and No One Cares," *The Guardian*, July 20, 2015. See also: Paula Kennedy, "Row over Nazi History Consumes Hungary," *BBC News*, January 23, 2014, http://www.bbc.com/news/world-europe-25864058 (last accessed on August 10, 2016).

39. This is the focus of "United Europe—Divided Memory," one of the six research fields of the Institute for Human Sciences (*Institut für die Wissenschaften vom Menschen*) in Vienna: http://www.iwm.at/research/focus-iv-united-europe-divided-history/ (last accessed on August 10, 2016).

40. "EU Referendum: Boris Johnson stands by Hitler EU comparison," BBC.com, May 16, 2016, http://www.bbc.com/news/uk-politics-eu-referendum-36295208 (last accessed on June 2, 2017).

41. Jon Sharman, "Donald Trump's White House 'Blocked State Department Holocaust Memorial Statement That Mentioned Jews,'" *The Independent*, February 3, 2017.

42. "How Facebook Flouts Holocaust Denial Laws Except Where It Fears Being Sued," *The Guardian*, May 24, 2017.

43. According to a Kremlin transcript, Putin stated: "The Soviet Union signed a non-aggression treaty with Germany. People say: 'Ach, that's bad.' But what's bad about that if the Soviet Union didn't want to fight, what's bad about it?"; Tom Parfitt, "Vladimir Putin Says There Was Nothing Wrong with Soviet Union's Pact with Adolf Hitler's Nazi Germany," *The Telegraph*, November 6, 2014.

44. Timothy Snyder, *Bloodlands: Europe between Stalin and Hitler* (New York: Basic Books, 2010). See also "Forum: Timothy Snyder's *Bloodlands*," *Contemporary European History* 21, no. 2 (May 2012), and the discussion in chapter 12 in this volume.

Part I. Holocaust

1 Hitler's Generals in the East and the Holocaust

Johannes Hürter

From 1933 onward, the radical antisemitism of Adolf Hitler and his supporters was the state doctrine of the German Reich and led to the persecution and murder of those European Jews who fell within the German sphere of control. This doctrine penetrated all state institutions, including the Wehrmacht and its leadership. After the war, those responsible, outside of the Nazi Party and the *Schutzstaffel* (SS), claimed to have had nothing to do with these crimes. The initial depression and uncertainty in view of the impending tribunal was quickly overcome. Even during the Nuremberg Trial of the Major War Criminals in 1945–1946, the German functional elites regrouped in order to defend themselves against all valid accusations. Although they were deeply compromised, the elites succeeded, together with a broad front of political and journalistic supporters in an unprecedented act of historical and political manipulation, in establishing the power to interpret their Nazi past and in anchoring the myth of the "clean" ministerial bureaucracy and the "unsullied" Wehrmacht in the historical consciousness of the German Federal Republic.

The former generals of the Wehrmacht were particularly successful in shaping this myth.[1] In court and in countless memoirs and other publications, they claimed a strict separation of the good military aspects and the bad political aspects. They were helped in this by the fact that not only West German society but also the Western Allies had considerable interest in liberating the Wehrmacht from the stigma of their crimes. The generals were representing all German soldiers, if not the entire nation, which was rehabilitated in order to allow its integration into the Western defensive alliance. West German rearmament required the know-how of experienced professionals from Hitler's armed forces. Remembrance of the Wehrmacht was distorted to focus solely on military achievements. Responsibility for defeats and crimes was transferred to Hitler, the SS, and a very few black, or should one say brown, sheep among the generals, such as those who had been hanged in Nuremberg, namely the Wehrmacht generals Wilhelm Keitel and Alfred Jodl. In this exculpatory narrative, the highly professional military elite, which had remained "decent" to the last, and "our brave soldiers" were uncoupled from the policies of the Nazi regime and the crimes committed "in Germany's name." This was particularly so for the greatest crime of all, the Holocaust. A general like Erich von Manstein, who was highly regarded until his death in 1973 and for a long time thereafter, succeeded in making the grateful German public and his numerous Anglo-Saxon admirers believe that in 1941–1942 he had known nothing about the murder of around thirty thousand Jews under his jurisdiction on the Crimean Peninsula, let alone shared any kind of responsibility for this mass murder.[2]

The position of the generals within the Nazi system of rule had, in reality, nothing in common with the retrospective construction of an unblemished foreign body.[3] The military elite was the most important and most influential of the traditional elites who supported the National Socialist regime. These men were initiated at an early stage into Hitler's radical plans and played a central role in the project of a "Greater German Reich," which could only be realized by means of war. The generals willingly allowed themselves to be harnessed by a regime that aimed with extreme militancy for a racially homogeneous "national community," hegemony in Europe, and "living space" in the east. They did this not only from opportunism, egotism, and a thirst for glory or other base motives but also because Hitler's policies were compatible with the thinking in power-political, militaristic, and racist categories that were prevalent in this elite. Even without being Nazis, the overwhelming majority of the generals placed their professional expertise to the last at the service of the Nazi dictatorship—the resistance of a few officers against Hitler was ultimately a completely isolated phenomenon among their comrades. The 3,191 generals and admirals of the Wehrmacht[4] thus contributed decisively to the successes and the resilience of Nazi tyranny. The catalog of involvement in the criminal policies is long and eclipses any crimes known to have been committed by the other traditional elites. The generals—namely the Wehrmacht leadership (High Command of the Wehrmacht, or OKW), the army leadership (High Command of the Army, or OKH), and the most senior troop command at the front—contributed significantly to the planning, preparation, and implementation of illegal wars of aggression, racial-ideological campaigns of annihilation, and brutal occupation regimes. Even in their professional core area, namely the operational conduct of the war, they were responsible for numerous mistakes with catastrophic results.

The Holocaust did not take place without the Wehrmacht, either. This is clear from the facts alone.[5] A central site of the Holocaust was the German-occupied Soviet Union. It was here that the systematic murder of all Jews began. Approximately 2.5 million Jews fell into the territory controlled by the Wehrmacht, even if a large part were there only for a short length of time. During the first wave of killings until March 1942, around six hundred thousand Jews were murdered in the occupied Soviet territories, of which at least 450,000 were in territory under military administration. The second wave of killings from April 1942 to October 1943, which claimed the lives of around 1.5 million people, targeted above all the ghettos in territory under civilian administration. By contrast, about fifty thousand Jews who were murdered in 1942 during the German offensive against Stalingrad and in the North Caucasus died in areas under military jurisdiction, as did the fifty thousand Jewish Red Army soldiers selected and murdered by the Security Police in the Wehrmacht's prisoner-of-war camps. To be added to this number are another 350,000 Jews who were murdered under Romanian occupation. Even if most of the more than 2.4 million victims claimed by the Holocaust in the occupied Soviet Union alone (within the borders of June 1941) were accounted for by the German SS and police apparatus, more than half a million of them died with the military's administration, acquiescence, and frequently also support—sometimes including actual participation in the killing. Outside of the Soviet Union, the Wehrmacht was also directly or indirectly involved in the Holocaust. In Serbia, Wehrmacht units murdered almost all Jewish men—close to six thousand—who were held as hostages during the course of perverse antipartisan campaigns. In other parts of German-occupied Europe, especially in the territories under military administration in France, Belgium, and Greece, Wehrmacht agencies supported the disenfranchisement and deportation of the Jewish populations.

* * *

The persecution and murder of the Jews in the territories under military administration would have been very difficult to implement *against* the will of the Wehrmacht and in particular the generals. The stance of the generals in the east regarding the "Jewish question" was, therefore, very important. How antisemitic were they?[6] Until World War I, the antisemitism in the Prussian-German officer corps did not differ significantly from that of the other conservative elites in Germany and many other European states. Reservations toward the Jews corresponded to the mood of the time and were fed by various forms of resentment: religious and cultural resentment directed at the Jewish religion and orthodox eastern Jewry, dissimilatory resentment directed against the emancipation and assimilation of the German Jews, and biological resentment directed against the Jewish race. At this point, it was still anti-Judaism and dissimilatory antisemitism that predominated rather than the newer racist hatred of Jews. The directive of the Prussian War Ministry from October 1916 to the effect that all Jewish soldiers be recorded statistically in order to examine whether Jews shirked army service disproportionately more often was a discriminatory measure and at the same time an alarming indication of antisemitic tendencies within the military.[7] Toward the end of World War I, these tendencies became more intense, fueled by the exhortations to hold out made by the Pan-German League, whose propaganda was directed ever more frequently against the Jewish influence among enemies at home and abroad.

Various forms of antisemitism merged and radicalized noticeably once again during the period of upheaval in 1918–1919. The military defeat, the revolution, and the change of system to a republic were blamed in particular on the Jews, who were cast back into their traditional role of scapegoat. The fighting against Spartacists in the Reich and Bolsheviks in the Baltic, whether experienced firsthand or not, also counted among the negative experiences of the military elite. "Jewish Bolshevism" became a code phrase for the collapse of monarchy and power, internal order, and military strength. Open antisemitism spread from the Pan-German League and the racial nationalists to the conservatives. The fact that the liberal Weimar Republic enabled many assimilated Jews to reach prominent positions in politics, society, the economy, and culture appeared to confirm the prejudice of a Jewish republic. Furthermore, serious conflicts were sparked off regarding the immigration of Polish "eastern Jews," who more clearly corresponded to the cliché of the "racially foreign" (*rassefremd*) Jew than the German Jews did. Just how popular antisemitism was among sections of the population before Hitler's assumption of power was first demonstrated not by the successes of his party from the end of the 1920s but by the anti-Jewish proclamations of conservative parties and associations such as the Young German Order, the Reich Agricultural League, and the German Nationalist People's Party; many officers sympathized with the latter. For all their differences in terms of their manifestations, the nationalist conservatives, the Pan-German League, the racial nationalists, and the National Socialists were linked by a fundamental antisemitic consensus. It was clear to only a very few that Hitler's ideology and politics would ultimately lead to the attempt to completely exterminate the Jews in the regions under German control. The partial identity of antisemitic thinking made it easier, however, to perhaps internally reject the further steps in the direction of the Holocaust and nonetheless to accept these steps again and again in practice.

Symptomatic for the anti-Jewish stereotypes within the nationalist conservative elite of the officer corps is the record kept by Gotthard Heinrici, who would later be among the "ordinary" generals and commanders on the eastern front. This officer complained as early as October 1918 that Germany was being governed by a "clique of Jews and Socialists."[8] During the Weimar years, he was close to the German Nationalists and hoped, following the change of government on January 30, 1933, "that we have finished with the Marxian Jewish pigsty."[9] He regarded the antisemitic stance and policies of Hitler's new government as fundamentally necessary, but in his view the pogrom-like excesses of the *Sturmabteilung* (SA) and the boycott of April 1, 1933 went too far: "It was necessary to force the Jews out of their influential positions. Yet the means were inappropriate."[10] Heinrici initially registered without criticism the countless discriminatory measures directed against Germans of the Jewish faith during the months and years that followed. It was not until the large pogrom of November 9–10, 1938, (*Reichskristallnacht* or the Night of Broken Glass) that he was shocked, though not very deeply. Shortly thereafter, he learned from a speech by Alfred Rosenberg in Detmold of the consequences and objectives that loomed as a result of the National Socialists' hatred of Jews: "For an hour he talked about the horrible Jews. The Jewish question, he said, would only be solved when there were no more Jews in Germany. They would do everything to accomplish that. Anyway, it would be best if there weren't any Jews left in the whole of Europe."[11] This perspective may have scared him, but the contemptuous racial policies did not prevent his increasingly positive stance toward the Nazi regime and his "Führer" over the next two years. When General Heinrici was transferred to Poland with his army corps in spring 1941, he was irritated in his quarters in Siedlce not only by the bedbugs and lice but also by the "awful Jews," which he mentioned in the same breath.[12] Despite his knowledge of National Socialist anti-Jewish policies, the antisemitism of this general was clearly unabated at the beginning of the campaign in the east.

Even if not all generals were so decidedly antisemitic, there is no evidence that the unmistakable disenfranchisement and persecution of the German Jews up to 1941 was a decisive factor in the generals' assessment of the Nazi regime. As a rule, their attitude toward the Jewish part of the population was no better than detached and indifferent. The widespread unease regarding the Night of Broken Glass was just as unsustained as Erich von Manstein's rare criticism of the application of the "Aryan Paragraph" in the Wehrmacht in spring 1934.[13] Not until the crimes committed in Poland from September 1939 onward did any incomprehension become more evident. During the Polish campaign and the first months of the occupation period until February 1940, several army generals opposed the murders, which targeted above all the Polish "intelligentsia" but also around seven thousand Jews by the end of 1939 alone.[14] One can argue about whether they intervened out of fundamental political and ethical considerations or only because they were concerned about the discipline and morale of their troops, who in some cases participated in the attacks on Jews. Nonetheless, the conduct of generals such as Blaskowitz, Küchler, Manstein, Reichenau, and Weichs remains remarkable. Although their antisemitic resentments were directed above all against the orthodox "caftan Jews,"[15] they disagreed with the abuse and murder of these Jews, who were regarded as "harmless." As these crimes in Poland took place under their jurisdiction, they felt—unlike during the pogroms of 1933 and 1938 in the Reich—obliged to intervene. At the same time, this intervention already marked the outermost boundary of dissent that the generals allowed themselves against National Socialist anti-Jewish policies.

* * *

Although the violence against the Jewish population in the occupied Soviet Union far exceeded anything that had gone on in Poland before 1941, not only the central military authorities like the OKW and the OKH but also the army generals deployed against the Red Army could be integrated into the National Socialist program without resistance.[16] The fact that the eastern front was by far the most important theater of war for the role played by the Wehrmacht in the Holocaust justifies the focus on the military elite in this theater. The eastern generals at the outset of Operation Barbarossa were the sixteen commanders of army groups, armies, and panzer groups who exerted the most influence as the highest authorities of executive power in the army rear areas and the army group rear areas. There were also the 17 commanding generals of army corps (general commands) and 155 commanders of divisions (divisional commands), making a total of 218 officers—all born in the nineteenth century—who commanded more than three million soldiers.[17] Why, unlike in Poland, was there no further protest from these ranks? In addition to a certain resignation in view of the limited impact of their interventions in Poland in 1939–1940, the corruption of the generals as a result of the unexpected victory in the western campaign and the tributes, promotions, and material bequests (endowments) that followed, as well as the partial political and ideological identification with Nazi ideology, all played an important role. The doubts about Hitler's war policy now completely receded. As soon as the generals were gradually transferred eastward in order to prepare for the attack on the Soviet Union, criticism of the oppression and maltreatment of the Polish population and, especially, its Jewish component had faded away. Instead, it was "moral indifference" and the "paralysis of conscience, the stirring of which became inconvenient," that manifested themselves.[18] The enslavement, ghettoization, and pauperization of the Polish Jews were noted though they now scarcely provoked any sympathy or outrage, but rather revulsion about the sordid state of "Jew nests." Old aversions to the eastern Jews surfaced, without the cause of the misery, that is, German occupation policy, being reflected on or criticized.

The resentment of eastern Jews then coalesced in the Soviet theater of war with the enemy image of Jewish Bolshevism. The generals had already tolerated the disenfranchisement of the assimilated Jews in their own country and, after an initial period of acclimatization, thereafter also the brutal suppression of the Polish Jews. Thus, objections on principle were scarcely to be expected from them against the targeting of Soviet Jews, who were regarded as the pillars of the Communist system, from the outset in the combating of enemies by the Security Police. The further the Wehrmacht advanced eastward, the more they encountered big city Jews who had found their place in the modern Soviet state as functionaries, academics, salaried employees, and industrial workers. These assimilated Jews were generally regarded as far more dangerous than the Orthodox Jews in the shtetl culture. Most German generals were deeply permeated by the enemy image of Jewish Bolshevism. The old resentment from the years of revolution and upheaval between 1917 and 1923 could now be vocalized and reactivated by the Nazi regime. The German military elite had already registered the supposedly large Jewish influence in the Soviet Union long before 1941. The role of the Jews in the state, in the army and in society in the Soviet Union was, as a rule, greatly exaggerated and viewed in an exclusively negative light.

Hitler succeeded in mobilizing the generals not only against the Stalinist Soviet Union but also against the "Jewish-Bolshevik intelligentsia," which allegedly supported this state and therefore had to be removed. The antisemitic grid within the thinking of his generals was sufficient for them to see above all Jews in the cadre of the Bolshevik nemesis. Only a very few foresaw that Hitler's racial fanaticism was more far-reaching than "only" removing Jewish functionaries and intellectuals, and would soon cross the threshold to genocide. There was a widespread consensus that the "peoples of the Soviet Union," as the Army High Command formulated it, were "under *Bolshevik-Jewish leadership*."[19] Therefore, the Wehrmacht elite entertained the illusion that by neutralizing the "Jewish-Bolshevik" cadre it would deprive enemy resistance of its foundation and thus break it. This was not only part of the military elite's political and ideological thinking but also part of its military thinking. In this campaign, the Wehrmacht elite had no intention of flinching from tough measures or from finally eliminating the Bolshevik threat once and for all.

* * *

To what extent were the generals, overwhelmingly conservative, socialized, and educated in Imperial Germany, prepared to follow the policies of violence against the Jewish population in the occupied Soviet Union? The political images of the enemy and military calculations among the Wehrmacht elite fostered the acceptance of anti-Jewish measures. Soon after the German attack on June 22, 1941, however, the killing operations reached a dimension that could be justified neither with military or policing necessity nor with the political and ideological presuppositions of the generals, but rather broke the mold. At the outset of the campaign, it could not be predicted how the generals deployed in the east would react to this escalation of racial hatred of Jews, in spite of their fundamental antipathy toward Jewish Bolshevism. Their reaction was anxiously awaited by Hitler and the SS leadership. Ultimately, the generals of the Eastern Army possessed some room for maneuver in their area of command, which they could also have made use of against the actions of SS and police forces. The degree to which Himmler and Heydrich's murder squads were able to ply their bloody trade in an unrestrained and smooth fashion depended on the attitude of the generals.

Even before the campaign began, the generals were informed about plans for an extremely severe course of action against the Soviet Jews. There could be no doubt that the four Einsatzgruppen of the Security Police and the Security Service (*Sicherheitsdienst*, or SD), who were to "process" an enormous swath of territory from the Baltic Sea to the Black Sea with only 3,500 men, as well as other SS and police units envisaged for the military hinterland, would be deployed above all for this purpose. The infamous Wagner-Heydrich agreement of April 1941, as well as additional orders and discussions, gave cause for apprehension,[20] even if it did not necessarily indicate mass murder of noncombatant Jewish men and certainly not the genocide of all Jews. It was announced for the army areas merely that the Sonderkommandos of the Einsatzgruppen would tackle "particularly important individuals." Here, the military elite still had extensive possibilities for exerting influence, because the army commanders were permitted to preclude the deployment of the SS and the police if it threatened to disturb military operations. The Wagner-Heydrich agreement made absolutely no mention of a deployment in the combat zone. Furthermore, the Sonderkommandos were "subordinated to the armies with regard to marching, supplies and accommodation." In the army group rear areas, the tasks of the SS units extended further and were more independent of the military agencies. Even here, however, the Einsatzkommandos were subordinated logistically to the Wehrmacht. Thus, in the military area of operations there were enough points of leverage for curbing or even prohibiting unwelcome actions by the Security Police that clearly exceeded the wording of the prior consultations. The SS leadership was walking a tightrope. On the one hand, it left open the looming scope of the murder policies and the number of victims. On the other hand, it did not insist on a clear separation of security police tasks from the Wehrmacht. After the protests of individual generals in the Polish campaign, the SS leadership could by no means be certain that the most senior troop command would accept massacres within army formations and would not apply their remaining competences against the activities of the Einsatzgruppen.

* * *

The Holocaust in the Soviet Union, which marked the commencement of the systematic murder of the Jews in German-occupied Europe, passed through several phases of escalation in summer 1941, whereby dynamic processes on the ground and decisions made at the center interacted with each other.[21] Initially, almost exclusively Jewish men were murdered, then, increasingly, women and children; from mid-August (and in some places even earlier) to early October 1941, the transition was made to the indiscriminate killing of all Jews in the occupied Soviet Union. Before the German invasion, the Quartermaster-General of the Army, Eduard Wagner, had impressed on the troop commanders in the East that they should not concern themselves with the "political deployment" of the SS and the police, as long as the military situation did not absolutely require it.[22] This became all the more difficult, however, the more widely the anti-Jewish operations spread. It was impossible to isolate the mass murder of sections of the civilian population in the area of operations from the jurisdiction and the tasks of the Wehrmacht, meaning a strict division of labor was nothing more than an illusion. Moreover, Himmler's murder squads were reliant on "constant, close cooperation" with the Wehrmacht, in accordance with the Wagner-Heydrich agreement, in order "to align" the military and the policing tasks.[23] From the outset, the senior staffs were well informed regarding the measures of the SS and the police. Even if the documentation of this information exchange and cooperation largely fell victim to the shredder, self-censorship, and the effects of the war, the surviving files leave us in no doubt.

All four Einsatzgruppen and their subordinate units received greater scope for action than initially planned. Instead of using certain possibilities of interpretation contained in the prior consultations to restrict the operating radius of the SS and the police, the commanders of the German Army allowed the Einsatzkommandos to ply their trade not only in the army group rear areas but also in the army rear areas, and the Sonderkommandos not only in the army rear areas but also in the combat zone, contrary to the Wagner-Heydrich agreement. In this way, the army group and army leaderships fostered without any necessity the murderous actions of the SS formations, which advanced with the fighting troops and were able to operate immediately behind the front line. In the reports of the Einsatzgruppen, which were compiled in the Reich Security Main Office (*Reichssicherheitshauptamt*, or RSHA) to form the "Incident Reports USSR" (*Ereignismeldungen UdSSR*, or EM), the appraisal of the relationship with the Wehrmacht was correspondingly positive.[24] To interpret this as nothing more than attention-seeking misses the point. The military also cherished the cooperation. The internal settlement of a dispute within the Ninth Army sheds light on the relationship between the command authorities and the SS. In August 1941, an SS lieutenant from Sonderkommando 7a complained about a disparaging remark made by an officer regarding the activities of the Security Police and the SD. The officer, whose conduct was also "most severely" condemned by the army commander, General Adolf Strauß, was promptly reprimanded by the army command with arguments that were very characteristic for the attitude of the military elite:

> It is known to the military leadership that with regard to the treatment and dispatch of Jews and Bolshevik elements, special instructions have been issued on the orders of the Führer. Members of the Security Service, the police and the Waffen SS have been assigned to implement them and they are to act in accordance with their orders. The Wehrmacht can be grateful that it does not have anything to do with such matters. Understanding can be expected from the Wehrmacht for the members of the SS and the police, who have been commissioned with the implementation of these tasks. For them as well, the carrying out of the orders issued to them is a difficult task, and most of those involved would rather join with their comrades from the army to fight the

external enemy. Unprofessional and inept behaviour on the part of officers in this matter must be regarded as particularly offensive. Especially with the head of the Sonderkommando deployed in the area of the Ninth Army, SS Lieutenant Colonel Blume, who is in every respect an entirely irreproachable SS officer, there exists the best relationship of trust, which must not be disturbed in any way whatsoever.[25]

The Chief of the Army General Staff, General Franz Halder, recalled after the war the positively enthusiastic reaction of the chiefs of staff of the individual army groups and armies during the large top-level meeting in Orša in mid-November 1941, when he asked, "What's the situation with Himmler's men, I was told: 'These people are worth their weight in gold, because they secure the rear lines of communication and in this way save us having to deploy troops for this task.'"[26] The high commands regarded the specialists from the Security Police and the SD as useful helpers in the combating of enemies (Gegnerbekämpfung) and safeguarding the areas behind the front. For this reason, they opened the door to the army areas wider than expected and even let them enter the combat zone. At the time of the meeting in Orša, the total murder of all Jews in the occupied Soviet territories was already at an advanced stage. Halder and the OKH had known about it for a long time. One colleague of Quartermaster-General Wagner, who had to summarize the reports of the RSHA, would never "forget it when General Wagner listened or when he added up the numbers of murder victims reported by the SD, those 'liquidated,' in the language of the SS, and took note of the territories that had been reported as 'free of Jews.'"[27]

The command authorities in the area of operations also received enough information, not only from SS and police officers but also from their subordinate units. The mass executions did not take place hidden from view. Some soldiers participated in them, while many others observed them as eyewitnesses.[28] There were enough witnesses whose impressions were passed on, at least in part, as far up as the high commands. They supplemented the routine reports by the Ic (intelligence) departments, counterintelligence troops, Secret Field Police, field gendarmerie, and other agencies working together with the Security Police. Several mass shootings took place in the vicinity of military headquarters. These events could be neither overlooked nor ignored. They were repeatedly a topic for conversation. The Einsatzgruppen staffs and their commandos were furthermore frequently stationed near or even in the localities in which the high commands of the army groups and armies were located. Alongside official contacts, various informal contacts could therefore arise, such as personal relations, mutual invitations, or collective vacations. Off-duty relationships with SS personnel and policemen, regardless of whether they were distanced or emphatically comradely, offered the possibility to learn even more about their tasks and operations.

The generals and their staffs could thus obtain an idea of the murderous activities of the SS and police forces. On this basis they had to decide to what extent they made use of their—admittedly limited but, if interpreted assertively, nonetheless effective—military jurisdiction vis-à-vis the Einsatzgruppen and, in part, also the battalions of the Order Police (*Ordnungspolizei*) and the brigades of the Waffen SS. In particular in the army zones, they could "consent or preclude,"[29] tolerate and support Himmler's "ideological troops," or drastically limit their room for maneuver.[30] They furthermore had the option to mark out the limits of cooperation at the lower levels. The administrative instructions and orders issued by the high commands to their subordinate formations and units had significant importance for the regional structuring of occupation rule and were by no means always predetermined by the regulations of the central authorities. In this respect, too, the senior troop command in the east possessed considerable scope for action. Again, however, it scarcely ever used this scope for action against the policies of mass murder in the operations zone, although these policies became ever clearer and more horrifying.

This stance of the senior staffs, ranging from passive to affirmative, impacted the cooperation of their subordinate departments with the SS and the police. Without the energetic assistance of the Wehrmacht at the front and in the communications zone, the policies of annihilation in the occupied Soviet Union could not have been executed so quickly or so extensively.[31] The commandos of the Einsatzgruppen, which were weak in terms of personnel strength, could not be immediately on the spot on the vast eastern front wherever the Wehrmacht conquered and occupied a city or town. For this reason, the first measures against Jews and communists were very frequently taken by the Wehrmacht. This was especially true for the Secret Field Police (*Geheime Feldpolizei*), which was the military security police and thus part of the Wehrmacht, though the counterintelligence troops and field gendarmerie also arrested, interrogated, and executed often just as rigorously as Heydrich's Security Police. These crimes took place directly in the area of authority of the high commands, to whom the military police was subordinated. The military administration—above all, the field and local headquarters (*Feld- und Ortskommandanturen*)—then registered and marked the Jews. They then incarcerated them in ghettos; disenfranchised, expropriated, and underfed them; deployed them for forced labor; frequently robbed them; and, in some cases even without the involvement of the Security Police, murdered them in the course of reprisals or as hostages.

Parallel to this, the mass shootings by the SS and police began from the first days of the campaign. Due to the rapid advance and the large spaces, many Jewish communities were initially omitted. But the murderers ultimately visited these places as well or returned to them in order to complete their tasks. They could then profit from the preliminary organizational work done by the military departments, since the Jews and other adversaries had in the meantime been apprehended. The further assistance of the military related above all to logistical support. As and when needed, lorries, ammunition, and cordons were provided. The agencies of the Wehrmacht stationed locally also acted as henchmen in the roundup and selection of the Jews, their escort to the execution site, and the burial of their corpses. Their soldiers sometimes even participated directly in the shooting operations performed by SS commandos, though this type of military assistance was too much for the troop command, which issued counterorders. At least in this respect, the planned division of labor was retained. The integration of the Eastern Army into the murder program of the SS and police was nonetheless extensive enough. The cooperation functioned—in spite of some conflicts and individual acts of resistance—to the last. It was promoted from an ideological viewpoint and was flanked by long-standing antisemitic indoctrination and agitation in the internal training and papers of the Wehrmacht, as well as in the propaganda distributed across the occupied territories.[32]

* * *

Why did the Wehrmacht command authorities tolerate, or rather accept and, in some cases, even support the killing of hundreds of thousands of Jews in territories under their control? One possible answer was given in postwar testimony by Rudolf-Christoph von Gersdorff, who belonged to the military opposition against Hitler. As the counterintelligence officer of Army Group Center, he, like the entire staff of the army group, including the commander Fedor von Bock, was informed in detail in July 1941 of the activities of Einsatzgruppe B under SS Brigadier Arthur Nebe.[33] The operations of July 1941, and not just the systematic murder of Jewish women and children months later, already constituted mass murder, and the high command could have energetically protested against them—but it did not. From a psychological point of view, it is therefore understandable that Gersdorff denied the real extent of his knowledge about the events of the opening phase of the eastern campaign. One statement made to the Public Prosecutor's Office in Munich about the allegedly very low number of shootings of Jews in the reports of Einsatzgruppe B sheds a characteristic light on the attitude of conservative officers to the shooting operations against Jews in the Soviet Union: "The figures were on a scale that, in view of the size of Nebe's operations zone, was quite conceivable, i.e. one could without further ado take the view that the shootings were related to the war. This was all the more the case when I learned that there were very many Jews among the operatives and that criminality within the Jewish population was greater and more active than within the remaining Russian population."[34] The former Field Marshal Erich von Manstein argued in retrospect in a similar vein: "It was really the case that the Jewish communities supplied a large percentage of partisans, saboteurs and dangerous people.... The fact that the Jews had reason to hate us naturally caused us to be vigilant in order to prevent this hatred from being turned into action."[35]

From this type of antisemitic point of view, the partial persecution and removal of Jews appeared to be a military necessity in the struggle against Jewish Bolshevism. It was not only "Jews in Party and state positions"[36] but also Jewish men of military-service age from the middle and upper classes (Jewish intelligentsia) that were classified as potential adversaries who might at any moment constitute a serious threat in the rear of the front and therefore had to be tackled promptly and preemptively by the limited number of security forces. As long as the racist security work of the SS and police was directed only against alleged functionaries, partisans, and saboteurs, as well as the Jewish intelligentsia, and furthermore justified as reprisals for crimes committed against German soldiers, there was virtually no resistance to it. The Einsatzgruppen made every effort in their reports to Berlin and to the military command authorities to cloak their murders in a pseudolegitimacy, although the dimensions of the shootings flouted any form of proportionality.

Nonetheless, the generals and their colleagues put aside their reservations against the already blatantly criminal police activities during the first months. The reason for this conduct is to be found not only in the ideological images of the enemy and in considerations of military necessity but also in the hopes for a lightning victory in the east. The military leadership wanted to successfully complete this highly risky campaign quickly, by all available means and without internal disputes—in order to then be transferred back to the West and, if possible, have nothing more to do with ethnic policies in the East. Military reasoning initially had absolute priority over political and ethical considerations. The fate of a suspect minority in a foreign country was of little consequence. On the contrary: many officers not only looked away but instead saw in the execution of supposedly dangerous adversaries, which Jewish functionaries and the intelligentsia were widely viewed as, an unpleasant but necessary building block in the realization and consolidation of the military victory. After all, in this "total" struggle against an ideological nemesis, a brutal approach was chosen in other areas as well, for example in the economic exploitation or the treatment of prisoners of war.[37]

Only when the hopes for a brief campaign were revealed as illusory and the transition was made to indiscriminate genocide (from mid-August 1941), did this understanding partially fade. Once the SS and police forces began targeting Jewish women and children ever more frequently and, ultimately, systematically killing all Jews in the occupied Soviet territories, some officers were troubled or even appalled. In some cases, their previously blunted conscience began to stir again and their indifferent or even approving stance toward the anti-Jewish operations changed—especially because at the same time news from back home filtered through to the effect that the persecution of German Jews had considerably intensified and led to the first deportations from the Reich to the East. Internal discussions took place in the command authorities, and, in a few cases, objections were voiced. However, the reaction to the gradual escalation of the killings of Jews was neither the same everywhere nor was it always critical. The majority continued to justify and support the murders—or at least tolerated them without objection. Alongside the argument of "combating of enemies," the supply and accommodation situation, which had drastically deteriorated in many operations zones of the Eastern Army and appeared to improve as a result of a decimation of the population, increasingly came to the fore. Overall, the military command authorities and the military administration remained integrated into the policy of murder either directly or indirectly, by means of active participation or passive toleration. This integration was in some instances reluctant and combined with unease but took place in other cases out of conviction and self-initiative—until, soon after the turn of the year 1941–1942, most Jews in the territories controlled by the Wehrmacht, around half a million people, were dead.

* * *

Two examples from many should suffice to illustrate how broad the spectrum was of the generals in the East who were directly or indirectly involved in the Holocaust, and that they did not necessarily have to be Nazis in order to function in the framework of the war of annihilation. The furthest degree of serving as an accessory to mass murder was marked by the commander of the Sixth Army, Field Marshal Walter von Reichenau.[38] In his operations zone, the Holocaust by bullets assumed the most grievous proportions. Here two factors combined: the still large Jewish population in the Ukrainian cities conquered by the Sixth Army, in spite of escape and evacuation, and Reichenau's particular radicalism. Given that he sympathized with Hitler already before 1933 and made every effort after the Nazi takeover of power to incorporate the armed forces into the new state, the conduct of this especially politicized and ideological general should come as no surprise. The fact that he could be independent to the point of renitence and had protested against shootings of Jews during the Polish campaign is somewhat bemusing, but it cannot alter the overall negative impression of his personality.

Reichenau worked well with Sonderkommando 4a of Einsatzgruppe C under the likewise particularly radical SS Colonel Paul Blobel; he gave direct murder orders, for example, against around ninety children in Belaya Tserkov[39] and supported the large anti-Jewish massacres in Kiev and Kharkov. On October 10, 1941, only ten days after the shooting of 33,771 Jews in Babi Yar, Kiev, in the operations zone of his own army, he demanded in his notorious order on the "Conduct of the Troops in the Eastern Region" complete understanding from his soldiers "for the necessity of the hard but just atonement against Jewish sub-humanity."[40]

The Reichenau order, with its plea for genocide, was in no way rejected by the less radical, conservative generals but was instead recommended by the superior military entities—the commander of Army Group South, Field Marshal Gerd von Rundstedt, and the OKH—to the other army commands to be circulated and emulated.[41] The order was subsequently announced along the entire front, as a rule with affirmative covering letters from other commanders. Some generals, for example, Hermann Hoth (Seventeenth Army) and Erich von Manstein (Eleventh Army) were even inspired by it to issue their own radical orders.[42]

Even if Reichenau's proximity to National Socialism was confirmed in horrific fashion in the occupied Soviet Union, National Socialist sentiments were by no means a prerequisite for the involvement of the generals in crimes. This is demonstrated not only by the adoption without objections of the Reichenau order among the other armies but also the conduct of numerous generals who were considerably less Nazified but nonetheless not "anti-Reichenaus" in the special situation of the war in the east. Even in the case of a general such as Carl-Heinrich von Stülpnagel, the predecessor to Hoth as commander of the Seventeenth Army who would later belong to the resistance of July 20, 1944, and is therefore assigned to a "different Germany" than his friend Reichenau, his distance to Nazi policies decreased during the first months of the war in the east.[43] For Stülpnagel, too, the Soviet Jews were the pillars of the Stalinist regime and had to be targeted. In his orders, he therefore directed the repressive measures of the Wehrmacht against the Jewish population.[44] At the same time, Stülpnagel recommended better "enlightenment about the Jews" in order to increase understanding for anti-Jewish operations.[45] With his policy of treating the Jews as security risks and scapegoats he facilitated measures against the Jews—even if it remains unclear to what extent he accepted the murders themselves.

It is noticeable, however, how well Stülpnagel's army command worked together with the Security Police. The large pogroms in western Ukraine (L'vov, Zolochov, Tarnopol, etc.) took place in the operations zone of the Seventeenth Army. According to the files of the Reich Security Main Office, the army command had itself suggested "first of all to use the anti-Jewish and anti-communist Poles living in the newly occupied territories for self-cleansing operations."[46] Furthermore, the army command repeatedly transferred to the Security Police the task of retaliating to acts of sabotage, for example, in Kremenchug,[47] where 1,600 Jews were ultimately murdered. It is also striking whom the army leadership cited as "suspects" on September 7, 1941, and against whom one should not be afraid of proceeding with all severity: "Jews of both genders and all ages."[48] This was shortly before the transition from the selective to the complete eradication of the Jews in the operations zone of Army Group South via the massacre of Kamenets-Podolskiy (August 26–28, 1941, 23,600 victims).[49] There can be no talk of Stülpnagel exerting a moderating influence on the treatment of the

Jews in his army zone. On the contrary: the wording of his orders protected and indeed promoted anti-Jewish operations and the corresponding initiatives of his colleagues. If fewer Jews were ultimately killed in Stülpnagel's jurisdiction than in the operations zones of other armies, it was mainly because the Seventeenth Army did not conquer any large cities after L'vov. To draw conclusions about his conduct in the German-Soviet war in 1941 from his active resistance in 1944 is an anachronistic fallacy, which is unfortunately to be found frequently in research on the resistance.[50]

* * *

The murder of around half a million men, women, and children of Jewish descent in the eastern operations zone would scarcely have been possible without the participation of the Wehrmacht, particularly in a logistical and administrative respect. Even if one takes into account that overall only a small proportion of the many million men of the Eastern Army were directly involved in the Holocaust and that there was a formal—though in practice frequently watered down— division of labor between the army and the SS and police apparatus, the participation of the Wehrmacht in the genocide in the occupied Soviet Union remains evident and comprehensive. Both the magnitude and the spatial expansion of the murder as well as the degree and functional structure of cooperation between Wehrmacht, SS, and police were decisively influenced by the conduct of the generals and their staffs. If intervention against the murders of Jews were to have any chance of success at all, then it had to come from the senior troop command of the generals in the east. In spite of all limitations in executive authority, it was especially the commanders of the army groups and the armies who fundamentally possessed enough in the way of formal competence and informal options to consent or preclude, impede or promote, protest or remain silent.

The fact that they did not use the scope of action remaining open to them in favor of the helpless victims, indeed as a rule did not even make any *attempt* to do so, provides a measure of the responsibility of the military elite for this first, so important, and groundbreaking stage in the genocide. It is certainly true that the Holocaust and the euthanasia were mass crimes committed by the state and were located in the arcane area of competence of the political leadership. This means that any serious attempt to thwart, undo, or at least dilute the fundamental decisions of the state leadership would have required an energetic protest or even a putsch by substantial parts of the Wehrmacht and would not necessarily have succeeded even then. For united action by the entire military leadership or at least the senior troop command on the eastern front, the prerequisites had long since been lacking after the generals had so deeply given themselves over to Hitler and his regime.

On the ground, in the operations zones, however, the generals deployed in the east could certainly have pursued a systematic obstruction of the racial-ideological murders. Clear protest or resistance on the part of several particularly prominent generals would at least have set an example and perhaps encouraged other commanders to engage in obstruction. After the experiences of the Polish campaign, Hitler, Himmler, Heydrich, and their executive organs must have feared a certain degree of opposition to their plans. During the first weeks of Operation Barbarossa, the SS and police behaved as though they wanted to test bit by bit what was possible in the new theater of war. The opening phase of the eastern campaign was thus of decisive importance for the further policies of murder. But when the military high commands learned of the mass murder of Jewish men, they were either silent or justified and even facilitated it. This clearly demonstrated that the leading command authorities of the Wehrmacht on the eastern front would not offer any resistance to the persecution of the Jews. This stance was an ominous sign for the gradual radicalization and expansion of the executions toward genocide. The murder of the Jewish "intelligentsia" and men of military-service age already announced the systematic "extermination," for those Jews who initially survived could all the more easily be categorized as potential "avengers" or "useless eaters"—all the more so when the campaign unexpectedly lasted much longer. This underlines the evident and eminent importance of the failure to set limits to the murders during the opening phase of the German-Soviet war. Therein lies the greatest responsibility and joint guilt of the generals for the murder of the Soviet Jews and for the Holocaust overall. In this way, they became Hitler's generals completely.

Of course, not every action taken and certainly not every word spoken against the anti-Jewish policy ordered by the highest authorities could be recorded in the service files or in private annotations. What good were internal discussions in intimate circles and clenched fists in pockets if—aside from the few known exceptions of officers beneath the rank of general—the discontent was not turned into actions, or at least none that might somehow have made themselves felt or had an impact. Solely for Field Marshal Fedor von Bock, the commander of Army Group Center, three very timid interventions have been proven, one against executions in the vicinity of his headquarters, then one against the "selections" of Jewish prisoners of war by the Security Police in the transit camps of the Wehrmacht, and finally against the burdening of supply lines by rail transports of Jews.[51] Yet in all three cases, the protection of human life was not at the forefront of his thinking but rather the motive of having as little to do with these things as possible. The case of Bock, who remained loyal to his Führer to the end, is an example of how a nationalist conservative general, whose surroundings tended ever more to opposition and, ultimately, even to resistance, was unable to bring himself to adopt a decisive stance against the Nazi crimes committed under the protection and safeguard of his troops. Even in the case of generals who were later active in (Stülpnagel, Hoepner) or at least on the margins of (Kluge) the coup against

Hitler and had to forfeit their lives for it, there is no indication that the murder of the Soviet Jews had any kind of deep impact on their attitude toward the dictator and his regime. Their conduct in 1941 in fact suggests otherwise.

Some army commanders even went beyond the passive toleration of the murder of Jews. Reichenau's agitating and murderous orders, the initiatives for pogroms and antisemitic propaganda by Stülpnagel and numerous other examples prove that proximity (Reichenau) or distance (Stülpnagel) to the Nazi regime was not necessarily decisive. Other things—alongside human weaknesses such as blind subordination, exaggerated assimilation, ambition, venality, conflict avoidance, or indifference—were crucial. Nationalist conservative generals and National Socialist functionaries possessed in their thinking a mutual stock of ideological grids, from which the deeply entrenched anti-Bolshevik and antisemitic sentiments coalesced disastrously in the eastern theater of war. The anti-Jewish stereotypes alone would surely not have been sufficient to acquiesce in or support the eliminatory policies of the Nazi regime in the occupied Soviet Union. Ideological components were supplemented by the military calculation prioritizing the security and the supply of German troops over all humanitarian considerations in this "total war" for "all or nothing," which the campaign in the east was classified as from the outset and all the more so the longer it lasted. With the removal of the Jewish population, both a security threat and a contributing factor to the grave accommodation and food problems appeared to disappear. This type of justification for the murder of the Jews overlapped with National Socialist ideology and propaganda but it was not necessarily based on this. It could also be founded on nationalist conservative mentalities and military motives. It remains undisputed, however, that without Hitler and his fanatical supporters there would have been no genocide against the Soviet Jews.

All in all, we can verify a shockingly smooth integration of Hitler's generals in the east (and their advisors) into the National Socialist program of murder. They frequently also possessed knowledge about the further course of the Holocaust, which was expanded in 1942 from the Soviet Jews to all Jews in German-occupied Europe, initially above all in Poland. The deportations of German Jews from October 1941 to the east were already well-known and constituted a subject in communications with the home front. It remains unclear when exactly and in what detail the troop generals learned of the industrial mass killing of people in the General Government. Baron Maximilian von Weichs, deployed from 1941 to 1945 as commander in the east and in the Balkans, admitted after the war that he had heard rumors about the death camps in Poland and personally broached the subject during a meeting with Himmler. The Reichsführer SS had apparently answered: "Those are not rumors, it is the truth." The general furthermore recalled "that Himmler, even showing a certain pride, related that the exterminations were carried out in a very humane fashion. People were loaded onto railway cars without knowing that they were going to a death both painless and sudden."[52]

This information prevented neither Weichs nor the vast majority of other field marshals and generals from condemning the assassination attempt of a few officers on Hitler on July 20, 1944,[53] and loyally serving the Nazi state to the end. Himmler did not have to mince his words on January 26, 1944, when speaking at an indoctrination conference for commanders of all parts of the Wehrmacht in Poznań. The manuscript for his speech states: "Jewish question ... complete solution, cannot allow any avengers for our children to emerge."[54] The generals gathered there greeted Himmler's speech with great applause. At other ideological policy training sessions in May and June 1944, the Reichsführer SS confessed that the "Jewish question" had been "solved without compromise in accordance with the mortal struggle of our people for the survival of our blood."[55] Himmler continued, "In this circle I can again address this in all openness with a few sentences. It is good that we had the toughness to exterminate the Jews in our domain."[56]

The knowledge of this gigantic state crime, which had begun immediately after the German attack on the Soviet Union in the operations zone of the Wehrmacht, had scarcely any noticeable impact on the generals, specifically those troop commanders who had borne the greatest responsibility on the eastern front in 1941 and 1942. On July 26, 1945, when the gas chambers of Auschwitz had long since become a subject for the global public, the US Army eavesdropped on a conversation in which two prominent captive generals, the former commanders in the German-Soviet war Heinz Guderian and Baronet Wilhelm von Leeb, discussed the merits and drawbacks of National Socialism. The exchange of views ended with the conclusion: "GUD: The fundamental principles were fine. L: That is true."[57]

—Translated from German by Alex J. Kay

JOHANNES HÜRTER is a Research Fellow at the Institute of Contemporary History Munich–Berlin and Professor of Modern History at the Johannes Gutenberg University in Mainz. Among other works, he has published *Wilhelm Groener: Reichswehrminister am Ende der Weimarer Republik (1928–1932)* (1993) and *Hitlers Heerführer: Die deutschen Oberbefehlshaber im Krieg gegen die Sowjetunion 1941/42* (2006).

Notes

1. See Johannes Hürter, "Die Wehrmachtsgeneralität und die 'Bewältigung' ihrer NS-Vergangenheit," *Forum für osteuropäische Ideen- und Zeitgeschichte* 18, no. 1 (2014): 17–30. See also Alaric Searle, *Wehrmacht Generals, West German Society, and the Debate on*

Rearmament 1949–1959 (Westport, CT: Praeger, 2003); on the political and societal context see Norbert Frei, *Vergangenheitspolitik. Die Anfänge der Bundesrepublik und die NS-Vergangenheit* (Munich: C. H. Beck, 1996).

2. See Oliver von Wrochem, *Erich von Manstein: Vernichtungskrieg und Geschichtspolitik* (Paderborn et al.: Schöningh, 2006).

3. See Manfred Messerschmidt, *Die Wehrmacht im NS-Staat. Zeit der Indoktrination* (Hamburg: Deckers, 1969); Klaus-Jürgen Müller, *Das Heer und Hitler. Armee und nationalsozialistisches Regime 1933–1940* (Stuttgart: Deutsche Verlags-Anstalt, 1969); Johannes Hürter, *Hitlers Heerführer. Die deutschen Oberbefehlshaber im Krieg gegen die Sowjetunion 1941/42* (Munich: Oldenbourg, 2006); Jürgen Förster, *Die Wehrmacht im NS-Staat. Eine strukturgeschichtliche Analyse* (Munich: Oldenbourg, 2007).

4. This number is taken from Reinhard Stumpf, *Die Wehrmachts-Elite. Rang- und Herkunftsstruktur der deutschen Generale und Admirale 1933–1945* (Boppard am Rhein: Boldt, 1982), 46: 2,344 army generals, 556 air force generals, 291 admirals in the Imperial Navy.

5. The figures that follow are based on the (somewhat divergent) data provided in Dieter Pohl, *Die Herrschaft der Wehrmacht. Deutsche Militärbesatzung und einheimische Bevölkerung in der Sowjetunion 1941–1944* (Munich: Oldenbourg, 2008), 243–282; Dieter Pohl, *Verfolgung und Massenmord in der NS-Zeit 1933–1945*, 3rd rev. ed. (Darmstadt: Wissenschaftliche Buchgesellschaft, 2011), 63–110; *Die Verfolgung und Ermordung der europäischen Juden durch das nationalsozialistische Deutschland 1933–1945*, vol. 7: *Sowjetunion mit annektierten Gebieten I. Besetzte sowjetische Gebiete unter deutscher Militärverwaltung, Baltikum und Transnistrien*, vol. ed. Bert Hoppe and Hildrun Glass (Munich: Oldenbourg, 2011), 13–49 (introduction).

6. On the following see Hürter, *Hitlers Heerführer*, esp. 509–517.

7. See Werner T. Angress, "Das deutsche Militär und die Juden im Ersten Weltkrieg," *Militärgeschichtliche Mitteilungen* 19 (1976): 77–146.

8. Heinrici's diary, entry for October 17, 1918, quoted in Johannes Hürter, *A German General on the Eastern Front: The Letters and Diaries of Gotthard Heinrici 1941–1942* (Barnsley: Pen and Sword, 2014), 13–14.

9. Heinrici to his parents, Berlin, February 17, 1933, quoted in Hürter, *A German General on the Eastern Front*, 16.

10. Heinrici to his parents, Berlin, April 1, 1933, quoted in Hürter, *A German General on the Eastern Front*, 18. However, only a few days later he again defended the "necessary" coercive measures and "even some hardships," and praised Hitler and Goebbels: "They carried out the boycott against Jews with great skill!" Heinrici to his parents, Berlin, April 9, 1933, quoted in Hürter, *A German General on the Eastern Front*.

11. Heinrici to his mother, January 16, 1939, quoted in Hürter, *A German General on the Eastern Front*.

12. Heinrici to his wife, April 22, 1941, quoted in Hürter, *A German General on the Eastern Front*, 60: "It is not very nice here, bad cold weather, spring is not in sight, bugs and lice are everywhere, just as the awful Jews with the Star of David on their sleeves."

13. See Hürter, *Hitlers Heerführer*, 139–140.

14. See Hürter, *Hitlers Heerführer*, 177–188. See also Helmut Krausnick and Hans-Heinrich Wilhelm, *Die Truppe des Weltanschauungskrieges. Die Einsatzgruppen der Sicherheitspolizei und des SD 1938–1942* (Stuttgart: Deutsche Verlags-Anstalt, 1981), 80–106; Alexander B. Rossino, *Hitler Strikes Poland: Blitzkrieg, Ideology, and Atrocity* (Lawrence: University Press of Kansas,

2003); Jochen Böhler, *Auftakt zum Vernichtungskrieg. Die Wehrmacht in Polen 1939* (Frankfurt am Main: Fischer, 2006).

15. Even retrospectively: see Weichs, "Erinnerungen," vol. 3, in Bundesarchiv-Militärarchiv, Freiburg im Breisgau (hereafter BArch-MA), N 19/7, fols. 18–19, where he writes regarding the ghetto in Łódź: "Extremely dirty houses and cabins. The well-known type of caftan-Jew could be seen in droves here."

16. The overview that follows regarding the shared responsibility of the German generals for the Holocaust in the Soviet Union is based on Hürter, *Hitlers Heerführer*, 517–599, where numerous examples and pieces of evidence can be found.

17. Figures according to the table on the wartime dispositions on June 22, 1941, in *Das Deutsche Reich und der Zweite Weltkrieg*, ed. Militärgeschichtliches Forschungsamt, vol. 4: *Der Angriff auf die Sowjetunion*, supplement (Stuttgart: Deutsche Verlags-Anstalt, 1983), Table 2, including the—soon deployed—reserves, though without the Romanian formations attached to the Eleventh Army. The figures were supplemented by the Army High Command Norway/Command Post Finland (two corps, four divisions). The admirals of the Imperial Navy and the generals of the Luftwaffe deployed in the east are not addressed in this chapter. The German admirals resembled the army generals in their structure and their (nationalist conservative) political and ideological orientation, while the Luftwaffe generals were younger, more socially heterogeneous and had more affinity with the Nazis.

18. Krausnick and Wilhelm, *Die Truppe des Weltanschauungskrieges*, 112.

19. Order issued by the command of the Seventeenth Army, June 16, 1941, with enclosed pamphlet, "Wichtig für alle Führer und Soldaten im Falle eines Krieges mit der Sowjetunion!" [Important for all officers and soldiers in the event of war with the Soviet Union], in BArch-MA, RH 20-17/276.

20. Order issued by Brauchitsch, "Regelung des Einsatzes der Sicherheitspolizei und des SD im Verbande des Heeres" [Regulations on the deployment of the Security Police and the SD within army formations], April 28, 1941, reproduced in Gerd R. Ueberschär and Wolfram Wette, eds., *"Unternehmen Barbarossa." Der deutsche Überfall auf die Sowjetunion 1941: Berichte, Analysen, Dokumente* (Paderborn: Schöningh, 1984), 303–304. For an example of other unmistakeable statements see the order issued by the OKW, "Richtlinien für das Verhalten der Truppe in Russland" [Guidelines for the conduct of the troops in Russia], May 19, 1941, Gerd R. Ueberschär and Wolfram Wette, eds., *"Unternehmen Barbarossa,"* 312–313: "(1). Bolshevism is the mortal enemy of the National Socialist German people. It is against this subversive worldview and its carriers that Germany is fighting. (2). This struggle demands ruthless and energetic measures against Bolshevik agitators, irregulars, saboteurs, Jews, and the complete elimination of all active or passive resistance."

21. Essential: Peter Longerich, *Politik und Vernichtung. Eine Gesamtdarstellung der nationalsozialistischen Judenverfolgung* (Munich: Piper, 1998), 293–418; for an overview see: Pohl, *Verfolgung und Massenmord*, 70–79. For new arguments for an earlier initiation of genocide in the north (end of July), also fostered by positive collaboration with the Wehrmacht, see: Alex J. Kay, "Transition to Genocide, July 1941: Einsatzkommando 9 and the Annihilation of Soviet Jewry," *Holocaust and Genocide Studies* 27, no. 3 (winter 2013): 411–442.

22. Notes made by the chief of staff of Army Group North, Major General Kurt Brennecke, regarding a discussion on June 4, 1941, at the OKH in Zossen, June 9, 1941, in National Archives and Records Administration, Washington, DC (hereafter NARA), T 312/805. On this occasion, Wagner confirmed once again, however, that the army remained the "highest

authority" (Brennecke, NARA, T 312/805) in the area of operations and that his commanders could "consent or preclude, depending on the military circumstances" (notes made by the chief of staff of the Seventeenth Army, Colonel Vincenz Müller, regarding this discussion, June 6, 1941, in BArch-MA, RH 20-17/23).

23. Order issued by Brauchitsch, "Regelung des Einsatzes der Sicherheitspolizei und des SD im Verbande des Heeres," April 28, 1941, reproduced in Ueberschär and Wette, eds., "Unternehmen Barbarossa," 303–304.

24. See the essential edition of the Incident Reports and other Einsatzgruppen documents: Klaus-Michael Mallmann, Andrej Angrick, Jürgen Matthäus, and Martin Cüppers, eds., *Dokumente der Einsatzgruppen in der Sowjetunion*, vol. 1: *Die "Ereignismeldungen UdSSR" 1941* (Darmstadt: Wissenschaftliche Buchgesellschaft, 2011); vol. 2: *Deutsche Besatzungsherrschaft in der UdSSR 1941–45* (Darmstadt: Wissenschaftliche Buchgesellschaft, 2013); vol. 3: *Deutsche Berichte aus dem Osten* (Darmstadt: Wissenschaftliche Buchgesellschaft, 2014). See also Peter Klein, ed., *Die Einsatzgruppen in der besetzten Sowjetunion 1941/42. Die Tätigkeits- und Lageberichte des Chefs der Sicherheitspolizei und des SD* (Berlin: Edition Hentrich, 1997).

25. Notes on a discussion made by the chief of staff of the Ninth Army, Colonel Kurt Weckmann, August 22, 1941, in Central Archives of the Russian Ministry of Defense, Podolsk (TsAMO RF), fond 500, 12454/236.

26. Peter Bor, *Gespräche mit Halder* (Wiesbaden: Limes, 1950), 197–198.

27. Walter Bußmann, "Politik und Kriegsführung. Erlebte Geschichte und der Beruf des Historikers," *Fridericiana. Zeitschrift der Universität Karlsruhe* no. 32 (1983): 3–16, here 11. Occasionally, Halder also attended the presentations. See also Bußmann's remarks on the agreements reached before the beginning of the eastern campaign: "I am not able to answer the question as to whether the OKH at that point in time, i.e. during preparations for 'Barbarossa,' was aware of the consequences that, as we know, culminated in the 'final solution.' Whoever knew about the 'program,' and this was generally accessible in the various publications and proclamations, could not and must not harbour any illusions, even if it did not suffice for them to imagine that a genocide was being carried out."

28. See chapter 8 in this volume.

29. See note 22.

30. This is proven by the example of the Eleventh Army, which during the first weeks of the campaign imposed on Einsatzgruppe D, much to the resentment of its commander Otto Ohlendorf, every march route, every place of action and even, in some cases, its range of tasks. From August 1941, however, this army command also allowed the SS and the police in its area of jurisdiction considerable freedom. See Hürter, *Hitlers Heerführer*, 526–528.

31. On cooperation between the Eastern Army, the SS and the police see the overviews in Krausnick and Wilhelm, *Truppe des Weltanschauungskrieges*, 205–278; Pohl, *Herrschaft der Wehrmacht*, 243–282. A comprehensive study of the participation of the Wehrmacht in the Holocaust in the Soviet Union is yet to be written. A detailed analysis using the example of Belarus: Christian Gerlach, *Kalkulierte Morde. Die deutsche Wirtschafts- und Vernichtungspolitik in Weißrußland 1941 bis 1944* (Hamburg: Hamburger Edition, 1999), 503–774. Using the example of Lithuania: Christoph Dieckmann, *Deutsche Besatzungspolitik in Litauen 1941–1944* (Göttingen: Wallstein, 2011). Using the example of several divisions: Christian Hartmann, *Wehrmacht im Ostkrieg. Front und militärisches Hinterland 1941/42* (Munich: Oldenbourg, 2009), 635–698.

32. See Jürgen Förster, "Geistige Kriegführung in Deutschland 1919 bis 1945," in *Das Deutsche Reich und der Zweite Weltkrieg*, ed. Militärgeschichtliches Forschungsamt, vol. 9/1: *Die deutsche Kriegsgesellschaft 1939 bis 1945. Politisierung, Vernichtung, Überleben* (Munich: Deutsche Verlags-Anstalt, 2004), 469–640, here passim.

33. See Johannes Hürter, "Auf dem Weg zur Militäropposition. Tresckow, Gersdorff, der Vernichtungskrieg und der Judenmord. Neue Dokumente über das Verhältnis der Heeresgruppe Mitte zur Einsatzgruppe B im Jahr 1941," *Vierteljahrshefte für Zeitgeschichte* 52 (2004), 527–562. The author's theses provoked a controversy in Germany regarding the conduct of later resistance fighters during the first months of the German-Soviet war. On this see Manuel Becker, Holger Löttel, and Christoph Studt, eds., *Der militärische Widerstand gegen Hitler im Lichte neuer Kontroversen* (Berlin: LIT, 2010); Rafaela Hiemann, "Widerstand und kumulative Erinnerungskonstruktion: Rudolf-Christoph Freiherr von Gersdorff," in *Life Writing and Political Memoir—Lebenszeugnisse und Politische Memoiren*, ed. Magnus Brechtken (Göttingen: V&R unipress, 2012), 145–201.

34. Transcript of the Public Prosecutor's Office attached to Regional Court Munich I on the hearing of Gersdorff, Cologne, May 4, 1959, in Staatsarchiv München, Stanw. 32970/5. See also Gerlach, *Kalkulierte Morde*, 1121.

35. Statement from 1949, quoted in Oliver von Wrochem, "Ein unpolitischer Soldat? Generalfeldmarschall Erich von Manstein," in *Karrieren im Nationalsozialismus. Funktionseliten zwischen Mitwirkung und Distanz*, ed. Gerhard Hirschfeld and Tobias Jersak, (Frankfurt am Main/New York: Campus, 2004), 185–204, here 190.

36. Heydrich to the higher SS and police leaders, Berlin, July 2, 1941, in Klein, ed., *Einsatzgruppen*, 325.

37. See the overviews of the war of annihilation in the East: Pohl, *Herrschaft der Wehrmacht*; Christian Hartmann, *Operation Barbarossa: Nazi Germany's War in the East, 1941-1945* (Oxford: Oxford University Press, 2013).

38. See the detailed coverage in Hürter, *Hitlers Heerführer*, 576–588.

39. See Helmuth Groscurth, *Tagebücher eines Abwehroffiziers 1938-1940. Mit weiteren Dokumenten zur Militäropposition gegen Hitler*, ed. Helmut Krausnick and Harold C. Deutsch (Stuttgart: Deutsche Verlags-Anstalt, 1970), 534–542.

40. Reichenau's order "Verhalten der Truppe im Ostraum" [Conduct of the troops in the eastern region], October 10, 1941, reproduced in Ueberschär and Wette, ed., *Unternehmen Barbarossa*, 339–340.

41. Rundstedt's order, October 12, 1941, reproduced in Ueberschär and Wette, ed., *Unternehmen Barbarossa*, 340; OKH order, October 28, 1941, reproduced in Ueberschär and Wette, ed., *Unternehmen Barbarossa*, 340–341.

42. Hoth's order "Verhalten der deutschen Soldaten im Ostraum" [Conduct of the German soldiers in the eastern region], November 17, 1941, reproduced in Ueberschär and Wette, ed., *Unternehmen Barbarossa*, 341–343; Manstein's order, November 20, 1941, reproduced in Ueberschär and Wette, ed., *Unternehmen Barbarossa*, 343–344.

43. See Hürter, *Hitlers Heerführer*, 570–575, where more evidence is provided.

44. See, for example, Stülpnagel's order "Behandlung feindlicher Zivilpersonen (Partisanen, jugendliche Banden) und der russischen Kriegsgefangenen" [Treatment of enemy civilians (partisans, gangs of youths) and Russian prisoners of war], July 30, 1941, in BArch-MA, RH 20-17/276.

45. Stülpnagel's position paper "Stellung und Einfluss des Bolschewismus" [Standing and influence of Bolshevism], August 12, 1941, in NARA, T 312/674 (2).

46. "Ereignismeldung UdSSR Nr. 10" [Incident report USSR no. 10], Chief of the Security Police and the SD, Berlin, July 2, 1941, reproduced in Mallmann et al., eds., *Ereignismeldungen UdSSR*, 64–66, here 64.

47. Seventeenth Army, "Tätigkeitsbericht" [Activity report] Ic/AO, July 22, 1941, in Archiv des Instituts für Zeitgeschichte, Munich, MA 1564, NOKW-2272.

48. Order of the Seventeenth Army "Überwachung des Zivilverkehrs" [Surveillance of civilian interaction], in BArch-MA, RH 20-17/276.

49. See Klaus-Michael Mallmann, "Der qualitative Sprung im Vernichtungsprozeß. Das Massaker von Kamenez-Podolsk Ende August 1941," *Jahrbuch für Antisemitismusforschung* 10 (2001), 239–264.

50. This applies not only to the tendentious biographies of the two eastern front generals and later resistance fighters Erich Hoepner and Carl-Heinrich von Stülpnagel by Heinrich Bücheler, *Hoepner. Ein deutsches Soldatenschicksal des Zwanzigsten Jahrhunderts* (Herford: Mittler E.S. & Sohn, 1980); *Carl-Heinrich von Stülpnagel. Soldat—Philosoph—Verschwörer. Biographie* (Berlin/Frankfurt am Main: Ullstein, 1989) but also, for example, to the standard work by Peter Hoffmann, *Widerstand, Staatsstreich, Attentat. Der Kampf der Opposition gegen Hitler* (Munich: Piper, 1969).

51. See Hürter, *Hitlers Heerführer*, 555–556, 564–565, and 594–595.

52. Hearing of Weichs by the Seventh US Army, May 30, 1945, in Bundesarchiv Koblenz, All.Proz. 2/FC 6180 P (Weichs). Original in English.

53. See Weichs's diary, entry for July 21, 1944, in BArch-MA, N 19/3, fols. 187–188: "A stab in the back like in 1918 but worse because it comes from a source from which one would have expected the opposite."

54. Heinrich Himmler, *Geheimreden 1933 bis 1945 und andere Ansprachen*, ed. Agnes F. Petersen and Bradley F. Smith (Frankfurt am Main: Propyläen, 1974), 201. On this meeting and Himmler's speech see also Förster, "Geistige Kriegführung," 602–605; Rudolf-Christoph Freiherr von Gersdorff, *Soldat im Untergang* (Frankfurt am Main: Ullstein, 1977), 146.

55. Speech by Himmler in Sonthofen, May 5, 1941, quoted in Peter Longerich, *Heinrich Himmler. Biographie* (Berlin: Siedler, 2008), 715. For similar remarks see Himmler's speech in Sonthofen on May 24, 1944, Longerich, *Heinrich Himmler*.

56. Speech by Himmer in Sonthofen, June 21, 1944, Longerich, *Heinrich Himmler*, 716.

57. Manuscript of conversation wiretapped by the Seventh US Army, July 26, 1945, in NARA, RG 238. Original in English.

2 Jews Sent into the Occupied Soviet Territories for Labor Deployment, 1942–1943

Martin Dean

It is widely assumed that the Einsatzgruppen of the German Security Police dealt fairly rapidly with the Jews of the occupied Soviet territories and that by the time of the liquidation of the Smolensk ghetto in the summer of 1942, there were almost no more Jews to be found behind the German front lines, especially in those parts of the Soviet Union that remained under German military administration.[1] A few exceptions to this assumption have been the subject of research since the partial opening of the Soviet archives to Western researchers. These include the camps for Jews established in southern Ukraine (under German civil administration) in 1942–1943, along the so-called Transit Highway (*Durchgangsstrasse*, or DG) IV, where Romanian Jews were brought in to supplement the dwindling numbers of Ukrainian Jews. There was also a network of concentration camp sub-camps in Estonia, which held thousands of Jews sent there for the extraction of shale oil, including even some brought in from Hungary in the summer of 1944.[2] The historian Christian Gerlach identified several transports of Polish Jews from the Warsaw ghetto in 1942 that were sent to destinations including Minsk, Bobruisk (now Babruysk), Mogilev (now Mahiliou), and Smolensk, mainly for skilled labor deployments.[3]

One fairly well documented example of Jews being sent into occupied Russian territory from the German Reich for use as labor is the so-called *Osteinsatz*, or deployment to the east, of Jews from Silesia in the winter of 1941–1942. This concerned a group of more than 300 Jews taken mostly from the *Reichsautobahn* (RAB) camps at the end of 1941. They were deployed to Sebezh and several other places in western Russia for the purpose of converting the railway lines to a narrower gauge behind the German front lines. Surprisingly, the survivors were sent back to Silesia after only three months, following an outbreak of typhus among the group. This story has been told by Bella Guttermann in her article "Jews in the Service of the Organisation Todt," but she characterizes it as a unique experiment that was not repeated.[4]

This essay will discuss briefly again the main features of the *Osteinsatz* to Sebezh, described by Guttermann, but will also look at several other similar labor deployments of Jews from the Warthegau, Warsaw, and other parts of pre-1939 Poland (some via the Baltic States) in 1942–1943. These case studies will be examined in conjunction with German policies on the establishment of forced labor camps in the occupied Soviet territories and the use of Jewish labor in those regions. It seems that the ad hoc use of available Jewish labor in occupied Russian territory occurred on more than one occasion and was even practiced by the Central Construction Office (*Zentralbauleitung*) of the Waffen-SS, which, for example, brought skilled Jewish craftsmen from Warsaw and Minsk to work in Smolensk and at other sites. Due to the paucity of contemporary German documentation, evidence of these labor deployments is drawn mainly from survivor testimony, including more recent video testimonies collected by the University of Southern California's (USC) Shoah Foundation Visual History Archive. In some cases, additional corroboration can be found in postwar German trials and also the reports of the Soviet Extraordinary State Commission (ChGK). Of particular value in recreating these events has also been the opening of the International Tracing Service (ITS) archives, which contain information on the paths of persecution for a large proportion of Jewish survivors.

The existence of more than three separate construction projects in occupied central and northern Russia in 1942–1943, requiring the importation of Jewish labor from the West, might appear rather surprising. Yet it demonstrates that certain aspects of the German war economy did receive temporary priority over the general policy of destruction directed toward the Jews. In particular, the useful nature of these Jewish workers probably also explains why those who survived were generally evacuated, rather than killed, once these tasks were completed or cut short by the advancing Soviet front. Indeed, we know about these camps mainly from the reports of Jewish survivors.

There was in fact a widespread policy of ghettoization in German-occupied eastern Belorussia and Russia in the second half of 1941 and the first months of 1942. The German authorities established more than a hundred ghettos in eastern Belorussia and around fifty ghettos on occupied Russian territory. Most of these ghettos only existed for a few weeks or months before they were liquidated by units of Einsatzgruppe B in mass shooting operations. However, due to the severe winter of 1941–1942, shortages of personnel, and the effects of the Soviet winter offensive before Moscow, the elimination of these ghettos dragged on into the spring and summer of 1942.[5]

These mass shootings reflected a policy of complete annihilation toward the native Jewish population in these regions, which was more or less completed by the summer of 1942. In eastern Belorussia, the last ghettos to be liquidated were in Khotimsk on September 3–5, and, according to local research, in Sloboda, in October 1942. The last ghettos on Russian territory west of Moscow were liquidated in the summer of 1942, including those in Rzhev and Smolensk in July. Only in very few places were a limited number of skilled workers retained after the ghetto liquidations. For example, in Petrovichi, a few Jewish specialist workers were kept alive at the time of the ghetto liquidation, but these people were subsequently shot.⁶ Given the thoroughness of these extermination operations behind the central and northern sectors of the Eastern Front, it might be reasonable to assume that these regions would remain *judenrein* (purged of Jews) for the remainder of the occupation.

Despite the German emphasis on excluding Jews from the skilled labor force in the occupied Soviet territories, which was enforced quite rigorously in occupied eastern Belorussia and Russia under Wehrmacht occupation, there was some Jewish forced labor in the short-lived ghettos in these regions.⁷ In Smolensk in particular, hundreds of Jews from the ghetto performed forced labor for almost one year. Smaller forced labor camps for Jews existed, for example, also in Chashniki (eastern Belorussia) and at Oster near Roslavl.⁸ However, for certain specific construction projects, the relevant German offices decided to use Jewish laborers who had already been assembled (and to some extent also selected and trained) in the forced labor camps for Jews (ZALfJs) and ghettos that still existed further to the west. In Generalkommissariat Weissruthenien, for example, a number of larger ghettos and/or ZALfJs existed well into 1943, including those in Głębokie (Hlybokaye), Krasne (Krasnae), Lida, Minsk, and Nowogródek (Navahrudak).⁹

This importation of Jews for labor purposes into the military-occupied areas of eastern Belorussia and Russia raises the question of whether it was part of a deliberate policy of "destruction through work," or if urgent military-related construction may have temporarily overridden Himmler's plans for complete annihilation. Recent scholarship has become more nuanced and is careful to avoid interpreting all Jewish labor deployment simply as "destruction through work." As Christopher Browning has cautiously put it: "the German use of slave labor was not a matter of consensus and varied so much according to time and place that no single phrase (such as 'destruction through labor') can capture some presumed consistency and essence of Nazi ideological policy."¹⁰ The examples described below tend to confirm the view that the treatment of Jewish forced laborers, even in the east, varied considerably according to the German organizations in charge and the nature of the labor assignment. First to be examined will be the *Osteinsatz* of Silesian Jews in Russia, which was among the initial labor deployments to the east. In January 1942, a group of around 350 Jewish forced laborers sent from the Gross Masselwitz forced labor camp for Jews in Breslau, Upper Silesia, arrived by train in Sebezh (located about 170 kilometers, or 106 miles, south of Pskov) in order to work on narrowing the gauge of the railway line between Sebezh and Velikie Luki under the supervision of the Organisation Todt (OT).

The men had been selected in the ZALfJs of Sakrau, Brande, Eichtal, and Auenrode, where they had worked for the Reichsautobahn on road construction. They were placed in quasi-uniforms of the OT, prior to their deployment to the east and were even given some marching drills, under the command of an older Jew, who had served as an officer in the Austrian army, Julius Siegel. On the day of their departure, the Jews marched twelve kilometers (seven and a half miles) under the escort of ethnic German guards from the Gross Masselwitz camp to the railway station in Breslau (Wrocław), where they boarded freight cars and departed. As Bela Guttermann has noted: "the men's identity was masked in order to conceal the decision [by the OT] to include Jews in the task force to the East."[11]

The outward rail journey lasted more than a week, passing through Königsberg, Kaunas, and Vilnius to reach Sebezh. Max Borenstein recalled that in the boxcars they received just one bucket of coal to last twenty-four hours and were allowed out only briefly each morning to answer the call of nature.[12] In Sebezh, the OT had set up a collection and transit camp at this railway junction. Although conditions were thirty degrees (Celsius) below freezing, the Jews were put to work straight away, clearing snow and relaying track to the narrower German gauge. Max Borenstein recalled that here the Jews still slept in the boxcars, where they received straw and a blanket. Due to the extreme conditions, people were dying every day. David Fischel remembered working from seven in the morning to around three or four in the afternoon, when it got dark. Probably at the end of the trip, Fischel became sick with typhus in Sebezh and was seen there by the Jewish doctor Wolf Leitner, who, however, had no real medicines with which to treat him.[13]

According to Guttermann's analysis, based on testimonies at Yad Vashem, around fifty men were selected in Sebezh and remained working there throughout the period of the deployment, while the main group traveled on to Chikhachevo and from there to Idritsa (twenty-four kilometers, or fifteen miles, east of Sebezh).

Max Borenstein recalled that in Idritsa, the Jews were accommodated in a former Russian military camp. On arrival, they had to clean up the camp, as the corpses of some previous inmates (probably Soviet POWs) were still lying in the bunks; other corpses were reputedly lying under a huge mound of snow and ice. The main problem was that the entire camp was still infested with "typhoid" [sic this should be typhus, carried by lice, MD]. Here the Jews again worked along the railroad changing the gauge. From Idritsa, Borenstein recalls moving further east to another small town named Mayevo (eighty kilometers, or fifty miles, east of Sebezh).[14] Other than in Idritsa, the Jews generally remained in the boxcars to sleep. The very cold weather and problems with typhus meant that increasing numbers of Jews became sick. Dr. Leitner encouraged them to keep moving all the time, so as not to freeze up and die in the snow.[15]

The main group passed through at least one more site near Velikie Luki, before being sent north to the village of Chikhachevo (140 kilometers, or 87.5 miles, north-northeast of Sebezh). According to Guttermann's summary, "in Chikhachevo... they received better treatment, as the entire task force—soldiers, civilian workers, forced laborers, and Jews—shared the same living conditions. The terrible winter blunted the antipathy, and the anti-Jewish abuse stopped. Only those doing sloppy work were punished."[16]

By this time, however, after several weeks, among the Jews the typhus infections had begun to produce a number of fatalities. Soon the OT decided to reunite the Jews at Chikhachevo with the initial group in Sebezh,[17] where Dr. Leitner tried to treat those who had become sick and separate them from the healthy, to stop the spread of the disease. However, now only around half of the men were still capable of working. Not long after the entire group was gathered in Sebezh, a German doctor recommended that they be returned to Germany, even though the OT commander wanted them to continue their work. Initially, the OT officials in charge issued instructions only to evacuate the healthy Jewish workers, but after protests by Dr. Leitner, the Wehrmacht doctors were so scared that the epidemic might spread, they decided to send them all back by rail as a group.[18]

The healthy workers literally dragged the sick men some three kilometers (1.8 miles) to board the railroad cars. The Jews received small rations for the journey, but suffered especially from a lack of water along the way. More prisoners died during this trip back and the group was disinfected twice along the route in Vilnius and Kaunas. In March 1942, after ten days of traveling, only between 120 and 150 men returned to Breslau and the Gross Masselwitz camp. "Upon their arrival, the other prisoners stared at them in astonishment, finding them shaggy and bearded, dehydrated and pale." A few days later, they were transferred to the St. Annaberg camp to be treated by Dr. Shmuel Mittelmann of Sosnowiec. Another twelve men died here, but the remainder recovered and were dispersed among ZALfJs Gräditz, Markstädt, and Bunzlau, where they earned a degree of respect from the other prisoners for having survived the *Osteinsatz*.[19]

Even before this deployment by the OT to narrow the gauge of the Russian railroads, there had been an earlier transfer of Jews into the newly occupied Soviet territories, shortly after the start of Operation Barbarossa. The first group of Jews to arrive in ZALfJ Palemonas in Lithuania in the summer of 1941 consisted of Polish Jews, who had already been working for the OT on road construction for several months. These Jews had worked first in Praust (Pruszcz Gdański) near Danzig before the German invasion of the Soviet Union, and then were sent to Palemonas together as a group with the same OT supervisors from the Praust camp. Albert Kowit from Ozorków, who was among this initial group, worked first around Palemonas clearing the forests, in preparation for converting a single-track railroad into double tracks.[20]

Then in the spring of 1942, additional Polish Jews were sent to Palemonas from various RAB-camps in Danzig-West Prussia.[21] Boris Kot, who was sent to Palemonas in the summer of 1942 from the Kaunas (Kovno) ghetto, recalls that there were Jews from the Litzmannstadt (Łódź) and Vilnius (Vilna/Wilno) ghettos in the camp. Some sources indicate that at times there were as many as three hundred, or even five hundred Jews in ZALfJ Palemonas. The barracks were very overcrowded with people sleeping in three-tiered bunk beds.[22] For example, Jews were also sent in May 1942 to Palemonas from the Borowensee (aka Owśnice) camp in Danzig-West Prussia, where they had been engaged in road construction and clearing snow from the highway.[23]

From Palemonas, the Jews from the Warthegau were then sent on to a series of more than ten separate smaller camps in Latvia, where they were mainly employed cutting railway ties from the forests or performing railroad construction work. Information about these camps in Latvia comes almost exclusively from a handful of Jewish survivors. For example, Jewish survivor Irving/Ignatz Kurek was sent from his hometown of Ozorków via Sdroien (Zdroje) and then Palemonas on to camps in Latvia in Saunags and Mazirbe. Regarding Saunags, Kurek stated that he was there with only a small group of Jews, building a camp for others. He stayed there for a couple of months and also mentions that the work involved preparing railroad ties.[24]

A more detailed description of the camp has been given by survivor Mendel Sznajder. In Saunags, the Jews were used by the Germans to cut down trees for making wooden railroad ties. It was a small camp for just over fifty people, who were housed in two buildings that were surrounded by just a small amount of barbed wire. While in Saunags, Sznajder, who learned some Latvian, came into contact with local Christians, who belonged to a sect of Pentecostalists. As he was trusted by the German foreman, he was even able to attend a service there in April 1943, at which Mrs. Sandbergs offered prayers for all the congregation and also specifically for the Jews in their midst, that they would be freed and allowed to join their families. Mendel Sznajder was very moved by this solidarity expressed by these Latvian Christians. From Saunags, Sznajder was transferred to Mazirbe, where his group did the same thing, cutting railway ties. From there, he was sent on to a collection camp in Talsen, before going on to another camp in Gawesen, where the Jews again did the same kind of work in the forests.[25]

Another similar OT camp for Polish Jews was located in Roja in Latvia. David Grabin explained that in Roja the Jews were used by the Germans to make wooden railroad ties from trees. Grabin's job was to decide what size of railroad tie could be made from a particular tree trunk and then saw it into the appropriate size chunks. The work was supervised by Germans from the OT and the Jews were guarded by Lithuanians. The food rations were never enough, he continued, but generally the treatment was fair. At the end of 1942, he was sent on to another camp on the coast in Plensums (Plieņciems). These lumber camps in Latvia were not large, consisting of groups of maybe fifty to hundred Jewish men. Men would leave the work site or the camp at times to beg for food from the local farmers.

Regarding the aforementioned camp at Gawesen in southwestern Latvia, Mendel Sznajder recalled that a senior OT official named Forster came to Gawesen to conduct an investigation into conditions there. At that time, there were about one hundred sick Jews among the group of just a few hundred men. Sznajder told Forster that the reason for so many people getting sick was the lack of food. At that time Sznajder had made a deal with the guards, so that people could sneak out of the camp to beg for extra food from the local population. However, one of Sznajder's friends, named David, was shot by a Ukrainian camp guard while returning to the camp from one of these foraging trips.

Jews from the Warthegau passed through the following camps run by the OT in Latvia: Engure, Eleja-Meitane, Gawesen, Kaltene, Mazirbe, Mērsrags, Plieņciems, Roja, Saunags, and Upesgrīva. Conditions were comparatively better than in many other ZALfJs or concentration camp subcamps, as the men had some access to additional food from the local population and relatively good relations with the OT officials that supervised the work, scattered in smaller groups. But when they were concentrated again at the Eleja-Meitane camp for railroad construction work in 1943, an outbreak of typhus occurred and the death rate went up. This may have been because they were joined here by other Jews from the Baltic States, who had previously been in the Riga ghetto. Almost all of the Polish Jews that survived these Latvian camps were evacuated by the SS to Germany in 1944, via the Riga-Kaiserwald and Stutthof concentration camps.

These transfers of Polish Jews from the Warthegau, first to Danzig-West Prussia and then on into Lithuania and Latvia for various construction projects, are of particular interest, as it appeared quite logical for the same OT work group to take with them their Jewish workers when deployed into Lithuanian and Latvian territory following the invasion of the Soviet Union. A few of these Jews survived the war, as the German authorities in Lithuania and Latvia had decided by 1942 that a certain amount of Jewish labor was still required for the sake of the war effort,[26] which meant that some of these Jews were eventually also evacuated from the Baltic States in 1944, when the advance of the Red Army threatened to cut them off from further retreat. Although the survival rate was not high, these men were among very few people who survived at all from some of the ghettos in the Hohensalza region of the Warthegau.

In early 1942, the Central Construction Office of the Waffen-SS established a forced labor camp for Jews in the city of Smolensk. The camp was based in the western part of the city on the territory of the unfinished Soviet Railway

Workers' Hospital. The Jewish inmates built and renovated the hospital for use as a rest and recuperation hostel for members of Einsatzgruppe B.

SS-Untersturmführer Johannes Weizenhöfer, the head of the local branch office (Aussenstelle) in Smolensk of the Zentralbauleitung, was also in charge of work at the camp. In January 1942, he had been transferred from the offices of the Higher SS and Police Leader (HSSPF) for Central Russia in Mogilev to work for Einsatzgruppe B in Smolensk. Initially, he used Russian workers and Soviet POWs for the construction projects, but due to a shortage of labor, soon he received permission from SS-Brigadeführer Erich Naumann, the head of Einsatzgruppe B, to collect a group of Jewish workers from the Minsk ghetto. Therefore, Weizenhofer brought about 250 to 300 skilled Jewish craftsmen (including masons and carpenters), as well as twenty Jewish women for office cleaning, from the Minsk ghetto to Smolensk by truck. He also requisitioned about another 150 Jewish workers from the Smolensk ghetto, so that about 400 prisoners were interned in the camp by the spring of 1942.

The camp was guarded by local Russian auxiliary police, who had been trained at the police leadership camp in Orsha. Every morning the Jewish camp elder, a rabbi, was required to submit a list of the sick and disabled prisoners. Those people unfit for work were then shot by members of the Security Police or by the police auxiliaries on the territory of the Railway Workers' Hospital. Weizenhöfer, in his postwar interrogation, noted that at least thirty to forty Jewish inmates were shot during his time at the camp, up until early September 1942. He added also that on the authority of Naumann, the Jews in the camp were excluded from the liquidation of the Smolensk ghetto on July 15, 1942, which was carried out in part using gas vans. Some of the remaining clothing and shoes from the ghetto were taken to the camp, to be used by the Jewish workers. When Weizenhöfer was transferred from Smolensk in September 1942, SS-Untersturmführer Behr succeeded him in charge of construction work for the SS in Smolensk.[27]

During the summer of 1942, additional Jews were brought to ZALfJ Smolensk as most of the ghettos in Generalkommissariat Weissruthenien (White Ruthenia / western Belorussia), further to the west, were being liquidated. Dr. Pavel Kesarev, who worked in the hospital for the civilian population in Smolensk during the occupation, recalled that in the summer 1942, more than a thousand Jewish craftsmen were brought from the former territory of Poland. Some of the sick were brought to his dispensary. He said that the Jewish prisoners were rebuilding the Smolensk Railway Workers' Hospital for the Gestapo.[28]

Testimonies and other documentation from at least eight survivors reveal that Jews were brought to ZALfJ Smolensk from a variety of other camps and ghettos, including from Dworzec and Slonim in Generalkommissariat Weissruthenien,[29] and also from Grójec, via the Warsaw ghetto. The precise dates of these transfers are hard to determine from the testimonies, but most seem to date from the summer of 1942, although it is possible that some Jews selected from ghettos outside Minsk were included in the initial batch of workers in early 1942. As the testimonies diverge somewhat regarding the work conducted, it is conceivable that there was more than one ZALfJ in Smolensk, but more likely the Jews were split up into various groups performing different kinds of work.

For example, Joseph Himmelstein-Stone recalls being sent from the Dworzec labor camp to ZALfJ Smolensk in June 1942, via the Minsk ghetto. He traveled by rail from Dworzec to Minsk with his father, but they did not work there, it was only a transfer station. In Smolensk, he and his father worked as tailors fixing the uniforms of dead German soldiers and cleaning barracks. His father fell ill and died in December 1942, and Joseph recalls that at some point control of the camp was transferred from the Wehrmacht to the SS. He says at least one high-ranking officer showed some kindness and gave him some bread, probably because of Joseph's young age. In June 1943, Joseph was transferred to another camp in Mogilev, where he also cleaned the barracks.[30]

Another survivor transferred from Dworzec, Jacob Fishkin, also recalls being sent to Smolensk by rail in the summer of 1942. On the journey, the Jewish workers received some food, as they were needed as laborers. In Smolensk, he worked with his father repairing the boots of German soldiers. After some time, a new group of guards entered the camp, and regular selections were conducted of those who could not work properly, so the number of workers continually declined. He notes that of around seven hundred Jews in the camp when he arrived, only one hundred were still alive when he left. From Smolensk, he was also transferred to a camp in Mogilev, sometime after the German defeat in Stalingrad.[31] Izak Levit reported that there were groups of tailors, furriers, and cobblers working for the Wehrmacht in the camp, which held around 250 Jews altogether and was surrounded with barbed wire, guarded by the SS and Russian auxiliaries.[32]

Another group of Jewish workers was selected at the Umschlagplatz (collection point) in the Warsaw ghetto, probably in September 1942, and sent from there to Smolensk. The group contained around eighty Jews from Grójec, who had been kept in a labor camp there as skilled craftsmen working for the Wehrmacht, after the transfer of the other Jews from the Grójec ghetto to the Warsaw ghetto, in February 1941. Three survivors of the Grójec group have reported on their experiences in ZALfJ Smolensk.[33]

They traveled at least five days in cattle trucks before arriving in Smolensk. Henry Silberstein worked there as a skilled craftsman, completing the tin roof of a large unfinished Soviet hospital. He slept in a three-tiered bunk in barracks and received coffee and bread for breakfast, and a soup for lunch. He recalled an SS officer, who was an engineer, commenting that the Jews from Warsaw did better work than the locals.[34]

In the joint account of the Hamer brothers from Grójec and also in Silberstein's testimony, there are reports of numerous killings of Jews in the camp. Sometimes at night, German SS and their Russian auxiliaries would enter the barracks and select mostly sick workers, subjecting them to abuse or demands for money, before taking them out and shooting them. Silberstein recalls that one night the guards found money in a jacket he had been given and then took away his badge with a number, which was effectively a death sentence. Through the intervention of a respected Jewish carpenter, Hershel, Silberstein managed to retrieve his badge. Then the next night two other Jews were hanged following a similar selection. Other prisoners were taken out and shot in a ditch located near the barracks and one man had his head split open. On another occasion, the Hamer brothers note that the SS requisitioned Jewish girls from the camp for a banquet, which meant that they would be raped and then killed. A girl named Mania managed to avoid this fate by getting her German drunk till he was unconscious, so she could escape; but her father in the meantime had committed suicide, choosing to go with eighteen others selected to be killed, as he feared the worst for his daughter. The few survivors of the Grójec group were sent via Minsk on to Lublin in the second half of 1943. Only three of them reportedly returned to Grójec at the end of the war.[35]

According to the testimony of a local inhabitant, who lived on Red Navy Street, in the fall of 1942 many of the prisoners were killed and buried on the hospital grounds. A Soviet exhumation, conducted on October 22, 1943, after the city's liberation, uncovered an estimated 1,500 corpses on the territory of the Railway Workers' Hospital in Smolensk.[36] ITS records indicate that only a handful of Jews survived the war, although more were evacuated from ZALfJ Smolensk via Minsk to various concentration camps and subcamps further west, where a number perished in turn.

The last major labor deployment of Jews into occupied Russia originating from Polish ghettos was from ZALfJ Schischmaren (aka Žiežmariai) in Lithuania in the spring of 1943. As many as a thousand Jews had been collected here, both men and women, mainly from the ghettos located southeast of Wilno/Vilnius, including Oszmiana, Holszany, and Smorgonie, which had survived into late 1942 thanks to their transfer from Generalkommissariat (Gk) Weissruthenien to Gk Litauen (Lithuania) in the spring of 1942, that is after the clearing of the countryside (*das flache Land*) of Jews in Gk Litauen, which had been completed by the end of 1941. In Schischmaren, the male and female Jewish workers had been doing highway construction work for the OT.[37]

In the spring and summer of 1943, there were several deployments from ZALfJ Schischmaren to places including Pskov (then in Gk Estland, now in Russia) and also Mokrovo, which is located in northern Russia about 120 kilometers (75 miles) northeast of Pskov. From the spring of 1943 until the fall of that year, the occupying German forces operated a ZALfJ in Mokrovo. Information on this little-known camp comes mainly from four female Jewish survivors interviewed in the 1990s by the USC Shoah Foundation (VHF).

Rachel Lendzin recalled the journey from Schischmaren to Mokrovo: "The [Jewish] workers were taken first by truck, and then by rail cars to Mokrovo … it took about two days and one night, there were about 100 people in each railcar, we couldn't move. Every eight hours or so, they would open the doors and there would be two pails of water for the entire car, so everyone got a spoonful of water." Halfway through the trip, there was an explosion under Rachel's railcar and several people fell on top of her. The Germans unloaded the Jews from the car, and the Jews thought that the SS officers were going to shoot them. Russian partisans had placed a bomb under the rail lines. Within four hours, the rail lines were fixed and they were loaded back onto the train and taken to Mokrovo.[38]

The Mokrovo camp consisted of four sleeping barracks and a kitchen located between two forests. The men and women were quartered separately. They wore the clothes they still had from home bearing Jewish stars. They slept in bunk beds and each day received four slices of bread and a good soup. The food was put in a metal can and they would eat wherever they could sit down. There was a place outside where the workers could wash themselves.[39]

According to Miriam Lederman, the camp was always in need of fresh water, which was delivered to the camp in huge trucks, like gasoline trucks. The Jewish workers sometimes would go with the Germans to help fill up the trucks with water. Liza Pariser recalled that it was a new camp when her group arrived and that it was a very marshy area with lots of mosquitoes.[40]

Liza noted that the workers had to cut down trees to prepare the land for a railroad. According to the ITS's *Verzeichnis der Haftstätten*, the work was supervised by the OT. Rachel Lendzin states that at Mokrovo the workers were not treated badly. Everyone had a different job, and the group Rachel was in also cut down trees. The group after her, made up of boys, put dynamite under the roots. Another group's job was to unload sand from wagons. Five or six girls would lift a rail and put it in place, then carry the wood over. "It was hard labor," Rachel said, "but they didn't beat us … when we came back from work they counted us … then they didn't bother us." The Jews also had Sundays off. After work, they would sit and talk, reminiscing about home and school, but never about their families. Sara Engor reports that the workers were laying rail lines and ordinary soldiers from the Wehrmacht supervised and guarded them. Sara Benusiglio (née Riebstein), however, recalls there being Estonian SS guards. Miriam Lederman was fortunate to get a job in the kitchen, where the work was less arduous.[41]

The survivors mention an internal Jewish hierarchy within the camp, naming Motel Mirski as having been in charge. Rachel Lendzin recalled that three people were killed during her time at Mokrovo. A friend of hers was bitten by a snake, but a Russian doctor drained the poison out, so she was able to recover. One of the victims was the father of Liza Pariser. After an accident, his leg became infected, but initially the Germans took him to a nearby hospital where his leg was amputated. Liza even managed to visit him by traveling on the water trucks with the Germans, but eventually she heard from her aunt, who also visited him from the camp, that he had been forced to dig a ditch and then was shot.[42]

Survivors mention occasional exchanges of fire between the German soldiers and Soviet partisans at night near the camp and also on the journeys to collect water. Miriam Lederman recalls that one night Russian partisans came to the barracks and said they would come back later to take out as many people as they can. "But nobody trusted each other," Miriam says, "and the Judenrat said the partisans could never take all of the people, so they didn't agree to it, and that was the end of it."[43]

In the fall of 1943, after around six months in the camp, the Jews were transferred to other camps further to the West. Rachel Lendzin recalls being sent to Petschur in Estonia (aka Petseri or Pechory, now in Russia). Other survivors mention being transferred to a camp in Kūdupe, Latvia. Almost all of the known survivors (all women) subsequently passed through Kaiserwald concentration camp in late 1943 or early 1944.[44]

Pskov (Pleskau in German) is located about 272 kilometers (170 miles) southwest of Leningrad (now St. Petersburg) on the Velikaia River. At the start of 1942, authority was transferred from the Wehrmacht to a German civilian administration. Pleskau became part of Gebiet Petschur and was incorporated into Generalkommissariat Estland, within Reichskommissariat Ostland.

According to the contemporary diaries of Herman Kruk (Vilnius/Vilna/Wilno ghetto) and Avraham Tory (Kaunus/Kovno ghetto), reports were circulating in May and June 1943, that a number of healthy workers from the "Zezmer" camp (ZALfJ Schischmaren) were being transferred to Pskov on the orders of the road construction company that ran the Zezmer camp.[45] At that time, more than a thousand Jews were reportedly in ZALfJ Schischmaren, and it seems likely that at least one hundred were transferred to the labor camp in Pskov. What is known about the camp is derived mainly from fragmentary survivor testimonies, but postwar compensation claims from more than six survivors, who were all sent to ZALfJ Pskov from Schischmaren, serve to firm up a rough outline of the camp's history.

Cypa Gutman made a report to the ITS in 1951, which outlined several key details. The camp was surrounded by barbed wire and guarded by members of the SS. According to Gutman, the camp held around five hundred people, of whom about half were women. The work conducted there consisted of construction work on the railroad.[46]

Syma Freund recalled in the 1990s being in ZALfJ Pskov for about six months. She was taken to the camp by train and worked, while living in the camp, more than eight hours a day. She recalled that the Russians bombed the trains, but not the camp, where she slept in bunk beds (pritches) within the barracks. The camp had SS guards and she recalled there were many mosquitoes that made her scratch their itching bites. From Pleskau, she subsequently was sent to Kaiserwald concentration camp in Riga.[47]

Syma Schwarz (née Golub) recalls that on her arrival in the camp many people were completely exhausted from the journey and some died soon afterward. She said that she worked on a farm while staying in the camp and could get some extra food at her work on the sly. Her mother and sister stayed in the barrack as they were sick with typhus. All their belongings had been taken away on arrival. The soup she ate had potatoes or bread in it and tasted good, but there was not enough. In the camp, some prisoners heard from listening secretly to the radio that the Russian forces were not far away.[48]

The prisoners of the Pskov camp give a variety of subsequent destinations. It seems that most were sent on from Pskov either to ZALfJ Kudeb (Kūdupe), on the eastern border of Latvia, or to ZALfJ Petschur (Pechory), still in Estonia, although some mention both of these places. Most were then sent on via Riga-Kaiserwald or other concentration camps to the Stutthof main concentration camp in the summer of 1944.[49]

The time period given by survivors for their stay in Pskov varies quite a bit, but it seems likely that they all arrived as one group from Schischmaren in around June 1943, and departed a few months later. The chronology given by Fruma Schkop (b. 1927 in Krewo) appears to be roughly correct. She was transferred from Zezmary (Schischmaren) to Pskov in June 1943, and then on to Pechory (Petschur) in October 1943.[50]

Similar examples of forced labor camps for Jews that existed in 1942 and 1943 can be documented also for eastern Belorussia. As noted above, some Jews from ZALfJ Smolensk were sent on to ZALfJ Mogilev and were also evacuated from there. Jews were also sent in 1942 from the Warsaw ghetto to the Waldlager in Bobruisk, where they remained until October 1943. There are additional reports of Jews from the Szczuczyn ghetto (near Lida) being sent to a ZALfJ near Borisov in September 1942, although it seems very few of these people survived.[51]

Several aspects of these deployments are of interest, although the experiences of surviving prisoners do not differ very much from those of Jews in the ghettos and concentration camps of the Baltic States, more than twenty thousand of which were evacuated to Stutthof concentration camp in the summer of 1944.[52] Those working directly for the OT or the Wehrmacht appear to have been treated better than those directly subordinated to the SS, notably those working on construction in Smolensk or Bobruisk, where sick prisoners were regularly shot, and arbitrary brutality and murder were daily events. In Bobruisk, for example, reportedly only 90 out of 1,500 Jews survived the deployment of just over one year.[53]

From the deployment in May 1942 of 403 Jews from Slonim to work in Mogilev, we know from detailed survivor testimonies that skilled workers or those with functions within the camp had much better chances of survival than those performing manual labor. On arrival in Mogilev, the Slonim Jews were taken "to a labor camp in a bombed-out military installation called 'Dimitrov.'" The Germans separated the Slonim Jews into two categories. Sixty of the prisoners were put to work as craftsmen. Here the work conditions were tolerable. They were not beaten by the guards and were given a little extra food. The other 343 prisoners were sent to work on a construction project known as the Government House. They traveled each day to a worksite outside the camp in trucks. These laborers were abused severely by the guards and were subjected to starvation and periodic selections. Due to these conditions, by late 1943, only 29 of the 403 Jews from Slonim were still alive in the camp. After evacuation to camps in Minsk, Lublin, and Radom, where most died of typhus, the few still alive were then transferred to the Ebensee sub-camp of Mauthausen concentration camp. Only a handful of the 403 Slonim Jews sent to Mogilev survived the war.[54]

Against this high rate of attrition, conditions in the brief *Osteinsatz* around Sebezh in early 1942, but also those experienced by the Jews working for the OT at Mokrovo and Pskov in northern Russia in 1943, appear to have been less dire. The *Osteinsatz* still lost about half of its number in just over two months, but this was mainly due to the extreme weather conditions, poor food, accommodation, and clothing. It was especially due to the outbreak of a typhus epidemic. It seems the doctors decided in this case not to conduct selections, and even the sick were transported home. In Pskov and Mokrovo, where death rates were low, the few fatalities that are known resulted mainly from accidents and disease, rather than the systematic brutality of the overseers and guards, as was the case in the SS-run camps in Smolensk, Bobruisk, and Mogilev. By the time of the deployments from ZALfJ Schischmaren, in May or June of 1943, it must have been clear to many Germans that they desperately needed any laborers doing key infrastructure work, as the fortunes of war had certainly turned against them after Stalingrad.

The main explanation for why most of these camps have remained largely unknown until now lies in the sources. Most relevant German documentation has not survived and there was clearly little incentive for the responsible offices to stress their dependence on Jewish labor, as indicated by the efforts of the OT to put the Jews into uniforms. Most of the details about these camps have been pieced together from Jewish survivor testimony. A few of these accounts have been available for some time, but given the notorious effectiveness of the Einsatzgruppen in rapidly cleansing the East, few historians even thought to look for examples of Jewish labor being utilized behind the Eastern Front in 1942–1943.

The availability of many more testimonies in the last few years, thanks to the USC Shoah Foundation collection, and especially also to the summaries of compensation claims, now accessible from the ITS archives, has made it possible to trace more completely the paths of these Jews deployed to the east. The number of survivors was in most cases literally just a handful, but they serve as key witnesses to the inevitable complexity and inherent contradictions of German labor policies with regard to Jewish workers behind the Eastern Front, which cannot be adequately described by the phrase "destruction through work."

MARTIN DEAN worked from 1992 to 1997 for the Metropolitan Police War Crimes Unit in London. His publications include *Collaboration in the Holocaust* (2000), *Robbing the Jews* (2008) and, as volume editor, *The USHMM Encyclopedia of Camps and Ghettos 1933–1945*, vol. 2: *Ghettos in German-Occupied Eastern Europe* (2012).

Notes

1. The opinions stated in this chapter are those of the author and do not necessarily reflect those of the US Holocaust Memorial Museum or the US Holocaust Memorial Museum Council. Much of the information for this chapter was collected as part of the research for forthcoming volumes of *The USHMM Encyclopedia of Camps and Ghettos 1933–1945*, which is a project of the Mandel Center at the USHMM under the direction of Geoff Megargee. Special thanks go to Alexander Kruglov, Hermann Weiss, Rachel McNellis, and many other people who have assisted with this project in a variety of ways.

2. See Andrej Angrick, "Annihilation and Labor: Jews and Thoroughfare IV in Central Ukraine," in *The Shoah in Ukraine: History, Testimony, Memorialization*, ed. Ray Brandon and Wendy Lower (Bloomington: Indiana University Press, in association with the US Holocaust Memorial Museum, 2008), 190–223; and Anton Weiss-Wendt, "The Business of Survival: Baltic Oil Ltd. and Jewish Forced-Labor Camps in Estonia," *Yad Vashem Studies* 36, no. 2 (2008), 45–71.

3. Christian Gerlach, *Kalkulierte Morde: Die deutsche Wirtschafts- und Vernichtungspolitik in Weissrussland 1941 bis 1944* (Hamburg: Hamburger Edition, 1999), 762–763.

4. Bella Guttermann, "Jews in the Service of Organisation Todt in the Occupied Soviet Territories, October 1941–March 1942," *Yad Vashem Studies* 29 (2001): 65–109, see 106.

5. *The United States Holocaust Memorial Museum Encyclopedia of Camps and Ghettos 1933–1945*, vol. 2 *Ghettos in German-Occupied Eastern Europe*, vol. ed. Martin Dean, series ed. Geoffrey P. Megargee (Bloomington: Indiana University Press, in association with the US Holocaust Memorial Museum, 2012), 1640–1644 (Eastern Belorussia Region) and 1782–1788 (Occupied Russian Territory).

6. Guttermann, "Jews in the Service of Organisation Todt in the Occupied Soviet Territories, October 1941–March 1942," 1681 (Khotimsk), 1733–1734 (Sloboda), 1811–1812 (Petrovichi), 1819 (Rzhev), and 1820–1824 (Smolensk).

7. See, for example, Martin Dean, "Ghetto Labor in Generalkommissariat Weissruthenien and the Military Occupied Territories of Eastern Belorussia and Russia,"

in *Arbeit in den nationalsozialistischen Ghettos*, ed. Jürgen Hensel and Stephan Lehnstaedt (Osnabrück: fibre, 2013), 265–271. On the overall labor policy regarding Jews in eastern Belorussia, see Gerlach, *Kalkulierte Morde*, 584–585.

8. *The United States Holocaust Memorial Museum Encyclopedia of Camps and Ghettos 1933–1945*, vol. 2 *Ghettos*, 1658 (Chashniki); Report "Korück 559," report on antipartisan actions, May 25–31, 1942, in Yad Vashem Archives, M-29, FR/38, 7 (Oster).

9. *The United States Holocaust Memorial Museum Encyclopedia of Camps and Ghettos 1933–1945*, vol. 2 *Ghettos*, 1190–1193 (Głębokie), 1217–1218 (Krasne), 1225–1228 (Lida), 1233–1237 (Minsk), and 1247–1251 (Nowogródek).

10. Christopher Browning, *Remembering Survival: Inside A Nazi Slave-Labor Camp* (New York: W. W. Norton & Company, 2010), 153.

11. Guttermann, "Jews in the Service of Organisation Todt," 83–87.

12. USC Shoah Foundation Visual History Archive (hereafter VHF), # 29907, Testimony of Max Borenstein.

13. VHF, # 12911, Testimony of David Fischel. "ZAL Sebesz" is mentioned also in International Tracing Service (hereafter ITS), 6.3.3.2, TD 247966, by a former inmate of the Eichtal RAB camp.

14. VHF, # 29907, Testimony of Max Borenstein.

15. VHF, # 29907, Testimony of Max Borenstein; ITS, 6.3.3.2, TD 161458, Samuel Grinbaum; Guttermann, "Jews in the Service of Organisation Todt," 91.

16. Guttermann, "Jews in the Service of Organisation Todt," 95.

17. Guttermann, "Jews in the Service of Organisation Todt," 95–97.

18. Guttermann, "Jews in the Service of Organisation Todt," 97–98.

19. Guttermann, "Jews in the Service of Organisation Todt," 98–103.

20. Christoph Dieckmann, *Deutsche Besatzungspolitik in Litauen 1941–1944* (Göttingen: Wallstein, 2011), 1091–1092; VHF, # 16707, Testimony of Albert Kowit.

21. ITS, CNI, Abram DOBRZYNSKI (b. January 23, 1929 in Ozorkow); VHF, # 33275, Testimony of Abraham Dobin (aka Dobrzynski).

22. Dieckmann, *Deutsche Besatzungspolitik*, 1092, gives the figure of 300 Polish Jews in the OT camp; VHF, # 33275, gives the figure of 500.

23. ITS, 6.3.3.2, TD 360709, David Grabinski; VHF, # 30601.

24. VHF, # 14966, Testimony of Irving Kurek.

25. VHF, # 46107, Testimony of Mendel Sznajder.

26. See Dieckmann, *Deutsche Besatzungspolitik*, 1009–1011 (Lithuania); Andrej Angrick and Peter Klein, *Die "Endlösung" in Riga: Ausbeutung und Vernichtung 1941–1944* (Darmstadt: Wissenschaftliche Buchgesellschaft, 2006), 202.

27. USHMM, RG-14.101M, fol. 2000, fr. 353–377 (Bundesarchiv Aussenstelle-Ludwigsburg (BA-L), B 162/25005), 6–20, Interrogations of Johannes Weizenhofer on March 12, 1960 and October 12, 1962.

28. State Archives of the Russian Federation (hereafter GARF), 7021-44-15, 63 (verso), statement of Dr. P.I. Kesarev on October 4, 1943 to Medical General–Lieutenant Prof. N. N. Burdenko.

29. Re: Dworzec, see notes 26 and 27. ITS, 6.3.3.2, TD 529840, Meir Kulisewski (Slonim); TD 405892, Schlomo Schuchotowicz (Slonim).

30. VHF, # 20123, Video testimony of Joseph Himmelstein-Stone; ITS, 6.3.3.2, TD 510449, Joseph Stone (or Himmelstein), b. January 1, 1930.

31. VHF, # 11294, Video testimony of Jacob Fishkin.
32. ITS, 1.1.0.7, fol. 76, 459.
33. Josef Hamer and Abram Hamer, "Di lezte Oyszidlung," in *Megilat Gritse*, ed. I. B. Alterman (Tel Aviv: Gritse Association in Isreal, 1955), 294–298; VHF, # 12115, Video testimony of Henry Silberstein; see also ITS, 6.3.3.2, TD 299593, Josef Hamer; TD 299591, Abram Hamer; and TD 498091, Henry Silberstein. These sources give conflicting dates for the period in Smolensk, but since the Hamer brothers report being there for around eleven months, the period from summer 1942 until summer 1943, just before the Soviets recaptured the city, seems likely. It is not clear from the yizkor book whether other Jews came from Warsaw with the Grójec group, as they were selected among four hundred Jewish workers at the "Umschlagplatz," but the other Jews are not mentioned subsequently.
34. VHF, # 12115.
35. VHF, # 12115; I. B. Alterman, *Megilat Gritse* (Tel Aviv: Gritse Association in Isreal, 1955), 294–298; Jewish Historical Institute, Warsaw (AŻIH), 301/4802, Testimony of Adam Bitter, 1950. The rape of Jewish women by German personnel was clearly against Nazi racial laws, nonetheless, it took place in dozens of different locations in the occupied East; see, for example, *The United States Holocaust Memorial Museum Encyclopedia of Camps and Ghettos 1933–1945*, vol. 2 Ghettos, 1139, 1180, 1199, 1368, 1381, 1450, 1471, 1475, 1546, 1561, 1655, 1679, 1727, 1765, 1789, 1798, 1801, 1812, and 1822.
36. GARF, 7021-44-15, 63 (verso); and 7021-44-1083, 2. This figure may be too high, as probably not more than a thousand Jews passed through the camp.
37. VHF, # 24713, Testimony of Liza Pariser; VHF, # 3411, Testimony of Tania Rozmaryn.
38. VHF, # 10678.
39. VHF, # 10678.
40. VHF, # 40439, Testimony of Miriam Lederman; VHF, # 24713, Testimony of Liza Pariser.
41. VHF, # 24713; # 10678; # 39994, Testimony of Sara Engor; ITS, 1.1.0.7, fol. 76, 284; # 40439.
42. VHF, # 10678; # 24713.
43. VHF, # 40439.
44. VHF, # 10678; ITS, 1.1.0.7, fol. 76, 284; ITS, 6.3.3.2, TD 495273; TD 13653, Rachel Traurig.
45. Herman Kruk, *The Last Days of the Jerusalem of Lithuania: Chronicles from the Vilna Ghetto and the Camps, 1939–1944*, ed. Benjamin Harshav (New Haven, CT/London: YIVO Institute for Jewish Research/Yale University Press, 2002), 558; Avraham Tory, *Surviving the Holocaust: The Kovno Ghetto Diary* (Cambridge, MA: Harvard University Press, 1990), 320–321, 328, and 372.
46. ITS, 1.1.0.7, fol. 76, 338.
47. VHF, # 18162, Testimony of Syma Freund; see also ITS, 6.3.3.2, TD 412790, Syma Freund, b. November 11, 1925.
48. VHF, # 18162, Testimony of Syma Schwarz (née Golub); see also ITS, 6.3.3.2, TD 971072, Syma Schwarz.
49. ITS, 6.3.3.2, TDs 412790, 971072, 339822, 266124, 289657, 762096, 382086.
50. ITS, 6.3.3.2, TD 339822, Fruma Szkop, b. September 15, 1930 in Krewo.
51. Mario Wenzel, "Zwangsarbeitslager für Juden in den besetzten polnischen und sowjetischen Gebieten," in vol. 9: *Der Ort des Terrors: Geschichte der nationalsozialistischen Konzentrationslager*, ed. Wolfgang Benz und Barbara Distel (Munich: C.H. Beck, 2008), 146;

C. E. Volochinsky, Y. Shwartz, S. Poliaczek, et al., eds., *Sefer Zikaron li-Kehilot Shts'uts'in, Vasililishki, Ostrin, Novidvor, Roz'anke* (Tel Aviv: Irgun Yots'e Ostrin be-Yisra'el, 1966), 88. See also Gerlach, *Kalkulierte Morde*, 762–763; and http://rememor.eu/wp-content/uploads/2015/06/p06_therkel_straede_EN.pdf (re: Waldlager Bobruisk).

52. Geoffrey P. Megargee, ed., *The United States Holocaust Memorial Museum Encyclopedia of Camps and Ghettos 1933–1945*, vol. 1: *Early Camps, Youth Camps, and Concentration Camps and Subcamps under the SS-Business Administration Main Office (WVHA)* (Bloomington: Indiana University Press, in association with the US Holocaust Memorial Museum, 2009), 1420.

53. Wenzel, "Zwangsarbeitslager für Juden in den besetzten polnischen und sowjetischen Gebieten," 146; see also ITS, 6.3.3.2, TD 277274.

54. Nachum Alpert, *The Destruction of Slonim Jewry* (New York: Holocaust Library, 1989), 135; ITS, CNI, Israel Judelewicz (b. April 6, 1905); VHF, # 1553.

3 Were the Jews of North Africa Included in the Practical Planning for the "Final Solution of the Jewish Question"?

Dan Michman

To what extent were the Jews of North Africa included in the *practical* planning for the "Final Solution of the Jewish Question," that is, of Nazi Germany's extermination policy as it developed from 1941 onward? On one hand, historians have reflected on this issue only in general terms, when contemplating the overall contours of the Nazi enterprise. In the twin areas of Jewish survivor discourses and debates on restitution, on the other hand, it has been a point of intense dispute. Therefore, a systematic analysis is a desideratum. In this chapter, I will try to answer this question on the basis of our current understanding of the evolution of the Final Solution of the Jewish Question and a close reading and analysis of the so-called Protocol of the Wannsee Conference. I will also try to answer this question by introducing unstudied and unnoticed archival material.

The Historiography of the Final Solution

In the study of the foundations, development, and consolidation of the master plan for the mass murder of the Jews, a study in which extensive energies have been invested over the past few decades, scholars in the last decade have arrived at a broad consensus concerning certain essential points, even though many details are still disputed. In contrast with the scholarly conceptions proposed in the initial stages of research immediately following the end of World War II, the basic and highly significant consensus is that the Nazis' operation of mass murder developed not in accordance with any organized plan but rather in a gradual, constantly expanding fashion.[1] Initially, there were the preparations for the invasion of the Soviet Union (beginning in 1940) and there was a gradual crystallization of an approach that was based on various components in Adolf Hitler's worldview, which he first formulated immediately after World War I (in his so-called first political writing of September 1919, in *Mein Kampf* and in his unpublished second book). In accordance with that worldview, the invasion of Soviet Russia

(Operation Barbarossa) was not simply a military campaign aimed at territorial expansion or at the attainment of influence but rather a military operation with ideological dimensions, with the Soviet Union symbolizing the fortress of Judeo-Bolshevism. Thus, in preparation for this new war, special ideological fighting units were set up: the *Einsatzgruppen* of the Security Police and the *Sicherheitsdienst* (SD), the intelligence service of the *Schutzstaffel* (SS), which were first created in 1938. In the first weeks of Operation Barbarossa, which was launched on June 22, 1941, the mode of action for the large-scale elimination of actual or suspected political enemies, many of whom were Jews and most of whom were men, gradually established itself. In mid-July 1941, in the wake of the repeated successes of the German forces, Hitler apparently instructed those in his immediate circle, including Heinrich Himmler, to step up the confrontation with the Jews and to explore the possibility of extensive operations against them. This instruction led to the document dated July 31, 1941, in which Hermann Göring officially authorized Reinhard Heydrich to investigate the possibility of carrying out a "comprehensive solution" (*Gesamtlösung*) of the Jewish question in Europe.[2] From reports compiled by the Einsatzgruppen and from other sources, it seems clear that, by mid-August 1941, a change had already taken place in the dimensions and systematic nature of the murders. From mid-August 1941, and in some places earlier, massive numbers of men, women, and children were massacred and entire areas were "mopped up"; similarly, the number of Jews murdered and recorded by the Einsatzgruppen increased astronomically. One of the low points in this period was the massacre at Babi Yar, near Kiev, on September 29–30, 1941, when 33,771 Jews were murdered. That same month, the initial plans for the construction of the first extermination camp at Chelmno were drafted and work began on the planned deportation of Germany's Jews, against whom severe policy measures were already being undertaken. In the meantime, the scope of massacres throughout the occupied areas of the Soviet Union widened. On November 28, Hitler held a meeting with the Mufti of Jerusalem, Haj Amin Al-Husseini. In their conversation, Hitler hinted that, if German forces managed to advance through the Caucasus Mountains, actions against the Jews would extend to that region as well. In a meeting with Nazi Party leaders on December 12, Hitler told this broadly based group that, "with regard to the Jewish question" (*bezüglich der Judenfrage*), he intended to "clean the table" (*reinen Tisch zu machen*).[3] In the first half of 1942, the plan to exterminate the Jews was expanded and began to include other parts of Europe, initially Poland, then Western Europe and, in the end, the rest of the continent.

The Wannsee Conference and Its Importance

In the context of these events, a discussion (*Besprechung*) was held on January 20, 1942, in a villa on the shores of Lake Wannsee, on the outskirts of Berlin; the meeting was attended by senior officials representing various SS departments and government ministries in the Third Reich and the subject under discussion was the "final solution of the Jewish question in Europe." In post-Holocaust discourse and writings, this gathering is invariably referred to as "the Wannsee Conference" (*Wannseekonferenz*),[4] a label that assigns to this meeting an image that greatly exceeds its true importance.[5] The document that records the proceedings of this meeting and which Adolf Eichmann worded, is termed the "minutes" (*Protokoll*) of the Wannsee Conference, although it is not a faithful record—Protokoll—of what actually transpired at that gathering, because the minutes were repeatedly reworked by Eichmann.[6] During the first decades of Holocaust research, the document was regarded by many as the smoking gun attesting to the existence of a carefully worked out plan for the execution of the Final Solution of the Jewish Question. This mistaken approach is still commonly encountered outside the community of Holocaust scholars.

Ever since the early 1990s, especially after the opening of research opportunities in the former Eastern European communist countries and in the wake of new research by many Holocaust scholars, a major change has occurred in the study of the Nazis' anti-Jewish policies in general, and the crystallization of the Final Solution in particular. As a result, the meeting at Wannsee has undergone various reevaluations and its precise place in the development of those policies has become an issue of serious debate among senior scholars of the Final Solution. Today it is clear that, with regard to the Final Solution, no organized and orderly decision-making process took place under Hitler's direction, although it is absolutely clear that he set the goal and provided the guidelines for the launching of actions that led to the extermination of the Jews, as Heydrich explicitly pointed out at the Wannsee meeting with the words "Following the Führer's initial consent" (*nach entsprechender vorheriger Genehmigung durch den Führer*).[7] The so-called minutes were an internal document, not one intended for the general public. The very fact that terms such as "extermination" or even "shooting" or "liquidation" are not used in such an internal document arouse questions and have sparked vigorous debates regarding the issue as to whether the systematic murder of all Jews was indeed the clear-cut meaning of the Final Solution, as understood at that moment by all participants. The absence of these terms is particularly blatant, when one compares the explicit and unambiguous terms used not only in reports filed by Einsatzgruppen commanders in the various regions of the Soviet Union but also in certain statements made by Hitler himself.[8] Nonetheless, there is a consensus among most Holocaust scholars that Heydrich convened the meeting in order to establish both his authority to implement the operation aimed in fact at the liquidation of the Jews and the need for coordination between all those involved in this operation, namely, the representatives of all the government ministries and nongovernment agencies participating in one or the other capacity in the execution of the "Final Solution of the Jewish Question," which was gradually evolving.[9]

The Wannsee Conference Minutes and the Number of Jews in the "Unoccupied Part of France"

One of the more familiar parts of the aforementioned "minutes" is especially important for any discussion of North African Jewry and the Holocaust: the table listing the number of Jews in the various countries destined to be included in the "Final Solution of the Jewish Question." The table, which has become iconic in popular Holocaust representations, is divided into two sections: Germany proper and all countries under direct German rule, and allies or satellites of Germany, and countries that were not (apparently: not yet) occupied (such as England, Portugal, Sweden, and Switzerland). The second section lists both parts of France: "Occupied France" with 165,000 Jews, which was under German control and the "unoccupied part of France," that is, Vichy France, with seven hundred thousand Jews.[10]

The latter figure of 700,000 is an exaggerated one for the number of Jews in unoccupied continental France and therefore raises serious questions. Some scholars have suggested that the figure also includes the Jews of North Africa. German historian Peter Longerich, who has made the inquiry into the evolution of the Final Solution one of his major research goals, insists that it includes Jews in the French colonies in North Africa.[11] However, following that statement, Longerich does not offer any referral or any arithmetical explanation. Moreover, his 772-page book refers to French African Jews in only two paragraphs, where he presents other factual information without making any mention of Wannsee or the question of French African Jewry's inclusion in the Final Solution.[12] Thus, it would appear that Longerich in fact does not believe that the Jews of North Africa were actually included in the planning of the Final Solution. Similarly, although not as insistently, Saul Friedländer writes in his book, *The Years of Extermination: Nazi Germany and the Jews, 1939–1945*, that "regarding France, Heydrich, in his initial listing, had mentioned seven hundred thousand Jews from the Vichy zone, which *probably* meant the inclusion of the Jews of French North Africa" (my emphasis).[13] However, in his book, Friedländer makes no reference to Tunisia or Algeria, and Moroccan Jews are mentioned only once—in a citation of Heydrich's comments in October 1941: Friedländer quotes Heydrich as saying that "these Jews" (Spanish Jews in France, whom Spain proposed transferring to Morocco) "would also be too far out of the direct reach of measures for a basic solution to the Jewish question to be enacted after the war." These comments indicate that the Final Solution (to be carried out *after* the war!) was defined as solely pertaining to Europe.[14] These two historians and other scholars who tend to interpret the figure of seven hundred thousand as including the Jews of French North Africa (significantly, Michel Abitbol, the leading scholar of the fate of North African

Jewry during World War II, is not included in this group)[15] do not back up their interpretation with any evidence from the period immediately preceding the preparation of background material for the Wannsee meeting.[16]

In contrast, another important group of historians argues explicitly that the Jews of North Africa were *not* included in the planning of the Final Solution. Raul Hilberg, one of the most prominent of Holocaust scholars, stated in the first edition of *The Destruction of the European Jews*, with reference to the German presence in Tunisia in 1942 and 1943, that "Tunisia was in Africa, and that the 'final solution' by its very definition was applicable only to the European continent."[17] In his discussion of the Wannsee Conference, he does not mention North African Jews.[18] Similarly, Leni Yahil, when discussing the Wannsee Conference, does not make any reference to North African Jewry, although she does say that the figures of Jews in Europe as listed in the aforementioned table are "problematic."[19] Moreover, in her book, North African Jews are mentioned only incidentally.[20] According to highly respected scholars of the Holocaust in France, the figure of the Jews in Vichy France does not include the Jews of North Africa. Michael Marrus and Robert Paxton, who discuss the minutes of the Wannsee Conference in their groundbreaking book on the Vichy government and the Jews, briefly comment that the minutes include an absurdly high figure for the number of Jews in unoccupied France.[21] Asher Cohen, in his comprehensive book on the Holocaust in France, and Daniel Carpi, in his study on the Italian authorities and the Jews of France and Tunisia during World War II, extensively discuss the number of Jews in wartime France. According to those two scholars, the citing of this high figure in the minutes apparently (Carpi stresses this adverb) stemmed from the exaggerated estimates of the number of Jews in Vichy France that were current during the first months of 1941 among experts on Jewish affairs in the General Commissariat on Jewish Questions (*Commissariat Générale aux Questions Juives*). On the basis of these estimates, Eichmann's aide in France, Theodor Dannecker, stated in a report dated July 1, 1941, that "estimates of the number of Jews range from four hundred thousand to eight hundred thousand."[22] A detailed discussion of Dannecker's figures can be found in Ahlrich Meyer's book on the Final Solution in France. According to Meyer, the figure of seven hundred thousand refers only to the Jews in southern France and does not include the Jews of North Africa. He believes that the figure is an average (*Mittelwert*) that emerged from Dannecker's calculations and he adds that the latter's report reached the desk of Franz Rademacher, the official in the Reich Ministry of Foreign Affairs who was responsible for Jewish affairs (Section D III) and who was Eichmann's counterpart. Meyer notes that it is impossible to find any additional route for the delivery or direct transmission of Dannecker's figures to Eichmann.[23]

How Were the Statistical Estimates Prepared for the Wannsee Meeting?

In research on the Nazis' anti-Jewish policy in general, immense importance is attached to the minutes of the Wannsee meeting, and, since the mid-1990s, great interest has been shown in the role that the meeting at Wannsee played in the crystallization of the Final Solution. It is therefore very surprising that, despite this fact, scholars have paid scant attention to the manner in which the figures on the various countries were compiled by Eichmann and his aides. The manner of compilation, not the de facto assumptions of Holocaust researchers, is the key to our explanation. A notable exception is the highly significant chapter by Christoph Kreutzmüller on the figure for the Jews of the Netherlands that appears in the minutes.[24] If we want to measure the validity of the figures in the Wannsee table, we must note the following. On the one hand, the table presents countries with very exact figures for the Jewish population, such as Germany, Austria, the Netherlands (the figure for the Jews there includes Jews of mixed race), and Estonia (which is labeled "free of Jews").[25] On the other hand, the figures for some of the other countries are highly exaggerated, especially for territories in the Soviet Union that were not yet occupied: five million. For the hitherto occupied areas of the Soviet Union, where tens of thousands of Jews had already been murdered (a fact that the Einsatzgruppen reported and which Eichmann knew about), 857,500 Jews are still listed—which means that altogether the number of Jews in pre-June 1941, would have had to be about six million![26] It can thus be concluded that there is a need for carefully examining each of the figures appearing in the Wannsee table. Moreover, in the table presented to the participants at the meeting, there is a blatant error, which no doubt caused the participants to grimace (as Kreutzmüller has already pointed out): In the table, in the category of countries that had not yet been occupied, Serbia is included, although it had been placed under German occupation nine months earlier.[27]

How were the figures presented at the meeting compiled? On August 6, 1941, the Central Office for Jewish Emigration (*Zentralstelle für jüdische Auswanderung*) in Berlin, which was part of the network of branches of Eichmann's office (Section IV B4), ordered the heads of the Jewish umbrella organization in Germany, the Reich Association of Jews in Germany (*Reichsvereinigung der Juden in Deutschland*) to quickly compile precise figures on the size of each Jewish community in the world.[28] The Jewish leaders were given this command three weeks after Hitler's meeting with a number of high-ranking officials in the Nazi regime on July 16 (Hermann Göring, Hans-Heinrich Lammers, Martin Bormann, Alfred Rosenberg, and Wilhelm Keitel), which, according to many leading Holocaust scholars, marked the beginning of the process that led to the Final Solution, and only a few days after Göring's letter to Heydrich of July 31.[29] (The letter was apparently written jointly by Heydrich and Eichmann and, for official reasons, was presented to Göring simply so that he could sign it; as noted at the beginning of this chapter, the letter authorized Heydrich to explore the possibilities for a "comprehensive solution to the Jewish question in the areas of German influence in Europe.")[30]

The instructions issued by Eichmann's Central Office to the Reich Association of Jews in Germany on August 6 were apparently part and parcel of the endeavor to clarify how the term Jew (*Judenbegriff*) was defined in different countries throughout the world with the goal to create uniformity in the term, in order to be able to have all relevant Jews included in the comprehensive policy that was now being developed. This is how some Holocaust scholars interpret the Central Office's directive.[31] Although this interpretation is not misguided as such, it does not tell the whole story. Indeed, the subject of the letter that the Reich Association sent in reply to the directive the following day, on August 7, is "Definition of the term 'Jew' in those countries where there are Jewish laws" (*Begriffsbestimmung des "Juden" in Ländern mit Judengesetzen*).[32] The letter's appendix—which is really the most important part of the letter—is entitled "The number of Jews, in absolute terms and as a percentage of the general population, in certain countries by region [continents], in alphabetical order, with an appendix on the definition of the term 'Jews' in those countries that have Jewish laws, in accordance with the regulations that have been published."[33] In other words, the statistics had become the principal element and the figures that were submitted referred to the entire world, not just to Europe! Apparently, the only explanation is that oral instructions (perhaps transmitted by telephone?) accompanied the written ones; this was a common practice in the Nazi regime. This initiative demonstrates the swift response and creativity of the *Eichmann-Männer* vis-à-vis the new winds blowing from Hitler's direction, as well as their more distant perspective, which went beyond the immediate target (the European continent). Six days after their initial response had been sent, an additional letter was submitted by the Reich Association to the Central Office together with a long appendix that supplemented both the statistics and the sources. The two statistical lists (dated August 7 and 13, respectively) are very detailed. Some of them are handwritten and include most of the countries and continents in the world, providing considerable detail on the United States (with the figures given for major metropolitan centers) and even on Palestine (with the Jewish population broken down by region, including, for example, the Negev region in southern Palestine).[34]

The Data Gathered on North Africa and the Definition of the Problem

The figures submitted for the Jews of the countries of North Africa in the first list were as follows: Egypt—70,000, Ethiopia—80,000, Algeria—115,000, Morocco—181,000, and Tunisia—66,000. For some reason, Libya is not included, although there is a figure for "the rest of Africa"—1,000, a remarkably low figure, which is hard to explain (South Africa is mentioned separately with a Jewish population of 95,000; this figure could, perhaps, relate to tiny Jewish communities, such as in Rhodesia [now Zimbabwe] to which some German Jews fled toward the end of the 1930s).[35] The second list repeats the figures but provides details under the rubric "Miscellaneous": "Various British [territorial] possessions—3[,000], Various Italian [territorial] possessions—43[,000; apparently, the reference here is to Libya], Tangier—12[,000]."[36] With regard to the countries that are the subject of the present discussion, there is no difference between the two lists. If we add the figure given for both the occupied and unoccupied parts of France—280,000—to the figure for the Jews of Algeria, Morocco, and Tunisia, we arrive at a total of 643,000, a number that does not fit with the totals supplied in the table in the Wannsee meeting minutes (where the figures are seven hundred thousand plus 165,000). Moreover, in the two lists, no distinction is made between the occupied and unoccupied parts of France; this fact is important, as will be explained below.

Eichmann continued to gather and update the figures. As he testified at his trial in Jerusalem, the compilation of figures was completed by late November or early December 1941,[37] because the meeting was originally scheduled for December 9 but was postponed due to the Japanese attack on Pearl Harbor. Eichmann therefore had additional time to update the figures. However, the day after the Pearl Harbor attack, a demand (*Anforderung*) was issued to the Reich Association to submit additional figures. On December 11, 1941, an amendment was received for the figures on France. Those figures were based on the statement made by the Commissioner General for Jewish Affairs (*Commissaire Général aux Questions Juives*) in France, Xavier Vallat, following the founding of an obligatory organization for all French Jews (UGIF—*Union Général des Israélites de France*). His statement was published, it was noted, in the German newspaper, *Frankfurter Zeitung*, on December 4 and brought to Eichmann's attention.[38] The *Frankfurter Zeitung* reported:

> The French homeland (i.e., Continental France) has 335,000 Jews
>   This figure breaks down into two almost-equal parts:
>   Occupied France—165,000
>   Unoccupied France—170,000.
>
> In France's North African possessions
>   Approximately 360,000 Jews reside, according to the following breakdown:
>   Morocco—160,000
>   Algeria—150,000
>   Tunisia—50,000[39]

Both the figures and the way they are presented are important for the present discussion. The figure for the Jews in the unoccupied parts of France plus the figure for the Jews in France's North African possessions total 530,000, a figure that is very different from the figure submitted six weeks later at Wannsee (but close to the number given in the August lists, if we deduct the figure for the Jews in occupied France). However, the *phrasing* of the text, including the distinction between the two parts of France (occupied and unoccupied) that appears in the opening part of the statement is identical with that which appears in the Wannsee minutes, and the same is true for the *figure given for the number of Jews in occupied France*: 165,000. The only difference between the texts in this particular section concerns the figure for the Jews in unoccupied France: 170,000 in the newspaper report as opposed to seven hundred thousand in the Wannsee minutes. As noted above, in accordance with the figures in Eichmann's possession, the latter figure does not represent the addition of the Jews in France's North African possessions. What happened here?

Solution to the Problem

In order to solve the problem of the unreasonable figure, we must first of all take into account the entire document's phrasing and logic. Throughout the Wannsee minutes, the emphasis is on a Final Solution of the Jews solely in *Europe* (*Endlösung der europäischen Judenfrage*). This emphasis appears in Heydrich's introductory remarks and is repeated verbatim four times in the minutes. Even in the verbatim comments on the implementation of the Final Solution, only the countries of Europe are mentioned and, when the Soviet Union is referred to, the following statement is made: "The influence of the Jews in the Soviet Union in all spheres of life is a well-known fact. Approximately five million Jews live in the European part of the Soviet Union, and nearly a quarter of a million Jews live in the Asian part." In the table of figures, the emphasis on Europe appears whenever there is the possibility of any doubt. For example: "Turkey (the European part)." Nevertheless, with regard to each country with possessions beyond its original territory, those possessions are specified. Thus, it is explicitly stated that the Jews of Sardinia are included in the figure for the Jews of Italy and, with regard to Albania, details are given under the rubric "Italy" too.[40] With regard to the Jews of Romania, it is stated that the figure includes the Jews of Bessarabia. In other words, the Wannsee table does not include any country that has territories outside Europe, while territories that do not naturally belong to a given country are mentioned explicitly. One might argue that, at the time, the French colonies in North Africa were perceived as an integral part of France and were automatically included in the figure for France. However, that argument can be refuted by reference to the figure for the Netherlands—which at the time possessed East India (Indonesia), Surinam, Curaçao, and Aruba—and by the figures for England, Portugal, and Spain, which all had numerous colonies all over the world (including in North Africa). With regard to these four European countries, the figure clearly and explicitly refers only to the Jews living in their European territories. Furthermore, one might also seek to argue that the North African territories controlled by the Vichy regime were an integral part of France in the eyes of its citizens. However, such an argument is imprecise. Not all of France's colonies enjoyed an equal status. While Algeria was considered a province or département (or actually had three provinces), Tunisia and Morocco both had the status of a protectorate.

The limiting of the figures to Europe should come as no surprise. All of the documentation prior to the Wannsee meeting is saturated with the emphasis that the Nazis wanted—at least in this period—a comprehensive or final solution of the Jewish question in *Europe*. The major change that took place in the latter half of 1941 was the fact that the idea of the systematic murder of the Jews throughout Europe gradually coalesced in the wake, and on the basis, of Nazi Germany's experience in the territories of the Soviet Union, when Germany introduced systematic organizational and technical methods in its operations in those territories. During that period, the vision that Hitler presented in his famous speech in the Reichstag on January 30, 1939, began to be realized. In that speech, he declared: "If the international Jewish financiers in and outside Europe should succeed in plunging the nations once more into a world war, then the result will not be the Bolshevizing of the earth, and thus the victory of Jewry, but rather the annihilation of the Jewish race in Europe!"[41]

Indeed, the "annihilation of the Jewish race in Europe" was the known vision that went into effect in 1941 and 1942. It should be pointed out that Hitler repeated what he had said in his January 1939 speech on various occasions in the following years.[42] Moreover, in the second week of September 1941, those words were the Nazi Party's "slogan of the week" and they appeared in posters in all of the Party's branches.[43] Earlier that year, on January 21, 1941, Eichmann's representative in France, Theodor Dannecker, had written in a memorandum to all the departments of the Reich Security Main Office (*Reichssicherheitshauptamt*—RSHA) of the SS that, "in accordance with the will of the Führer, there will be a need, when the war is over, to bring about a final solution of the Jewish question in all the European territories under Germany's rule or supervision."[44] Similarly, Paul Zapp, speechwriter for Reichsführer SS Heinrich Himmler, wrote: "The political and diplomatic leadership of Adolf Hitler has laid the foundations for the European solution of the Jewish question."[45] In late 1941, five days before the original date of the Wannsee meeting, the aforementioned Franz Rademacher, head of the Jewish desk (*Judenreferat*) in the German Ministry of Foreign Affairs, which was the counterpart of Eichmann's department in the RSHA, prepared the draft of a speech for the permanent secretary in the Foreign Ministry, Ernst von Weizsäcker; the speech was signed by his deputy, Martin Luther. Rademacher wrote that "we must utilize the opportunity offered by this war in order to completely cleanse Europe of the Jewish question."[46]

If the Wannsee meeting's minutes discuss the Final Solution of the Jewish Question in Europe alone, one cannot read into the strange figure for the Jews of unoccupied France a message that contradicts the spirit of the minutes. Is it at all possible that there was a typing error in this document? Such a possibility is regarded sometimes by scholars as illogical. Could an error have been made in a German administrative document, especially in the case of the minutes of such an important conference, on which, in the eyes of many, the entire plan of the Final Solution hinges!? The answer, of course, is yes. It *is* possible that mistakes slipped into official German documents and there are many instances of such mistakes, just as there are instances of mistakes in all documents, whether private or administrative. However, in the particular case of the Wannsee meeting's minutes, we have already pointed out errors—that is, we have shown that the preparation of the figures was imprecise. Moreover, as we have seen, the Wannsee meeting was a gathering of senior officials but not those at the highest level, and its participants did not decide on the execution of the Final Solution of the Jewish Question. The purpose of the gathering was quite different; the meeting was convened in order to ensure that Heydrich had the authority he required and that there was sufficient coordination between the various agencies involved. It is interesting to note that, with regard to the Wannsee meeting's minutes, we do have the testimony of the person who drafted them—although it was delivered nineteen years after the minutes were written up. Eichmann himself admitted that the minutes contained errors, especially with regard to the subject of the present discussion. At his trial in Jerusalem, Eichmann was asked to comment on the minutes and he was asked numerous questions about them. When the prosecutor, Gideon Hausner, asked him about the table of figures, Eichmann replied, "With regard to the figures, I only now—that is, only recently—discovered that the figures were not quite right. For instance, regarding France. But I do not know—perhaps it is also possible that I erred when I recorded the figures."[47] This is, in fact, the most reasonable and logical explanation, especially since, in the Reich Association's "amendment letter" of December 11, 1941, one can see a dash and a dot above it after the figure of 170,000. At first glance, the dash and the dot seem to imply the insertion of an additional digit; a zero might thus have been added at the end of the figure during a first round of copying, which then creates the number 1,700,000. Since the Wannsee document was typed, that is, there was at least one additional stage of manual copying, it is quite possible that the copier—when seeing the unreasonable number 1,700,000—deliberately left out the first digit—1. This is one possible—indeed, hypothetical—explanation, although there might be another reason; in any event, it is quite clear that an error was made.

Would the Jews of North Africa Have Been Included in the Final Solution if Germany Had Conquered That Part of the World?

Can it be understood from the above discussion that the Final Solution would not have been applied to the Jews of North Africa if they had come under firm Nazi control? Clearly, historians cannot provide unambiguous answers when they are asked to speculate. Nevertheless, in light of the scant data in our possession and the manner in which the Final Solution plan developed, one can hazard a guess. A few years ago, German scholars Klaus-Michael Mallmann and Martin Cüppers uncovered evidence for the existence of a special SS unit, the Task Force Egypt (*Einsatzkommando Ägypten*), headed by SS officer Walter Rauff. This unit was to operate behind the regular forces of Erwin Rommel in Egypt and then proceed to Palestine. When Rommel failed to invade Egypt and Palestine and was forced to retreat, Rauff was assigned to Tunisia. While there, first anti-Jewish measures were implemented along the lines that had become common in anti-Jewish policies immediately after the occupation of other countries.[48] Additionally, we are in possession of a statement made by Dr. Gebhardt von Walther, who was attached to the German consulate in Tripoli and who wrote in a May 12, 1942, report on the "Jewish question in Libya" that "there is no doubt that, when the time comes, the Jewish question will also be solved in Tripolitania."[49] Moreover, we know today that the master plans for the Final Solution were neither clear nor organized and that the Final Solution instead developed as a result of internal dynamics from the moment that Hitler gave the green light, as the circles of killing gradually widened. The first indications that we have pointed out hint at the high probability that the Nazi regime would have applied the policies that developed in Europe beyond its borders, had it succeeded in establishing a solid presence outside the continent. The first indication of such a probability can be found in the implementation of the Final Solution in the Crimea and the North Caucasus.[50] After all, Hitler's struggle was in the final analysis a war against world Jewry (*das Weltjudentum*) and not just against European Jewry.[51] Moreover, we have seen that figures were gathered on Jews throughout the world for Eichmann's office. However, this scenario never occurred. The discussion at Wannsee, as Ian Kershaw explains, was an interim stage in the coalescence of the Final Solution. In January 1942, only preliminary preparations for the execution of the Final Solution had been made; however, the decision to kill Europe's Jews had already been taken.[52] This stage referred solely to Europe's Jews; even though the vision of a "global solution to the Jewish question" was there, Jews in areas beyond the perimeter of the European continent, including the Jews of North Africa, had *not* been included at this point in time in the practical implementation of the campaign and were therefore not included in the Wannsee meeting discussion.

DAN MICHMAN is Emeritus Professor of Modern Jewish History at Bar-Ilan University, and also serves as Head of the International Institute for Holocaust Research at Yad Vashem, Israel. Among his recent books are *Holocaust Historiography: A Jewish Perspective. Conceptualizations, Terminology, Approaches and Fundamental Issues* (2003) and *The Emergence of Jewish Ghettos during the Holocaust* (2011).

Appendices[53]

Table 3.1. The numbers of Jews in Europe and Africa, as presented in the reports of the Reich Association of Jews in Germany to the Central Office for Jewish Emigration, Berlin, August 7 and 13, 1941.

EUROPA [EUROPE]	
Deutschland [Germany]	
Altreich [Old Reich]	167,245
Ostmark [Austria]	52,549/(44,000)
Protektorat [Protectorate of Bohemia and Moravia]	75,000
Ost-Oberschlesien [East Upper Silesia]	115,000
Wartheland	360,000
Generalgouvernement [Government General]	1,500,000
Estland [Estonia]	4,500
Lettland [Latvia]	96,000
Litauen mit Wilna [Lithuania with Vilnius]	300,000
Belgien [Belgium]	80,000
Denemark [Denmark]	7,000
Griechenland [Greece]	90,000
Luxemburg [Luxembourg]	900/(945)
Niederlande [Netherlands]	135,000
Norwegen [Norway]	1,500
Russland (ehemals polnischer Teil) [Russia (former Polish part)]	1,200,000
Bessarabien und Nordbukowina [Bessarabia and North Bukovina]	500,000
Bulgarien [Bulgaria]	50,000
England	340,000
Irland [Ireland]	3,700
Finnland [Finland]	1,800
Frankreich [France]	280,000
Italien [Italy]	52,000
Albanien [Albania]	200
Jugoslawien [Yugoslavia]	68,000
Kroatien [Croatia]	29,000
Montenegro und Serbien [Montenegro and Serbia]	39,000
Portugal	2,500
Rumanien (ohne Bessarabien) [Romania (without Bessarabia)]	275,000
Rusland (UdSSR) [Russia (USSR)]	3,020,000
Schweden [Sweden]	8,000
Schweiz [Switzerland]	18,000
Slowakei [Slovakia]	89,900
Spanien [Spain]	4,500
	(*Continued*)

Table 3.1. (*Continued*)

Turkei (europaischer Teil) [Turkey (European Part)]	60,000
Ungarn (mit Karparto-Ukraine, Siebenburgen und Teilen der Slowakei) [Hungary (with Carpatho–Ukraine, Transylvania and parts of Slovakia)]	750,000
Europa insgesamt [Total for Europe]	**9,707,394**
AFRIKA [AFRICA]	
Ägypten [Egypt]	70,000
Äthiopien [Ethiopia]	80,000
Algier [Algiers]	115,000
Marokko [Morocco]	181,000
Sudafr. Union [South African Union]	95,000
Tunis [Tunisia]	66,000
Sonst. Britische Besitzungen [Other British territories]	3,000
Sonst. Italienische Besitzungen [Other Italian territories]	43,000
Tanger [Tangiers]	12,000
Übrige Länder [Remaining countries]	9,000/1,000
Afrika insgesamt [Total for Africa]	**666,000**

Report dated December 11, 1941, from the Reich Association of Jews in Germany to Eichmann's department, containing updated figures on the Jews in France, with a division between the occupied and unoccupied parts, and in French North Africa.

Aus der
Frankfurter Zeitung vom 4. Dezember 1941.

Nach einer Aeusserung des Generalkommissars für die Judenfrage, Vallat, werden von dem neuen Gesetz (Zusammenfassung im "Verband der Juden in Frankreich")

im französischen Mutterlande 335000 Juden

betroffen und zwar fast zu gleichen Teilen

im besetzten Gebiet 165000
im unbesetzten Gebiet 170000.

In den

nordafrikanischen Besitzungen Frankreichs

leben etwa 360000 Juden und zwar

in Marokko 160000
in Algier 150000
in Tunis 50000.

Notes

1. For summaries of the dominant approaches today, see Christopher Browning (with contributions by Jürgen Matthäus), *The Origins of the Final Solution: The Evolution of Nazi Jewish Policy, September 1939–March 1942* (Lincoln, NE/Jerusalem: University of Nebraska and Yad Vashem, 2004); Saul Friedländer, *The Years of Extermination: Nazi Germany and the Jews, 1939–1945* (New York: HarperCollins, 2007); Ian Kershaw, *Fateful Choices: Ten Decisions That Changed the World, 1940–1941* (London: Allen Lane, 2007), 431–470 and 569–575; Dan Michman, "The 'Final Solution to the Jewish Question,' its Emergence and Implementation: The State of Research and its Implications for Other Issues in Holocaust Research," in *Holocaust Historiography: A Jewish Perspective—Conceptualizations, Terminology, Approaches and Fundamental Issues* (London: Vallentine Mitchell, 2003), 91–126; Peter Longerich, *Holocaust: The Nazi Persecution and Murder of the Jews* (Oxford: Oxford University Press, 2010), 257–421.

2. The document was drafted by Heydrich, who submitted it to Hermann Göring for his signature. A photograph of the document is presented in Gedenk- und Bildungsstätte Haus der Wannsee-Konferenz, ed., *Villenkolonien in Wannsee 1870–1945: Großbürgerliche Lebenswelt und Ort der Wannsee-Konferenz* (Berlin: Gedenk- und Bildungsstätte Haus der Wannsee-Konferenz, 2000), 113.

3. According to Joseph Goebbels's diary: Elke Fröhlich, ed., *Die Tagebücher von Joseph Goebbels*, part II, vol. 2 (Munich: Saur, 1996), 498.

4. In a letter dated January 19, 1992, that Dr. Robert M. W. Kempner wrote to the team of the memorial site, House of the Wannsee Conference (Haus der Wannsee-Konferenz), he described the manner in which the minutes were found during the preparation of the documentation for the so-called Ministries Case, the 1947 trial at Nuremberg of members of the German ministerial bureaucracy. He depicted how he and his colleagues were so excited when they discovered the "Minutes of the meeting on the Final Solution of the Jewish Question from January 20, 1942, which afterwards became known throughout the world as the Wannsee Conference" ("Wir waren aufgeregt, als wir ein Protokoll über die später als Wannseekonferenz weltbekannt gewordene Sitzung über die Endlösung der Judenfrage vom 20. Januar 1942 entdeckten"). For a photograph of the letter see the website of Haus der Wannsee-Konferenz.

5. Götz Aly and Susanne Heim, *Vordenker der Vernichtung. Auschwitz und die deutschen Pläne für eine neue europäische Ordnung* (Frankfurt am Main: S. Fischer, 1995), 60, state that the term "conference" was already used in German bureaucratic internal discourse before the end of the war ("Im amtsinternen Sprachgebrauch wurde dieses Treffen als 'Konferenz der Staatssekretäre' bezeichnet"), but do not provide any source; in any case, there is no evidence to suggest that this was the term used at the time, in 1942.

6. A photograph of the minutes has been printed in many places and the minutes have also been translated into several languages. A high-quality reproduction of the document can be found in the catalog published by the museum of Haus der Wannsee-Konferenz: *Die Wannsee-Konferenz und der Völkermord an den europäischen Juden. Katalog der ständigen Ausstellung* (Berlin: Haus der Wannsee-Konferenz, 2006), 199–213. At his trial in Jerusalem in 1961, Eichmann gave testimony concerning the meeting and made a number of comments on the minutes themselves.

7. Haus der Wannsee-Konferenz, ed., *Die Wannsee-Konferenz und der Völkermord an den europäischen Juden. Katalog*, 203 (p. 5 of the original minutes).

8. For different interpretations of the venue and significance of the meeting and for discussions of these interpretations (as well as bibliographical references regarding the participants), see especially Mark Roseman, *The Villa, the Lake, the Meeting: Wannsee and the Final Solution* (London: Penguin, 2002), 1–6 and 55–96.

9. In a recent chapter, Gerhard Wolf proposed viewing this meeting also in another context, that of Heydrich attempting "to reclaim lost influence in the broader field of Nazi population policies by aligning the treatment of 'enemy populations' with the grander vision of a 'German East'. This Nazi dystopia not only called for destroying Jewish existence in Europe, but demanded that even the way in which Jews were killed would serve the Nazi cause." This possible additional dimension does not undermine the question of the geographical limits of the planning as discussed at Wannsee. See: Gerhard Wolf, "The Wannsee Conference in 1942 and the National Socialist living space dystopia," *Journal of Genocide Research* 17, no. 2 (2015): 153–175; the quote is from page 153.

10. Haus der Wannsee-Konferenz, *Die Wannsee-Konferenz und der Völkermord an den europäischen Juden. Katalog*, 204.

11. Peter Longerich, *Politik der Vernichtung: Eine Gesamtdarstellung der nationalsozialistischen Judenverfolgung* (Munich-Zürich: Piper, 1998), 469. Longerich repeats this argument in a more incisive manner in *The Unwritten Order: Hitler's Role in the Final Solution* (London: Tempus, 2002), 96: "Included in the 700,000 Jews for unoccupied France are those of the North African colonies." He repeats this argument word for word in *Holocaust*, 307.

12. Longerich, *The Unwritten Order: Hitler's Role in the Final Solution*, 545.

13. Friedländer, *The Years of Extermination*, 340.

14. Friedländer, *The Years of Extermination*, 285.

15. Michel Abitbol, *Les Juifs d'Afrique du Nord sous Vichy* (Paris: G.-P. Maisonneuve et Larose, 1983); Michel Abitbol, *Les Juifs d'Afrique du Nord sous Vichy* (Paris: Riveneuve éditions, 2008).

16. Edith Shaked, who teaches the Holocaust at Pima Community College in Tucson, Arizona, argues that the Jews of North Africa were included in the figure of 700,000 and presents as the main document proving this point an entry in Himmler's appointments diary, dated December 10, 1942: "Juden in Frankreich 600–700,000 abschaffen" ("dispose of 600,000 to 700,000 Jews in France"). The entry has a checkmark appearing alongside it, signifying Himmlers's authorization of this plan. In my opinion, this diary entry cannot be offered as evidence, because it was written eleven months *after* the Wannsee meeting and refers to a document he apparently received from Heydrich or from his own aides (it can be assumed that the Jews who had already been deported from France in 1942 were deducted from that figure). See Edith Shaked, "The Holocaust: Reexamining the Wannsee Conference, Himmler's Appointment Book, and Tunisian Jews," *The Nizkor Project*, http://www.nizkor.org/hweb/people/s/shaked-edith/re-examining-wannsee.html. It should also be noted that Shaked primarily focuses on the fate of Tunisian Jewry and she makes no mention of Algerian or Moroccan Jewry or of the differences between the various colonies of North Africa. On Himmler's diary, see Peter Witte, Michael Wildt, Martina Voigt, Dieter Pohl, Peter Klein, Christian Gerlach, Christoph Dieckmann, and Andrej Angrick, eds., *Der Dienstkalender Heinrich Himmlers 1941/42* (Hamburg: Christians, 1999).

17. Raul Hilberg, *The Destruction of the European Jews* (Chicago: Quadrangle Books, 1961), 411.

18. Hilberg, *The Destruction of the European Jews*, 264–265. Hilberg did not change his phrasing in the later editions—see the third edition: Raul Hilberg, *The Destruction of the European Jews* (New Haven/London: Yale University Press, 2003), vol. II, 687.

19. Leni Yahil, *Die Shoah: Überlebenskampf und Vernichtung der europäischen Juden* (Munich: Luchtehand, 1998), 436.

20. See the index in Yahil, *Die Shoah: Überlebenskampf und Vernichtung der europäischen Juden*.

21. Michael Marrus and Robert Paxton, *The Vichy Regime in France and the Jews* (New York: Basic Books, 1981), 222.

22. Asher Cohen, *Persécutions et sauvetages: Juifs et Français sous l'Occupation et sous Vichy* (Paris: Cerf, 1993), 132–133; Daniel Carpi, *Bein Shevet le-Hessed. Ha-Shiltonot ha-Italkiyim vihudei Tzarefat ve-Tunisiya be-Milhemet ha-Olam ha-Sheniya* (Jerusalem: Merkaz Shazar, 1993), 23n31 (Hebrew).

23. "Ohne daß sich der weitere Übermittlungsweg oder eine direkte Weitergabe der Statistik von Dannecker und Eichmann nachwiesen ließe"; Ahlrich Meyer, *Täter im Verhör: Die "Endlösung der Judenfrage" in Frankreich 1940–1944* (Darmstadt: Wissenschaftliche Buchgesellschaft, 2005), 86–88.

24. Christoph Kreutzmüller, "Die Erfassung der Juden im Reichskommissariat der besetzten niederländischen Gebiete," in *Besatzung, Kollaboration und Holocaust: Neue Studien zu Verfolgung und Ermordung der europäischen Juden*, ed. Johannes Hürter und Jürgen Zarusky (Munich: Oldenbourg, 2008), 21–44.

25. Haus der Wannsee-Konferenz, *Die Wannsee-Konferenz und der Völkermord an den europäischen Juden. Katalog*, 204 (p. 6 of the original minutes).

26. In Soviet Russia's census for 1937, 2,715,108 Jews were listed for the entire Soviet Union. See Mordechai Altshuler, *Soviet Jewry on the Eve of the Holocaust: A Social and Demographic Profile* (Jerusalem: Centre for Research of East European Jewry, Hebrew University of Jerusalem, 1998), 2. Peter-Heinz Seraphim's book on the Jews of Eastern Europe, which was published in 1938 and was a basic source for the experts on Jewish affairs in the SS, notes that in 1926 there were 2,476,000 Jews in the European part of Soviet Russia. See Peter-Heinz Seraphim, *Das Judentum im osteuropäischen Raum* (Essen: Essener Verlag, 1938), 290.

27. Kreutzmüller, "Die Erfassung der Juden," 41.

28. Letter from Reichvereinigung der Juden in Deutschland to Zentralstelle für jüdische Auswanderung, August 7, 1941, in Bundesarchiv Berlin, R 8150, 25, 1. My thanks to Dr. Wolf Kaiser from the memorial and educational site, Haus der Wannsee-Konferenz, for giving me a copy of this document. The appendix to the letter appears on 2–20.

29. Browning, *Origins of the Final Solution*, 281–312 and 353–423; Gerhard Weinberg, *Germany's War for World Conquest and the Extermination of Jews* (Washington, DC: USHMM/Center for Advanced Holocaust Studies, 1995), 10.

30. This famous letter has been published in many places since its submission as document 710-PS at the Trial of the Major War Criminals at Nuremberg: *International Military Tribunal*, vol. 26, 266–267.

31. Cornelia Essner, *Die "Nürnberger Gesetze" oder die Verwaltung des Rassenwahns 1933–1945* (Paderborn: Schöningh, 2000), 335–341; Michael Wildt, *Generation des Unbedingten. Das Führungskorps des Reichssicherheitshauptamtes* (Hamburg: Hamburger

Edition, 2002), 607–617; Gideon Botsch, "Der Weg zum Massenmord an den Juden Europas," in *Die Wannsee-Konferenz und der Völkermord an den europäischen Juden. Katalog*, ed. Haus der Wannsee-Konferenz, 72–86.

32. See note 25.
33. See note 25.
34. Letters from Reichvereinigung der Juden in Deutschland to Zentralstelle für jüdische Auswanderung, August 7 and 13, 1941, in Bundesarchiv Berlin, R 8150, 25; for the specifications mentioned here see the second report, 21–65.
35. Letters from Reichvereinigung der Juden in Deutschland to Zentralstelle für jüdische Auswanderung, Letter from the Reich Association to the Central Office, August 7, 1941, 8. For the Jewish population in Rhodesia see: https://www.jewishvirtuallibrary.org/zimbabwe-virtual-jewish-history-tour.
36. Aforementioned letter from the Reich Association to the Central Office, August 13, 1941 (see note 28), 25.
37. Eichmann's response to Judge Yitzhak Raveh, Session 106, July 21, 1961. The German version appears in Kurt Pätzold and Erika Schwarz, *Tagesordnung. Judenmord: Die Wannsee-Konferenz am 20. Januar 1942* (Berlin: Metropol, 1992), 196.
38. Unfortunately, we could not find the issue of this newspaper where this information was published. However, this does not change the fact that it was quoted and used by Eichmann's office.
39. Bundesarchiv Berlin, R 8150, Bd. 28, 11.
40. Quotes from Haus der Wannsee-Konferenz, *Die Wannsee-Konferenz und der Völkermord an den europäischen Juden. Katalog*, 204–205 (pp. 6–7 of the original minutes).
41. The original German text reads: "Ich will heute wieder ein Prophet sein: Wenn es dem internationalen Finanzjudentum in und außerhalb Europas gelingen sollte, die Völker noch einmal in einen Weltkrieg zu stürzen, dann wird das Ergebnis nicht die Bolschewisierung der Erde und damit der Sieg des Judentums sein, sondern die Vernichtung der jüdischen Rasse in Europa"; see Max Domarus, *Hitler—Reden und Proklamationen 1932–1945: Kommentiert von einem deutschen Zeitgenossen*, vol. II (Munich: Suddeutscher, 1965), 1057. For the English translation see: Jeremy Noakes and Geoffrey Pridham, eds., *Nazism 1919–1945: A Documentary Reader*, vol. 3 (Exeter: University of Exeter Press, 1988), 1049.
42. On this point, see Ian Kershaw, *Hitler 1936–1945: Nemesis* (London: Allen Lane, 2000), specifically, the index, under "Hitler" and "Prophecy."
43. Peter Witte, "Zwei Entscheidungen in der 'Endlösung der Judenfrage': Deportationen nach Lodz und Vernichtung in Chelmno," in *Theresienstädter Studien und Dokumente 1995*, ed. Miroslav Karny, Jaroslava Milotova, Raimund Kemper, and Michael Wögerbauer (Prague: Theresienstädter Intiative/Academia, 1995), 46.
44. "Gemäß dem Willen des Führers soll nach dem Kriege die Judenfrage innerhalb des von Deutschland beherrschten oder kontrollierten Teiles Europas einer endgültigen Lösung zugeführt werde"; cited in Browning, *Origins of the Final Solution*, 114–115.
45. "Die politische und diplomatische Führung Adolf Hitlers hat die Grundlagen für die europäische Lösung der Judenfrage geschaffen"; cited in Wolfram Meyer zu Utrup, *Kampf gegen die "jüdische Weltverschwörung." Propaganda und Antisemitismus der Nationalsozialisten 1919 bis 1945* (Berlin: Metropol, 2003), 449n120.
46. "Die Gelegenheit dieses Krieges muss benutzt werden, in Europa die Judenfrage endgültig zu bereinigen"; Luther to Weizsäcker, December 4, 1941, in Yad Vashem Archives

(hereafter YVA), 051.463, and cited in Eckart Conze, Norbert Frei, Peter Hayes, and Moshe Zimmermann, *Das Amt und die Vergangenheit: Deutsche Diplomaten im Dritten Reich und in der Bundesrepublik* (Munich: Blessing, 2010), 186.

47. Eichmann's response to prosecutor Gideon Hausner, at the session that took place on July 18, 1961. Cited in German in Pätzold and Schwarz, *Tagesordnung*, 194.

48. Klaus-Michael Mallmann and Martin Cüppers, "'Beseitigung der jüdisch-nationalen Heimstätte in Palästina': Das Einsatzkommando bei der Panzerarmee Afrika 1942", in *Deutsche, Juden, Völkermord. Der Holocaust als Geschichte und Gegenwart*, ed. Jürgen Matthäus and Klaus-Michael Mallmann (Darmstadt: Wissenschaftliche Buchgesellschaft, 2006), 153–176; and Klaus-Michael Mallmann and Martin Cüppers, *Halbmond und Hakenkreuz* (Darmstadt: Wissenschaftliche Buchgesellschaft, 2006); Peter Lieb, "Erwin Rommel. Widerstandskämpfer oder Nationalsozialist?," *Vierteljahrshefte für Zeitgeschichte* 61, no. 3 (2013): 303–343. Several memoires and diaries shed light on German anti-Jewish policies from the perspective of the persecuted Jews: Robert Borgel, *Étoile jaune et croix gammée* (Paris: Le Manuscrit, 2007); Paul Ghez, *Six mois sous la botte* (Paris: Le Manuscrit, 2009); Jacob-André Guez, *Au camp de Bizerte. Journal d'un Juif tunisien interné sous l'occupation allemande, 1942–1943* (Paris: L'Harmattan, 2001); Clément Houri, *L'Occupation de la Tunisie par les armeés de l'axe, 20 novembre 1942–1947 mai 1943: Vue de Cremieuxville (banlieue de Tunis)—Journal* (Jerusalem: Institut Ben-Zvi and Yad Vashem, 2013) (Hebrew).

49. Rauff to the German Embassy in Rome, May 12, 1942, in YVA, JM/2213.

50. Kiril Feferman, *The Holocaust in the Crimea and the North Caucasus* (Jerusalem: Yad Vashem, 2016).

51. The continuation of the citation presented above from Zapp's draft of Himmler's speech (see note 40), speaks of the beginning of a solution to the global Jewish question (*Lösung der Weltjudenfrage*). In the summer semester of 1943, Theodor Scheffer organized a scholarly conference on the Jewish Question at the pedagogical-political department of the University of Jena. At the conference, Scheffer stated that, "as far as we are concerned, the matter does not end with our having solved the Jewish Question in the Reich in an extensive manner. This is a global question that is closely connected to the unique nature of both the current war and the continual intensification of the battles in the course of the war" ("Es ist für uns nicht damit abgetan, daß wir die Judenfrage im Reich weitgehend gelöst haben. Sie ist eine Weltfrage, mit der dieser Krieg und seine immer heftiger werdenden Kämpfe zusammenhangen"). Cited in Uwe Hoßfeld, Jürgen John, Oliver Lemuth, and Rüdiger Stutz, eds., *Kämpferische Wissenschaft. Studien zur Universität Jena im Nationalsozialismus* (Cologne: Böhlau, 2003), 530–531. In other words, in terms of the Nazis' "vision," a wide range of persons who believed in that vision ideologically spread the idea of the Final Solution beyond Europe's borders even before Germany was in a position to implement it.

52. Kershaw, *Fateful Choices*, chapter 10.

53. The documents are presented in their entirety in Norbert Kampe and Peter Klein, eds., *Die Wannsee-Konferenz am 20. Januar 1942. Dokumente, Forschungsstand, Kontroversen* (Cologne/Weimar/Vienna: Böhlau, 2013), 20–24.

Part II. Sinti and Roma

4 "The Definitive Solution to the Gypsy Question": The Pan-European Genocide of the European Roma

Wolfgang Wippermann

On December 8, 1938, the Reichsführer *Schutzstaffel* (SS) and Chief of the German Police in the Reich Ministry of the Interior, Heinrich Himmler, announced the "definitive solution to the Gypsy question" (*endgültige Lösung der Zigeunerfrage*). This solution was supposed to be achieved "on the basis of the character of this race" (*aus dem Wesen dieser Rasse heraus*). In the process, "the racially pure Gypsies and the half-castes" were "to be dealt with separately" (*die rassereinen Zigeuner und die Mischlinge gesondert zu behandeln*). This was justified with reference to the "findings" of "racial-biological research."[1] The research in question was that carried out by Robert Ritter. He claimed to have proven with his "racial-biological research" that the Roma belonged to an "inferior race." Ritter furthermore argued that the "half-castes" possessed an even more inferior character to the "racially pure Gypsies." They had emerged, after all, from sexual relations between Roma and antisocial, criminal members of the German nation. The "half-castes" possessed, therefore, not only inferior "Gypsy" blood but also likewise inferior "antisocial and criminal blood."[2]

All those people were regarded as "Gypsy half-castes" (*Zigeuner-Mischlinge*) whose parents, grandparents, or even great-grandparents included a woman or a man who, for whatever reason, had been identified as a "Gypsy." This classification was by no means carried out exclusively by the notoriously antiziganist "Gypsy police" but also via many other stuffy officials and pious pastors, who had handed their relevant files and church registers over to the "Gypsy researchers" surrounding Robert Ritter. With their help, Ritter and his colleagues succeeded in recording all thirty thousand German Sinti and Roma and classifying them according to racist criteria in the corresponding half-caste gradation. This affected not only the racially pure Roma but also the half-, quarter-, and eighth-part "Gypsies." They all fell victim to the "definitive solution to the Gypsy question ... on the basis of the character of this race."[3]

The National Socialists commenced their preparations for this "definitive solution" immediately after coming to power. From 1933, the German Sinti and Roma were discriminated against and persecuted for racist reasons. This approach was legitimated by pointing to various racial laws and regulations. The legislation was applied to the Sinti and Roma in a very arbitrary fashion. This can be seen from the example of the Law for the Prevention of Offspring with Hereditary Diseases (*Gesetz zur Verhütung erbkranken Nachwuchses*) from July 14, 1933, which envisaged the forced sterilization of people suffering from so-called hereditary diseases. Blindness, deafness, schizophrenia, and feeble-mindedness were counted among these diseases. However, it was incumbent on physicians to prove the occurrence of these medical conditions. These findings were then examined by the specially created Hereditary Health Courts (*Erbgesundheitsgerichte*). In the case of German Sinti and Roma, however, this did not happen. Instead, they were subjected to forced sterilization on the grounds of their allegedly inherent antisocial behavior. This reasoning is to be regarded as racist. Nonetheless, not one of the forcibly sterilized Sinti and Roma has been indemnified for the suffering they were subjected to during the Nazi era. The application of racist forced sterilization laws to the Sinti and Roma has not been viewed as a racially motivated injustice for the simple reason that the entire forced sterilization law of the National Socialist state has not been interpreted by today's German state as racist and thus unjust.

From late 1935 onward, the Nuremberg race laws, which were actually directed against German Jews, were also extended to German Sinti and Roma. Sinti and Roma were counted among those who were designated in several decrees of the Reich Minister of the Interior as "carriers of non-German or non-related blood" (*Träger nicht deutschen oder nicht artverwandten Blutes*).[4] For this reason, they were prohibited from marrying or engaging in sexual intercourse with people of German or related blood. Whoever violated this ban was convicted of "race defilement" (*Rassenschande*) and sentenced to a lengthy term of penal servitude. This illegal and racially motivated practice was authorized in the *Commentary on the German Race Laws*. In this commentary, published in 1936 and written by Dr. Hans Globke and Dr. Wilhelm Stuckart, the following sentence can be found: "In Europe, it is generally only Jews and Gypsies who are of alien blood."[5]

Sinti and Roma were also affected by the decree of the Reich and Prussian Minister of the Interior from December 14, 1937, on the "preventive suppression of crime by the police" (*Erlass über die vorbeugende Verbrechensbekämpfung durch die Polizei*).[6] Thousands of Sinti and Roma were labeled as antisocials for racial reasons and taken into "preventive police custody" (*polizeiliche Vorbeugungshaft*) or sent to various concentration camps in April and June 1938. Hardly any of them survived internment in a camp. Their murder was willful. The racially motivated and clearly illegal abduction of alleged antisocial Sinti and Roma and their incarceration in concentration camps was already an integral component of the "definitive solution to the Gypsy question … on the basis of the character of this race."[7]

On September 21, 1939, the participants of a "Gypsy conference" (*Zigeunerkonferenz*) in Berlin discussed other and more radical methods to bring about the "definitive solution to the Gypsy question."[8] Some of the ministerial officials and "Gypsy researchers" proposed the sterilization of all those German Sinti and Roma still incarcerated. This suggestion was abandoned, however, as too laborious and too expensive. Instead, it was decided that the German Sinti and Roma, as well as those from Austria, which had been annexed to the German Reich a year earlier, would be deported eastward. In order to facilitate the deportation of the Sinti and Roma, they were ordered on October 17, 1939, to no longer leave their places of residence. This was in any case no longer possible for those Sinti and Roma who were interned in the "Gypsy camps" (*Zigeunerlager*) that had existed in various large German cities since 1935.

In early 1940, the Governor General in occupied Poland, Hans Frank, opposed the expulsion of all German Sinti and Roma to "his" General Government, which comprised the core territories of the vanquished and shattered Polish state, whereupon Frank and Himmler negotiated a compromise.[9] Instead of all thirty thousand German Sinti and Roma, only 2,500 were deported to occupied Poland in April 1940, from the western and northern parts of the German Reich.

Himmler did not order the deportation of those Sinti and Roma still in Germany until December 16, 1942. This order was implemented in early 1943. Most of the Sinti and Roma were deported to Auschwitz. Unlike the other prisoners, the Sinti and Roma were not separated according to gender and age. Instead, the Sinti and Roma had to live—or, rather, vegetate—with their wives and children in a "Gypsy camp" separated off from the rest of Auschwitz. Before they were gassed, the adult Sinti and Roma had to watch as their children slowly and tortuously died of starvation and epidemics. On July 31, 1944, the last inhabitants of the "Gypsy camp" in Auschwitz were gassed. Among them were not only German but also many foreign Sinti and Roma.[10]

The vast majority of the altogether five hundred thousand Roma who fell victim to the genocide were not murdered, however, in Auschwitz and in the other concentration and extermination camps. They were shot to death in the Eastern European countries invaded and occupied by German troops. This was by no means done only by the murder squads of the Einsatzgruppen, who followed in the wake of the regular combat troops, but also by members of the police battalions and the Wehrmacht. After and while they herded together the Jews and shot them on the spot, they did the same with the Roma. This did not take place in stationary or mobile gas vans but rather through the deployment of machine guns and other small arms. The corpses of the Roma (and Jews) shot from close range were not burned in the crematoria of the concentration camps but rather buried in remote forests. However, in order to combat the spread of the dreaded typhus and to remove evidence of Nazi crimes after the war had definitively turned against Germany, the corpses were exhumed, to be then burned in the open and on grates produced from railway tracks.

The murder of Jews and Roma was justified with the same, or at least comparable, racist ideology and prejudices. This can be demonstrated by way of example with reference to an October 26, 1941, letter from the chief of the Military Administration in Serbia, Dr. Harald Turner. In this letter, Turner ordered the taking of Jews and Roma as hostages and then their murder.[11] Turner's letter began with a declaration of hostility: "Jews and Gypsies" constituted "an element of insecurity and thus of endangerment to public order and safety" (*ein Element der Unsicherheit und damit der Gefährdung der öffentlichen Ordnung und Sicherheit*). Therefore, the Jews had to be annihilated, because "the Jewish intellect has caused the war." Turner invoked here Hitler's speech to the Reichstag on January 30, 1939, in which he had effectively declared war on "international Jewry" and threatened it with the "annihilation of the Jewish race" (*Vernichtung der jüdischen Rasse*). Roma had not been mentioned in the speech. (In general, Hitler rarely commented on "Gypsies.") Nonetheless, Turner also regarded the Roma as members of an "inferior race." Picking up where the (unnamed) "Gypsy scholars" (*Zigeunerforscher*) had left off, Turner declared: "As a result of his internal and external construction, the Gypsy cannot be a useful member of a community of nations" (*Der Zigeuner kann aufgrund seiner inneren und äußeren Konstruktion kein brauchbares Mitglied einer Völkergemeinschaft sein*). Whereas the "Jewish element play a significant role in leading the gangs," by which he meant the Serbian partisan formations, "it is especially the Gypsies who are responsible for particular cruelties and for the intelligence service" (*gerade Zigeuner für besondere Grausamkeiten und den Nachrichtendienst verantwortlich sind*). Turner was unable to present proof of his accusations. Nonetheless, on August 29, 1942—ten months after his aforementioned order—he reported to his superiors with a murderous pride: "Serbia [is the] only country in which the Jewish question and the Gypsy question [have been] solved."[12]

In this way, Turner confirmed that the Roma had been handled in the same way as the Jews—murdered. What he did not say, however, was how, with which methods, and according to which criteria the Jews and Roma had been seized. Answers to these questions can be found in the reports that Turner's colleagues composed about the murder of Polish and Soviet Jews and Roma. In these reports, they freely admitted that they killed all people they regarded as Jews and "Gypsies." In the case of the Jews, their physical appearance sufficed to condemn them.

Not all but many of the Eastern European Jews were recognizable as Jews because of the way they wore their hair and beards and due to their attire. They indeed corresponded to the image that antisemites visualized when it came to "the Jews." Moreover, most Jews lived in villages, towns, and certain quarters of the larger cities, which were almost exclusively inhabited by Jews. However, none of this applied to the Roma, or at least not in the same way. Some of them did not correspond to the way in which the antiziganists visualized the "Gypsies," because they did not wander about "like the Gypsies" but had instead become sedentary and had also adapted themselves to their fellow citizens in their other modes of behavior. This applied to a substantial number of Soviet Roma, who had not only been encouraged but indeed forced by the Soviet authorities to settle down and adjust themselves in general to the Soviet social order.

As they could not immediately be identified as "Gypsies," those Soviet Roma who were sedentary and socially assimilated were not murdered at once. The murder squads of the Einsatzgruppen, police battalions, and specific units of the Wehrmacht initially concentrated on the murder of the Jews as well as those Roma who still roamed around the country, as "the Gypsies" were allegedly accustomed to do; the Roma were identified and stigmatized as "Gypsies" on account of their way of life and their clothing. The fact that it was these itinerant Roma who were shot first and most of all, however, was a cause of irritation to some of the "Gypsy scholars" in the Reich. They argued that these Roma were "racially pure Gypsies," who were not as dangerous or "racially inferior" as the "half-castes" (*Mischlinge*). Himmler, of all people, shared this view. In 1942, when the annihilation of the Soviet Roma had already begun and that of the Serbian Roma had already been concluded, Himmler planned in all seriousness to exempt the German and Austrian "racially pure Gypsies" from extermination, because they have "generally not behaved so anti-socially and in their cult valuable German blood has survived, which must be studied."[13] To this end, the Roma were to be brought to a type of "Gypsy reservation" (*Zigeuner-Reservat*), where they would be subjected to special examinations carried out by the "Gypsy scholars." This did not come to pass because Hitler put an end to Himmler's insane plan.

Nevertheless, the German agencies responsible for the murder of the Soviet Roma appear to have been aware of Himmler's plans for a reservation. This assumption is supported by the documented fact that the murder squads were instructed by their superiors not to murder the "racially pure Gypsies" if their racial purity had been established. Therefore, the orders already issued by different people and different institutions to treat the Roma "like the Jews," that is, to murder them, were countermanded. This led to a chaotic situation. This situation was overcome, however, because of what the historian Hans Mommsen has called "cumulative radicalisation."[14] The most radical form and variation of the final solution prevailed. All those Jews and Roma who could be seized were murdered.[15]

In the process, the German murderers also obtained support from members of several Soviet peoples. On the Crimea it was the Tatars, whose representatives were asked by Otto Ohlendorf's Einsatzgruppe D which of the Roma—who lived among the Tatars, spoke their language, and, like the Tatars, were Muslims—were "Gypsies." Without necessarily desiring or knowing this, these Tatars became in this way accessories to genocide.¹⁶ Yet this was not unique to the Tatars. Various Balts and Ukrainians either volunteered for or were forced to assist in the murder of Jews and Roma. Due to their collaboration in genocide, a number of Tartars, Balts, and Ukrainians were severely punished by the Soviet authorities after 1945. Individual Balts and Ukrainians were sentenced to death and executed. The Crimean Tatars were collectively deported to the Asian parts of the Soviet Union, without their individual guilt or innocence being verified. From the point of view of the Soviet authorities, they had all collaborated with the German fascists. As this did not apply to all Tatars, the Soviets had in this way repaid an old (German) injustice with a new (Soviet) injustice. This should of course be criticized, although it should not lead to the condemnation as unfounded and unjust of all punitive and retaliatory measures taken by the Soviet authorities against actual collaborators.

It is rather the far too mild treatment of Western European collaborators in the genocide of Jews and Roma that was unfounded and unjust. Only very few Dutch, Belgian, and French police officials who arrested Jews and Roma and handed them over to the German murderers were punished for their criminal acts. This was intentional. These European countries simply did not want to acknowledge that many of their citizens had been involved in one way or another in the murder of Jews and Roma. Some of them had even taken part voluntarily, without being forced to do so by the Germans.¹⁷

Worth mentioning here is the French collaborationist regime based in Vichy. It delivered not only Jews and Roma to the German murderers but also arrested thousands of foreign Jews and French Roma on its own account and interned them in camps in unoccupied France, where many of them died.¹⁸ The camp for Jews in the southern French municipality of Gurs is notorious. Less well known are the various "Gypsy camps," known as *camps aux nomades*. They were located in the immediate vicinity of the Gurs camp, and the treatment of the Roma incarcerated there appears to have been little different from the treatment of the Jews in the Gurs camp. However, whereas the Gurs camp was dissolved immediately after the liberation of France in 1944, the inmates of the "Gypsy camps" were not liberated for another two years, until 1946.

Fascist Italy also participated in the genocide of the European Roma (and Jews).¹⁹ Immediately after promulgating racial laws directed against the Africans in the Italian colonies in 1937, Italy extended them to include Italian Jews and Roma. Jews and Roma were discriminated against for racial reasons and incarcerated in camps during the war, of which several were designated *campi di concentramento*—concentration camps. These camps existed in all parts of Italy and in the Croatian and Slovenian territories of Yugoslavia conquered by Italian troops. Toward the end of the war, the authorities of the fascist Republic of Salò handed over to the Germans a not insignificant number of Jews and Roma, who were then deported to German concentration and extermination camps.

This also applies to Tiso's clerical fascist regime in Slovakia, which permitted not only the seven thousand Slovakian Jews but also an unknown number of Roma to be deported to German extermination camps.[20] In neighboring Hungary, Ferenc Szálasi's Arrow Cross movement delivered five hundred thousand Hungarian Jews and an unknown number of Roma to Adolf Eichmann, who had traveled to Hungary especially for this purpose. Eichmann then had the Jews and the Roma deported to German extermination camps. A further fifty thousand Jews and an unknown number of Roma were moreover massacred on the spot by the Hungarian fascists.[21]

The crimes of the Hungarian fascists were eclipsed, however, by those committed by the Croatian fascists. The Ustaša regime led by Ante Pavelić murdered hundreds of thousands of Jews, Roma, and Serbs. These murders were carried out in the notorious Jasenovac concentration camp, in which Roma composed by far the largest group of prisoners, and also in all parts of the formally independent state of Croatia, where the fascists of the Ustaša shot Jews, Roma, and Serbs. This took place with the knowledge, and indeed the approval, of members of the Catholic Church.[22]

The campaign of annihilation pursued by the so-called Iron Guard, the Romanian fascist party, against Romanian Jews even before the outbreak of World War II was at least tacitly condoned by the Romanian Orthodox Church.[23] During the war it made no effort to prevent the deportation of Romanian Roma to those Soviet territories conquered by the Romanian army (or, rather, reconquered, because they had previously belonged to Romania).[24] To this day, it is not known how many Roma died as a result. Romanian historians do not even really want to know. Some even dispute the fact that Romania played any part in the genocide of the Roma (and the Jews).

In this, they are not on their own. Many Eastern and Western European historians and politicians simply do not want to accept that their countries were involved in the genocide of the Jews and the Roma in one way or another. The European collaboration in the pan-European genocide of the European Roma (and Jews) constitutes a taboo topic for European historical scholarship. Why is that the case? And how did it come about?

In order to answer these questions, we must know and criticize the fact that not only the European collaboration with Nazi Germany but also the pan-European genocide of the European Roma itself was for a long time concealed and denied. This concealment and denial was started by the contemporaries to the genocide. Although the genocide of the Roma was public knowledge, hardly anyone criticized it. No one helped the persecuted Roma. Not one of the European resistance movements took a stand for the Roma. All the European and non-European states refused to grant Roma refugees asylum. There simply was no Romani migration.

While not all of the mistakes and failures made before 1945 could be corrected or rectified after the war, some of them could have been. Yet this did not happen. The victorious powers of World War II even failed to punish the German perpetrators for their crimes and indemnify the surviving Roma for their suffering. In 1945–1946, they refrained from addressing the genocide of the European Roma at the trials of the major German war criminals in Nuremberg. This was the case although numerous documents had been collected during the trial preparations with which the racist intentions and motivations of the genocide could have been proven. Yet the Allies did not do so and evidently did not want to do so. Why was this?

It is tempting at first glance to assume that the Allies failed to do so because they would have had to admit that they made no effort to prevent the genocide, and instead stood by and watched while the Germans and other European nations participated in the genocide of the European Roma. However, Allied inaction against the mass murder of the Jews was similar, and yet this genocide *was* addressed at Nuremberg. It is more likely, therefore, that the Allies failed to address the genocide of the Roma because it would have meant them having to safeguard the rights of the surviving Roma in obtaining some kind of restitution for their suffering. The Allies wanted to avoid this at all costs. The Roma were not supposed to receive compensation. The Allies only very reluctantly allowed the Jews to—partially—force through their claims for restitution against Germany. This took place in 1952, when representatives of Jewish organizations and the Israeli state negotiated an agreement in Luxembourg with the chancellor of the Federal Republic of Germany, in which the Federal Republic committed itself to "making amends" (*Wiedergutmachung*) to the surviving Jews.

To this day, the Roma have not succeeded in obtaining this.[25] No agreement has been signed with their representatives comparable to the Luxembourg agreement of 1952. The German authorities have justified their refusal to sign a restitution agreement with the Roma by claiming that the European Roma, unlike the Jews, do not have their own state and have no universally recognized representatives who are authorized to conclude an agreement equivalent to that of Luxembourg. This argument is formally correct but is to be regarded from a moral perspective as reprehensible.

Also worthy of condemnation is the fact that the German authorities refused for a long time to make restitution payments to individual Roma who survived the genocide. This refusal was justified with the historically false claim that Sinti and Roma were not persecuted and murdered for racial reasons, as the Jews had been. In 1956, the Federal Court of Justice in Karlsruhe established a precedent when it ruled that the Sinti and Roma were persecuted because of their "anti-social characteristics" (*asoziale Eigenschaften*) and subjected to "particular restrictions" (*besondere Beschränkungen*).[26] In the eyes of the Federal Court of Justice, only the deportation of the German Sinti and Roma to Auschwitz extermination camp in spring 1943 had been illegal. In issuing this ruling, the highest German court of law denied the racially motivated persecution of the Sinti and Roma. This was an unspeakable scandal but one that was scarcely criticized by the German and European publics of the time. The Federal Court of Justice at least felt compelled on December 18, 1963, to partially revise its judgment of 1956.[27] The judges admitted that racial political motives may have contributed to the enactment of measures taken after Himmler's decree of December 8, 1938. Sinti and Roma were therefore now permitted to apply for indemnification for persecution that took place after December 8, 1938. Some German Sinti and Roma then indeed did this. Aside from a very few exceptions, foreign Roma, on the other hand, have not had the questionable pleasure of obtaining restitution.

This is well-known in all European countries, but it is not criticized by any of them. Political reasons, on the one hand, are the cause of this silence. The individual European countries evidently do not want to spoil things with the politically and economically powerful Germany. They, therefore, refrain from exhorting that nation to pay reparations to the Roma persecuted by it. Added to this is evidently the fear that the other European countries will themselves be prosecuted for their part in the pan-European genocide of the European Roma and thus be obliged to pay reparations to the survivors.

Those countries who refuse to do so are above all the same ones that not only persecuted Roma in the past but also discriminate against and persecute them in the present. The Roma in France and Italy are subjected to discrimination. The Roma in Croatia, Romania, Hungary, and several other former Communist states are persecuted. This is well known in the other European countries. Nonetheless, most of them refuse to grant asylum to the Roma, who are discriminated against and persecuted.

How is this all possible? How can the members of a people be discriminated against and persecuted in the present, whose people were subjected to genocide in the past? Has Europe forgotten this? Why does the pan-European genocide of the European Roma play such an insignificant role in European memory? These critical questions should be directed not only at European politicians but also at European historians. It is they, namely, who denied well into the 1980s the fact that the Roma were the subject of an intentional and racially motivated genocide. The Romani genocide—or Porajmos—has become a forgotten Holocaust, *l'holocauste oublié*, as the French historian Christian Bernadec has accurately called it.[28]

It is, above all, the German historians of National Socialism who are to blame for this state of affairs. For a long time, they refused to even address the genocide of the Roma. In all the handbooks and overviews of the history of the "Third Reich" that were published in the 1950s, 1960s, and 1970s, the genocide of the Roma is mentioned only in passing. The history books written for schoolchildren at the time generally contain the exceedingly laconic remark that "Gypsies were also persecuted." German (and Israeli) historians energetically disputed the argument that Porajmos and the Shoah are comparable because they were both intentional and racially motivated genocides.

Since the 1980s, the picture has changed. Various foreign historians have noted that the persecution of the Roma was intentional and racially motivated. These historians include Jerzy Ficowsky from Poland; Selma Steinmetz and Erika Thurner from Austria; Bernard Sijes from the Netherlands; and Christian Bernadec from France.[29] The biggest credit, however, for preventing the genocide of the Roma from falling into oblivion, goes to the Brits Donald Kenrick and Grattan Puxon, whose book *The Destiny of Europe's Gypsies* has become something of a standard work because it has been translated into several European languages and has also found an echo in various European countries.[30] Inspired by the demonstrations and historical-political activities of the Central Council of German Sinti and Roma, chaired by Romani Rose, several younger German historians have since published regional studies and overviews of the persecution of—especially—German Sinti and Roma.

Since the 1990s, however, there has been something of a countermovement. Some German and foreign historians claim to have established that the genocide of the Roma was not so intentional, racially motivated, and total as the genocide of the Jews, for which reasons the two genocides are scarcely comparable. Michael Zimmermann is among those who justify their claims in this way.[31] The murder of the Roma, he argues, was more improvised than intentional and was motivated in no way by racial considerations but rather sociopolitical ones. Furthermore, far fewer people fell victim to the genocide of the Roma—Zimmermann gives the figure of 96,000—because (and this is where his argumentation really becomes problematic) the "racially pure Gypsies" in Germany and the sedentary Roma in the east were both spared. This is not true. Zimmermann at least recognizes that the Roma were subjected to genocide. This was disputed by the American political science Guenter Lewy, however, in such a way that it can only be described as scandalous.[32] I strongly criticized his claims in a book in which I undertook (evidently for the first time) a comparison of the Shoah and the Porajmos.[33]

It should be pointed out here that research into the genocide of the Roma presented in the works cited earlier is not yet sufficient.[34] The murder of the Eastern European Roma and the collaboration of the Western and Eastern European states in the genocide are aspects that have been neglected.[35] Finally, it must be more closely examined whether the genocide of the Roma is really comparable with other European and non-European genocides. This is not possible without an intensive examination of research on comparative genocide and its methods. German historians have not yet been prepared to undertake such a task. They fear that the special nature of the genocide carried out by the Germans against the Roma (and against the Jews) might be obliterated by being placed in the context of a general history of genocide.[36]

More important, however, than all these controversies about the history of the pan-European genocide of the European Roma are the lessons that can be learned from the past and for the present. It is not only politicians but also historians who can learn and apply these lessons. They must address not only the past but also the present, because—unlike the past—the present can indeed be overcome. In regard to the subject of this chapter, overcoming the present involves the following: the pan-European genocide of the European Roma must be reappraised above all in order to assist today's European Roma to enforce their rights and protect them against new injustices. By "rights" I mean the claim of the Roma to restitution from all those European countries who participated in one way or another in the genocide of the Roma. The European Roma must be protected furthermore against the injustice that is being done to them today in several European countries, where they are once again being subjected to discrimination and persecution.

—Translated from German by Alex J. Kay

WOLFGANG WIPPERMANN is Adjunct Professor for Modern History at the Free University, Berlin. His books include *Europäischer Faschismus im Vergleich* (1983), *The Racial State: Germany 1933–1945* (with Michael Burleigh, 1991), *Totalitarismustheorien* (1997) and *"Auserwählte Opfer?": Shoah and Porrajmos im Vergleich. Eine Kontroverse* (2005).

Notes

1. Circular decree issued by the Reichsführer SS and Chief of the German Police in the Reich Ministry of the Interior, Heinrich Himmler, "Combatting the Gypsy plague" (*Bekämpfung der Zigeunerplage*), in *Ministerialblatt des Reichs- und Preußischen Ministers des Innern* 99, no. 51 (December 8, 1938): 2105–2110.

2. Robert Ritter, "Zur Frage der Rassenbiologie und Rassenpsychologie der Zigeuner in Deutschland," in *Reichsgesundheitsblatt* 13 (1938): 425–426.

3. On the following, see the overviews in: Till Bastian, *Sinti und Roma im Dritten Reich. Geschichte einer Verfolgung* (Munich: C. H. Beck, 2001); Martin Luchterhandt, *Der Weg nach Birkenau. Entstehung und Verlauf der nationalsozialistischen Verfolgung der "Zigeuner"* (Lübeck: Schmidt-Römhild, 2000); Wolfgang Wippermann, *"Auserwählte Opfer"? Shoah und Porrajmos im Vergleich. Eine Kontroverse* (Berlin: Frank & Timme, 2005); Michael Zimmermann, *Verfolgt, vertrieben, vernichtet. Die nationalsozialistische Vernichtungspolitik gegen Sinti und Roma* (Essen: Klartext, 1989); Michael Zimmermann, *Rassenutopie und Genozid. Die nationalsozialistische Lösung der Zigeunerfrage* (Hamburg: Christians, 1996).

4. Various decrees are reproduced in Wolfgang Wippermann, *Geschichte der Sinti und Roma in Deutschland. Darstellung und Dokumente* (Berlin: Pädagogisches Zentrum, 1993), 77 ff.

5. Wilhelm Stuckart and Hans Globke, *Kommentar zur deutschen Rassengesetzgebung*, vol. 1 (Munich/Berlin: C. H. Beck, 1936), 55: "In Europa sind regelmäßig nur Juden und Zigeuner artfremden Blutes."

6. Reproduced in: Wippermann, *Geschichte der Sinti und Roma in Deutschland*, 79.

7. See the circular decree issued by Heinrich Himmler, "Combatting the Gypsy plague" (*Bekämpfung der Zigeunerplage*), in *Ministerialblatt des Reichs- und Preußischen Ministers des Innern* 99, no. 51 (December 8, 1938): 2105–2110.

8. The minutes of this conference have not survived. On this and other conferences on the "Gypsy question," see Zimmermann, *Rassenutopie und Genozid*, 167–172.

9. Minutes of a discussion between Heydrich and (the representative of the Governor General Hans Frank) Arthur Seyß-Inquart on January 30, 1940, on matters relating to the deportation of Poles, Jews, and "Gypsies," reproduced in Wippermann, *Geschichte der Sinti und Roma in Deutschland*, 87–88.

10. Zimmermann, *Rassenutopie und Genozid*, 293 ff.

11. For this and the following see the circular letter from the Chief of the Military Administration in Serbia (Dr. Harald Turner), dated October 26, 1941, to all field and circuit commanders, reproduced in Wippermann, *Geschichte der Sinti und Roma in Deutschland*, 96.

12. Ernst Klee and Willy Dressen, eds., *"Gott mit uns." Der deutsche Vernichtungskrieg im Osten 1939–1945* (Frankfurt am Main: Fischer, 1989), 114: "Serbien einziges Land, in dem Judenfrage und Zigeunerfrage gelöst."

13. Letter from Martin Bormann to Heinrich Himmler, dated December 3, 1942, reproduced in Wippermann, *Geschichte der Sinti und Rom in Deutschland*, 94: "im allgemeinen nicht asozial verhalten hätten und in ihrem Kult wertvolles germanisches Brauchtum überliefert sei, das erforscht werden müsste."

14. Hans Mommsen, "Der Nationalsozialismus: Kumulative Radikalisierung und Selbstzerstörung des Regimes," in Bibliographisches Institut, ed., *Meyers Enzyklopädisches Lexikon*, vol. 16, rev. ed. (Mannheim: Lexikonverlag, 1976), 785–790.

15. Wolfgang Wippermann, "Nur eine Fußnote? Die Verfolgung der sowjetischen Roma. Historiographie, Motive, Verlauf," in *Gegen das Vergessen. Der Vernichtungskrieg gegen die Sowjetunion*, ed. Klaus Meyer and Wolfgang Wippermann (Frankfurt am Main: Haag & Herchen, 1992), 75–90; Martin Holler, *Der nationalsozialistische Völkermord an den Roma in der besetzten Sowjetunion (1941–1944)* (Heidelberg: Dokumentations- und Kulturzentrum Deutscher Sinti und Roma, 2009).

16. Martin Holler, "Extending the Genocidal Program: Did Otto Ohlendorf Initiate the Systematic Extermination of Soviet 'Gypsies'?," in *Nazi Policy on the Eastern Front, 1941: Total War, Genocide, and Radicalization*, ed. Alex J. Kay, Jeff Rutherford, and David Stahel (Rochester, NY: University of Rochester Press, 2012), 267–288, esp. 272–273.

17. Wolfgang Wippermann, *Niemand ist ein Zigeuner. Zur Ächtung eines europäischen Vorurteils* (Hamburg: Körber-Stiftung, 2015), 79 ff.

18. See Denis Pechanski, *Les Tsiganes en France, 1936–1946* (Paris: Librairie Académique Perrin, 1994).

19. See Amadeo Osti Guerrazzi, "Der italienische Faschismus und die 'Zigeuner,'" *Jahrbuch für Antisemitismusforschung* 18 (2009): 139–159.

20. See Karel Vodicka, "Die Zigeuner des Monsignore Tiso. Roma-Verfolgung im 'Schutzstaat' Slowakei 1939–1945," *Zeitschrift für Ostmitteleuropa-Forschung* 53 (2004): 46–82.

21. See János Bársony and Agnes Daróczi, *Pharrajimos: The Fate of the Roma during the Holocaust* (Budapest: International Debate Education Association, 2007); Melanie Barlai and Florian Hartlieb, "Die Roma in Ungarn," *Aus Politik und Zeitgeschichte* 29-30/2009 (July 13, 2009): 33-39.

22. Wolfgang Wippermann, *Faschismus. Eine Weltgeschichte vom 19. Jahrhundert bis heute* (Darmstadt: Primus, 2009), 161 ff.

23. See Viorel Achim, *The Roma in Romanian History* (New York: Central European University Press, 2004).

24. See Radu Ionid, *The Holocaust in Romania: The Destruction of Jews and Gypsies under the Antonescu Regime, 1940-1944* (Chicago: Ivan R. Dee, 2000); Viorel Achim, "Die Deportation der Roma nach Transnistrien," in *Rumänien und der Holocaust. Zu den Massenverbrechen in Transnistrien 1941-1944*, ed. Mariana Hausleitner, Brigitte Mihok, and Juliane Wetzel (Berlin: Metropol, 2001), 101-112.

25. Julia von dem Knesebeck, *The Roma Struggle for Compensation in Post-War Germany* (Hatfield: University of Hertfordshire Press, 2011).

26. Judgment of the Federal Court of Justice, dated January 7, 1956, reproduced in Tilman Zülch, ed., *In Auschwitz vergast, bis heute verfolgt. Zur Situation der Roma (Zigeuner) in Deutschland und Europa* (Reinbek: Rowohlt, 1979), 168-170.

27. Judgment of the Federal Court of Justice, dated December 18, 1963, reproduced in *Rechtsprechung zum Wiedergutmachungsrecht* 15 (1964): 209 ff.

28. Christian Bernadec, *L'holocauste oublié. Le massacre des Tsiganes* (Paris: Editions France-Empire, 1979).

29. Jerzy Ficowsky, *Wieviel Trauer und Wege. Zigeuner in Polen* (Frankfurt am Main: Internationaler Verlag der Wissenschaften, 1992); Selma Steinmetz, *Österreichs Zigeuner im NS-Staat* (Vienna: Europa Verlag, 1966); Erika Thurner, *Nationalsozialismus und Zigeuner in Österreich* (Vienna: Geyer Edition, 1983); Bernard Sijes, *Vervolging van Zigeuneers in Nederland 1940-1945* (The Hague: Nijhoff, 1978); Bernadec, *L'holocauste oublié*.

30. Donald Kenrick and Grattan Puxon, *The Destiny of Europe's Gypsies* (London: Basic Books, 1972).

31. Zimmermann, *Rassenutopie und Genozid*.

32. Guenter Lewy, *"Rückkehr nicht erwünscht." Die Verfolgung der Zigeuner im Dritten Reich* (Munich: Propyläen, 2001).

33. See Wippermann, *"Auserwählte Opfer"?*

34. In this context it is worth mentioning Luchterhandt, *Der Weg nach Birkenau*.

35. See Karola Fings and Frank Sparing, *"einziges Land, in dem Judenfrage und Zigeunerfrage gelöst." Die Verfolgung der Roma im faschistisch besetzten Jugoslawien 1941-1945* (Cologne: Rom, 1993); Holler, *Der nationalsozialistische Völkermord an den Roma*; Felicitas Fischer von Weikersthal, ed., *Der nationalsozialistische Genozid an den Roma Osteuropas. Geschichte und künstlerische Verarbeitung* (Cologne: Böhlau, 2008); Ionid, *The Holocaust in Romania*; Vodicka, "Die Zigeuner des Monsignore Tiso"; Anton Weiss-Wendt, "Extermination of the Gypsies in Estonia during World War II. Popular Images and Official Policies," *Holocaust and Genocide Studies* 17 (2003): 31-61; Guerrazzi, *Der italienische Faschismus und die "Zigeuner."*

36. Wippermann, *"Auserwählte Opfer?,"* 125 ff.

5 Deadly Odyssey: East Prussian Sinti in Białystok, Brest-Litovsk, and Auschwitz-Birkenau

Martin Holler

THE GEBIETSKOMMISSAR (Regional Commissioner) in Brest-Litovsk, Franz Burat, wrote in his June 24, 1943, situation report:[1] "The presence of the Gypsies, who were sent to me last year from the Białystok administrative district, has a very devastating effect. Begging and stealing are the main occupation of this rural plague. I consider it urgently necessary that these idlers be treated as the Jews are and request the appropriate authorization."[2] These "Gypsies" were in fact hundreds of East Prussian Sinti who had been deported to Białystok at the beginning of 1942 and later on, in spring and late summer of the same year, transferred to Brest, where most of them were kept in a "Gypsy camp" (*Zigeunerlager*). The severity of the quoted remark stands in stark contrast to the dominating image of Burat among scholars. In his groundbreaking study on anti-Jewish policy in occupied Brest-Litovsk, Christopher R. Browning has shown that both the *Gebietskommissar* and the SS and Police Garrison Commander (*SS- und Polizeistandortführer*) tried to save Jewish workmen from annihilation in their area of responsibility. After the first mass shootings of Jews conducted by task forces (*Einsatzgruppen*) and police battalions under German military administration at the beginning of the war, the area of Brest went through a relatively calm period of several months under civil administration, even when the second wave of extermination reached the General District (*Generalbezirk*) Volhynia and Podolia in 1942. Ultimately, however, the higher authorities enforced the mass killing of all remaining Jews in Brest, which they prioritized over the economic concerns of the local administration.[3]

The deportation of East Prussian Sinti to Brest as such was, in two respects, a unique event in the course of Nazi occupation: On the one hand, it was the only deportation of German Sinti and Roma into the occupational zone subordinated to Alfred Rosenberg's Reich Ministry for the Occupied Eastern Territories (*Reichsministerium für die besetzten Ostgebiete*, hereafter RMbO).[4] On the other hand, it was the only deportation of German citizens to the Reich Commissariat

Ukraine (*Reichskommissariat Ukraine*, hereafter also RKU), insofar as corresponding plans for the deportation of German Jews were not implemented.[5]

In this chapter, I will analyze the reactions of the civil administration of Brest-Litovsk to the unannounced transfer of Sinti from Białystok and its "Gypsy policy" between May 1942, and April 1944. In order to critically scrutinize the perspective of the perpetrators on the alleged "Gypsy problem," it is furthermore necessary to take the background and the conditions of the deportations from East Prussia to Białystok and from Białystok to Brest into account. Finally, I will describe the survival strategies of the affected Sinti on their forced odyssey through Eastern Europe.

The body of source material on the "Gypsy policy" in Brest is exceptionally good, since the situation reports of the *Gebietskommissar* in Brest-Litovsk and his subordinated administrative offices are largely preserved from late 1941 to the beginning of 1944.[6] Personal statements of Sinti survivors at Brest are rare, but in combination with the documents it is nevertheless possible to reconstruct the reactions of the victims.

In relation to Białystok, however, the situation is the exact opposite. The body of perpetrator files on the treatment of the East Prussian Sinti is limited, while numerous testimonies of survivors—most of them had escaped before the deportation to Brest—and Polish eyewitnesses provide a detailed insight into the horrible conditions in the prison of Białystok.

Registration, Categorization, and Deportation to Białystok

Sinti had lived in East Prussia for centuries and spoke Romanes as well as the local Low German. For several generations, the vast majority of the ethnic minority led a sedentary life and dealt with agriculture.[7] A large part of the approximately two thousand East Prussian Sinti worked as simple farm hands paid in kind, while several successful horse traders and farmers among them possessed their own house and farm. Further typical professions of local Sinti were bricklayer, bootmaker, artist, market trader, and vermin exterminator.[8] The landless usually lived in rented rooms or small rural huts; emergency shelters or caravans were the exception.[9] The director of the Research Center for Racial Hygiene and Population Biology (*Rassenhygienische und bevölkerungsbiologische Forschungsstelle*, hereafter RHF) in the Reich Ministry of Health, Dr. Robert Ritter, experienced severe difficulties in integrating the East Prussian Sinti, whose number he estimated at around 2,500,[10] into his pseudoscientific concept of especially inferior "Gypsy half-castes" (*Zigeunermischlinge*).[11] In particular, the obvious social integration of the "Gypsy bastard population" contradicted his racial theories. Hence, Ritter described the "Gypsies" of East Prussia as an exception to the rule, suggesting that they must have "absorbed the blood of sedentary and industrious people in the course of many centuries" and therefore seem to be despite "their racially foreign appearance ... little 'authentic,'" even though they still know the "romani chib" (Romani language). In order to substantiate his allegation, he named three purported distinguishing marks of "Gypsies" in other parts of Germany: defiance of traditional Romani taboos, regular school attendance of the children, and low musical talent.[12] Nevertheless, the East Prussian Sinti also came into the focus of the "complex of science and police" (Zimmermann). Responsible for their genealogical registration and anthropological examination at the RHF was the scientific assistant Dr. Sophie Ehrhardt,[13] who conducted two special expeditions for this purpose in 1940 and 1941. The Sinti were obliged by police summons—and in case of refusal by police force—to gather for the examination, in the course of which Ehrhardt and her assistants took photos, measured the body and head, and asked about family relations and ancestors. Furthermore, the police provided Ehrhardt's commission with church registers, statistics, and "Gypsy files."[14]

Altogether, the RHF examined and registered 1,087 East Prussian "Gypsies," divided into men (nos. 1–548) and women (nos. 549–1087).[15] The collected material included three-part portrait photo series (profile, frontal, and diagonal), morphological measuring cards, finger- and handprints, and genealogies. Both the morphological material and the extensive genealogical tables contained classifications of the mix degree (*Mischlingsgrad*), which followed in a slightly simplified manner the categories elaborated by Ritter for his race-diagnostic expert reports (*rassendiagnostische Gutachten*): "Z" meant pure Gypsy (*Vollzigeuner*); "ZM (+)" Gypsy half-caste with predominantly Gypsy blood (*Zigeuner-Mischling mit vorwiegend zigeunerischem Blutsanteil*); "ZM" "Gypsy half-caste with equal parts of German and Gypsy blood"; "ZM (–)" "Gypsy half-caste with predominantly German blood"; and "NZ" non-Gypsy (*Nicht-Zigeuner*). In case of doubt, categories such as "preliminary non-Gypsy" (*vorl. NZ*) were used.[16]

The practical initiative for repressive measures against the minority came from the Criminal Police Head Office of Königsberg (*Kriminalpolizeileitstelle Königsberg*), which applied to the Reich Criminal Police Office (*Reichskriminalpolizeiamt*, hereafter RKPA) of the Reich Security Main Office (*Reichssicherheitshauptamt*, hereafter RSHA) in April and May 1941 for the permission to deport the East Prussian "Gypsies" from their area of responsibility. In July 1941, the RSHA only authorized the establishment of a "Gypsy communal camp" (*Zigeunergemeinschaftslager*) in cooperation with the district leadership of the NSDAP (*Gauleitung*), since "a general and final solution of the Gypsy question ... currently cannot take place."[17] Subsequently, the local authorities surrounded existing "Gypsy" barracks at Contiener Weg in the southwest of Königsberg with barbed wire and delegated several policemen as guards.[18] A part of the adult inmates fit for work were compulsorily employed for minimal remuneration outside the camp. Later, the Sinti of Königsberg shared the fate of the other "Gypsies and Gypsy half-castes" in the German Reich: On March 28, 1943, a transport with 352 Sinti (192 women and girls, 160 men and boys) from Königsberg arrived at the newly established Gypsy Family Camp (*Zigeunerfamilienlager*) of the concentration camp at Auschwitz-Birkenau.[19] About 200–250 Sinti, however, remained in the Königsberg camp up to the end of the war. Between 1942 and 1945, several of the adult inmates underwent forced sterilization. In regard to East Prussia, however, the fate of the Sinti from Königsberg was an exception.[20]

The majority of Sinti and Roma in the East Prussia Province remained unaffected by internment measures up to the end of 1941. In the first two months of 1942, however, the local authorities started a large wave of arrests, whereby the police intruded around four or five o'clock in the morning into the houses of Sinti families and ordered them to pack their bags for resettlement to Poland. In some cases, the police officers tried to calm the situation by promising them that every family would receive a farm with a good piece of land.[21] At the railway station, where they had to enter cattle trucks, the affected Sinti understood that all the promises were completely meaningless.[22]

Between January and February 1942, district after district of the East Prussia Province was made "free of Gypsies" (*zigeunerfrei*) by deporting the Sinti to Białystok,[23] where they were concentrated in the prison of the town. In two cases, an escort command of the First Company of Reserve Police Battalion 13 met the arriving transports—around 100 Gypsies on January 5 and 125 Gypsies on January 31—at the station of Białystok and led the Sinti to the prison. The escorts took place "without incident," as the war diary of the company mentioned.[24] What the policemen perceived as proven routine, the unsuspecting victims experienced as traumatic shock. Amanda Dambrowski describes the reception in Białystok with the following words: "Around ten o'clock in the evening the train stopped. The doors were opened. SS men shouted: 'Out, out and on to the lorry!' We climbed them like crazy, the children cried.... As the lorry stopped, it was dark, we couldn't see anything. Polish SS men [*sic*] stood there with rubber truncheons, they drove us, beat us and the children, no matter where. Crying and screaming began."[25] When the transport from Allenstein (Olsztyn) arrived, the deportees had to line up in the knee-deep snow, while the guards ransacked their luggage for valuables. If an adult moved or a child began to cry, they were beaten with sticks; it took three hours, before the group was directed to the prison.[26]

Conditions inside the prison of Białystok were at that time disastrous. Besides starvation and cold, the hygienic conditions were life-threatening. In the overcrowded cells, dozens of people had to share a single wooden bucket instead of a lavatory. Dambrowski continues: "Ice and snow were on the walls; the windows had been knocked out. No heating stove. No water to drink. No bed. Nothing.... Nobody wanted to go on the bucket, many wept from shame. But they had to go anyway. And so it went day in, day out.... The children had diarrhoea. We lay so close to each other. When they wanted to go to the bucket, they had to step over the others. Thereby they lost their faeces and everybody, sometimes the one, sometimes the other, got some of it."[27]

In the wake of the unsanitary prison conditions in combination with malnutrition, diseases like typhus, spotted fever, and noma began to spread, which in particular took the lives of small children and elderly people.[28] Former Polish prisoners confirm the high mortality among the Gypsies from Germany caused by hunger and epidemic typhus. According to postwar statements of eyewitnesses, on some days up to twenty Sinti died. Polish inmates had to carry the corpses to the vegetable garden behind the prison walls and bury them in mass graves.[29]

As of spring 1942, some of the Sinti were used for clearing work outside the prison area, which enabled them to make contact with the local population and to ask for help or barter for foodstuffs, which they could smuggle into the prison.[30] Individual Sinti inmates even managed to escape.[31]

According to the Sinto Robert Adler, three months after his arrival in Białystok on February 14, 1942, approximately in mid-May, a commission came into the prison, headed by two female staff members of the RHF in the company of several police officers. One of the women interrogated the Sinti about their name, age, origin, and the like. Afterward, she carried out a physical examination by extensively scrutinizing the hands, the face (frontal and profile), and the back of the head, as Adler remembers. During the next day, the witness saw how three families, whom he knew from the daily yard exercise, were transferred to another cell block, and shortly afterward they were taken away from the prison.[32] The point in time at which the examination took place indicates that the selection of the RHF commission must have taken place in connection with the first transport of Sinti to Brest-Litovsk in May 1942, which will be described in detail below. Most likely, the head of the commission was Anna Tobler, since Sophie Ehrhardt had left the RHF by the end of March 1942. In a postwar witness statement, Tobler admitted that Ritter had sent her "in 1943 [sic] to the Gypsy Camp [sic] Białystok, in order to tell him about the conditions there." She could not tell, however, whether Ritter wrote to the RSHA about the bad conditions or not.[33]

A further selection took place in September 1942, immediately before the transfer of the remaining Sinti to Brest. Previously, individual families, especially landowners and relatives of Wehrmacht soldiers, had sent written petitions to German authorities, in which they asked for release or at least better prison conditions. Subsequently, single families, who had been rated "socially adapted" and whose home authorities agreed, were indeed allowed to return to East Prussia under certain prerequisites. The Dambrowski family, for example, was told that they would be released for "good behaviour, good repute among the neighbors in Goldap, and because they were farmers." The precondition for their return to East Prussia was, however, their "agreement" to sterilization. Shortly after their return, every family member from the age of twelve up was sterilized. Amanda Dambrowski, who was pregnant at that time, had to undergo a forced abortion. Furthermore, the house and farmland of the Dambrowskis was occupied by other families, so that the returnees had to live in wooden barracks.[34]

Anna Tobler was the only former RHF staff member who confessed after 1945 that she had been aware of the dramatic situation of the East Prussian Sinti in the prison of Białystok. Yet, the recorded genealogies of Ritter's Research Center show clearly that at least the high mortality rate among the imprisoned children must have been known to the staff, since cases of birth and death were added in some of the genealogical tables (*Sippentafeln*) up to the summer of 1942, partly with an exact date. Thus, the RHF must have been supplied with vital record changes, either by the prison authorities and the civil registry office of Białystok or by the RKPA and the East Prussian authorities. So far, the following picture emerges: In fifty-one cases we find the entry "† in Bialystok," including twenty children aged under five years alone, and a further five children up to the age of sixteen years. In two cases, we find the additional remark "court-martialed and shot" (*standrechtlich erschossen*), indicating failed attempts to escape.[35]

The Transfer to Brest-Litovsk

Białystok was only a stopover of several months on the odyssey of the East Prussian Sinti. During the year 1942, the survivors of the extreme prison conditions were transferred to the town of Brest. The *Gebietskommissariat* in Brest-Litovsk was established in September 1941, as part of the *Generalkommissariat* Volhynia and Podolia in the *Reichskommissariat* Ukraine.[36] Hence, like the Province of East Prussia and the Białystok district, Brest-Litovsk was subordinated to the authority of *Gauleiter* and *Reichskommissar* Erich Koch. The most important civil policymakers were Mayor Franz Burat,[37] who was *Stadtkommissar* in Brest-Litovsk (town commissioner, from September 1942 also *Gebietskommissar*), and Major Friedrich Wilhelm Rohde of the Urban Police, who was SS- und *Polizeistandortführer* Brest-Litovsk and *SS-Standartenführer*.[38] Until September 1942, *Gebietskommissar* Curt Rolle[39] also had a certain influence on the administration of the town, since he headed the employment office in Brest during the first months of the German civil administration. Responsible for security police matters was Ernst Berger, who headed the *Außenstelle Brest-Litowsk* of the Brest-Litovsk Branch of the KdS Rovno (*Kommandeur der Sicherheitspolizei und des SD Rowno*).[40]

As Christopher R. Browning has demonstrated, the local civil administration of Brest tried in 1942 by all means to preserve parts of the Jewish ghetto, in order to continue to exploit the manpower of skilled Jewish artisans. When in May 1942, the second and final wave of extermination of the Jewish population reached the *Generalbezirk* Volhynia and Podolia, Burat, Rolle, and Rohde began to emphasize in their situation reports to their superior authorities the extraordinary economic value of the Jewish workers in the ghetto, who, at the same time, caused no danger and showed a great willingness to work, despite their extremely low food rations. Furthermore, the Jewish craftsmen were irreplaceable for the extended workshop complex, which was under continuing construction in 1942. While *Stadtkommissar* Burat intended to spare only Jews capable of work, *SS- und Polizeistandortführer* Rohde argued for keeping the entire Jewish community of the ghetto. According to Browning, the efforts and pragmatic arguments of the civil administration could only delay the killing wave in the Brest area for a certain time, but they were not able to stop it, since the higher authorities prioritized a complete annihilation for ideological reasons. In mid-October 1942, the Security Police liquidated the ghetto of Brest-Litovsk by killing all remaining Jews, including the skilled workers. During the previous six weeks, the Security Police had already liquidated the smaller ghettos of the regional towns around Brest.[41]

As described below, the attitude of the civil administration in Brest-Litovsk toward the East Prussian Sinti was the exact opposite compared to the case of the Jews in the ghetto. Both Burat and—at least at the beginning—Rohde complained about the unannounced transfer of the "Gypsies from Białystok," who had to be supplied with food and accommodated in the town. Burat, especially, described this task as an extraordinary burden and tried everything to get rid of the deportees, but his attempts to convince the higher authorities remained unsuccessful. The treatment of the East Prussian Sinti in Brest can be divided roughly into four phases: Already in spring 1942, a first transport from Białystok with 150 Sinti arrived in Brest, apparently as a kind of test run. After a short time in prison and the checking of their identities, the deportees were released and treated like second-class Reich citizens; they received housing in the town, food supplies, and—although hesitantly—wages in accordance with German standards under civil administration. Shortly after the arrival of a second transport with a further 800 Sinti in September 1942, the norms for wages and supply were drastically reduced, and a guarded "Gypsy camp" was established. In early 1943, the Sinti were resettled to the former Jewish ghetto and partly used as forced laborers, while Burat in June 1943 openly demanded a radical "solution to the Gypsy problem," without receiving the permission for mass murder from his superior authorities. Finally, in April 1944, the remaining East Prussian Sinti were deported from Brest-Litovsk to the concentration camp at Auschwitz-Birkenau, where most of them were suffocated in the gas chambers in August 1944.

The German authorities in Brest-Litovsk were quite surprised when the first transport of Sinti arrived from Białystok in May 1942, since they had not been informed about it.[42] What puzzled them even more was the circumstance that the deported Gypsies turned out to be citizens of the German Reich. Rohde stated in June 1942, that among the inmates of the prison in Brest-Litovsk were momentarily "around 150 apprehended Gypsies who declare to be Reich Germans

(*Reichsdeutsche*). As far as they could prove this, they were in the meantime released and directly integrated into the labour process. The combing through of these Gypsies is not yet completed, so that the release of a further part has to be expected."[43]

The assertion that the "Gypsies" were "apprehended" reflects the traditional language standard of the police in regard to Sinti and Roma, although the Urban Police had simply met the deportees at the railway station and brought them to the prison.[44] *Stadtkommissar* Burat used a comparably stereotypical expression by stating that the "Gypsies" had been "expelled" (*abgeschoben*) from East Prussia via Białystok, and he called the deportees an "extraordinary nuisance."[45] Burat used similar coarse expressions in connection with disabled Jews, whose sustenance he described as "an extraordinary burden."[46] The second department of the *Stadtkommissariat*, in its turn, considered the behavior of the deported Sinti to be presumptuous and was worried about the German image among the local population:

> The settlement of Gypsies in Brest-Litovsk is a nasty thing. They threaten the reputation of Germanness (*Deutschtum*) per se. The provision of accommodations proceeded with some strange accompaniments. They demanded, for instance, decent apartments and dared to explain in the presence of locals that they have come to Ukraine in order to provide cultural and pioneering work. The locals who witnessed this remark could not resist grinning slightly, and they certainly had good reason to do so. When you meet these people on the street, they openly greet with the Hitler salute (*mit Deutschem Gruß*), which is anything but pleasant.[47]

Several details of this description are remarkable: First of all, the East Prussian Sinti of the first transport seem to have had a special status in Brest-Litovsk. The transfer from Białystok is no longer described as "expulsion," but as "settlement," and the German authorities helped the newcomers find lodgings in the town. Apparently, the Sinti were also allowed to move about freely. Secondly, the comments on the alleged behavior of the Gypsies have to be treated cautiously due to the stereotypical anti-Gypsyism of the German authorities. After the humiliating experience of the deportation and the horrible conditions in the prison of Białystok, it seems rather unlikely that the Sinti harbored any illusions about their actual status in Brest-Litovsk, even if the racial experts would have made corresponding promises during the selection in Białystok. On the other hand, it is possible that the ostentatious display of Germanness, including making the Hitler salute and giving a self-confident appearance by demanding decent apartments, was a consciously chosen survival strategy. The complaining words of *SS- und Polizeistandortführer* Rohde from the same period of time corroborate this impression:

> Meanwhile, I have released the so-called German Gypsies from prison and integrated them into the labour process. New difficulties appear insofar as the Gypsies assert on their own accord to be German subjects (*Reichsangehörige*).

> They demand, rightly or wrongly, ration cards for Germans, whereas so far they have been issued ration cards for the locals, which admittedly allowed them only to receive bread, since other foodstuff is not available. Furthermore, it is not yet clarified, whether pensions of German Gypsies unable to work can be payed further on here, since they have no means at all and therefore have to rely on begging and charity.⁴⁸

Rohde's insertion of "so-called German Gypsies" reveals his doubts and reluctance in regard to the identity of the deportees. On the other hand, he gives a rational explanation for the begging of Gypsies unfit for work, without any stereotypical interpretation. The *SS- und Polizeistandortführer* finally had no choice but to comply with the demands of the 150 East Prussian Sinti. Shortly after their release from prison, they received wages and food rations like other Germans in the town.⁴⁹ Unfortunately, the period of relative safety lasted only for a short while.

The main deportation of East Prussian Sinti from Białystok followed in September 1942. Shortly after, the Urban Police of Brest-Litovsk reported on the "establishment of a Gypsy camp" with eight hundred inmates.⁵⁰ The local resident and food supply registers of the town administration indicate that the 150 Sinti of the May transport were not put into the camp, but remained in their apartments.⁵¹ In any case, the total number of 950 Sinti deportees from Białystok suggests that a large part of the estimated two thousand Sinti deported from East Prussia had either not survived the disastrous conditions in the prison of Białystok or stayed back for other reasons.⁵² The "Gypsy camp" was situated on the grounds of a former prisoner of war (POW) camp, in which two-story wooden barracks served as accommodation.⁵³ It was surrounded by a barbed wire fence and guarded by ten local—presumably Polish—members of the Urban Police under the leadership of two German commanders.⁵⁴ According to eyewitnesses, a Sinto named Dombrowski became the camp elder. The newcomers had to work in various places, among them a cement factory and a dairy.⁵⁵ Three East Prussian Sinti can be found on the municipal vehicle fleet's list of drivers, and a further Sinto was even employed at the office of the major of the Urban Police.⁵⁶ Most of the able-bodied Sinti, however, were used for important construction projects, as a November 1942 report of the *Generalkommissar* for Volhynia and Podolia reveals: "At present, 2,200 workers are employed in various road and bridge construction works, among them 400 Gypsies and 200 forced laborers."⁵⁷ Some survivors have described their work for the German Railways (*Reichsbahn*) under the guard of armed railway policemen,⁵⁸ which might have taken place after the resettlement to the former ghetto in 1943, when the status of the East Prussian Sinti in Brest-Litovsk decreased.

The arrival of the Sinti transport from Białystok took place at a very critical moment in time. In the course of the second and final wave of extermination against the Jewish population in the RKU, the German Security Police had systematically liquidated the remaining ghettos of the district towns around Brest-Litovsk in August and September 1942. On October 15 and 16, 1942, finally, more than seventeen thousand Jews from the ghetto in Brest-Litovsk were murdered.[59] For this purpose, the local security police, Gendarmerie, and Urban Police had gathered together with the newly arrived members of Police Battalion 310, Police Company Nuremberg (*Polizeikompanie Nürnberg*), and the Forty-Eighth Motorized Police Battalion. All Jews remaining in Brest, including around two thousand highly skilled craftsmen, were rounded up and divided in groups. The Jews unfit for transport were selected and shot in the area of the ghetto, among them a lot of children and elderly people. The other Jews were transferred in freight trains around a hundred kilometers to the northeast, where they were shot and buried in prepared pits in a forest near Bronnaia Gora. After the operation, the grounds of the ghetto were combed through several times in order to find any last hidden Jews, who were then murdered as well.[60] Most likely, the East Prussian Sinti in Brest-Litovsk became to a certain extent witnesses of the horrible events in October 1942.

For the Sinti themselves, the situation also deteriorated, since they were made responsible for a typhus fever epidemic. In this context, *Gebietskommissar* Burat[61] complained in his situation report for October and November 1942 about the behavior of the *SS- und Polizeiführer*,[62] since the latter took—in disregard of the *Gebietskommissar*—the decision to allow some of the Gypsies to settle in the town instead of the camp. This led to, according to Burat, a spread of the disease throughout the whole town.[63] The *Gebietskommissar* managed, nevertheless, to contain the center of infection "with the available primitive means."[64] What these primitive means looked like is not explained in the situation report, but it is notable that at the side of the paragraph, two exclamation marks are added with a blue pencil, apparently by the *Generalkommissar* for Volhynia and Podolia or his deputy, to whom the report was submitted. This might indicate that the Sinti affected with typhus fever were not only isolated from other inmates, but shot. The Soviet survivor Georgii Mikhailovich Karbuk, who was incarcerated in the prison of Brest-Litovsk during the German occupation, witnessed one day how "a large group of German Gypsies were shot in the prison yard." Among the victims, he stated, were men, women, and children.[65]

In retrospect, *Gebietskommissar* Burat described the events differently: "The Gypsies who were expelled from the Białystok district, imported typhus fever (*Fleckfieber*). Especially in the prison, where the Gypsies had been temporarily accommodated, many cases of typhus fever (*Flecktyphus*) occurred, so that I was forced to place the so-called women's prison, which is situated separately from the main prison, exclusively at the disposal of those affected with typhus fever."[66]

Given the catastrophic hygienic conditions in Białystok's prison, where many East Prussian Sinti had already died of typhus fever, the spread of this infectious disease to the deportees in Brest-Litovsk is not surprising. At the same time, typhus fever was in any case widespread in the town of Brest, particularly in the often-overcrowded camp for (unfit) laborers repatriated from the Reich (*Arbeiterrückführerlager*). In these cases, the local administration also resorted to the isolation of affected inmates in order to contain the spread of infection.[67]

The situation report of the employment office of Brest-Litovsk for November 1942, reveals that the Sinti ran the risk of ultimately losing their status as nationals of the German Reich: "At the moment, the wage-setting for Gypsies causes some difficulties. Thus far, wages typical in the [General] Government or the East Prussian rates have been payed. The reduction of the wage rates to those of the local population led to considerable dissatisfaction, which is unfortunately often even stirred-up by the employers, who take sides with the Gypsies."[68]

The solidarity of the German employers in Brest-Litovsk indicates that they regarded the East Prussian Sinti as their own compatriots, and also that they were content with the performance of their employees. Meanwhile, it must have been clear to both sides—civil administration officials as well as employers—that the reduction of the wage rates to the level of locals would have life-threatening consequences for the affected Sinti. In the very same report, the employment office openly admitted how precarious the situation for local workers really was: "Every effort was made to ensure that the wages laid down in decrees and collective agreements are not exceeded. However, these wages do not offer any incentive for regular labour to the local workforces, since they are insufficient to cover the subsistence due to the extremely high prices on the free market.... It has a very negative impact on the population's willingness to work, if you earn more money by selling two eggs on the black market than a skilled worker does for a day's work."[69]

For the inmates of the guarded Gypsy camp, the situation was even worse, since they were cut off from the local population of Brest and could not even take part in the unofficial barter trade in order to organize some additional food.

With the beginning of 1943, the *Gebietskommissariat* Brest-Litovsk intensified its efforts to get rid of the East Prussian Sinti. Particularly interested in such a solution was the employment office, which demanded the site of the Gypsy camp in order to establish a forced labor camp for "work-shy" locals. It was planned to deport the Sinti to eastern Ukraine: "The transfer of theses Gypsies to Dnepropetrovsk is now authorized by the *Generalkommissariat*, but the transport failed so far due to the missing provision of heating stoves for the railway wagons."[70] Seemingly, the German Reich nationality had—probably for the last time—saved the East Prussian Sinti from this transport under life-threatening conditions in freezing cold. Meanwhile, the destination of the planned deportation was a rather logical choice. The *Generalkommissariat* Dnepropetrovsk was industrially the most valuable part of the RKU, particularly because of the hydroelectric dam "Dneproges." In the course of the "Ivan programme" and due to the large-scale deportations of forced laborers to the German Reich, the civil administration of this area had to face permanent shortages of manpower.[71] Thus, the attempt to resettle the Sinti from Brest to Dnepropetrovsk might also have been based on economic concerns. In any case, the deportation plans as such meant a further aggravation of their situation. Finally, these plans were abandoned, potentially because of the negative development on the eastern front. After the defeat at Stalingrad, the German Wehrmacht was on the retreat, and in February 1943, the front approached eastern Ukraine. In autumn 1943, the Red Army already reached the *Generalbezirk* Dnepropetrovsk.

Meanwhile, in February 1943, the civil administration found a new temporary accommodation for the Sinti: "During the reference month, the original forced labour camp could at last be used again, after the Gypsies, who had been living here so far, had been resettled to the previous ghetto after consultation with the SD [actually Security Police; MH]."[72] From the employment office's point of view, an appropriate solution was found in this way, but for the Sinti the resettlement to the "blood-warm ghetto"[73] was a bad omen. Furthermore, it seems that the surveillance was strengthened, since according to witnesses the Sinto Hermann Klein was shot for leaving the ghetto site.[74]

In reaction to the growing partisan activity and the disastrous supply situation, the *Gebietskommissar* in Brest-Litovsk radicalized his policy toward the local population under his control step by step, especially in connection with work demands and forced labor.[75] With regard to the Sinti, the *Gebietskommissar* in Brest-Litovsk wanted to adopt an even more radical line. After the plans to deport them eastward had ultimately failed, Burat openly demanded their physical annihilation: "The presence of the Gypsies, who were sent to me last year from the Białystok administrative district, has a very devastating effect. Begging and stealing are the main occupation of this rural plague. I consider it urgently necessary that these idlers be treated as the Jews are and request the appropriate authorization."[76]

The murderous intention behind the expression "be treated as the Jews are" is obvious, since the Jewish population of Brest and its surroundings had been murdered long before. At the same time, Burat's enumeration of traditional anti-Gypsy stereotypes—"begging and stealing," "rural plague" (*Landplage*), "idlers" (*Tagediebe*)[77]—in order to legitimize his demand is ideologically connoted with traveling Gypsies, although the East Prussian Sinti were sedentary and lived under conditions (barbed wire, armed guards) in which traveling, stealing, and begging were not even imaginable. Actually, the argumentation of the *Gebietskommissar* tells us more about himself than about the affected inmates of the Gypsy camp in the Brest ghetto. Burat's image of "typical Gypsies" is obviously rooted in his professional activity as mayor of a provincial town in East Prussia of the prewar period and shaped the frame of reference of his administrative correspondence on Gypsies with his superior authorities, even when it comes to applications for physical extermination. In this particular case, however, his argumentation is extremely perfidious and even cynical, since he himself caused the development he criticizes: the gradual reduction of wage payments, social benefits, and supply rates, which Burat had enforced against the will of German employers on the ground, created a desperate situation for the affected Sinti. Yet, the *Gebietskommissar* interprets the increasing incapacity for work not as a consequence of permanent exploitation and malnutrition, but rather ascribes it to "the Gypsies" as alleged essential characteristics—"[work-shy] idlers." Most likely, Burat's real motivation was based on economic concerns, the more so as the supply of the local population—and even of the German officials—became more and more difficult to ensure. Furthermore, in 1943 the Urban Police in Brest was thinned out to the maximum, so that the guarding of the "Gypsy ghetto section" was hard to manage.[78]

Burat did not succeed with his radical demands, but the situation of the East Prussian Sinti in the former ghetto of Brest remained fragile. It took another six to eight months, however, before a definite decision about their further fate was made. At that time, in early 1944, the security situation in the district of Brest-Litovsk, which meanwhile belonged to the *Generalkommissariat* White Ruthenia, was already largely out of control. Due to the strong partisan activity, most individual district regions had lost their direct connection, since streets were mined, bridges destroyed, phone and electricity lines cut off, and so on. Even in the town of Brest, the German control over the local population decreased inexorably. The thinned-out police forces were no longer able to prevent or punish escapes or refusals to work.[79]

Hence, the final decision to deport the East Prussian Sinti to Auschwitz-Birkenau was, in my opinion, less connected with the mass deportations of Sinti and Roma from the Reich since 1943—or, as Michael Zimmermann asserts, the internal discussions at the Reich Ministry for the Occupied Eastern Territories and the *Reichskommissariat* Ostland about an official decree on sending all "roaming Gypsies and Gypsy half-castes" to concentration camps,[80]—than with the German preparatory measures in reaction to the approaching front: the Red Army recaptured Brest already in July 1944. On March 21, 1944, Burat wrote in his situation report to the *Generalkommissar* for White Ruthenia under the heading "*Judentum* (Jewry)" very briefly about the upcoming deportation of the Sinti from Brest-Litovsk: "There are no [more] Jews in the district, but only around a thousand Gypsies. These shall be deported in the near future to the Protectorate of Bohemia and Moravia, as the SD informs."[81] The exact number of "Gypsies" remaining in Brest was at that time 880 persons, as a "list of evacuees" of the urban registration office later showed.[82] Assuming a total number of 975 "Gypsies" in Brest-Litovsk (950 arrivals in May and September 1942, 13 arrivals in 1943,[83] 12 childbirths),[84] the number decreased until April 1944 by 95 persons.

We can conclude that these persons died in Brest-Litovsk between May 1942, and April 1944.[85] In the current case, however, such statistics can only provide a rough approximation, since the numbers given in the German situation reports could be rounded figures, whereas the registration lists of the town's administration are not completely recorded.

Auschwitz-Birkenau

In fact, a train with the remaining East Prussian Sinti left Brest in April 1944, and was directed to the concentration camp at Auschwitz-Birkenau. At that time in the Gypsy Family Camp (*Zigeunerfamilienlager*) of Auschwitz II, Section B II e, which had been established in late February 1943, around six thousand of originally nineteen thousand inmates were living; the others had died in the course of a year due to permanent malnutrition and catastrophic hygienic conditions.[86] On April 16, 1944, the new arrivals from Brest-Litovsk were added to the "Camp Register of Gypsies," separated by gender: 445 women and girls received the numbers Z-10086 to Z-10530, while 407 men and boys were given the numbers Z-9384 to Z-9790.[87] The total number of 852 newly registered Gypsies from Brest means that twenty-eight of the 880 deportees did not arrive (alive) at Auschwitz-Birkenau. Whether they died on the way or—less likely—managed to escape, is not recorded.

According to the "Camp Register," thirty-five "Polish Gypsies" were among the East Prussian Sinti.[88] The names of these Polish Roma can also be found in various documents of the town's administration in Brest, including the deportation list.[89] Judging from the birthplaces, most of them originated from the Białystok district and adjacent areas,[90] thus there are grounds for the assumption that these Polish Roma had also been deported from Białystok to the Gypsy camp in Brest-Litovsk, whether together with the German Sinti or separately.

Apparently, the administration of Birkenau had prepared the camp section for the transfer from Brest-Litovsk. On April 15, 1944—one day before the arrival of the East Prussian Sinti—1,317 inmates of the *Zigeunerfamilienlager*, who had been selected as fit for work, were deported to other concentration camps in the Reich.[91] It seems obvious that this transfer had the purpose of making room for new inmates at Section B II e. Furthermore, due to the negative course of the war, it was no longer possible to recruit enough forced laborers from the occupied eastern territories, so the German industry and the labor camps increasingly had to resort to concentration camp prisoners.[92] Karola Fings and Frank Sparing, however, interpret the transfer of Sinti and Roma from Birkenau to other camps as a clear sign for the German preparation to liquidate the *Zigeunerfamilienlager*, implying a corresponding order in April 1944,[93] but their argumentation does not include the arrival of the East Prussian Sinti during the same period. It is definite, in any case, that in mid-April 1944, the—relative—"special status of the Sinti in

Auschwitz ended," since selections for work deportations had never taken place before in Section B II e, as Martin Luchterhandt correctly emphasizes.[94]

Most scholars assume that the decision to liquidate the *Zigeunerfamilienlager* completely was not made until mid-May 1944, and that it was connected to the upcoming arrival of the first transports with Jews from Hungary. Rudolf Höß, who had already been the camp commander of Auschwitz-Birkenau from May 1940 to November 1943, returned on May 8, 1944, to his former domain in order to prepare for the mass murder of hundreds of thousands of Hungarian Jews. Wherever the capacity of the gas chambers and crematoria was not sufficient for an extermination measure of such massive scale, the SS had to organize temporary accommodation facilities inside the camp for some of the arriving Jews. Apparently, the barracks of Section B II e were regarded as one of the appropriate sites.[95] The first attempt to liquidate the *Zigeunerfamilienlager* failed, however, due to the resistance of the Sinti and Roma, who had been warned by prisoner functionaries, as the Polish former political prisoner and office clerk at the Gypsy camp, Tadeusz Joachimowski, remembered after the war: On May 16, 1944, the SS imposed a block detention at B II e, and in the evening, several lorries entered the *Zigeunerfamilienlager*. SS men surrounded the barracks and ordered the Gypsies to come out in groups, block by block. However, the inmates, who were armed with metal tools and stones, refused to leave the barracks and entrenched themselves. Some of the adult Sinti, who had served in the Wehrmacht at the beginning of the war, threatened that they would not die without a struggle but rather take some of the killers with them. The SS men were completely confused about this reaction, and after consultation with the camp commander they decided to withdraw.[96]

During the following days, the camp administration conducted new selections of Sinti and Roma. More than 1,500 persons, among them many former Wehrmacht soldiers and their families, were transferred to the base camp Auschwitz I on May 23, 1944. One day later, a further deportation of young and able-bodied Sinti and Roma (aged between seventeen and twenty-five years) from the *Zigeunerfamilienlager* took place: eighty-two "Gypsy men" were transferred to Flossenbürg concentration camp,[97] among them thirty-four East Prussian Sinti and four Polish Roma, who had arrived from Brest-Litovsk in April 1944.[98] One hundred sixty-one "Gypsy women" were deported to the concentration camp Ravensbrück,[99] among them twenty-two East Prussian Sintizze and one Polish Romni from Brest.[100]

At the beginning of August 1944, the SS started its second attempt to liquidate the *Zigeunerfamilienlager*. Prior to the liquidation, a last selection of young inmates took place, and these inmates were transferred to the earlier selected families at Auschwitz I. The SS told them that they would be brought to Hindenburg (Zabrze) in order to build barracks for a new Gypsy Camp with better sanitary facilities; later on, the remaining relatives would follow them. The train with the workforces left Auschwitz I on July 31, 1944, but took the direction of Birkenau and stopped near Section B II e, where the Sinti and Roma were allowed to say goodbye to their relatives and friends. This event, unique in the history of Auschwitz-Birkenau, obviously aimed to have a calming effect on the affected people in order to prevent any renewed resistance. Yet, two days after the train left, the SS imposed a block and camp detention. The Polish nurses and educators were gathered and transferred to other sections of Auschwitz II. In the evening, SS men surrounded the barracks and forced the inmates block by block to climb onto lorries, which brought the men, women, and children to the gas chambers of the crematoria. Up to the last moment, the victims desperately protested, asked for mercy, and resisted, but it did not help.[101] The operation lasted the whole night. The following day, the SS combed the whole area of Section B II e and found a woman and two children in hiding places; they became the last victims of the former *Zigeunerfamilienlager*. Altogether, 2,897 Sinti and Roma were gassed and burned in the night of August 2–3, 1944.

How many East Prussian Sinti had been among the victims and how many had been selected for work beforehand, remains unclear in regard to the existing sources.[102] Moreover, in autumn 1944, several return transports from Buchenwald to Auschwitz took place: among the 1,188 prisoners who were transferred on October 5, 1944, from Buchenwald concentration camp to Auschwitz II (Birkenau) and probably gassed on the same day there were 800 "Gypsy men."[103] Shortly after, on October 18, 1944, 217 "Gypsy women" and a further woman were sent back from Buchenwald to Auschwitz-Birkenau.[104] Even those Sinti and Roma who stayed in Buchenwald and Ravensbrück had rather low chances of survival. The male prisoners fit for work were partly sent to Mittelbau-Dora, a subcamp of Buchenwald concentration camp, where the extremely hard forced labor in the tunnel system reduced the average life expectancy to a few weeks. In the Ravensbrück Women's Concentration Camp, numerous "Gypsy" women and girls died of illnesses and malnutrition or from the cruel experiments of sterilization by x-rays and injections into the uterus.[105]

It seems likely that only a few dozen of the deported East Prussian Sinti survived the Nazi persecution. It has not been possible so far to calculate a definite number. The documents of the International Tracing Service and of German compensation offices allow us at least to examine individual fates, but a systematic analysis of this type of source is still a desideratum.

The surviving East Prussian Sinti suffered in many respects from the consequences of the war and the Nazi persecution: First of all, they shared the traumata of most German Sinti and Roma—the experience of humiliation and persecution, deportation, concentration camp, loss of many relatives, sterilization, and eventually the denied recognition as victims of racist persecution. Secondly, they lost their homes in East Prussia forever.

Conclusion

Although most East Prussian Sinti outside Königsberg had been sedentary peasants for generations and regarded by Robert Ritter as "untypical Gypsies," they were arrested and deported by the German police to Białystok in early 1942. Due to the terrible conditions in the prison of Białystok, many Sinti inmates died of malnutrition and diseases, especially small children and elderly people. The RHF, which cooperated with the German police, was well informed about the high mortality rate, as entries in its genealogical tables reveal. Most likely, Ritter's race specialists even took part in selections at the Białystok prison. Single families were allowed to return to East Prussia on the condition that they were sterilized, while a first group of 150 Sinti was deported to Brest-Litovsk in May 1942.

The local German authorities were confused by the unannounced arrival of Gypsies from Białystok, who even turned out to be of German Reich nationality. After a short time in the prison of Brest, the deportees received accommodation in the town as well as German wages and food supplies. This relatively privileged status ended, however, soon after the arrival of a further transport of around eight hundred East Prussian Sinti from Białystok, who were sent to a newly established Gypsy camp in Brest. The reduction of wages and food supplies to the level of locals threatened the Sinti with starvation.

It is unmistakable that in the case of Brest-Litovsk the initiative for a radical solution to the self-created "Gypsy problem" came from the *Gebietskommissar* himself. While Burat had attempted (in vain) to prevent the complete liquidation of the Jewish ghetto for economic reasons, he tried everything in order to get rid of the East Prussian Sinti. After initial hesitation with regard to their German nationality, he decided to deprive them step by step of their rights, beginning with the establishment of the guarded camp and followed by the reduction of wages and food supplies. When plans for a deportation of the German Gypsies from Brest to Dnepropetrovsk in 1943 failed, Burat openly demanded their physical extermination by proposing to the *Generalkommissar* for Volhynia and Podolia that they be treated "as the Jews are." It was a different matter with the *SS- und Polizeistandortführer* in Brest-Litovsk, Rohde, who—after some initial skepticism—adopted a rather moderate position in regard to the Sinti deportees. Hence, the example of Brest-Litovsk demonstrates that the civil administration in the *Reichskommissariat* Ukraine could sometimes even have a much more radical attitude toward the "Gypsy question" than the SS. In the perception of *Gebietskommissar* Burat, Gypsies were "antisocial elements" and "useless eaters," regardless of their actual working capacity and the support by their German employers in the town. Obviously, the fact that among the German Gypsies in Brest were skilled workers and experienced farmers in no way fit into Burat's worldview. All in all, the example of Brest-Litovsk relativizes to a certain degree Mikhail Tyaglyy's assumption that the genocidal intent with regard to "Gypsies" was mainly, if not exclusively, a matter for the Security Police and the Wehrmacht, while the civil administration was more interested in exploiting the work force.¹⁰⁶ Especially at the *Gebietskommissar* level, stereotypical images of the Gypsies as such might have dominated and led to harsh anti-Gypsy attitudes. Unfortunately, so far, only the case of Brest-Litovsk allows binding statements on that question, thanks to the extraordinarily detailed record of bureaucratic correspondence from 1941 to 1944.

Indeed, the anti-Gypsy policy in the *Reichskommissariat* Ukraine was in general rather contradictory. On May 8, 1942, the deputy of *Reichskommissar* Ukraine, Dargel, ordered that henceforth "Gypsies are to be treated generally like Jews. A decree concerning a potential placement in ghettos will be issued later."¹⁰⁷ Here, the term "Gypsies" is used without any distinction. In two implementing orders, however, the *Generalkommissar* for Volhynia and Podolia concentrated on "itinerant Gypsies," who ought to be arrested, imprisoned, and engaged for useful labor. Horses and wagons of the Gypsies were to be confiscated.¹⁰⁸ Meanwhile, in July 1942, data on the Roma population were collected in Volhynia: on behalf of the *Gebietskommissar* in Stolin, the rural rayon administration of Vysotsk ordered the village administrations to submit information on all "Gypsies" living in the area, including information about their way of life, profession, ownership of land, and even whether they were "real Gypsies or half-castes."¹⁰⁹ Whether the village elders knew about the purpose of such inquiries is not clear, but at least they had the power to save Gypsies by ignoring their presence. In the current case of Vysotsk rayon, all nine village elders answered that no Gypsies live in their area. In other regions of the *Generalbezirk* Volhynia and Podolia, however, the mass murder of Roma started in spring and summer 1942 almost simultaneously. So far, seventeen mass shootings of Roma are known from this area, with a total of nearly a thousand victims, according to Soviet investigations.¹¹⁰

At the same time, it must be pointed out that compared to the local Roma in the *Generalbezirk* Volhynia and Podolia, the deported East Prussian Sinti had been granted an exceptional status from the very beginning. This also applies to the final deportation to Auschwitz-Birkenau in April 1944, which had been labeled as an evacuation by the local administration of Brest-Litovsk. With their arrival at the *Zigeunerfamilienlager*, the deportees from Brest-Litovsk returned to the course of the regular Nazi persecution of German Sinti and Roma, which ended in the gas chambers of Auschwitz-Birkenau.

MARTIN HOLLER, MA, studied history and Slavic (Polish and Russian) literature. He is the author of various works on the fate of Roma in Nazi-occupied Europe, including the monograph *Der nationalsozialistische Völkermord an den Roma in der besetzten Sowjetunion 1941–1944* (2009). Holler has also contributed to several source edition projects on German history and the Holocaust.

Notes

1. I am grateful to Dr. Frank Reuter of the Documentation and Cultural Center of German Sinti and Roma as well as Karol Usakiewicz of the Institute of National Remembrance (Białystok branch) for their helpful comments and for supplying me with several copies from Polish archives. I would also like to thank Dr. Karola Fings of the National Socialism Documentation Center of the City of Cologne for valuable suggestions.

2. Situation report for May–June 1943, *Gebietskommissar* in Brest-Litovsk to *Generalkommissar* for Volhynia and Podolia, June 24, 1943, Bundesarchiv Berlin-Lichterfelde (hereafter BArch Berlin), R 94/8, unpaginated (as in the entire record group R 94).

3. See the chapter by Christopher R. Browning, "German Killers: Orders from Above, Initiative from Below, and the Scope of Local Autonomy—The Case of Brest-Litovsk," in *Nazi Policy, Jewish Workers, German Killers* (Cambridge/New York: Cambridge University Press, 2000), 116–142.

4. Far-reaching plans of the Reich Criminal Police Office (*Reichskriminalpolizeiamt*, hereafter RKPA) for large deportations of "Gypsies" to Riga in the *Reichskommissariat* Ostland (hereafter RKO) were not realized. See Martin Luchterhandt, *Der Weg nach Birkenau. Entstehung und Verlauf der nationalsozialistischen Verfolgung der "Zigeuner"* (Lübeck: Schmidt-Römhild, 2000), 195.

5. At the beginning of 1942, concrete preparations for the deportation of German Jews to the District Area (*Kreisgebiet*) Shepetovka in order to use them as forced laborers for road building failed due to the resistance of *Gebietskommissar* Dr. Worbs. Eventually, the deportation plans from Germany to RKU were generally abandoned. See Dieter Pohl, "Schauplatz Ukraine. Der Massenmord an den Juden im Militärverwaltungsgebiet und im Reichskommissariat 1941–1943," in *Der Deutsche Krieg im Osten 1941–1944. Facetten einer Grenzüberschreitung*, ed. Christian Hartmann, Johannes Hürter, Peter Lieb, and Dieter Pohl (Munich: R. Oldenbourg, 2009), 155–196, here 175.

6. BArch Berlin, R 94/6, 7, and 8; Gosudarstvennyi Arkhiv Brestskoi Oblasti (State Archive of the Brest Oblast, hereafter GABO), f. 201.

7. Sedentary Sinti farmers could be encountered in East Prussia already in the first half of the nineteenth century. See Carl von Heister, *Ethnographische und geschichtliche Notizen über die Zigeuner* (Königsberg: Gräfe und Unzer, 1842), 144–155.

8. Jana Mechelhoff-Herezi and Uwe Neumärker, "Nachwort. 'Heimat im deutschen Osten'—Leben, Verfolgung und Vernichtung der ostpreußischen Sinti," in Reinhard Florian, *Ich wollte nach Hause, nach Ostpreußen! Das Überleben eines deutschen Sinto*, ed. Jana Mechelhoff-Herezi and Uwe Neumärker (Berlin: Stiftung Denkmal für die ermordeten Juden Europas, 2012), 93–109, here 94–95; Sophie Ehrhardt, "Zigeuner und Zigeunermischlinge in Ostpreußen," *Volk und Rasse* 17, no. 3 (March 1942): 52–57, here 53; Sophie Ehrhardt, "Über Sesshaftigkeit und Grundbesitz ostpreussischer Zigeuner. In dieser Fassung an Dr. R. Ritter geschickt—am 16.6.1942" [unpublished manuscript, copy from 1980], Universitätsarchiv Tübingen (hereafter UAT), 288/5, unpaginated.

9. In the Lomse quarter of Königsberg, two communal Gypsy barracks accommodated several Sinti families. The building of such wooden barracks was connected with the restrictions on enlargement of the fortress city, which caused a permanent lack of housing space. See Bruno Schwan, *Die Wohnungsnot und das Wohnungselend in Deutschland* (Berlin: Carl Heymanns, 1929), 168–171, with illustrations on 169 and 171.

10. "Übersicht über die in Deutschland lebenden Zigeuner und Zigeunermischlinge," undated [1940]. BArch Berlin, ZSg 142/70, unpaginated.

11. On the abstruse racial theories of Ritter see among others "Arbeitsbericht Dr. Ritters an die Deutsche Forschungsgemeinschaft," January 20, 1940, BArch Berlin, R 73/14005, unpaginated; Benno Müller-Hill, *Tödliche Wissenschaft: Die Aussonderung von Juden, Zigeunern und Geisteskranken 1933–1945* (Reinbek bei Hamburg: Rowohlt Taschenbuch, 1984), 59–64; Michael Zimmermann, *Rassenutopie und Genozid. Die nationalsozialistische "Lösung der Zigeunerfrage"* (Hamburg: Christians, 1996), 135–138.

12. See Robert Ritter, "Die Zigeunerfrage und das Zigeunerbastardproblem," *Fortschritte der Erbpathologie, Rassenhygiene und ihrer Grenzgebiete* 3 (1939): 2–20, here 12. The apparent incompatibility of theory and reality led Ritter to ignore the example of East Prussian "Gypsies" in his subsequent publications. See Zimmermann, *Rassenutopie*, 137. This could also be the reason why Sophie Ehrhardt's aforementioned second contribution on the topic ("Über Sesshaftigkeit und Grundbesitz ostpreussischer Zigeuner") remained unpublished.

13. Sophie Ehrhardt (1902–1990) graduated in zoology with a doctoral thesis on the behavior of ants. In 1935, she became assistant of the race specialist H. F. K. Günther in Berlin. From October 1938 to March 1942, Ehrhardt worked for Robert Ritter in the RHF. Afterward she moved to Tübingen and began to work at the University's Institute for Racial Biology, which was renamed after 1945 to Anthropological Institute. Ehrhardt continued her work and became a nontenured professor in 1957, before retiring in 1968. See "Lebenslauf von Sophie Ehrhardt," 1980, UAT, 288/5; Bernd Grün, *Sophie Ehrhardt (1902–1990)* (2005), http://www.uni-tuebingen.de/frauenstudium/daten/biographien/Biogramm_SophieEhrhard.pdf (last accessed on August 16, 2015); Hans-Joachim Lang, "'Ein schöner Einblick in die Forschungsarbeit.' Vorbereitende Beiträge Tübinger Wissenschaftler für die Zwangssterilisation und Ermordung deutscher Sinti," in *Sinti und Roma und Wir. Ausgrenzung, Internierung und Verfolgung einer Minderheit*, ed. Ulrich Hägele (Tübingen: Kulturamt, 1998), 75–90.

14. See Sophie Ehrhardt, "Kurzer Reisebericht über meine Untersuchungen an Zigeunern in Ostpreussen," September 10, 1980, UAT, 288/5; Ehrhardt, "Über Sesshaftigkeit."

15. The card record system was based on numerical and alphabetical order. See BArch Berlin, R 165/7, 8, and 9.

16. See BArch Berlin, R 165, passim.

17. "Reichssicherheitshauptamt an Kriminalpolizeileitstelle in Königsberg vom 22. Juli 1941—auf dortige Schreiben vom 1.4.1941 und 18.5.1941 betr. Abschiebung der ostpreußischen Zigeuner." Printed in Reichssicherheitshauptamt, Amt V, ed., *Sammlung der auf dem Gebiete der vorbeugenden Verbrechensbekämpfung ergangenen Erlasse und sonstigen Bestimmungen*, BArch Berlin, RD 19/28-15, fols. 237–237a. The reference letters of the *Kriminalpolizeileitstelle Königsberg* are not recorded.

18. It is possible, however, that the barracks in Königsberg were already fenced off in 1938, as several survivors stated. See *Rechtsprechung zum Wiedergutmachungsrecht* 9 (1962): 4–5. Generally, the history of this camp needs further investigation.

19. See Danuta Czech, *Kalendarium der Ereignisse im Konzentrationslager Auschwitz-Birkenau 1939–1945* (Reinbek bei Hamburg: Rowohlt, 1989), 452; State Museum of Auschwitz-Birkenau in cooperation with the Documentary and Cultural Center of German Sintis and Roms, Heidelberg, eds., *Memorial Book: The Gypsies at Auschwitz-Birkenau*, Vols. 1 and 2 (Munich: K.G. Saur, 1993), Camp Register of Gypsies at Auschwitz-Birkenau (females),

Nos. Z-5963 to Z-6154, 410–423; Camp Register of Gypsies at Auschwitz-Birkenau (males), Nos. Z-5397 to Z-5458, and Z-5462 to Z-5559, 1046–1057.

20. A further specific victim group were young men, who in June 1938 had been arrested during Operation Workshy Reich (*Aktion Arbeitsscheu Reich*) and taken to concentration camps, where they were marked with the black triangle of alleged "antisocial elements" (*Asoziale*). Furthermore, arbitrary single arrests and compulsory employments could take place since December 1937 in the framework of the decree on Crime Prevention by the Police (*Vorbeugende Verbrechensbekämpfung durch die Polizei*); in most cases, the affected individuals were later also transferred to concentration camps. All these measures affected likewise several hundred Sinti and Roma throughout Nazi Germany. See Wolfgang Ayaß, *"Asoziale" im Nationalsozialismus* (Stuttgart: Klett-Cotta, 1995), 138–165 and 196–197. Concerning East Prussia Sinti, only single cases are recorded.

21. See "Erinnerungsbericht des Sinto Franz Wirbel," 1979, Archiwum Państwowego Muzeum w Oświęcimiu (Archive of the State Museum of Auschwitz-Birkenau, hereafter APMO), 165739/783, ark. 3–26, here 3; "Zeuge Robert Adler," May 26, 1983, BArch Ludwigsburg, B 162/21080, fols. 202–207, here fols. 202–203; "Zeuge Hermann Dambrowski," November 10, 1983, BArch Ludwigsburg, B 162/21080, fol. 239.

22. See Franz Wirbel, "Die Rückkehr von Auschwitz," *Pogrom. Zeitschrift für bedrohte Völker* 12, no. 80–81 (March–April 1981): 142–143, here 142; Zimmermann, *Rassenutopie*, 228. For the deportation from Sensburg a passenger train was used. See "Zeuge Robert Adler," May 26, 1983, BArch Ludwigsburg, B 162/21080, fols. 202–207, here fol. 203.

23. Under German occupation, the *Bezirk Bialystok* was subordinated to *Gauleiter* Erich Koch in his function as Chief of Civil Administration (*Chef der Zivilverwaltung*). The district had a special status with a rather provisional character, since Nazi plans for an incorporation into East Prussia were never implemented.

24. See "Kriegstagebuch Nr. 3 der 1. Komp. des Res.Pol.Batl. 13 vom 5. und 31. Januar 1942," BArch Berlin, R 20/76, fols. 542 and 553.

25. Amanda Dambrowski, "Das Schicksal einer vertriebenen ostpreußischen Sinti-Familie im NS-Staat," *Pogrom. Zeitschrift für bedrohte Völker* 12, no. 80–81 (March–April 1981): 72–75, here 72. Most survivors reported about the shouting and beating by the guards when they arrived in Białystok.

26. See "Erinnerungsbericht Wirbel," APMO, 165739/783, ark. 3–4.

27. Dambrowski, "Das Schicksal," 73.

28. See "Erinnerungsbericht Wirbel," APMO, 165739/783, ark. 4; Dambrowski: "Das Schicksal," 73–74.

29. See "Protokół przesłuchania Michała Bury w OKBZH w Białymstoku," March 7, 1968, Archiwum Instytutu Pamięci Narodowej, Oddział w Białymstoku (Archive of the Institute of National Remembrance Branch in Białystok, hereafter AIPN Bi), 1/52, ark. 5; "Protokół przesłuchania Mikołaja Hryniewickiego w OKBZH w Białymstoku, May 11, 1968, AIPN Bi, S 2/68/1, ark. 20"; "Protokół przesłuchania Franciszka Zdanowicza w OKBZH w Białymstoku," January 12, 1972, AIPN Bi, 1/52, ark. 70; "Protokół przesłuchania Filipa Stepaniukaw OKBZH w Białymstoku," August 15, 1972, AIPN Bi, 1/53, ark. 143. Exhumations, which IPN conducted in cooperation with the public prosecutor of Białystok between 2013 and 2015 at the former garden of the prison (today remand center), revealed sixty-five pits with at least 359 human remains, including approximately 30 percent children. The scale of bodies comprised victims of both Nazi occupation and Stalinism, the murders

took place between 1939 and 1956. With the help of DNA comparisons with relatives, it was possible to identify almost two hundred persons. See Marcin Zwolski, "Ekshumacje z dołów śmierci w Białymstoku," *Kresowiacy* (August 27, 2015), http://kresowiacy.com/2015/08/ekshumacje-z-dolow-smierci-w-bialymstoku/ (last accessed on September 27, 2015); Marcin Zwolski, *Searching and Identifying the Victims of the Crimes of Totalitarian Regimes: Remand Centre in Białystok 2013-2014. Information material for the Conference "Searching and Identifying the Victims of the Crimes of Totalitarian Regimes: Polish Experiences in the European Context (Białystok, June 25-26, 2015)," Based on the Exhibition by the Branch Commission for the Prosecution of Crimes against the Polish Nation of the Institute of National Remembrance (IPN) in Białystok* (Białystok: IPN, 2015). The identification via DNA comparison did so far not take place in relation to the skeletons of children. In all probability, most of the young victims could turn out to be Sinti, since the usual inmates under German occupation—and Stalinism—had been adult men. Only in the case of Gypsies and Jews, whole families had been put into the prison of Białystok.

30. Dambrowski, "Das Schicksal," 74; Zimmermann, *Rassenutopie*, 229.

31. See "Erinnerungsbericht Wirbel," APMO, 165739/783, ark. 4–10; Guenter Lewy, *The Nazi Persecution of the Gypsies* (New York: Oxford University Press, 2000), 83.

32. "Zeuge Robert Adler," May 26, 1983, BArch Ludwigsburg, B 162/21080, fols. 204–207. Adler speaks in his entire interrogation about the year 1941 instead of 1942; for unknown reasons, the interrogators did not bring his attention to this obvious mistake.

33. See Hohmann, *Robert Ritter*, 537. The trip to Białystok, however, must have taken place in 1942, since in 1943 the East Prussian Sinti were situated in Brest.

34. "Zeuge Paul Dambrowski," July 27, 1983. BArch Ludwigsburg, B 162/21080, fols. 218–219; Dambrowski, "Das Schicksal," 74.

35. BArch Berlin, R 165/134–165.

36. Only in 1944, after the Red Army had recaptured large parts of the *Generalkommissariat* Volhynia and Podolia, the *Gebietskommissariat* Brest-Litovsk became part of the *Generalkommissariat Weißruthenien* (General District White Ruthenia [Belarus]) in the RKO.

37. Franz Burat (1896–1973), communal politician; 1931 joined the NSDAP; as of 1936 mayor of Ragnit (Tilsit district); September 1939 to February 1940 acting mayor of Zichenau (Ciechanów); September 1941 to 1942 *Stadtkommissar* in Brest-Litowsk, then *Gebietskommissar* in Brest-Litowsk until July 1944; 1945 to 1953 in Soviet captivity; 1963 to 1973 member of the District Committee Tilsit of the *Landsmannschaft Ostpreußen* ("Homeland Association of East Prussia"). See BArch Berlin, former BDC, NSDAP-Zentralkartei; "Vernehmung des Bürgermeisters a.D. Franz Burat," November 19, 1962, BArch Ludwigsburg, B 162/29839 (AR 1.040/72), fol. 8; Browning, *Nazi Policy*, 193 and 205.

38. Friedrich Wilhelm Rohde (1893–1975), merchant; 1915 to 1918 soldier; 1927 NSDAP entry; as of August 1933 member of the Urban Police; SA member until 1935; 1939 SS entry; November 1941 to December 1942 SS- *und Polizeistandortführer* Brest-Litovsk; as of 1943 combating of Soviet partisans within *Kampfgruppe von Gottberg* (Combat Group von Gottberg). See BArch Berlin, former BDC, SSO file Friedrich Wilhelm Rohde; Browning, *Nazi Policy*, 193–194 and 205–206.

39. Curt/Kurt Rolle (born 1903), *SA-Standartenführer*; 1932 NSDAP and SA entry; April 1920 to March 1934 *Reichswehr* (Army); as of April 1934 full-time SA officer; September 1939 to 1941 military service; September 1941 to 1942 *Gebietskommissar* in Brest-Litovsk,

afterwards *Gebietskommissar* in Staro-Konstantinov; postwar investigations of the Public Prosecutor's Office led to no results, since the residence of Rolle could not be detected. See BArch Berlin, former BDC, SA file Kurt Rolle; BArch Berlin, former BDC, PK/P 121; BArch Ludwigsburg, B 162/4835 (AR-Z 334/59), fol. 750; Browning, *Nazi Policy*, 193, 205, and 212.

40. Ernst Berger (1904–1960), senior police detective; 1933 SA membership for six months; 1936 SS entry; 1937 NSDAP entry; 1928 police service; 1933 Gestapo official; as of February 1942 head of the *KdS-Außenstelle Brest-Litowsk*; Berger committed suicide on June 18, 1960 after his release from custody. See BArch Berlin, former BDC, SSO file Ernst Berger; BArch Ludwigsburg, B 162/4835 (AR-Z 334/59), fol. 745; Browning, *Nazi Policy*, 194 and 212.

41. Browning, *Nazi Policy*, 179–217, esp. 193–205.

42. Situation report of the *Stadtkommissar* in Brest-Litovsk for June 1942, BArch, R 94/6.

43. Situation report of the *SS- und Polizeistandortführer* Brest-Litovsk for May 15 to June 15, 1942, BArch Berlin, R 94/6.

44. Stereotypical police terminologies concerning Gypsies had a long tradition in the German Reich. See the examples in Zimmermann, *Rassenutopie*, 376.

45. Situation report of the *Stadtkommissar* in Brest-Litovsk for June 1942, BArch Berlin, R 94/6.

46. See Situation report of the *Stadtkommissar* in Brest-Litovsk for May 1942, BArch Berlin, R 94/6; Browning, *Nazi Policy*, 197.

47. Situation report of the *Stadtkommissariat* in Brest-Litovsk, department II, for June 1942, BArch Berlin, R 94/6.

48. Situation report of the *SS- und Polizeistandortführer* Brest-Litovsk for June 15 to July 15, 1942, BArch Berlin, R 94/6.

49. This follows indirectly from a later report of the employment office in Brest-Litovsk, in which the standard wages of the Sinti are reduced to the level of the local population. See Situation report of the *Gebietskommissar* in Brest-Litovsk, employment office, for November 1942, BArch Berlin, R 94/7.

50. Situation report of the *Schutzpolizei-Dienstabteilung* (Service Department of the Urban Police) Brest-Litovsk, BArch Berlin, R 94/7.

51. See the various registers in GABO, f. 201, op. 1. The addresses of these Sinti did not change even in 1943, when the inmates of the Gypsy camp were transferred to the former ghetto, but they were included in the deportation to Auschwitz-Birkenau in 1944. See the various registers in GABO, d. 583, ll. 99–1050b.

52. Michael Zimmermann assumes that an unknown number of East Prussian Sinti could have been among the Polish Roma who were deported in March and May 1943 from the Białystok district to the concentration camp at Auschwitz-Birkenau and gassed without registration. See Zimmermann, *Rassenutopie*, 459–460. This would mean that some of the East Prussian Sinti stayed back in Białystok in 1942, be it because they were needed as forced laborers or for other reasons. However, it is not possible to provide documentary proof of this assumption.

53. See Luchterhandt, *Der Weg*, 197; Donald Kenrick and Grattan Puxon, *The Destiny of Europe's Gypsies* (London: Sussex University Press, 1972), 98.

54. Situation report of the *Schutzpolizei-Dienstabteilung* Brest-Litovsk, October 12, 1942, BArch Berlin, R 94/7.

55. Kenrick and Puxon, *The Destiny*, 98; GABO, f. 201, op. 1, d. 548, l. 57.

56. See "Namentliches Verzeichnis der Angestellten, Fuhrmänner und Arbeiter des Fuhrparkes Stralo Brest," May 21, 1943, GABO, f. 201, op. 1, d. 6678; GABO, f. 201, op. 1, d. 548, ll. 59–600b.

57. Situation report for September–October 1942, *Generalkommissar* for Volhynia and Podolia to *Reichskommissar* Ukraine, November 1, 1942, BArch Berlin, R 6/687, fols. 6–85, here fol. 70. The date of the report and the differentiation between "Gypsies" and "forced laborers" suggest that the "400 Gypsies" were indeed East Prussian Sinti. This observation contradicts Christian Gerlach's assumption that the statement of *Generalkommissar* Schöne proves that "travelling Roma" "after their arrests were partly used as forced laborers in work gangs." See Gerlach, *Kalkulierte Morde*, 1067.

58. Lewy, *The Nazi Persecution*, 83; Luchterhandt, *Der Weg*, 197; Zimmermann, *Rassenutopie*, 229; "Zeuge Hermann Dambrowski," November 10, 1983, BArch Ludwigsburg, B 162/21080, fol. 240.

59. The exact number of victims of the ghetto liquidation is most likely 17,893, as the registration office's statistics on the population figure demonstrate very vividly: On October 15, 1942, 16,934 Jews with "permanent residence" (*stałych mieszkańców*) and 959 Jews with "temporary residence" (*czasowych mieszkańców*) were registered in Brest-Litovsk. For the next day, the same numbers appear, but they are crossed out. Finally, from October 17, 1942 on, the column for Jewish residents remained empty. GABO, f. 201, op. 1, d. 502, ll. 150b-16.

60. See Browning, *Nazi Policy*, 203–204; Gerlach, *Kalkulierte Morde*, 716–717; E. [Evgenii] Rozenblat, *"Zhizn' i sud'ba" brestskoi evreiskoi obshchiny XIV-XX vv.* (Brest: Beloruskii Fond Kul'tury, 1993), 33–37.

61. In the course of an administrative reform on September 1, 1942, the *Stadtkommissariat* and the *Gebietskommissariat* Brest-Litovsk had been united under the name *Gebietskommissariat*. In his new function as *Gebietskommissar* in Brest-Litovsk, Burat was responsible for both the town and the surrounding district, while his former colleague Curt Rolle became *Gebietskommissar* in Staro-Konstantinov.

62. As in the document. Most likely, Burat meant *SS- und Polizeistandortführer* Rohde.

63. Situation report of the *Gebietskommissariat* Brest-Litovsk, department II, for October 1942, BArch Berlin, R 94/7. It seems that Rohde henceforth generally followed a softer line in the Gypsy question than Burat.

64. Situation report of the *Gebietskommissariat* Brest-Litovsk, department II, for October 1942, BArch Berlin, R 94/7.

65. Paul Kohl, *"Ich wundere mich, daß ich noch lebe." Sowjetische Augenzeugen berichten* (Gütersloh: Mohn, 1990), 39. Christian Gerlach was the first historian to point to the possible link between this mass shooting and the occurrence of typhus fever in late 1942. See Gerlach, *Kalkulierte Morde*, 1066. However, Karbuk does not mention any date or approximate time period, so that clear proof cannot be provided. East Prussian Sinti survivors did not mention any mass shootings during their stay in Brest-Litovsk, but this might be explained by an earlier isolation of the infected, due to which contact to the others was lost. At the same time, the investigation files of the Soviet Extraordinary State Commission dealing with similar Nazi crimes in Brest-Litovsk do not contain information about the potential shooting of Gypsies in the prison. See State Archive of the Russian Federation (Gosudarstvennyi Arkhiv Rossiiskoi Federatsii, GARF), f. 7021, op. 83, d. 10; GABO, f. 501, op. 1, dd. 41, 298.

66. Situation report of the *Gebietskommissar* in Brest-Litovsk for November–December 1942, BArch Berlin, R 94/7.

67. Situation report of the *Gebietskommissar* in Brest-Litovsk for November–December 1942, BArch Berlin, R 94/7.

68. Situation report of the *Gebietskommissar* in Brest-Litovsk for November–December 1942, BArch Berlin, R 94/7.

69. Situation report of the *Gebietskommissar* in Brest-Litovsk for November–December 1942, BArch Berlin, R 94/7.

70. Situation report of the *Gebietskommissar* in Brest-Litovsk, employment office, for January 1943, BArch Berlin, R 94/8.

71. On the "Ivan programme" see Kim Christian Priemel, *Flick. Eine Konzerngeschichte vom Kaiserreich bis zur Bundesrepublik* (Göttingen: Wallstein, 2007), 465–467.

72. Situation report of the *Gebietskommissar* in Brest-Litovsk, employment office, for February 1943, BArch Berlin, R 94/8. In the run-up to the mass murder of the Jewish population of Brest, the *KdS-Außenstelle* had taken over the legal responsibility for the ghetto in August 1942. See Browning, *Nazi Policy*, 201. Evidently, the site of the former ghetto remained under the control of the Security Police even after its liquidation.

73. This is how the survivor Franz Wirbel, whose relatives were affected, expressed it after the war. See Wirbel, "Die Rückkehr von Auschwitz," 142.

74. See Luchterhandt, *Der Weg*, 197.

75. Situation report of the *Gebietskommissar* in Brest-Litovsk for May–June 1943, BArch Berlin, R 94/8.

76. Situation report of the *Gebietskommissar* in Brest-Litovsk for May–June 1943, BArch Berlin, R 94/8.

77. On the development and changes of anti-Gypsy stereotypes in Germany and Europe see among others Klaus-Michael Bogdal, *Europa erfindet die Zigeuner. Eine Geschichte von Faszination und Verachtung* (Berlin: Suhrkamp, 2011); David Mayall, *Gypsy Identities 1500–2000: From Egypcyans and Moon-men to the Ethnic Romany* (London: Routledge, 2004); Wolfgang Wippermann, *"Wie die Zigeuner." Antisemitismus und Antiziganismus im Vergleich* (Berlin: Elefanten Press, 1997).

78. Complaints about the extremely limited personnel resources of the *Schutzpolizei* grew in 1943 and 1944 permanently. See BArch Berlin, R 94/8.

79. This severe problem had bothered the civil administration already since mid-1943, and the situation continued to get worse day by day. See the work situation reports of the *Gebietskommissar* in Brest-Litovsk, June 25, 1943 and January 25, 1944, BArch Berlin, R 94/8.

80. See Zimmermann, *Rassenutopie*, 315. Zimmermann's argumentation is untenable for two obvious reasons: firstly, the East Prussian Sinti were no "roaming Gypsies and Gypsy half-castes," as even Robert Ritter had to admit; secondly, they had been kept in a camp already since September 1942.

81. Situation report of the *Gebietskommissar* in Brest-Litovsk for January–March 1944, BArch Berlin, R 94/8.

82. See "Verzeichnis der Personen, die Brest-Litowsk verlassen haben" (Register of persons who have left Brest-Litowsk), June 12, 1944, GABO, f. 201, op. 1, d. 583, ll. 99–105ob. The "evacuation" as such had already taken place two months before.

83. At the end of March 1943, two families—one with five children, the other with four—arrived in Brest-Litovsk and received "the permission of the *Stadtkommissar* [actually *Gebietskommissar*; MH]" to register in the town, as the registration office of the town

administration expressed it. Whether this was an additional deportation or—as the term "permission" suggests—the result of an approved application for family reunion, does not emerge from the document. See the entries from March 26 and 30, 1943, in "Verzeichnis der nach Brest-Litowsk ankommenden Personen" (Register of persons arriving in Brest-Litowsk), GABO, f. 201, op. 1, d. 584, ll. 4 and 8.

84. Childbirths were also registered in the *"Verzeichnis der nach Brest-Litowsk ankommenden Personen."* In the period from August 16 to November 16, 1943, eight "Gypsy" children were born, between January 25 and April 1, 1944, another four. See GABO, f. 201, op. 1, d. 586, fol. 46, 64, 710b, 940b, 96, 1190b; ibid., d. 654, ll. 2, 90b, 13, 440b.

85. Only two entries of death can be found in the lists of the registration office, both cases concern "Gypsy women." See the entries from June 30, 1943, and March 6, 1944, in "Verzeichnis der Brest-Litowsk verlassenden Personen," GABO, f. 201, op. 1, d. 586, l. 260b; GABO, f. 201, op. 1, d. 654, l. 32.

86. The high mortality demonstrates that the granted "privileges" for Sinti and Roma in Birkenau (families stay together, civilian instead of inmate clothing, nursery, music band, temporary additional rations for pregnant women and babies, etc.) ultimately had no relevance for survival. See Luchterhandt, *Der Weg*, 282–286; Zimmermann, *Rassenutopie*, 331–338.

87. See Czech, *Kalendarium*, 758; *Memorial Book*, part 1 (females), 676–705; part 2 (males), 1284–1311. The numbers were also tattooed on the left forearm.

88. Sixteen female inmates (Z-10268 to Z-10270 and Z-10272 to 10284) and nineteen male inmates (Z-9421 to Z-9423 and Z-9564 to Z-9579). See *Memorial Book*, part 1 (females), 688–689; part 2 (males), 1286–1287 and 1296–1297.

89. See GABO, f. 201, op. 1, d. 583, ll. 99–1050b.

90. Ten persons were born in Barglow (Bargłów Kościelny), three in Augustow (Augustów), one in Jaminy, and one in Wizna. Four persons originated from nearby Lida, which under Nazi occupation belonged to the *Generalkommissariat* White Ruthenia.

91. Eight hundred eighty-four men were transferred to Buchenwald, 473 women to Ravensbrück. See Czech, *Kalendarium*, 756.

92. Michael Zimmermann considers the economic need to be the main motive for the selections at the *Zigeunerfamilienlager* in 1944. See Zimmermann, *Rassenutopie*, 340.

93. See Karola Fings and Frank Sparing, *Rassismus—Lager—Völkermord. Die nationalsozialistische Zigeunerverfolgung in Köln* (Cologne: Emons, 2005), 327.

94. See Luchterhandt, *Der Weg*, 299.

95. See Christian Gerlach and Götz Aly, *Das letzte Kapitel. Der Mord an den ungarischen Juden* (Stuttgart/Munich: Deutsche Verlags-Anstalt, 2002), 256.

96. See Czech, *Kalendarium*, 774–775.

97. In the Camp Register of Flossenbürg, the arrivals from Birkenau received the numbers 10361 to 10442, but without the usual categories Z (*Zigeuner*) or ASO (*Asozialer*). Instead, sixty-five inmates were registered as Reich Germans, eight as Czechs and six as stateless. The fact that all of them had been inmates of the Gypsy Family Camp arises solely from their names. See Norbert Aas, *Sinti und Roma im KZ Flossenbürg und in seinen Außenlagern Wolkenburg und Zwodau* (Bayreuth: Bumerang, 2001), 31.

98. See *Memorial Book*, part 2 (males), 1286–1309.

99. See APMO, Sygn. 66, KL Ravensbrück, ark. 134–138.

100. See *Memorial Book*, part 1 (females), 676–705.

101. See Lucie Adelsberger, *Auschwitz. Ein Tatsachenbericht* (Berlin: Lettner, 1956), 109–115; Filip Müller, *Sonderbehandlung. Drei Jahre in den Krematorien und Gaskammern von Auschwitz* (Munich: Steinhausen, 1979), 239–243.

102. The Camp Register of Gypsies ends with July 21, 1944, so that individual fates cannot be reconstructed. See *Memorial Book*, part 1 (females), 727. Transfer lists of the concentration camps Buchenwald and Ravensbrück, to which the transport of August 1944 was directed, are only partly recorded.

103. See Czech, *Kalendarium*, 895.

104. See Czech, *Kalendarium*, 910.

105. See Zimmermann, *Rassenutopie*, 345–348 and 357–358.

106. Mikhail Tyaglyy, "'Zigeuner sind im allgemeinen wie Juden zu behandeln.' Évolution de la politique anti-tsigane du Commissariat du Reich Ukraine au cours de printemps et de l'été 1942," in *Roms, Tsiganes, Nomades: Un malentendu européen*, ed. Catherine Coquio and Jean-Luc Poueyto (Paris: Éditions Karthala, 2014), 165–175, here 174; Mikhail Tyaglyy, "Nazi Occupation Policies and the Mass Murder of the Roma in Ukraine," in *The Nazi Genocide of the Roma: Reassessment and Commemoration*, ed. Anton Weiss-Wendt (New York/Oxford: Berghahn, 2013), 120–152, here 146.

107. *Reichskommissar* in Ukraine, department II a, to *Generalkommissar* in Brest-Litovsk, Zhitomir, Kiev, Nikolaev, and Dnepropetrovsk regarding "Treatment of Jews," May 8, 1942, Derzhavny Arkhiv Volynskoï oblasti (State Archive of Volhynia Oblast, DAVO), f. R-2, op. 1, spr. 8b, ark. 156.

108. Order of the *Generalkommissar* for Volhynia and Podolia regarding Gypsies, May 15, 1942; *Generalkommissar* for Volhynia and Podolia to all *Gebietskommissare* and the *Stadtkommissar* in Brest-Litovsk regarding "Wandering tradesmen and Gypsies," May 21, 1942. See Tyaglyy, "Nazi Occupation Policies," 131.

109. Tyaglyy, "Zigeuner," 171–172. As Tyaglyy correctly suggests, the reference to "half-castes" most likely indicates that the initial order to collect information came from the RMbO, since Otto Bräutigam had demanded similar information on Roma in a letter to RKO in June 1942.

110. See Aleksandr Kruglov, "Genotsid tsygan v Ukraine v 1941–1944 gg.: statistiko-regional'nyi aspekt," in *Golokost i Suchasnist'* 2, no. 6 (2009): 83–113, here 97–98.

Part III. "Useless Eaters"

6 Soviet Prisoners of War in SS Concentration Camps: Current Knowledge and Research Desiderata

Reinhard Otto and Rolf Keller

State of Research

Soviet prisoners of war constitute one of the largest groups of victims of National Socialist violence. The German Wehrmacht refused to treat them according to the rules of international law, first and foremost the Geneva Convention on Prisoners of Wars (POWs) from 1929. Insufficient supplies of food and accommodation, brutal treatment and intentional murder by the army and *Schutzstaffel* (SS) resulted in the death of at least 2.6 million and perhaps even 3.3 million Red Army soldiers from a total of between 5.3 and 5.7 million Soviet POWs in German captivity.[1]

This is a fact that has been known for decades but has likewise been ignored by the German public to a large extent, although the fate of these POWs is so well researched, at least in parts, that the crime as such cannot be denied. Nevertheless, the controversy over compensation for the few POWs still alive and also the question of a memorial for the victims clearly demonstrate the difficulties in accepting this.

In 1978, German historian Christian Streit published the first study about this topic with a considerable impact on later research. In his book, he documented in detail the criminal policy of the German state, as well as the indifference of the German population toward the fate of the Soviet POWs.[2] His study initiated further investigation into many POW camps and aspects of captivity, which were summarized by Rolf Keller at the latest in his doctoral thesis about the assignment of captured Soviet soldiers.[3] All these books and essays show that in archives in Germany and abroad historians will find a lot of sources even for detailed research. A relevant sample of documents has been recently published.[4]

In all those years since 1978, one aspect has been almost entirely neglected: the release of Soviet POWs to the Gestapo and the SS and their transfer to concentration camps. In 1998, Reinhard Otto published a detailed study about the cooperation of the Wehrmacht and the Gestapo in annihilating Soviet POWs but there has been almost no further research since then. Military historians and historians concerned with the concentration camps have simply ignored this vital issue.[5] In fact, this was also true before the end of the Cold War. The few chapters published on this topic were written by historians from socialist countries such as the Soviet Union, Poland, and East Germany and are largely based on the memories of former POWs and/or concentration camp inmates. Both survivor groups emphasize the heroic resistance of these men and women, who had always been a role model for the inmates of other nations. Since the 1990s, several concentration camp memorials, like Dachau and Sachsenhausen, have sporadically published essays about Red Army soldiers but they refer only to their respective camps and do not view this particular victim group in its overall context. As late as 2004, a conference at the Flossenbürg memorial dealt with this subject for the first time, and since 2008, its results have been published.[6]

Nevertheless, it is obviously unrealistic to consider this special group of inmates only in the context of a single concentration camp; its sheer dimensions seem to be largely underestimated. Numerous exhibitions have provided the final impetus for purposeful overall research: from 2010 to 2012, work was undertaken to revise the Mauthausen concentration camp exhibition and in 2013–2014 for a memorial at the rifle range of Hebertshausen concentration camp near Dachau, where at least four thousand Soviet POWs were murdered up to July 1942. Reinhard Otto was tasked with both projects. At the same time, the Sachsenhausen memorial was planning an exhibition to show the history of the "Inspectorate of the Concentration Camps" (*Inspektion der Konzentrationslager*, or IKL) in which Rolf Keller emphasized the topic "Selection and Murder of Soviet Soldiers in the Concentration Camps of the SS." In all these projects, relations inside the concentration camp system became apparent up to the conclusion of central planning inside the IKL and the delegation of specific functions of particular concentration camps concerning the Soviet POWs. More fundamental is the awareness of close cooperation between Wehrmacht and SS and the intersecting of the military POW organization with the concentration camp system, which was primarily seen in the research carried out on Mauthausen.

The archival situation for specifying the role of the Wehrmacht and the relations inside the concentration camp system is not bad because the concentration camp memorials have gathered most personal information in databases, and the individual files of the Soviet POWs maintained by the Wehrmacht have been revealed in a huge project since 2000.[7]

It has never been asked how many Red Army soldiers in total were at some point among the inmates of the concentration camps. One essential reason for this might be the problem of defining this group because it is inhomogeneous and can be divided into several subgroups. A first classification is possible by using the inmate category "prisoner of war" (*Kriegsgefangener*)—there were many who were brought to the concentration camps as such and classified in this way thereafter (abbreviation "*Kgf.*"). Others had been "released" previously and came as "civilians" to the SS camps. At least 34,000 Soviet soldiers belonged to the first group: about 26,000 so-called labor Russians (*Arbeitsrussen*) from October 1941 on, in addition a minimum of 4,500 "ex-legionnaires" (*Exlegionäre*) as well as roughly 3,500 disabled POWs in the Lublin-Majdanek concentration camp, of whom 1,250 were transferred to Mauthausen in July 1944.

Those who had been released before being sent to a concentration camp fall into a sub-classification. There is the group of POWs who were brought to the SS camps explicitly to be executed as soon as possible—so-called special treatment (*Sonderbehandlung*)—and were therefore not registered as camp inmates. First of all, the "selected" (*Ausgesonderte*) have to be mentioned, POWs who had been selected from among all POWs in 1941–1942 because of the fact that they belonged to certain ideologically "unbearable" groups.[8] This crime, based on operational orders (*Einsatzbefehle*) nos. 8 und 9, was planned jointly by the High Command of the Wehrmacht (*Oberkommando der Wehrmacht*, or OKW) and the Reich Security Main Office (*Reichssicherheitshauptamt*, or RSHA). The operational orders were suspended on August 1, 1942, but nevertheless remained in effect and so it could transpire that after this date "unbearable" Soviet POWs were transferred to a concentration camp and "liquidated" sometime after arrival.[9] Another group that should be named are the so-called K inmates (*K-Häftlinge*), officers, mostly Soviets, who escaped from captivity but were later captured. The "bullet order" (*Kugelbefehl*) from March 4, 1944, stipulated that officers who had fled and were captured again, with the exception of Brits and Americans, were to be officially deregistered with the Wehrmacht Information Office (*Wehrmachtauskunftstelle*, or WASt) as "fled and not captured again" (*geflohen und nicht wiederergriffen*) but in fact brought to Mauthausen. Nearly all of these, at least 2,500 men, died by being shot or from starvation.[10]

Finally, there is a group, sent to the concentration camps after summer 1942, whose size cannot be measured. After being released from captivity, they were sent to concentration camps for different individual reasons such as close contact to German women, refusal to work or "insubordination" (*Widersetzlichkeit*), but an execution was only to be carried out in the case of crimes such as murder or cannibalism.[11] Relevant for this new approach was the necessity of labor deployment. They came as civilians, just like all the other inmates, but in the different camps different terms were used for them. Thus, in Flossenbürg, one can find the "released POWs" (*entl. Kgf.*), Soviet POWs whose former status was still visible although they had been handed over to the Gestapo. By contrast, in Mauthausen, such inmates were called "political Russians" (*Polit. Russen*) or "civilian Russians"

(*Zivilrussen*), so that no one could recognize their POW past from the moment of transfer. In these cases, it is only possible to establish their POW background if one obtains the corresponding Wehrmacht documents. A good example for that is a network of resistance of about 500 soldiers, mostly officers, in the vicinity of the military hospital Ebelsbach (Lower Franconia), discovered by the Gestapo in the summer of 1944. They came to Mauthausen as "civilian Russians" and many of its members were shot.[12] It has so far been possible to establish at least four thousand inmates in Mauthausen as former POWs; in Flossenbürg one can find about 3,100 "released or former POWS." But it is not obvious whether the different terms used in both concentration camps mean the same thing. At least 15,000 people in Mauthausen from a total of 38,000 Soviet inmates can be counted as POWs or former POWs. As far as these and the other concentration camps are concerned, detailed and, in part, fundamental historical research is necessary, last but not least with regard to the total number of POWs brought to the concentration camps by the Gestapo after being released. At present, this figure cannot be established.

An exception is the case of about 500 "reactivated" people: POWs who had been selected for "special treatment" until summer 1942. But, instead of being murdered, they were transferred to Mauthausen-Gusen concentration camp to work in the respective quarries. After their arrival, they were registered a second time, whereupon the concentration camp reported this registration to the WASt. Taken together, the total number of Soviet POWs in German concentration camps will come to more than one hundred thousand, a dimension that should cause more historical research than has been the case to date.

Soviet POWs in Concentration Camps and the Role of the Wehrmacht

In the case of the first group mentioned, those who were indicated as prisoners of war in the concentration camps, the question arises as to whether and how far the Wehrmacht could wield its influence even in the SS camps. According to international law, captured military personnel were exclusively subordinated to the army, and only the army could dispose of their labor. The easiest group to investigate is that of the so-called labor Russians, because it is the largest. Well-known data on this group leads us to new conclusions, but it is still too early to form a coherent picture. This must be the focus of further research.

The "Labor Russians"

On October 4, 1941, the OKW ordered several POW camps to hand over about 26,000 Red Army soldiers to the SS in order to exploit them for work in the concentration camps.[13] Today, historians agree that the OKW officially insisted on being informed about all changes concerning the POWs including cases of death, but in practice the military leadership was willing to neglect this fact. One part of the order indicated that the POWs were subordinated to the SS in all matters from the moment of delivery. Research suggests that it was, in fact, a complete transfer, and the OKW therefore did not take charge of those POWs again at any point in the future.[14] Looking at this order and at the living conditions of the POWs in the SS camps in detail, a new picture emerges of the historical situation, because the Wehrmacht evidently had—or at least could have had—far more influence inside these parts of the concentration camps (called SS-POW Labor Camps—*SS-Kriegsgefangenen-Arbeitslager*) than has so far been assumed.

At first, the OKW decided that according to their rules all these POWs should remain under the card index control of the WASt, so that the Wehrmacht had a lasting overview of that group. It worked just like a normal transfer from one military POW camp to another: the POW was accompanied by his file card, his objects of value, his money and his clothes, and, most of all, all cases of death and transfers to other concentration camps were to be announced to Berlin using precise OKW rules and forms. Therefore, additional advice in the order of October 4, 1941, was actually unnecessary. It stipulated that from the moment of transfer, all these POWs were subordinated to the SS in every respect, not least in medical and economic concerns. The purpose of this decree was rather to make the concentration camp commanders familiar with matters they were normally not accustomed to.[15] On October 11, 1941, the Inspector of the Concentration Camps passed on the OKW order to his commanders as a matter of routine.[16] He nevertheless added an internal caveat a few days later: in cases of unnatural death, the SS court officer in charge should send a report to him but not to the WASt. The latter institution was only supposed to receive information in the way the OKW had laid down in the instruction of October 4, 1941.[17] The circumstances of death were consequently masked vis-à-vis the military authorities, and therefore the message was more a formal act than an explicit piece of information, but the SS obeyed this bureaucratic behavior to the letter from this point on.

The special role of this new group in the concentration camps was apparent in that they were housed in a special area, called the SS-POW Labor Camp, which was separated from the rest by barbed wire. All other inmates were strictly forbidden to enter that zone. One can compare it with the strict ban on contact between civilians and POWs in military POW camps.[18] Flossenbürg camp was to receive special barracks from the High Command of the Army (*Oberkommando des Heeres*, or OKH) in autumn 1941 for housing the "labor Russians," which were different from those types of barracks used in the concentration camps. They were probably directly paid by the Wehrmacht or in an indirect way by means of the assignment of material. Because of a lack of resources, the barracks were ultimately not made available until March 1942 at the earliest.[19]

The concentration camp bureaucracy dealt with the "labor Russians" completely differently from all other inmates. They were a special group of prisoners in the camp statistics. They were not registered as inmates with a typical concentration camp number but stayed there with the tag number they had received from the Wehrmacht after their capture. In Auschwitz, at least, the camp administration established a peculiar series of POW numbers, called "Russian prisoners of war" (*Russische Kriegsgefangene*, or RKG),[20] while in Mauthausen a block of numbers was reserved for them, but even in these camps the essential number was the Wehrmacht tag number, and it was this that was sent to the WASt to inform that institution about all personal changes, such as deaths or transfers. The WASt staff handled the files of the dead "labor Russians" in the same way it handled those of normal POW camps. The special role of this group in the concentration camps can be explicitly seen by the initiation of death books used only for them, and in these books the inmate known as the camp clerk (*Lagerschreiber*) entered only the tag number. Death books of Soviet POWs still exist in excerpts or are preserved in their entirety for Auschwitz, Buchenwald, Mauthausen/Gusen, and Neuengamme.

The concentration camps were not at all part of the Wehrmacht's POW organization, but now they had been assigned a peculiar role. Their administrations were responsible to the WASt for maintaining the register for the entire time the "labor Russians" remained in a given camp, and they had to observe the registration guidelines. But that was incompatible with their self-concept and accordingly that of the SS headquarters in Oranienburg and Berlin because they would have become subordinate to the Wehrmacht in certain aspects of their work. By creating the POW Labor Camp, these institutions were something new in formal aspects not foreseen in army directives. Therefore, the military POW camps occasionally had some bureaucratic problems. Thus, Stalag XIII B Weiden (Upper Palatinate) referred to Flossenbürg concentration camp as a work detachment on the personal cards of the POWs, and Auschwitz was Labor Commando No. 46 of Stalag 308 Neuhammer (Lower Silesia) in early October 1941. Two thousand Soviet POWs were transferred from Stalag VI C Bathorn to the SS Works in Gusen-Linz, which was officially impossible under formal agreements. It was impossible because POWs were not allowed to be transferred to nonmilitary institutions or public enterprises. In such cases, this had to be recorded in the section "work detachment" on the personal cards. But the outward impression was that this behavior worked according to military rules and international law because the OKW had not resigned itself to giving up its rights concerning the POWs. They were only on loan and could be reclaimed at any time. With this constraint, the Wehrmacht could fulfill the SS request for manpower without any problems.

Evidence of the Wehrmacht's maintenance of this formal claim is that an inspection of the POW Labor Camp in Mauthausen by the responsible Commander of the Prisoners of War (*Kommandeur der Kriegsgefangenen*) of Military District XVII Vienna took place on April 23, 1942. While he understood his authority for such an inspection to be self-evident,[21] this certainly did not extend to caring for decent living conditions, although this obligation was stipulated in the same regulation: of those two thousand Red Army soldiers who arrived at Mauthausen on October 22, 1941, only 247 were still alive on the day of his inspection, in Gusen a mere 164 from 1,993. Most had died of malnutrition, exhaustion and illnesses, while other POWs had been executed.[22]

At any rate, the concentration camp adhered to the OKW guidelines until the end of the war.[23] When a Soviet POW died, the WASt received a death certificate just as it did from one of the army's officer camps or those for enlisted men. As prescribed, the personal cards were sent to that institution, where a stamp or a handwritten entry added on the front gave evidence of the last POW Labor Camp or concentration camp the POW had been in. In each case of transfer to another concentration camp, the WASt was also informed. The status of the few surviving "labor Russians" normally stayed the same; they remained POWs.

All these features of Red Army soldiers in concentration camps mentioned above should be at least—partly—found in the case of other soldiers who were transferred there at a later date. In the first place, this is true for members of the so-called Indigenous Formations (*Landeseigene Verbände*, or LeV), legionnaires of the Wehrmacht who were taken to Mauthausen-Gusen concentration camp explicitly for punishment purposes.

Members of the "Indigenous Formations" (LeV)

On September 25, 1943, a transport of sixty-seven "political Russians" arrived at Mauthausen concentration camp. However, barely two weeks later, on October 7, 1943, a "notification of change" read: "According to an order from the Political Department [Gestapo branch office], those sixty-seven inmates listed on the list of arrivals of September 26, 1943, are *Russian POWs* (not political Russians), and from today on, they will have this status as such."[24] In addition, their date of arrival was changed to October 7, 1943, exactly the day on which they had again become POWs. Their personal cards were stamped "POW Labor Camp Mauthausen-Gusen." These men were members of the Indigenous Formations, who had been transferred from Kauen/Kowno (Lithuania) to this concentration camp.

In spring 1942, the first experiments began for the formation of new armed units, for which the personnel were to be recruited from among "Turkic peoples," later Caucasians as well. They were supposed to support the Germans in fighting against the Soviet Union. These units were called eastern legions (*Ostlegionen*), while the legionnaires were referred to as members of the Indigenous Formations. Most of all the legions were founded and trained in special camps in the General Government. On becoming a member of such a legion, a man's status changed from a POW to a soldier of the German Wehrmacht and he swore on oath to be a faithful follower of Adolf Hitler.[25]

But there was a lot of suspicion directed toward the legionnaires concerning their combat strength as well as their discipline, as a result of which their units were sent to fight only quite late in the war. Based on racial prejudices, rough and harsh treatment seemed to be appropriate for them from the beginning. If a legionnaire did something wrong he could be severely punished, and after having served his sentence, he was expelled from the Wehrmacht and transferred back to the status of a POW. The term ex-legionnaire was often used for these former members of the Indigenous Formations.

In some main camps, special compounds were established for these now former legionnaires, called "special camps," whose purpose was laid down in an order of October 29, 1943.[26] In addition, there were also "politically unreliable" former soldiers, who had not committed any crimes. Nevertheless, they were not to be transferred to a legion because of their uncertain political attitude. Their transfer to a special camp had to be accompanied with the special comment "politically unreliable." However, these compounds were only used for a temporary accommodation of six weeks at most. The final destination of all those POWs who were sentenced to detention in a special camp was in fact Mauthausen concentration camp. There they were to work under the hardest conditions, as the commander of the prisoners of war in the General Government wrote on December 2, 1943. From the moment of their arrival the SS was in charge of them.[27]

After the first transport on September 25, 1943, mentioned above, further transports of former legionnaires arrived at Mauthausen right up until almost the end of the war, totaling about 4,500 people. They all came to the POW Labor Camp Mauthausen-Gusen, which was marked by a stamp on the front of their personal card, the reverse of which sometimes reads "Special Camp Mauthausen." In the Mauthausen arrival lists they were named "*Kgf.*," and counted in the statistics with this status. Unlike the "labor Russians," they received a regular inmate number in addition to their identity tag and frequently both numbers were conveyed to the WASt, which was constantly informed about the situation of the former legionnaires. In contrast to the "labor Russians," they were not isolated from the other concentration camp inmates but instead lived together with them in the same barracks and worked in the same labor detachments. In case of death, the name and the military tag number were noted in the death book of the Soviet POWs. At least two death sentences were carried out in Mauthausen on September 13, 1944, that had been imposed by the Military Court of the Senior Field Headquarters 372 in Lublin (*Kriegsgericht der Oberfeldkommandantur 372 Lublin*) on April 11 of the same year.[28] In other cases, death penalties were confirmed by military courts in principle, but the execution was in fact foregone "in favor of" transfer to a "special camp" and labor deployment there under the harshest conditions.[29]

To show that Mauthausen concentration camp was designed as part of the penal system of the Wehrmacht, there exists an interesting parallel to the fate of the legionnaires. Even before World War II began, German soldiers who had been expelled from the Wehrmacht as "unworthy of engaging in combat" (*wehrunwürdig*), were transferred to a concentration camp where they were classified as "SAW [*Sonderabteilung Wehrmacht*—special section Wehrmacht] inmates." This was considered the harshest punishment possible in such cases of misconduct. In wartime, such soldiers were sent to a penal camp or penal battalion; if this sentence was not deemed to have contributed to their personal improvement, their transfer to a concentration camp was seen as the last chance to make them real servicemen. From July 17, 1944, SAW delinquents could be placed on probation instead of being executed; they would then be taken to a concentration camp for strategic employment. The OKH commented on this as follows: in cases in which the execution of a death warrant was pointless in terms of military discipline, and if the convict was not deemed useful as a soldier at all, he could be handed over to the SS Security Service (*Sicherheitsdienst*, or SD) for employment. This situation was called interim detention I (*Zwischenhaft I*), and the only prison for those soldiers sentenced to death was Mauthausen concentration camp. In Mauthausen, they were categorized as "protective detainees" but with the additional specification of interim detention. Nevertheless, they remained servicemen; in the camp statistics, they formed the special SAW group.[30]

It is apparent that Mauthausen had a similar function for the former legionnaires. There were no penal units or camps in the German POW organization. The only possibility of implementing a sentence against a POW found guilty of a serious crime was to transfer him to an army prison or, in more serious cases, to a civilian institution for penal servitude. Due to their expulsion from the Wehrmacht, the members of the Indigenous Formations were no longer soldiers, but POWs anyway, and thus their crimes had to be punished in a special way. Presumably, under the influence of the OKW and the OKH, a military punishment department of the harshest sort came into being in Mauthausen, which was actually not planned in the POW system. Nevertheless, as usual, the army insisted on its power of control over this group of POWs.

In the case of the SAW prisoners, as well as the former legionnaires, the military leadership thought to stimulate the SS to do the dirty work for the army in the concentration camp. There must have been longer negotiations beforehand. The first reference to Mauthausen in military documents in this respect is dated December 2, 1943, although the first legionnaires had arrived at the camp ten weeks earlier (September 25, 1943).[31] It is implausible that the SS helped the army for altruistic reasons; its aim was rather to acquire more forced laborers, especially people in comparatively good physical condition.[32]

When compared to the "labor Russians," it is evident that the terms of transfer of Soviet POWs to a concentration camp were largely the same. This must have been part of the negotiations between the OKW/OKH and the SS, as well. No reference to the order of October 4, 1941, has been found to this day, but in the meantime the regular presence of Red Army soldiers in a concentration camp had become a matter of course and especially in terms of bureaucratic concerns. The reason for the incorrect assessment of the first group of legionnaires might be seen in the uncertainty of the Political Section of Mauthausen as to whether they were real POWs or not. That would explain the later alteration of their inmate status.

The "Reactivated" Soviet POWs

The findings to date might help us to understand the situation of one group of Soviet concentration camp inmates who had an exceptional position between the real POWs ("labor Russians" and former legionnaires) and those who were not registered as inmates at all (selected and K inmates). First of all, their peculiar status will be distinctively shown by the following example.

As evidenced by his German POW personal card, the twenty-four-year-old Belarusian farmworker Mikhail Ivanovich Dudin, a private, was captured near Slonim in the first days of the war against the Soviet Union. In mid-July 1941, he was brought to POW main camp *Stalag* 326 Senne in Eastern Westphalia, and a few weeks later his odyssey continued with a transfer to camp V C Malschbach in southwestern Germany, where he had to work in a detachment in the small town of Lauffen (Neckar). According to the operational orders nos. 8 and 9, at the turn of the year 1941–1942 an operational commando (*Einsatzkommando*) of the State Police Regional Headquarters in Stuttgart checked all Red Army soldiers working there with regard to their "ideological compatibility" and adjudged Dudin to be "unbearable." Therefore, the camp commander released him from captivity on January 26, 1942, and handed him over to the *Einsatzkommando*, which sent him to Dachau concentration camp a few days later.

Regarding this process, one would fully expect him to have been executed at the rifle range of Hebertshausen, but in his case something very unusual actually happened: Dudin was not murdered but "reactivated" as a POW, which means he was returned to his former status. He received a completely new second personal card, the same Wehrmacht form like the first. On the front, someone has written with a typewriter "based on the specifications of the POW newly created in 'POW Labor Camp Mauthausen-Gusen'." On the reverse, there is a notification in the transfer column: "17.2.1942 from Dachau concentration camp to POW Labor Camp Mauthausen-Gusen." There, his status was changed again by a formal transfer from the POW Labor Camp to Mauthausen concentration camp on August 25, 1942. Thus, Dudin was released from captivity a second time and ultimately transformed into a normal concentration camp inmate. He died in Gusen on April 19, 1943.[33]

Until now, 374 men with a biography comparable to that of Mikhail Dudin can be found among the Mauthausen inmates. They arrived there between January 22,

1942 and June 16, 1942, coming from Buchenwald, Dachau, Flossenbürg, Groß-Rosen, or Auschwitz, as well as Sachsenhausen. From the end of March 1942 onward, even if they officially arrived as POWs, they nevertheless received a new personal card just like those who had arrived before that date, and just like on the card of Dudin one can read: "based on the specifications of the POW newly created in 'POW Labor Camp Mauthausen-Gusen'."[34] Before they were transferred to Mauthausen they stayed in that concentration camp, where they would normally have been executed within one month, in Dachau within about eight weeks.

The origins of this policy can probably be traced back to an order by Reichsführer SS Heinrich Himmler, issued on November 15, 1941. In it, he agrees to the following decision: "the execution of those POWs (in particular commissars) can be delayed for those who are able to work in quarries, according to their physical constitution." Officers in charge of protective custody and the camp physician were to separate POWs destined for work from the execution transports after their arrival, but later it was also necessary to obtain permission for the delay from the "Chief of the Security Police and the SD," that is, Heydrich.[35] As far as Buchenwald concentration camp is concerned, a corresponding document exists. Its commandant had submitted a request to Berlin on December 16, 1941, concerning 138 selectees. The answer was given five weeks later (January 20, 1942): all of the 138 should be moved to Mauthausen immediately.[36] It has since been possible to ascertain most of their names. It is quite absurd to see Dudin and his comrades being, as it were, reactivated to the status of POWs.

These 138 selectees had been separated in a Wehrmacht camp by an *Einsatzkommando*, released from captivity and signed off at the WASt, evidently by sending their personal cards to that institution, similar to the behavior in cases of death. They did not exist anymore. Therefore, further inquiries were impossible in the former camp as well as in the WASt, where queries like that would have caused considerable confusion. Thus, the new second registration must be based on Mauthausen's own initiative and it is astonishing to see that German concentration camp bureaucrats trusted the specifications of POWs who did not even have their military identity tags any longer.[37] But it did not matter; the concentration camp leadership knew that they would never leave the camp.

To answer the question as to why this happened is difficult. Up to the end of February 1942, more than 300 reactivated POWs arrived at Mauthausen. To house this relatively large group among all the other inmates apparently seemed to be inopportune, not least because of their special background. Only the compounds of the "labor Russians" offered the possibility to accommodate them. But, after their release, they were still civilians and they could not be brought as such to the military department of the concentration camp, which might have meant conflict with the Wehrmacht. The problem was to be solved only by their reinstatement to the status of POWs, which was indeed impossible without military support. As mentioned above in connection with the "labor Russians," the concentration camps had received file cards to announce all their changes to the WASt, but new registrations were not allowed for them, and so the respective forms had to be requested from the army. This could explain why Mauthausen is the only camp in which the presence of reactivated Soviet POWs can be verified. Nonetheless, from their arrival on there were two different groups in the POW Labor Camp Mauthausen and Gusen. The IKL instructed Mauthausen concentration camp to consider this fact. On March 28, 1942, it fixed the announcement of Soviet POWs in a teletype to Berlin. At the end, it stated: "Those prisoners of war whose execution was deferred and were [instead] deployed in Mauthausen's quarry are to be deducted from the above report."[38] Thus, they were not part of the monthly statistics of the concentration camp, but clearly of the ration count.[39]

Most of those reactivated POWs died from sickness (or at least this is how their death was formally recorded), were executed or allegedly shot while attempting to escape. This was true of at least 319 from 375 POWs actually known with this special status. Only a few survived, and so the employment demanded in Himmler's order of November 15, 1941, is not worth mentioning. Why sixty of them were transferred from the POW Labor Camp to the concentration camp, which meant the loss of their POW status again, and another fifty on November 18, 1942 again, is so far unclear.[40]

The Disabled Soviet POWs in Lublin and Mauthausen

In the concentration camps Lublin-Majdanek and Mauthausen, one can find a further group of Soviet POWs that is different from those mentioned above. In mid-1942, the German military authorities had discovered that released POWs, among them disabled people, had become itinerant beggars in the occupied territories in the East. The OKW thought that they might be dangerous in the future because they might become members of gangs (*bandenanfällig*). Therefore, it ordered on September 22, 1942, that Soviet POWs who could be released because they were not capable of work, be handed over to the Higher SS and Police Leader responsible for that particular territory. According to instructions from the Reichsführer SS and Chief of the German Police, they were to arrange further transfer or rather employment.[41] About three months later, on January 6, 1943, Reichsführer SS Himmler told his subordinates to bring such POWs to a special compound of the Lublin-Majdanek concentration camp, which was to resemble a military hospital. Soviet medical doctors and paramedics had to take care of them, with the aim of making them employable in the Lublin camp itself, completely or in part. In a supplement, Himmler pointed to the potential of using this measure as a propaganda tool.[42]

From May 21, 1943 onward, transports of disabled POWs arrived at Lublin, mostly amputees, but among them some who were willing to collaborate with the Germans. They came from camps and working detachments in the surroundings of Lublin as well as in the occupied Belarusian territory and Estonia, altogether about 3,500 invalid Red Army soldiers. Today, most of them are known by name, and some information is available about their kind of disability, the living conditions in Lublin and the work of the military hospital staff.[43] These sources prove that this hospital could not be used for propaganda at all. By July 24, within two months of their arrival, more than 30 percent of the POWs had died, not because of their disability but because of tuberculosis resulting from lack of food and poor accommodation. "A weight of 37 kg was no rarity for POWs with a normal height," an army physician stated after liberation, and another reported that many of the disabled were accommodated in the quarantine hut, where they became infected by TBC. There had been no medicine or bandage material at all.[44]

On July 24, 1944, the Red Army approached Lublin-Majdanek concentration camp, which was hastily evacuated. One thousand two hundred and fifty of the surviving POWs had been sent to Mauthausen ten days before. According to the degree of their injuries, they were classified as to their capacity for work. Evidently, most of them stayed in the main camp because it was not possible to send them to work detachments far away. The names of those who died were recorded in the POW death book, as usual, but, in contrast to earlier practice, not with the military tag number but with the number given to them in Lublin-Majdanek. To date, we have evidence for the death of 228 disabled in Mauthausen.

The Situation of the Soviet POWs in the Concentration Camps

In 1941, primarily, the status *Kgf.* meant an essentially lower position compared with the other concentration camp inmates. These POWs were placed in a special compound of the concentration camp, which, in addition, was fenced off by barbed wire, and so it was like a prison inside a prison. To enter their barracks or to establish contact with them was strictly forbidden. The camp commandant of Buchenwald threatened those who violated this order with a transfer to the POW Labor Camp, which, for a certain time, was a punishment with implications that were evident to everyone.[45] The rations were much worse than those allocated to other inmates. At the same time that the POWs arrived there, the camp administration received instructions from the OKH ordering increased rations, but these were still grossly insufficient to improve the poor physical condition of the POWs.[46] To be sure, starvation was the most frequent cause of death for the "labor Russians." It is revealing that the rations were adjusted to match those of the normal inmates, just as the employment of the Red Army soldiers was being considered. The SS Economics and Administration Main Office (*Wirtschafts- und Verwaltungshauptamt*, or WVHA) stipulated in March 1942, that the "labor Russians" be treated like all other concentration camp inmates. A few weeks later, this order was expanded to include additional food for those performing hard labor and those who were forced to work long shifts or at night.[47]

The work of the POWs was similar to that of civilian convicts: building roads, draining swamps, working in quarries. But in their monthly report of November 1941, the German Earth and Stone Works (*Deutsche Erd- und Steinwerke*, or DESt) made the following note: "The camp Gross Rosen was allocated to Russian POWs. These Russians are in such bad physical condition that only minimal work can be demanded from them. They are worse than the worst inmates have been until today."[48] Emil Büge, inmate of Sachsenhausen concentration camp, reports the first employment of some hundred "labor Russians" at the Heinkel Works in Oranienburg on March 9, 1942. It was a complete failure because the administration was forced to bring them back to the concentration camp the following day due to their complete weakness.[49]

The fatal situation of the Red Army soldiers in the concentration camps can be traced back to the OKW specifications. Although these men were subordinated to the SS in respect to supplies, the latter did nothing to combat the malnutrition. At least, the IKL could have granted the rations of normal inmates. But both institutions had the same objective, the decimation of the Slavic subhumans. An increase in the food rations in March and April 1942, would not have been difficult because, on the one hand, there had been a greater need for forced laborers, and, on the other hand, the number of POWs to be fed had substantially diminished. On March 1, 1942, this group appeared in the OKW statistics for the first time. At this time, 7,479 from about 26,000 in October 1941, were still alive; one year later their number counted only 2,162.[50]

Around the same time, in the first half of 1943, the question arose as to how to deal with members of the Indigenous Formations who were presumably deemed unreliable in political terms or who had committed crimes. A simple return to captivity seemed an insufficient sanction. There were no special penal units in the German POW organization and to set one up would have been difficult due to a lack of personnel. Mauthausen concentration camp was classified as the only Level III camp, which meant a camp for those who were "barely educable" (*kaum noch erziehbar*) in National Socialist terms. Already the selected commissars had been transferred to this special camp; their work in the quarries was the harshest punishment, apart from execution, for those deemed to be ideologically dangerous. It was just this kind of camp that seemed suitable to punish former legionnaires and it was under SS command. To demonstrate its independence from the SS, the Wehrmacht used a new definition, which was nevertheless incorrect: "a special camp attached to Mauthausen/Upper Danube concentration camp."[51] It was the same with the term POW Labor Camp, which did not exist anymore. The former legionnaires were not concentrated in special barracks but distributed all over the camp.

Probably based on the experiences with the "labor Russians," some things changed. On arrival in Mauthausen, the ex-legionnaires were registered under a normal inmate number. Photos on personal cards show they had been given the typical concentration camp clothes. Their rations did not differ from those of other inmates. A mortality rate of 25 percent for former legionnaires was considerably lower than the average in Mauthausen. Thus, in 1943 and the following years, the status *Kgf.* did not necessarily mean an inferior position, as it did in the case of the "labor Russians." What it did indicate was that the legionnaires were a special group, officially subordinated to the Wehrmacht, who could be taken away from Mauthausen at any time by the military authorities. As a result of this, the concentration camp administration was forced to correct the information regarding the inmate status, which in theory only the Wehrmacht was allowed to change.[52] Furthermore, this redesignation of the former legionnaires suggests, with reference to the reactivated POWs, that their second release from captivity, and the change in their status to that of a civilian concentration camp inmate, could not have been undertaken without military permission.

The disabled Soviet soldiers of Lublin-Majdanek and Mauthausen do not match this pattern. Compared to all the other Soviet inmates in the latter camp, only a few died, which might have been due to the continuation of the relatively good treatment started in Lublin. Perhaps the transfer to Mauthausen, forced by the advance of the Red Army, did not alter the idea of using the inmates for propaganda purposes; it certainly does not seem to have impacted on the good medical care they had been receiving. Further research is necessary here.

Transfers Within the Concentration Camp System and the Special Role of Certain Camps

Transferred as a POW to a concentration camp, a Red Army soldier kept this status in the long run. At least, the following example would support this supposition. On March 27, 1942, a transport of 416 Soviet POWs left the main camp at Stalag VII A Moosburg near Munich with Buchenwald concentration camp as its destination. Having worked in the autumn of 1941 in that region, they had all been selected by policemen from the Munich and Regensburg Gestapo offices as "ideologically unbearable," and normally they would have been shot a few days later at the rifle range of Hebertshausen, belonging to Dachau concentration camp. But in their case some officers in Moosburg and in the administration of Military District VII in Munich refused to hand them over to the Gestapo, referring to Wehrmacht regulations and to international law. They did so because weeks before they had learned that 267 POWs who had previously been handed over had been murdered there. Their refusal caused a conflict between the Wehrmacht and the Gestapo that was finally resolved in Berlin by means of a compromise between the OKW and the Reich Security Main Office. It intended to verify the ideological classification of the POWs, but this time in Buchenwald to ensure impartiality.[53] All these 416 men were still POWs because their transfer to the Gestapo had been stopped. In the archives of the Buchenwald memorial, a list of the complete transport exists and it shows that they arrived as POWs on March 29, 1942.[54]

The further fate of these Red Army soldiers is shrouded in mystery but it appears most of them were killed by a method also employed in such places as Sachsenhausen and Auschwitz. About 330 of the 416 remained in Buchenwald. Probably, a second ideological check confirmed the first with the result that they were shot in Buchenwald's *Genickschußanlage*, a device to clandestinely shoot people in their necks from behind. They disappeared without a trace. Nevertheless, according to Soviet sources, about 120 men were liberated from that concentration camp in 1945, which means that their selection had been altered.[55] At least one of them was released from Buchenwald and returned to normal POW captivity; to this day, no other such case is known.

Seven weeks after their arrival, on May 19, 1942, the remaining POWs from Moosburg, about eighty people, were sent to Sachsenhausen concentration camp together with more than 900 other Soviet POWs. Most of them died there. In each case of death, a death certificate was issued exactly in accordance with the OKW order of October 4, 1941, mentioned above. The certificate was sent to the WASt. It is unusual, but eighteen of these men have left no traces in the records of Sachsenhausen. Their presence in that concentration camp can only be proven in an indirect way—via Auschwitz concentration camp. There, a transport of 250 men arrived, coming from Sachsenhausen on October 31, 1942, among them the aforementioned 18. Immediately after their arrival, between November 1, 1942 and November 13, 1942, the Auschwitz staff started to liquidate all of them systematically. Apparently, the execution was the only purpose of the transfer and although this was clear, all 250 were registered in Auschwitz as newly arrived POWs. The concentration camp administration filled out new personal cards, sometimes with erroneous information, sending them to the WASt with faked causes of death. The fate of all these men is completely unknown in Sachsenhausen and Auschwitz. Not even the names are known in the memorials today.[56] They can only be revealed by the personal POW documents, created by the Wehrmacht, located today mostly in former Soviet archives.

The course of events described above appears to be quite particular, but it is not an isolated case. Another example: a POW group of unknown quantity, registered in Stalag 332 Fellin (Estonia) came to Auschwitz on November 27, 1943, and was transferred to Lublin-Majdanek three weeks later (December 15, 1943). Perhaps they belonged to the disabled, but they did not belong to those who came to Mauthausen on July 14, 1944. The transfer was reported to the WASt. Unfortunately, only the most basic facts are known at present and it is not possible to explain them more fully, other than to say that it seems highly likely that groups of Soviet POWs were killed without leaving any records.

Research Desiderata

This chapter attempts for the first time to consider the Soviet POWs as part of the concentration camp system as a whole and has shed new light on its methods and operations. While a foundation for future research has been laid, the research thus far still only allows for a few conclusive explanations. The results concerning the legionnaires can be established as fact. Despite the amount of new evidence surrounding "labor Russians," the underlying system cannot be completely reconstructed. In the case of the reactivated and the disabled POWs our conclusions are still speculative. One reason for this is that, at this moment, there are hardly any files pertaining to these groups that could help to understand or explain the process of planning and decision making in the headquarters of the Wehrmacht and the SS.

It seems logical that there must have been a rationale behind the transports mentioned above. The systematic murder of 250 POWs cannot have happened by chance, not least because some of them had been explicitly selected for execution one year earlier. But such conclusions can only be reached if one is looking at the concentration camp system as a whole. Researching the situation of an individual concentration camp alone is not adequate for future research, as this chapter has demonstrated that the complex puzzle can only be reconstructed from archives at Buchenwald, Sachsenhausen and Auschwitz, in addition to Dachau and Neuengamme.[57] The issue of transporting Soviet POWs has not been addressed in the relevant concentration camp literature and could often not be considered because the connections to other concentration camps were not researched and seemingly beyond the realm of interest.

Moreover, there arises the question of a system behind the events surrounding the "labor Russians." In the beginning, they were transferred to nearly every concentration camp, most of them to Auschwitz and Mauthausen. After nine months, the first POW Labor Camp, Neuengamme, was liquidated, and the surviving POWs, as well as most of those from Buchenwald, were brought to Sachsenhausen. It was the same with Flossenbürg, from where 650 came to Mauthausen in September 1942, others later to Auschwitz. This transfer of POWs focused on at least three camps.

This leads us to the role of Mauthausen, which evidently had a special function within the system. Its penal character was apparent with respect to the former legionnaires and the reactivated POWs, as well as with the K inmates. Although the fate of the latter has been intensively researched in the last few years, the record is still unclear in many respects.[58] Precisely in view of its penal character, it is astonishing that the disabled POWs were also transported to Mauthausen and, what is more, that they appear to have been treated in a positive manner.

A great deal more research is necessary in respect to the influence of the Wehrmacht on the SS and the resulting treatment of Soviet POWs. Intensive but as yet unknown negotiations must have taken place between both organizations before the "labor Russians," the former legionnaires and the disabled POWs could be sent to camps run by the SS. Such negotiations would have been preceded by intensive discussions about the possibilities of military influence on parts of the concentration camps, not least on the special camp at Mauthausen. It is uncertain how far this influence reached; the inspection of Mauthausen by leading Wehrmacht officers is an indication that it was more pervasive than has so far been assumed, which leads us to the question of responsibility by the German military leadership for those POWs.

At the outset, we specified three major groups of Soviet POWs: the first group being those who came to concentration camps as POWs without the Gestapo being involved, and who retained this status thereafter ("labor Russians," ex-legionnaires, and the disabled). This group was analyzed at some length above. The second group consists of those who had been released from captivity and executed in the concentration camps, without being registered after their arrival. Regarding the K inmates, as stated above, there is a real lack of research.[59] By contrast, with respect to the selectees, much is known today. In their case, it is now possible to identify them individually because the respective documents have been revealed by a joint German-Russian-Belarusian-Ukrainian project. These people can be traced to the camp in which they had been executed, but only if this happened in Dachau, and, to some extent, in Mauthausen, but not at those camps where most were murdered: Sachsenhausen (16,000) und Buchenwald (8,000).[60] Their names should be made known for commemoration purposes as well as for political reasons.

The third group must also be discussed in terms of future research. This group concerns those Red Army soldiers who were transferred to the concentration camps after the suspension of the selections in the summer of 1942. They had been handed over to the Gestapo, but still ended up at a concentration camp for forced labor, not for execution. Given the example of the previous transfers to the Gestapo, this third group cannot be equated with the "labor Russians" or legionnaires. Importantly, in the concentration camps, different terms were used for members of this group, which makes it impossible to precisely define who belonged to it and who did not. Therefore, the first step of any future research must be to adopt explicit definitions by comparing these different terms in the individual concentration camps. That would also help to define the special functions of the different concentration camps.

While studying the fate of the Soviet POWs one should also not forget the presence of non-Soviet POWs in the German concentration camp system. Firstly, one can note the presence of "red Spaniards" (Republican soldiers of the Spanish Civil War, 1936–1939) in Mauthausen, who entered into German captivity in 1940 and were transferred to Mauthausen soon thereafter. There were also the so-called Italian Military Internees (IMIs) who were mostly to be found in

Buchenwald and Dora-Mittelbau. Additionally, British and Dutch parachutists were shot in Mauthausen in early September 1944. Their status should be the subject of research, as well.

REINHARD OTTO has researched and published widely on Soviet prisoners of war in German captivity and in Scandinavia during World War II. He was director of the memorial at former POW Camp 326 in Senne, Germany, between 1998 and 2006. From 2000 to 2006, he was the academic coordinator of a German-Russian-Belarusian project to unearth German documents concerning prisoners of war in former Soviet archives.

ROLF KELLER is head of the department "Memorials Development in Lower Saxony" at the Lower Saxony Memorials Foundation (*Stiftung niedersächsische Gedenkstätten*), Celle. His recent publications include *Sowjetische Kriegsgefangene im Deutschen Reich 1941–1942* (2011), *Sowjetische Kriegsgefangene im Arbeitseinsatz 1941–1945* (ed. with Silke Petry, 2013), and *"Ruhet in Frieden, teure Genossen ...": Der Friedhof des Kriegsgefangenenlagers Bergen-Belsen – Geschichte und Erinnerungskultur* (with Silke Petry, 2016).

Notes

1. The primary sources for ascertaining the total number of POWs and the number of dead are sparse and contradictory. See Reinhard Otto, Rolf Keller, and Jens Nagel, "Sowjetische Kriegsgefangene in deutschem Gewahrsam 1941–1945. Zahlen und Dimensionen," *Vierteljahrshefte für Zeitgeschichte* 56, no. 4 (October 2008): 557–602. We are grateful to Christian Streit and Rüdiger Overmans for their advice and comments on this text.

2. Christian Streit, *Keine Kameraden. Die Wehrmacht und die sowjetischen Kriegsgefangenen 1941–1945*, 4th rev. ed. (Bonn: Dietz, 1997 [1978]). The publication by Alfred Steim, *Die Behandlung der sowjetischen Kriegsgefangenen im Fall Barbarossa* (Heidelberg/Karlsruhe: Juristischer Verlag, 1981), has been unjustly neglected in comparison to the work by Christian Streit.

3. Rolf Keller, *Sowjetische Kriegsgefangene im Deutschen Reich 1941/42. Behandlung und Arbeitseinsatz zwischen Vernichtungspolitik und kriegswirtschaftlichen Zwängen* (Göttingen: Wallstein, 2011).

4. Rüdiger Overmans, Andreas Hilger, and Pavel Poljan, eds., *Rotarmisten in deutscher Hand. Dokumente zu Gefangenschaft, Repatriierung und Rehabilitierung sowjetischer Soldaten des Zweiten Weltkrieges* (Paderborn: Schöningh, 2012); Rolf Keller and Silke Petry, eds., *Sowjetische Kriegsgefangene im Arbeitseinsatz 1941–1945. Dokumente zu den Lebens- und Arbeitsbedingungen in Norddeutschland* (Göttingen: Wallstein, 2013).

5. Reinhard Otto, *Wehrmacht, Gestapo und sowjetische Kriegsgefangene im deutschen Reichsgebiet 1941/42* (Munich: Oldenbourg, 1998).

6. Johannes Ibel, ed., *Einvernehmliche Zusammenarbeit? Wehrmacht, Gestapo, SS und sowjetische Kriegsgefangene* (Berlin: Metropol, 2008), containing initial overviews by

Rolf Keller and Reinhard Otto, "Sowjetische Kriegsgefangene in Konzentrationslagern der SS. Ein Überblick," 15–43, and Jan Erik Schulte, "Die Kriegsgefangenen-Arbeitslager der SS 1941/42: Größenwahn und Massenmord," 71–90; in general also Streit, *Keine Kameraden*, 217–223. See furthermore Rolf Keller, "Sowjetische Kriegsgefangene im KZ. Zur Kollaboration von Wehrmacht, Gestapo und SS," in *Wehrmacht und Konzentrationslager*, ed. KZ-Gedenkstätte Neuengamme (Hamburg: Edition Temmen, 2012), 106–118.

7. Personnel cards and other card index records for prisoners located in numerous archives in the former Soviet Union can be accessed online at http://www.obd-memorial.ru (last accessed on January 22, 2018). For more information on this see Rolf Keller and Reinhard Otto, "Das Massensterben der sowjetischen Kriegsgefangenen und die Wehrmachtbürokratie. Unterlagen zur Registrierung der sowjetischen Kriegsgefangenen 1941–1945 in deutschen und russischen Institutionen. Ein Forschungsbericht," *Militärgeschichtliche Mitteilungen* 57, no. 1 (1998): 149–180, as well as Otto, Keller, and Nagel, "Sowjetische Kriegsgefangene in deutschem Gewahrsam 1941–1945."

8. Operational orders nos. 8 and 9 from July 17, 1941, and July 21, 1941, respectively: Nuremberg Documents (hereafter: Nbg. Doc.) NO 3414 and NO 3415, as well as the supplementary guidelines from August 27, 1941 (Nbg. Doc. NO 3448). All those considered to be "unbearable" elements in a criminal, political, or other respect, for example, the intelligentsia, commissars of the Red Army, Jews, leading public figures, were to be separated from the rest. As of July 31, 1942, at least 35,000 persons had fallen victim to the selections on Reich territory alone.

9. Commissars and politruks of the Red Army continued to be regarded as "unbearable," but they were to be sorted out already on the territory of the General Government and then sent to Mauthausen. On March 9, 1943, for example, sixty-three politruks from Stalag 319 Cholm were transferred to Mauthausen, of which fifty-six were executed on April 17 (Archiv der Gedenkstätte Mauthausen, Y_50_01 Syng_8, 105—Zugangsliste, Y_04_ISD-Exekutionsbuch).

10. International Tracing Service, Bad Arolsen (hereafter ITS), Allg. Informationen Mauthausen, Ordner 5, fols. 42–45 On the K inmates, see Matthias Kaltenbrunner, *Flucht aus dem Todesblock. Der Massenausbruch sowjetischer Offiziere aus dem Block 20 des KZ Mauthausen und die Mühlviertler Hasenjagd. Hintergründe, Folgen, Aufarbeitung* (Innsbruck/Wien/Bozen: Studien Verlag, 2012), as well as Christian Kretschmer, "'Gelungene Flucht—Stufe III.' Hintergründe, Entstehung und Opfer der 'Aktion Kugel'," in *Kriegführung und Hunger 1939–1945. Zum Verhältnis von militärischen, wirtschaftlichen und politischen Interessen*, ed. Christoph Dieckmann and Babette Quinkert (Göttingen: Wallstein, 2015), 227–262. On the number 2,500 see Andreas Kranebitter, *Zahlen als Zeugen. Soziologische Analysen zur Häftlingsgesellschaft des KZ Mauthausen* (Vienna: New Academic Press, 2014), 163–164.

11. On December 12, 1942, the State Police regional headquarters in Düsseldorf made available to its subordinated offices a summary of all regulations under the heading "Labor Deployment, and Treatment of Soviet-Russian Prisoners of War" (Nbg. Doc. NG 1841). On July 17, 1944 Military District VI Münster summarized all orders regarding the "Transfer of Prisoners of War to the Gestapo" (IMT, XXVII, 262–264, Nbg. Doc. 1514-PS).

12. Reinhard Otto, "Die 'Ebelsbacher.' Ein Widerstandskreis sowjetischer Kriegsgefangener und ihr Weg nach Mauthausen," in *KZ-Gedenkstätte Mauthausen/Mauthausen Memorial 2011*, ed. Bundesministerium für Inneres (Vienna: Bundesministerium für Inneres Referat IV/7/a—KZ Gedenkstätte Mauthausen, 2012), 27–40.

13. Bundesarchiv-Militärarchiv, Freiburg im Breisgau (hereafter BArch-MA), RW 48/v.12, fols. 184–189. The prisoners of war were sent to Auschwitz (10,000), Buchenwald (2,000), Flossenbürg (2,000), Groß Rosen (2,500), Gusen (2,000), Mauthausen (2,000), Neuengamme (1,000), and Sachsenhausen (2,500). Around 2,000 were sent to Lublin-Majdanek in the General Government. Preparations were also made in Dachau for the arrival of 4,000 prisoners of war, but they never arrived.

14. See Streit, *Keine Kameraden*, 220ff.; Otto, *Wehrmacht*, 186–200; Keller, *Kriegsgefangene*, 406–417.

15. See "Zweck und Gliederung des Konzentrationslager" (undated), Bundesarchiv (hereafter BArch), NS 3/391, fol. 9, where the procedure in the case of the death of prisoners of war (Russians) on the basis of the OKW decree from October 4, 1941 is described: submission to the WASt of a notification of death, half of the identity disc, and a green index card.

16. BArch ZA, ZB 6307, with the note that the corpses were to be cremated, and the urns labeled by the identity disc number. Urn lids from Flossenbürg are known. Additional information on the OKW order was sent to the concentration camp commandants on October 23, 1941 (Nbg. Doc. NO 1239).

17. Hauptstaatsarchiv Düsseldorf, RB 53, G.J. Nr. 187.

18. On the history of the construction of the SS POW camps see Jan Erik Schulte, "Vom Arbeits- zum Vernichtungslager. Die Entstehungsgeschichte von Auschwitz-Birkenau 1941/42," *Vierteljahrshefte für Zeitgeschichte* 1 (2002): 41–70; Jan Erik Schulte, "Die Kriegsgefangenen-Arbeitslager der SS 1941/42," in *Einvernehmliche Zusammenarbeit?*, ed. Johannes Ibel (Berlin: Metropol, 2008), 71–90.

19. Johannes Ibel, "Sowjetische Kriegsgefangene im KZ Flossenbürg," in *Einvernehmliche Zusammenarbeit?*, ed. Johannes Ibel (Berlin: Metropol, 2008), 119–157, here 135. In autumn 1941 the SS applied to the OKH for contingents of construction materials. "Bericht von Hans Kammler, Chef des SS-Hauptamtes Haushalt und Bauen, zum Stand der Bauarbeiten der Kriegsgefangenenlager Lublin und Auschwitz (19.12.1941)," in Majdanek Memorial Archive, Fotokopie 41. On November 12, 1941 a discussion took place on this issue in the War Economy and Armaments Office (BArch-MA, RW 19/178).

20. The prisoners came from Stalag 308 Neuhammer, and Stalag 318 Lamsdorf. A transport list for 1,600 people from Lamdsorf can be found in Central Archives of the Russian Ministry of Defense (TsAMO RF), 58/18004/922, http://obd-memorial.ru/html/info.htm?id=73126533 (last accessed on 2 June 2017). Stalag = *Kriegsgefangenen-Mannschafts-Stammlager*, a POW camp for enlisted men.

21. The activity report of the administrative head of Mauthausen states: "The Inspector of the Prisoner of War Camps General Schäfter inspects the camp." Bertrand Perz, ed., *Verwaltete Gewalt. Der Tätigkeitsbericht des Verwaltungsführers im Konzentrationslager Mauthausen 1941 bis 1944* (Vienna: Bundesministerium für Inneres Referat IV/7/a—KZ Gedenkstätte Mauthausen, 2013), 58, and 89. According to the *Heeresdruckvorschrift* 38, no. 5, 41, the Commander of the Prisoners of War in the Military District had the right to inspect camps. This related first and foremost to the "building structure of the camp, administrative, sanitary and organizational matters." As early as March 25, 1942 the camp had been inspected by three commanding generals (Bertrand Perz, ed., *Verwaltete Gewalt. Der Tätigkeitsbericht des Verwaltungsführers im Konzentrationslager Mauthausen 1941 bis 1944*, 86). It is not known whether such inspections also took place in other concentration camps.

22. See the cases of death recorded on a daily basis for Mauthausen and Gusen, where particular data stand out. A diagram can be found in Kranebitter, *Zahlen als Zeugen*, 203.

23. See the notification of death for Nikolaj Kurenkow (VII A 91599) from February 5, 1945, issued in Oranienburg, http://obd-memorial.ru/html/info.htm?id=301094070&page=3 (last accessed on June 2, 2017).

24. Mauthausen Memorial Archive (hereafter AMM), 50_2_Syng_09_120, and 162. This was subsequently added to the arrival report.

25. No research has been carried out on the ex-legionnaires. This applies to almost the same extent to the eastern legions. See Joachim Hoffmann, *Die Ostlegionen 1941–1943* (Freiburg: Rombach Druck- und Verlagshaus, 1986).

26. BArch-MA, RH 53/52-23, fols. 190–191. The order from October 29, 1943 was sent for information purposes also to the head of *Amtsgruppe D* (Concentration Camps) in the SS Economics and Administration Main Office WVHA in Oranienburg. POW camps with sections for ex-legionnaires: Stalag 336 Kauen, Stalag 355 Proskurow, and Stalag 366 Siedlce (for those expelled from the eastern front), Stalag XII A Limburg (for those expelled from the west) as well as Stalag XVII A Kaisersteinbruch (for those expelled from the south and the southeast).

27. BArch-MA, RH 53/23-52, fol. 164. Inmates were sent to this special camp for murder, suspected murder, rape, theft, subversion, and so on. Those for whom there was no instruction that they should be sent to a special camp were transferred to the normal labor deployment. From early 1941, Mauthausen, as a concentration camp of Level III, was foreseen for the incarceration of inmates from whom no improvement was expected; see the secret letter from the chief of the Security Police and the SD, Reinhard Heydrich, on the classification of the concentration camps, January 2, 1941 (IMT, XXVI, 695–697, Nbg. Doc. US-492).

28. In the Mauthausen death register the cause of death is listed as: "Hanged on the orders of the Military Court." AMM, Y31_315. Oddly, it is only referred to as a special camp. Mauthausen is virtually never referred to by name.

29. See 352/48896 Gosalischwili Wassilij, sent to Mauthausen on October 29, 1943, where he died on September 21, 1944, http://obd-memorial.ru/html/info.htm?id=272089148 (last accessed on June 2, 2017).

30. According to Hans-Peter Klausch, "Von der Wehrmacht ins KZ: Die Häftlingskategorien der SAW- und Zwischenhaft-Gefangenen," in *Wehrmacht und Konzentrationslager*, ed. Gedenkstätte Neuengamme (Bremen: Edition Temmen, 2012), 67–105 (quotes 86–87).

31. A still unknown, related ordinance from June 28, 1943 suggested that such considerations were evidently already circulating before June of that year; BArch-MA, RH 53/23-52.

32. One thousand one hundred and thirty-three legionnaires from 4,449 known died in Mauthausen (25 percent) compared to about 15,000 out of 37,500 Soviet inmates in total, civilians and POWs (40 percent). This lower death rate will not have been caused by better treatment but rather by the legionnaires' better state of health upon arrival at the camp.

33. KGB Archives, Minsk, file number 10036401-10036410. See also Reinhard Otto, "Gestapo und sowjetische Kriegsgefangene," in *Kriegsgefangene des Zweiten Weltkrieges. Gefangennahme—Lagerleben—Rückkehr*, ed. Günter Bischof, Stefan Karner, and Barbara Stelzl-Marx (Vienna: Böhlau, 2006), 475–486.

34. KGB Archives, Minsk, file number 10036401-10036410. See also Otto, "Gestapo und sowjetische Kriegsgefangene."
35. IMT, XXXV, 163 (Nbg. Doc. 569-D).
36. Nbg. Doc. NO 1958.
37. Dudin cited his number completely correctly as V C 65043.
38. AMM, Y_1c 000001. On March 30, 1942, the headquarters passed this on to the administration of the concentration camps Mauthausen and Gusen.
39. The head of administration cited for March 1, 1942, 2,474 Soviet prisoners of war in Mauthausen and Gusen who needed feeding. On April 1, 1942, 1,429 prisoners were still alive in the two camps. Thereafter, the POWs were no longer listed separately in the statistics. Perz, ed., *Verwaltete Gewalt*, 83 and 86.
40. AMM, Y_50_01_Syng._7_000165, and 000239.
41. BArch, R 3091/20173.
42. BArch, NS 19/126, fol. 1.
43. See Tomasz Kranz, "Lublin-Majdanek—Stammlager," in *Der Ort des Terrors. Geschichte der nationalsozialistischen Konzentrationslager*, vol. 7, ed. Wolfgang Benz and Barbara Distel (Munich: C. H. Beck, 2008), 33–84, here 40.
44. ITS, 5.1. Trial 0102 Majdanek, 0055_82323153_1 and 0239_82323337_1.
45. Otto, *Wehrmacht*, 192.
46. Perz, ed., *Verwaltete Gewalt*, 58 (entries for October 22 and 24, 1941).
47. Order issued by the WVHA on March 18, 1942: BArch ZA, KZ/Hafta Groß Rosen 1/2.
48. Quoted in Isabel Sprenger, *Groß-Rosen. Ein Konzentrationslager in Schlesien* (Cologne: Böhlau, 1996), 194.
49. Emil Büge, *1470 KZ-Geheimnisse. Heimliche Aufzeichnungen aus der Politischen Abteilung des KZ Sachsenhausen Dezember 1939 bis April 1943* (Berlin: Metropol, 2010), 268.
50. BArch-MA, RW 6/534.
51. In the registers of identity discs and notifications of change among the eastern units, any mention of the Mauthausen camp was avoided. Instead, the prisoners were transferred to a special camp with no named location.
52. Until March 1944, the LeV-POWs were part of the OKW statistics (BArch-MA, RW 6/534); later statistics have not survived.
53. Otto, *Wehrmacht*, 208–229, contains a detailed portrayal of the so-called Meinel case, as well as references to source material and literature.
54. ITS, 1.1.05.1.0494 (the archival reference number is incomplete).
55. Efim A. Brodski, *Die Lebenden kämpfen. Die illegale Organisation Brüderliche Zusammenarbeit der Kriegsgefangenen (BSW)* ([East] Berlin: Deutscher Verlag der Wissenschaften, 1968), 79–80; Efim A. Brodski, *Im Kampf gegen den Faschismus. Sowjetische Widerstandskämpfer in Deutschland 1941–1945* ([East] Berlin: Deutscher Verlag der Wissenschaften, 1975), 248. Only very few are so far known by name.
56. The one and only reference to this transport was made by Emil Büge, who mentions in his diary a group of 247 Soviet POWs sent to Auschwitz to be murdered there. Büge, *1470 KZ-Geheimnisse*, 267.
57. Dachau concentration camp was prepared to execute the POWs from Moosburg. Part of the transport from Sachsenhausen to Auschwitz were several "labor Russians," who had been brought to Neuengamme concentration camp in October 1941. They came to

Sachsenhausen on June 24, 1942, after the POW Labor Camp in Neuengamme had been liquidated.

58. It is unknown whether all recaptured POWs were handed over to the Gestapo and brought to Mauthausen, because POWs as such can be found in other concentration camps, too.

59. It remains a matter of controversy whether the K inmates were registered in Mauthausen. On the current state of research see Kranebitter, *Zahlen als Zeugen*, 164–165.

60. It should not be too difficult, however, to ascertain the names of at least a third of those murdered in Buchenwald and Sachsenhausen concentration camps.

7 The Murder of Psychiatric Patients by the SS and the Wehrmacht in Poland and the Soviet Union, Especially in Mogilev, 1939–1945

Ulrike Winkler and Gerrit Hohendorf

Introduction

With the opening of the Memorial and Information Point at Tiergartenstrasse 4 in Berlin in September 2014, about three hundred thousand mentally ill and disabled people murdered in the National Socialist era were given—after a long period of repression and oblivion—a place in Germany's culture of remembrance.[1] While the "euthanasia" campaigns in Germany and Austria, "*Aktion T4*," the "child euthanasia" program and the patient murders through starvation, neglect, and overdoses of medication have, up to now, been well documented and are widely known,[2] this does not apply to the patient killings in the German-occupied territories of Poland and the Soviet Union—despite the fact that the National Socialist "euthanasia" program is closely associated with World War II. On September 1, 1939, the National Socialist leadership began not only an external war but also an internal war, one against the parts of the population regarded as economically useless and racially and genetically inferior.

While the active involvement of the Wehrmacht in the various forms of Nazi "euthanasia" in the so-called *Altreich* ("Old Reich," i.e., Germany within the borders of 1937) cannot be established, the picture changes if one takes the war against the Soviet Union into consideration.[3] This war was not only directed against the enemy's armed forces, but also against those parts of the civilian population who had previously been defined as racially or genetically inferior and as "useless eaters" (*unnütze Esser*).

The Start of the Patient Murders in Poland

Leaving aside the fact that even before the outbreak of war individual patients in hospitals and nursing homes in the German Reich had died from overdoses of medication, neglect, and starvation, then the first victims of Nazi "euthanasia" were in fact Polish psychiatric patients.[4] Three weeks after the German invasion of Poland, on September 22, 1939, the first patients were transported from the institution in Kocborowo (Konradstein) near Gdansk by the SS *Wachsturmbann* Kurt Eimann (1899–c.1980) and shot in a nearby forest. Until January 1940, between 1,600 and 2,000 people fell victim to this first major murder campaign.[5] In the following weeks and months, thousands of institutional patients were murdered by *SS-Sonderkommandos*, among others in Świecie (Schwetz), Owińska (Treskau), and Dziekanka (Tiegenhof). Tiegenhof was where Baltic German settlers found a place to live, but the "euthanasia" did not spare them either. Moreover, the central office dealing with the patient transfers set up in Tiegenhof served the bureaucratic administration and concealment of the murders. Here, false death certificates were issued for the patients murdered in the "Warthegau" and subsequently dispatched.[6]

In the former Polish Wartheland, the *SS-Sonderkommando* of Herbert Lange (1919–1945) initially used an improvised gas chamber in the Fort VII concentration camp in Poznań, where, in October–November 1939, patients from the Owińska institution were murdered with carbon monoxide gas.[7] Later, *Sonderkommando Lange* used mobile gas chambers to kill people: thus the patients of the institutions in Kościan (532 patients), Warta (499 patients), Gostynin (107 patients), and Kochanówka near Łódź (600 patients) were taken to the nearby woods, where they were asphyxiated to death in the gas vans. An infantry battalion was billeted in Kościan; Warta served as an institution that received ethnic Germans from Romania; and, after it had been vacated, Gostynin was placed at the disposal of the Wehrmacht. In the institutions at Tworki, Kulparkow, and Koberzyn, patients were killed mainly by starvation. The *Schutzstaffel* (SS) units were particularly brutal in the institution in Chełm. In January 1940, they drove the patients out of the wards to ultimately shoot them in front of the entrance door of the hospital. Members of the SS were henceforth accommodated there; it was later used as a military hospital. As with Tiegenhof, Chełm also served as a fictitious place of death for those Jewish psychiatric patients who were gassed as part of *"Aktion T4"* from the spring of 1940 onward. In this respect, a close connection between the T4 headquarters in Berlin and the SS units in the Occupied Eastern Territories can be established.[8] In total, at least 16,500 murdered Polish psychiatric patients—not counting the victims of starvation and neglect—should be assumed.[9]

The Murder of Pomeranian and East Prussian Patients in Poland

The actions against Pomeranian and East Prussian patients were conducted following a similar pattern: selection by German doctors, shooting or gassing of the chronically ill and disabled patients by the SS, and use of the vacated institutions for the purposes of the Wehrmacht and the SS. The NSDAP *Gauleiter* in

Pomerania, Franz Schwede-Coburg (1888–1960), had at least 1,400 supposedly incurable mental patients from the institutions in Stralsund, Lauenburg, Ueckermünde, and Treptow taken by the *SS-Wachsturmbann Eimann* to a wooded area near Wejherowo (Neustadt) and murdered. Incidentally, selection was carried out here not by the organizational headquarters of the Nazi "euthanasia" campaign, at Tiergartenstrasse 4 in Berlin, but was the responsibility of the doctors on site at the institutions.[10] The institutions in Lauenburg and Stralsund were placed at the disposal of the SS; the institution in Treptow served thereafter as a Wehrmacht hospital. Even the NSDAP *Gauleiter* of East Prussia, Erich Koch (1896–1986) made use of *Sonderkommando Lange* to get rid of about 1,600 of his institutional patients, who were deported in May and June 1940 to Soldau concentration camp and murdered in Lange's gas vans.[11]

With the intensified air attacks on the German Reich from 1942 onward, the institutions in the Warthegau and the General Government also served as places to where the patients of mental hospitals and nursing homes in the Rhineland, Westphalia and northwestern Germany could be transferred. Thus approximately eight thousand psychiatric patients from the Rhineland alone were transferred to, among other places, Kulparkow, Tiegenhof, and Tworki, in order to make room for "alternative hospitals" (*Ausweichkrankenhäuser*) for the German civilian population. Most of the transferred patients did not survive the war.[12]

The Halting of "*Aktion T4*" and the Beginning of the War of Annihilation against the Soviet Union

When the war against the Soviet Union began on June 22, 1941, "*Aktion T4*" had just reached its peak and was to be extended to cover the people of German origin in the Protectorate of Bohemia and Moravia.[13] But the campaign of gassing asylum patients to death was halted on August 24, 1941, by order of Hitler after the protest sermon given by the Bishop of Münster Count Clemens August von Galen (1878–1946), presumably to avoid jeopardizing the morale of the German population through a public debate about "euthanasia."[14] Nevertheless, the killings continued in a more decentralized way in the children's wards, in the *Hungerhäuser* (hunger houses) and in individual mental hospitals and nursing homes with a particularly high death rate until the war ended. It is, therefore, no wonder that the "euthanasia" program, which was based on a selection of the population according to their *Lebenswert* (life value), should significantly shape the actions of the *SS-Einsatzgruppen* and the Wehrmacht in the war against the Soviet Union.

The Murder of Psychiatric Patients in the Occupied Soviet Union

The approach taken by the German occupying forces toward mentally ill people in the territory of the Soviet Union can be compared to the killings in the Polish institutions. However, in the territory of the Soviet Union, there was much greater involvement of Wehrmacht troops and departments. For example, in late August 1941, Wehrmacht units, at the initiative of the medical department of the administrative sub-area headquarters (*Feldkommandantur*), shot the remaining 450–700 patients of the psychiatric hospital in Choroszcz, which had belonged to the Soviet Union since the Hitler-Stalin Pact of August 1939, and under German occupation became part of the *Bezirk Białystok*. The majority of the patients had been evacuated to various Soviet institutions before the war began in 1941, where—as it turned out—they were not safe.[15]

As a rule, the physical annihilation of psychiatric patients was carried out by the operational groups (*Einsatzgruppen*) and operational commandos (*Einsatzkommandos*) of the security police and the SD (security service), who were tasked with the political and racial cleansing of the occupied territories behind the front. In the attack on the Soviet Union in June 1941, four *Einsatzgruppen*, designated A, B, C, D, and in turn subdivided into operational commandos and special commandos (*Sonderkommandos*), were assigned to the army groups of the Wehrmacht. Along with the security divisions of the Wehrmacht, they were supposed to ensure the safety and the supply routes of the advancing frontline troops. They were furnished with far-reaching orders: "To be executed are all functionaries of the Comintern (as indeed the Communist professional politicians per se), the senior, middle and radical lower functionaries of the Party, the Central Committee, the regional and district committees, People's Commissars, Jews in Party and state positions, other radical elements (saboteurs, propagandists, snipers, assassins, agitators, etc.)."[16]

The fact that the murder of the patients of the psychiatric hospitals was also part of the remit of the *Einsatzgruppen* and *Einsatzkommandos* has, to date, been somewhat neglected in historical research. But the departments of the Wehrmacht in the army rear areas were also significantly involved in decisions regarding the fate of mentally ill people.[17] The murder campaigns of the *Einsatzgruppen*, which were supported by units of the regular police, the reserve police battalions, the Secret Field Police and by local auxiliary forces, were directed against Soviet Jews (initially Jewish men of military service age and as of August 1941, the entire Jewish population), Communist officials, partisans, and their supporters, Roma, so-called antisocial elements and also against the patients of psychiatric hospitals. The patients were not only victims of mass shootings: the Germans also used specially prepared gas vans or set up gas chambers; they poisoned the people with drugs, let them starve or freeze to death and did not hesitate, at least in once known case, to blow them up. Sometimes, these killing methods were combined.

The German occupiers regarded mentally ill people as uncontrollable, dangerous, a source of epidemics, and "useless eaters." They were a part of the population that could not be economically exploited for the purposes of the occupying forces. This view was widespread—not only within the SS, but also in the

Wehrmacht, which assumed the administration of the occupied territories (only the western parts of the occupied Soviet Union were subordinated to the civil administration under Reich Minister for the Occupied Eastern Territories Alfred Rosenberg in late summer 1941; throughout the occupation period, large territories remained under military administration). Thus, in September 1941, the Chief of the General Staff of the Army, Franz Halder (1884–1972), tersely wrote the following in his war diary regarding the psychiatric hospitals: "mental asylums [in the area of Army Group] North. Russians see the mentally deficient as sacred. Nevertheless, killing necessary."[18]

After negotiations with Heinrich Himmler (1900–1945), *Sonderkommando Lange*, which was familiar with the killing of mentally ill people, was ordered to Novgorod to murder the patients of the local psychiatric hospital.[19] In December 1941, the Eighteenth Army of Army Group North requested the liquidation by *Einsatzkommando 1b* of about 240 women suffering from mental illnesses, syphilis, and epilepsy in the Makarevo asylum on the grounds that the starved women could supposedly break out and would then be a source of disease: "What is more, the inmates of the institution, in terms of the German point of view, also represent objects of life no longer worth living."[20] While the liquidation of the Makarevo institution was justified with the threat to German soldiers, utilitarian considerations played the decisive role in the "elimination" of the roughly 1,300 patients of Kashchenko Psychiatric Hospital in the district of Leningrad by a task force of *Einsatzgruppe A* at the request of the High Command of the Eighteenth Army: the Wehrmacht was not prepared to feed the inhabitants of the institution, and the buildings were to be used as a hospital.[21]

Hitherto existing findings show a gradual radicalization of the measures carried out by the Wehrmacht and the *SS-Einsatzgruppen* against the mentally ill patients in the institutions. First, the military administration reduced the occupants' meals to below what was needed for subsistence. Thus, for example, the doctors at the psychiatric hospital in Vinnitsa, Ukraine, were instructed by the military government to hand out only 100 g of bread per patient and day. The food supplies of the hospital were confiscated by the Wehrmacht. In response to the doctors' protests, the *Gebietskommissar* in charge announced: "For the mentally ill, even 70 g of bread is too much." In autumn 1941, 800 patients were ultimately shot and 700 more killed by poison infusions. The institute's premises were finally used as a sanatorium and mess by the Wehrmacht.[22] This clearly shows a three-stage approach of the reduction in food rations to the final liquidation of the entire institution via the extermination of patients unfit for work in order to use the premises for the purposes of the Wehrmacht.

Mentally handicapped children were also among those murdered in the Soviet Union. In the summer of 1942, for example, the boys and girls of the orphanage in Jeissk, on the east coast of the Azov Sea, were loaded into gas vans by a commando of *Einsatzgruppe D* and killed in an agonizing way.[23] According to previous (preliminary) investigations, it can be assumed that German forces killed at least 17,000 psychiatric patients in the occupied territories of the Soviet Union.[24] Precisely how the patient killings took place in the area of the occupied Soviet Union is to be depicted on the basis of newly evaluated sources, using the psychiatric hospital in Mogilev as an example.

The Patient Murders in Mogilev: Sources

The most detailed source materials for the reconstruction of the murders of the patients of the psychiatric hospital in Mogilev and its agricultural colony in the years 1941 and 1942 are the records of interrogation[25] from the preliminary proceedings against Georg Frentzel (1914–1979).[26] The case of the former driver of *Einsatzkommando 8* of *Einsatzgruppe B* was brought before the District Court of Karl-Marx-Stadt (today: Chemnitz) in 1969. The accused had been investigated because, among other things, he was suspected of being involved in the murders of psychiatric patients in Mogilev. The arrest warrant against Frentzel, who had continued to work unmolested as a miner after his release from Soviet captivity on September 10, 1949, and had been a member of the Socialist Unity Party of Germany (*Sozialistische Einheitspartei Deutschlands*, or SED), was preceded by thorough and extensive observations of his family and professional environment by the Ministry of State Security (MfS). The discovery of Frentzel was the result of systematic research by the MfS since the mid- to late-1960s regarding a "series of criminal complexes or units involved in them, especially in the area of the *SS-Einsatzgruppen*."[27] In the course of these investigations, which are to be viewed in connection with the large concentration camp trials in West Germany—Auschwitz (I 1963–1965, II 1966, III 1973–1976), Sobibór (1965–1966), Treblinka (1964–1965)—the GDR came across with "astonishing regularity several dozen members of the respective *Einsatzgruppen* ... who had been living unmolested in East Germany for more than twenty-five years."[28]

On December 10, 1971, after a trial that had lasted for more than two years, Frentzel was sentenced to life imprisonment for war crimes and crimes against humanity.[29] In the course of the taking of evidence by the East German prosecutor at the time, former nurses and doctors from the Mogilev institute were flown to the GDR from Belarus and interrogated in detail. Their statements were also included in our study, as well as the statements made by the indicted and convicted doctors of the Mogilev hospital in July 1944 and November 1948. Written recollections of former doctors and nurses could also be resorted to; they are stored in the State Archives of Public Organizations of Mogilev Region, in the State Archives of the Russian Federation, the State Archives of Mogilev Region and in the Yad Vashem Archives in Jerusalem. All these sources were supplemented by the memories of the victims' families or villagers who broke their silence and reported on the murder of the patients only when a memorial was established on the hospital grounds in 2009. Finally, the "Operational Situation Reports of the Chief of the Security Police and the SD in the USSR," the "Incident Reports USSR"[30] and some documents of the Mogilev Health Office, copies of which were found in the central investigation proceedings regarding Frentzel, were also used. This extremely heterogeneous collection of sources promised, on the one hand, a detailed description of what happened, but also held in store a special challenge in terms of evaluation. Thus, the reports of the Frentzel trial in particular, in which the testimonies of the Belarusian doctors from the 1940s were incorporated, had to be critically examined, since all those questioned who had been assigned a specific role—either as (formerly) accused people or as witnesses—had testified.[31] Their descriptions, therefore, contained not only their subjectively colored memories, which had for the most part been peacefully integrated into the story of their own life, but were also often made with the intention to minimize the scope of their own complicity and to qualify their own responsibility. Even Frentzel, who was facing the threat of the death penalty, initially denied his complicity. Only under the crushing weight of the evidence did he finally admit his involvement in the patient murders and provided details.[32] Except for a small film sequence, in which those who were doomed to die are seen shortly before their gassing in mid-September 1941—waving at the camera, friendly and clueless—as well as the names of two, at least temporary, survivors—Antonina Miklashevskaia[33] and Natasha—little is known of the men, women, and children of the psychiatric hospital in Mogilev and its agricultural colony.

Einsatzkommando 8 in Mogilev

Mogilev, a town of 99,500 inhabitants, 250 kilometers east of Minsk, was taken by German troops on July 26, 1941, after fierce fighting with the defending Red Army.[34] *Einsatzkommando 8* had reached Minsk on July 8, 1941,[35] where a little later an advance commando (*Vorkommando*), the so-called Mogilev squad, was set up under the direction of Eugen Fleschütz.[36] The task of this squad, to which Frentzel belonged as a driver, was to "make quarters" in Mogilev for the rest of *Einsatzkommando 8*, which meant in concrete terms that the Jewish residents of the town had to deliver furniture, rugs, lamps, and so on to the German authorities—as was photographed by Frentzel.[37] Furthermore, the Jewish workers had to repair the teachers' training college, into which the "vanguard" had moved its headquarters.[38] Early in August 1941, other members of *Einsatzkommando 8*, which finally made Mogilev its base on September 9, 1941, followed.[39] The commando now totaled nearly ninety men, including thirty to forty police officers. Initially employed as a driver of the "*Sanka*" (ambulances),[40] in August 1941, Frentzel was promoted to the post of personal driver of Adolf Prieb (b. 1897), who served *Einsatzkommando 8* as chief interpreter. Until early in December 1941, Frentzel drove Prieb through Mogilev, including to the local psychiatric hospital on several occasions.[41]

The Patients of the Psychiatric Hospital and "Colony" in Mogilev

Founded in 1804, the "Mogilev Republican Psychiatric Hospital" was located in a suburb of Mogilev.[42] Women, men, and children suffering from mental illness lived in multistory buildings on its spacious grounds. While it was probably almost exclusively people who were not fit for work or only to a very limited extent who were admitted to the main institution itself, a few kilometers away, chronically ill people who had been classified as capable of work were employed in the "side business"[43] of the "psych. colony,"[44] an agricultural estate, established in 1932. The colony had a male and a female section;[45] children probably did not live there. The hospital and its affiliated colony could accommodate about a thousand people.

During the twenty-five-day battle for Mogilev, two buildings of the main institution came under German attack and an unknown number of patients was killed. As the German troops were supposed to "live off the land," little remained for the population of Mogilev and, for the most vulnerable, particularly for patients at the hospital, there was almost nothing left: many of them died of starvation.[46] But even the lives of the more resistant patients were in great danger, since they bore—in the National Socialist sense—a two-fold, some even a three-fold stigma. As so-called mentally ill people, they were considered as hereditarily ill, as citizens of the Soviet Union as inferior and, if they were members of the Jewish community, as sub-human. Since many patients were unable to work, they also were considered unnecessary dead weights, who stood in the way of the Wehrmacht's food and economic policy objectives. In the statements he made in 1970, Frentzel confirmed this view when he stated as the reason for the intended murder of the patients that "all those people who were of Jewish descent or another racial descent—except for the Aryan—were considered ... as inferior stuff and therefore destroyed."[47] A few days later, he reiterated his statement. He continued: "Through their illness, these people were afflicted with 'unhealthy hereditary factors,' therefore inferior, unable to work, and also represented useless eaters."[48]

The First Murder Campaigns in September and October 1941

Until the Germans' arrival in Mogilev, Dr. Meer Moiseevich Kliptsan (b. 1904)[49] had been the chief physician of the psychiatric hospital, in which, at that time, there were only a handful of doctors, including A. N. Stepanov and N. A. Pugach.[50] An unknown number of doctors at the institution had previously been called up to the Red Army; other doctors had—on the order of the chief physician—accompanied a group of patients to Smolensk,[51] thus ensuring at least their temporary survival. Several doctors, however, had left the hospital and fled eastward from the occupiers. After the Germans had arrested Dr. Kliptsan, probably because of his Jewish origin,[52] Dr. Stepanov was appointed head of the institution. Pugach became his deputy.[53]

Apparently, however, the hospital also soon became the focus of attention of the military administration, since shortly after taking office, the new chief physician received an order from the "med. san. department" of the city government of Mogilev "to cut staffing levels" and to sift through and categorize the patients.[54] For the selection, in which a doctor of the *Feldkommandantur* took part,[55] and the annihilation of the greater part of the psychiatric patients in Mogilev, there was a whole bundle of motives on the part of the Wehrmacht and *Einsatzkommando 8* on site. For example, they assumed there was danger of epidemics. The sick were also regarded as "nauseating"[56] by the head of *Einsatzkommando 8*, Dr. Otto Bradfisch (1903–1994), whereby one must bear in mind that the poor physical condition of the patients had to no small extent been brought about by the deliberate degradation of their living conditions by the occupiers. Finally, the interest in using the building for their own purposes played an important role.

By means of the example of Mogilev, the close hierarchically organized network of relationships between the German military administration that issued orders, the local authorities that passed on these orders, the hospital management that implemented the orders, and finally the staff of the *Einsatzkommando* that carried out the killings is clearly evident. The categories into which the hospital staff was supposed to divide the patients demonstrate an internal institutional hierarchy of victims, based on utilitarian considerations. The recording and selection of patients proceeded, according to the then chief physician, as follows:

> About three weeks prior to the annihilation of the first group of patients, which was effected by gas poisoning in the gas chamber, I called, on the instructions of the head of the med. san. department of Mogilev City Council, who was also called Stepanov, doctors Pugach and Makar Pavlovich Kuvshinov as well as doctor Maria Ivanovna Plotnitskaia together and told them of the instruction that I had received, namely to draw up lists of all patients who were in the hospital for the insane for treatment, and to specify the diagnosis of the disease and the state of health of each patient.[57]

Owing to supply problems in Mogilev, Stepanov continued, there was an unwillingness to continue to provide for "such a large number of patients."[58]

The patients incapable of working were supposedly to be evacuated to other areas; those fit for work were to be incorporated into the work activities and recently diagnosed sufferers allegedly included in the food supply.

In the end, just under 1,500 patients, children among them, were divided into the following categories: chronically ill and incapable of work (550), chronically ill and capable of work (550), as well as recently diagnosed sufferers who "needed treatment" (400).⁵⁹ The hundred patients in the agricultural colony were dealt with similarly. Fedor Vasil'evich Korso, a worker from Bykhov born in 1905, was also among those registered. Korso had taken part in the Soviet-Finnish War and had developed a psychosis as a result of a head injury. He was then admitted to the psychiatric hospital. His relatives subsequently tried to save him, but arrived too late.⁶⁰

The lists were handed over to the city council,⁶¹ and just one week later, three or four German officers entered the institution to seek out a room for the gassings. They chose the surgery room in hospital building No. 10.⁶² However, before the first mass murder of patients in the hospital took place, there was apparently something of a trial run. The main indication of this is a film found in the Berlin apartment of Arthur Nebe (1894–1945) at the end of the war; the approximately two-minute sequence shows patients in the Mogilev hospital being transferred to a previously prepared gas chamber.⁶³ Since 1937, Nebe had been Chief of the Reich Criminal Police (since 1939 Office V of the newly formed Reich Security Main Office) and from June to November 1941 head of *Einsatzgruppe B*, which murdered almost 45,500 people in Belarus during this period.⁶⁴ When he and Himmler visited the Novinki psychiatric colony near Minsk on August 15, 1941, the latter gave him the task of delivering the patients in the institution. Nebe was predestined for this task not only as head of *Einsatzgruppe B*, but also by his relevant experience in relation to the murder of patients in the Reich: after 1939, he was an important liaison between the Reich Security Main Office and the "euthanasia" headquarters T4. Among other things, he—along with his chief chemist Dr. Albert Widmann (1912–1986)—was responsible for supplying carbon monoxide gas to the killing centers. During his visit to Minsk, he was instructed by Himmler to try out new, less burdensome methods of killing, since the mass shootings that had been taking place since June had turned out to be very stressful for the members of the *Einsatzgruppen* and this had led to insubordination, excess drinking and mental stress reactions.⁶⁵ In addition, the selection and killing of patients at the psychiatric hospitals in Minsk had been coordinated with the new General Commissioner (*Generalkommissar*) for White Ruthenia, Wilhelm Kube (1887–1943).⁶⁶ Nebe, however, did not have to call on his men to shoot "mental patients," which is why he ordered the chemist Widmann and the munitions expert Hans Schmidt to Minsk.⁶⁷

In mid-September 1941, Nebe, Widmann and Schmidt tried to kill at least twenty-four patients of Minsk Psychiatric Hospital with explosives in a forest near Minsk. The victims were locked in a bunker, which was then blown up. When some patients who had survived the blast crawled out of the bunker, covered in blood, they were returned to it and killed with an even bigger explosive charge. The further use of explosives was subsequently rejected, as this killing method was unsafe for the perpetrators and the widely scattered body parts had to be gathered. The other patients in the psychiatric colony of Novinki were—just like the patients in the Second Clinical Hospital in Minsk—gassed or shot between September and December 1941.[68]

After the attempt to kill patients with explosives, Nebe and Widmann drove on to the psychiatric hospital in Mogilev,[69] which they viewed together with the Austrian SS doctor Dr. Hans Battista (1915–1995) and other unidentified members of staff. According to the judgment of the district court of Stuttgart against Widmann of September 1967, the doctors working there had been informed of the Germans' plans to kill patients with gas. It was all obviously just a matter of finding a suitable room and preparing it for the killings. On the very same day, the windows of the selected room were bricked up and two pieces of pipe that were to serve as the gas pipes inserted into the wall. The next day some patients were killed with gas in the presence of Nebe, an unidentified police officer as well as some SS officers. The management of these killings was in the hands of Widman, who controlled the gas pipes and "by his own hand smeared fresh mortar around the not quite airtight places around the gas supply nozzle."[70] Then a car of the Adler make was driven backward against the wall, where Widmann used a metal tube to attach the exhaust pipe to the short pieces of connecting pipe set into the wall. After that, the nursing staff had to collect the patients and lead them to the gas chamber. People went obediently and unsuspectingly with their familiar caregivers. As the Regional Court of Stuttgart in the trial against Widmann stated in 1967, an unknown number of women and men died a long and cruel death by suffocation.[71] The aforementioned film sequence apparently originates from this operation. It shows not only scantily clad men and women who are led to a building by nurses, but also two cars whose exhaust pipes were connected to a tube protruding from the wall by means of a hose. One of the vehicles (Pol 28545) seen in the film was an Adler car, that is, the make of the vehicle in which Widmann had traveled to Belarus.[72]

This first trial gassing was followed at the end of September (possibly in early October) by the murder of a large proportion of the patients, the first so-called *Aktion*. In 1970 Frentzel gave detailed information about how the mass killing proceeded. According to his statement, twenty members of *Einsatzkommando 8* were involved in the murder campaign.[73] "The fact that the former *SS-Sturmbannführer* Bratfisch [Bradfisch], former *SS-Hauptsturmführer* Prieb and the sarge of *Einsatzkommando 8*, former *SS-Oberscharführer* Strohammer, Karl, accompanied them was a matter of course."[74] The plans of the Germans had clearly been known in advance: former chief physician Stepanov said in 1948 that he knew about the murder plans and had asked his subordinates "what action they could take in order to save at least some of the patients from death."[75] No one, he said, suggested anything and even he, Stepanov, knew no way out of the "situation that had arisen."[76]

On the day of the murders, according to Frentzel's statement, a truck first went to the Jewish ghetto,[77] which had existed in Mogilev since September 25, 1941.[78]

There, the vehicle picked up about ten to fifteen men between thirty and forty years of age. Some of them were first driven to the vicinity of the village of Polykovichi and left there. They were supposed to wait for the arrival of the bodies from Mogilev in order to bury them in slit trenches and antitank ditches later.[79] The remaining six to eight Jewish men were taken to Mogilev hospital.[80]

The motorcade that included Frentzel had, in the meantime, arrived at that ward building in which the gas chamber had been set up. Frentzel remembered that there were two metal pipes inserted at "knee height"[81] in the building to which they connected the exhaust pipes of the parked vehicles. He observed that the patients—clothed only in a shirt or smock—were brought from the other buildings into the building in groups of five to twenty, sometimes more.[82] In each case, sixty to eighty of them were then crammed into the "gas chamber."[83] Frentzel noticed that the patients were weak and starving: "Going by the appearance of the patients, they weren't in very good shape. They were extremely emaciated and virtually feeble. They were a terrible sight."[84] Bradfisch described the patients' condition even more drastically. They were, he said, "invariably unclothed" and "afflicted with ulcers on which thousands of blowflies had settled."[85]

When the "gas chamber" was opened and when the vehicles were changed, a "strong odour" wafted out to the people standing outside.[86] The victims died an agonizing death. Natal'ia Nikitichna Kosakova, an employee in the psychiatric hospital, was in an adjoining room during the gassings. She "could hear the loud wailing and screaming of the victims. When the bodies were carried out of the 'gas chamber,' almost all of them had an unnatural posture. They were contorted, their clothes torn and they had clawed each other in their death throes. Their veins stood out, their faces had turned purple."[87]

On that day in late September or early October, it was not just the patients of the Mogilev institution who were murdered, but also the patients housed in the "colony for the insane." After the trucks had driven the dead bodies to Polykovichi and dumped them there, these patients were loaded on to the empty trucks and taken to the main hospital, where, according to Frentzel, they "were then annihilated by us in the gas chamber."[88] Subsequently, following the instruction of the "med. san. department" of Mogilev City Council, the word "evacuated"[89] was written behind the name of each murdered person in an attempt to conceal the facts.

At the end of this first murder campaign, Stepanov stated in 1948, a German officer, probably Prieb, gave a speech to the staff of the psychiatric hospital. He told his audience that "they [the Germans] were carrying out such exterminations in Germany, too, since the annihilated patients were of no use to anyone, neither to themselves nor to others, and this category of people was only to be destroyed."[90] The precise number of victims of the murder campaign in late September is still unknown. Stepanov testified in 1948 that, besides men and women, there were also "thirty children aged between five and twelve years old."[91]

in the group. Regarding the total number of victims, he stated that in the "first 'action' about 650 people, all chronically ill, whether able to work or not, as well as all patients of Jewish nationality without exception, regardless of the stage of their disease"[92] had been gassed. The Jewish death toll was, he said, about sixty.[93] Transcripts from Belarusian patient lists say the following about the number of patients in the hospital in Mogilev:

- On September 3, 1941, 910 patients were on the hospital premises in Mogilev. Dr. Stepanov specifies 916 patients for this day, including eleven Red Army members. At the same time, the chief physician noted six deceased.[94]
- Two months later, on November 2, there were only 217 patients in the Mogilev hospital, including six Red Army members. This means that 693 patients had been "moved," that is, probably murdered. It can be assumed that the patients in the colony were also included in these figures. However, the statistics of the chief physician on November 2 indicate that there were still eighty patients in the colony.[95]

Operational Situation Report No. 6 of the *SS-Einsatzgruppen* specifies for October 1941, that 836 "mentally ill people" had been shot dead in Mogilev.[96] Frentzel attributed the difference of 143 murder victims to the patients in the colony.[97] However, he could not explain why the official German report only talked of shootings and not of gassings. He insisted that it must refer to the "first action" mentioned by him,[98] and speculated that the verb used—"shot"—was intended to conceal the "actual method of execution."[99]

The "Second Action" in January 1942

Around 300 to 350 people were very probably exempted from the first action. According to Stepanov, they were "treated further,"[100] but the files at hand do not reveal what form this treatment took. Three and a half months later, probably in the "second half of January 1942,"[101] Prieb, however, apparently returned to the hospital and explained that the chronically ill now had to be "weeded out [for] evacuation."[102] This time, chief physician Stepanov claimed to have learned of the plans of *Einsatzkommando 8* only on the day his patients were murdered.[103] Matron Elizaveta Nikolaevna Laktsiutko recalled, however, that, on January 19 or 20, 1942, Germans had once again entered the hospital and measured how thick the walls of the building were.[104] The matron informed Dr. Kuvshinov, who thereupon discharged from his ward about forty patients who were able to orient themselves in the hope they would find their way to their families.

Einsatzkommando 8, said Frentzel, was informed of the *"Aktion"* the day before it took place.[105] Prieb, who had played such a leading role in the "first action," was absent this time.[106] In his place, SS-*Sturmscharführer* Fleschütz led the murder campaign in his role as head of the Mogilev squad. Frentzel and the other drivers were divided up as "sentries"[107] and formed—with the support of the policemen—a cordon outside the 2.5 to 3 m high wall of the institution, which was interspersed with boards.[108] This security measure was designed not only to prevent patients from escaping. There was also a fear, above all, of partisan raids.[109]

Since the enclosure around the site was slightly damaged, Frentzel could not see everything that went on, but was probably able to observe details of the procedure.[110] The people were, he said, driven out of the buildings to the trucks and loaded on to them.[111] The people doomed to die, including children and apparently even infants,[112] were in a pitiful state: "it's also true to say, like with the patients executed during the first 'Aktion,' that they were lean, that's to say emaciated. They were just skin and bones."[113] Although it was "extremely cold"[114] and there was a lot of snow on the ground, the "patients [were] driven to their execution without clothes."[115] Frentzel also stated that the patients "[had] to undress completely."[116] The Germans, however, had been dressed "appropriately," according to Frentzel.[117] They had also kept warm with alcohol, he continued. He reported that "we ... had taken schnapps to keep [us] warm in the course of the 'Aktion'." During the evacuation of the patients, the "sentries" had talked about the fact that this had been "the last measure there and that [soon] there would no longer be any sick Soviet citizens in the institution."[118] The people were driven to Pashkovo. The members of *Einsatzkommando 8* who were waiting for them there pushed them into a tank ditch and shot them. Use was also made of hand grenades. Frentzel explained that these explosives were needed to loosen the frozen soil so a pit could be dug.[119] Nevertheless, one female patient apparently managed to escape. A woman living in Novo-Pashkovo recalled that "a young woman named Natasha" wandered around in the village, sleeping a night here and a night there. Sometimes she hid in the cemetery, sometimes in villagers' homes. She stayed "quite a long time in the village," but in the end she "disappeared—no one knew where to."[120]

It is unclear how many people were killed in total in the case of the second action, either. Frentzel stated that the trucks had traveled back and forth between the institution and Pashkovo several times: "If it had been a matter of a few patients, then such an effort would certainly not have been 'necessary'," he commented. "In such a case we would have driven to the institution with one or two vehicles and loaded up the patients. After this had happened, we would have left the hospital grounds again and the matter would have been sorted."[121]

With the murder of the last patients from the Mogilev Psychiatric Hospital, the German occupying forces annihilated not only those whom they regarded as, in principle, unworthy of life. They also derived quite tangible benefits from their crimes. Before Frentzel and the other men left the premises, they took all the food that was still stored in the institution: "flour, legumes, and maybe also potatoes."[122] The looting of the civilian population by the chronically undersupplied troops of the Wehrmacht was—as already mentioned—commonplace and had also been firmly factored in by the military leadership.[123] Frentzel stated: "One fact was that when we were carrying out 'actions' we were always concerned about finding food in the homes of Soviet citizens. We just took it so we could improve our 'bill of fare'."[124] The buildings of the "evacuated" institute continued to be used: a German military hospital was set up in the psychiatric hospital; the medical and domestic staff were taken on to a large extent and now had to work for the Germans.[125]

Obliterating Traces

In the course of 1943, the Red Army moved farther and farther to the west. By the turn of the year 1943–1944, it had reached a line about 20 km east of Vitebsk, Orsha, and Mogilev. Given this development, the German occupying forces attempted to cover up the traces of their crimes, including in Novo-Pashkovo. Stepan Ivanovich Pilunov, a captured partisan, had to help with the disposal of the bodies.[126] He reported that he and other detainees in Mogilev prison were loaded on to military trucks and first taken to Pashkovo, where the Germans forced them to dig up the corpses, while other prisoners had to dig shallow pits for their incineration and chop wood for a pyre. This field crematorium was in operation for almost a month, he said. The disposal of the bodies, however, did not succeed entirely: the Soviet Extraordinary State Commission came across mass graves after the liberation of Belarus in September 1944.

Summary

The patient killings in the occupied Soviet territories continued the policy of the "annihilation of life unworthy of living" that had already been taking place in the German Reich since 1939. Between this systematic murder of institutional patients under the Nazi "euthanasia" program and the course of action in the German-occupied territories, there was not only an ideological link, but also continuities regarding personnel. This is particularly evident with the example of Mogilev, since the patient murders there, as in Minsk, can be traced back to an initiative of Himmler and Nebe. Nebe, as head of the Reich Criminal Police Office (*Reichskriminalpolizeiamt*), and his chief chemist Widmann had earlier been responsible for supplying carbon monoxide gas to the killing centers of the T4 program. Although it is true that the SS did not wish to be associated with the euthanasia program in the German Reich and the SS membership of the staff of the six gassing centers on German territory was not supposed to be evident to those on the outside, the killings of patients in the occupied territories of the Soviet Union—as had been going on in Poland already since 1939—show, however, that the *SS-Einsatzgruppen* basically recognized the alleged necessity of "destroying life unworthy of living" and actively conducted the killing of institutional patients.

The murders not only had ideological objectives, but also served very specific interests. Thus, the patients of the psychiatric hospital in Mogilev became subjects for new methods of killing. The longer the German occupation lasted, the more difficult the procurement of supplies for the German troops (*Einsatzkommando 8* among them) became and the more one required food, premises, medical supplies, and specialized personnel for the advancing German soldiers or the wounded, the less the mentally ill possessed—in the eyes of the German military and civil administration—a right to live. As "ballast existences" and "useless eaters," who were also seen as an alleged source of epidemics, they were completely annihilated in Mogilev, too. The patient murders that were set in motion with the assessment and selection of mentally ill people arranged by the city council served the immediate interests of the German occupying forces in Mogilev as well as in many other places in the occupied territories in the east.

ULRIKE WINKLER is a German historian and political scientist specializing in the history of Nazi Germany, the history of German social welfare, and disability history. Her books include *Männliche Diakonie im Zweiten Weltkrieg. Kriegserleben und Kriegserfahrung der Kreuznacher Brüderschaft Paulinum von 1939 bis 1945 im Spiegel ihrer Feldpostbriefe* (2007). In 2017, Dr. Winkler was appointed to the advisory board of the Foundation Memorial to the Murdered Jews of Europe, Berlin.

GERRIT HOHENDORF is Associate Professor, MD, psychiatrist, medical historian, and medical ethicist. He holds a permanent teaching position at the Institute for History and Ethics of Medicine, Technical University of Munich. He is jointly responsible for the content of the open-air exhibition at the Information and Memorial Point for the Victims of National Socialist "Euthanasia," Berlin.

Notes

1. See http://www.stiftung-denkmal.de/denkmaeler/gedenk-und-informationsort-fuer-die-opfer-der-ns-euthanasie-morde.html (last accessed on August 11, 2015). The virtual memorial can be found at http://www.gedenkort-t4.eu (last accessed on August 11, 2015). The English catalog appeared under the title: Foundation Memorial to the Murdered Jews of Europe, ed., *Memorial and Information Point for the Victims of National Socialist "Euthanasia" Killings* (Berlin: Stiftung Denkmal für die ermordeten Juden Europas, 2016); see also the catalog in Plain German: Stiftung Denkmal für die ermordeten Juden Europas und Stiftung Topographie des Terrors, eds., *Tiergartenstraße 4: Gedenk-Ort und Informations-Ort für die*

Opfer der national-sozialistischen "Euthanasie"-Morde, 2nd ed. (Berlin: Stiftung Denkmal für die ermordeten Juden Europas, 2015).
   2. See esp. Ernst Klee, *"Euthanasie" im Dritten Reich: Die "Vernichtung lebensunwerten Lebens"* (Frankfurt am Main: Fischer, 2010); Henry Friedlander, *The Origins of Nazi Genocide. From Euthanasia to the Final Solution* (Chapel Hill/London: University of North Carolina Press, 1995); and Gerrit Hohendorf, *Der Tod als Erlösung vom Leiden: Geschichte und Ethik der Sterbehilfe seit dem Ende des 19. Jahrhunderts in Deutschland* (Göttingen: Wallstein, 2013).
   3. See Hans-Walter Schmuhl, "Vergessene Opfer. Die Wehrmacht und die Massenmorde an psychisch Kranken, geistig Behinderten und 'Zigeunern'," in *Wehrmacht und Vernichtungspolitik: Militär im nationalsozialistischen System*, ed. Heinrich Pohl (Göttingen: Vandenhoeck & Ruprecht, 1999), 115–139.
   4. Tadeusz Nasierowski, *Zagłada osób z zaburzeniami psychicznymi w okupowanej Polsce: Początek ludobójstwa* (Warsaw: Neriton, 2008).
   5. Zdzisław Jaroszewski, ed., *Die Ermordung der Geisteskranken in Polen 1939–1945* (Warsaw: Wydawnictwo Naukowe PWN, 1993), 57–65; Volker Rieß, *Die Anfänge der Vernichtung "lebensunwerten Lebens" in den Reichsgauen Danzig-Westpreußen und Wartheland 1939/1940* (Frankfurt am Main: Peter Lang, 1995), 53–55.
   6. See Enno Schwanke, *Die Landesheil- und Pflegeanstalt Tiegenhof: Die nationalsozialistische Euthanasie in Polen während des Zweiten Weltkriegs* (Frankfurt am Main: Internationaler Verlag der Wissenschaften, 2015).
   7. See Klee, *"Euthanasie" im Dritten Reich*, 99–104.
   8. Annette Hinz-Wessels, "Antisemitismus und Krankenmord. Zum Umgang mit jüdischen Anstaltspatienten im Nationalsozialismus," *Vierteljahrshefte für Zeitgeschichte* 61, no. 1 (2013): 65–92, here 81–85.
   9. Jaroszewski, ed., *Die Ermordung der Geisteskranken*, 226–227.
   10. Rieß, *Die Anfänge*, 53–118.
   11. Sascha Topp, Petra Fuchs, Gerrit Hohendorf et al., "Die Provinz Ostpreußen und die nationalsozialistische 'Euthanasie': SS-'Aktion Lange' und 'Aktion T4'," *Medizinhistorisches Journal* 43, (2008): 20–55.
   12. Winfried Süß, *Der "Volkskörper" im Krieg: Gesundheitspolitik, Gesundheitsverhältnisse und Krankenmord im nationalsozialistischen Deutschland 1939–1945* (Munich: De Gruyter Oldenbourg, 2003), 327–339.
   13. Michal Šimůnek and Dietmar Schulze, eds., *Die nationalsozialistische "Euthanasie" im Reichsgau Sudetenland und Protektorat Böhmen und Mähren 1939–1945* (Prague: Trauner, 2008).
   14. Heinz Faulstich, *Hungersterben in der Psychiatrie 1914–1949. Mit einer Topographie der NS-Psychiatrie* (Freiburg: Lambertus, 1998), 273–288; as well as: Süß, *"Volkskörper,"* 127–151.
   15. Jaroszewski, ed., *Die Ermordung der Geisteskranken*, 147–151; as well as: Christian Gerlach, *Kalkulierte Morde: Die deutsche Wirtschafts- und Vernichtungspolitik in Weißrußland 1941–1945* (Hamburg: Hamburger Edition, 1999), 1067–1068.
   16. Quoted from: Peter Klein, ed., *Die Einsatzgruppen in der besetzten Sowjetunion 1941/42: Die Tätigkeits- und Lageberichte des Chefs der Sicherheitspolizei und des SD* (Berlin: Edition Hentrich, 1997), 325.
   17. Helmut Krausnick and Hans-Heinrich Wilhelm, *Die Truppe des Weltanschauungskrieges. Die Einsatzgruppen der Sicherheitspolizei und des SD 1938–1942* (Stuttgart: Deutsche Verlags-Anstalt, 1981), 543–544 and 548–552; Klee, *"Euthanasie,"* 310–312; Gerlach, *Kalkulierte Morde*,

1067–1074; Angelika Ebbinghaus and Gerd Preissler, "Die Ermordung psychisch kranker Menschen in der Sowjetunion: Dokumentation," in *Aussonderung und Tod: Die klinische Hinrichtung der Unbrauchbaren*, ed. Götz Aly, Angelika Ebbingshaus, Matthias Hamann, Friedemann Pfäfflin, and Gerd Preissler (Berlin: Rotbuch, 1985), 75–107; Johannes Hürter, "Die Wehrmacht vor Leningrad: Krieg und Besatzungspolitik der 18. Armee im Herbst und Winter 1941/42," *Vierteljahrshefte für Zeitgeschichte* 49 (2001): 377–440; as well as the recently published collection of papers: Alexander Friedman and Rainer Hudemann, eds., *Diskriminiert—vernichtet—vergessen: Behinderte in der Sowjetunion, unter nationalsozialistischer Besatzung und im Ostblock 1917–1991* (Stuttgart: Franz Steiner, 2016).

18. See Franz Halder, *Kriegstagebuch, Bd. III: Der Russlandfeldzug bis zum Marsch auf Stalingrad (22.6.1941–24.9.1942)*, ed. Hans-Adolf Jacobsen (Stuttgart: Kohlhammer, 1964), 252 ff.

19. See Christian Gerlach, "Militärische 'Versorgungszwänge,' Besatzungspolitik und Massenverbrechen: Die Rolle des Generalquartiermeisters des Heeres und seiner Dienststellen im Krieg gegen die Sowjetunion," in *Ausbeutung, Vernichtung, Öffentlichkeit: Neue Studien zur nationalsozialistischen Lagerpolitik*, ed. Norbert Frei, Sybille Steinbacher, and Bernd C. Wagner (Munich: De Gruyter, 2000), 175–208, here 194.

20. Quoted in Ebbinghaus and Preissler, "Die Ermordung," 78; as well as Hürter, "Wehrmacht," 435–436.

21. Hürter, "Wehrmacht," 436–438.

22. See Ebbinghaus and Preissler, "Die Ermordung," 95–96.

23. See Ebbinghaus and Preissler, "Die Ermordung," 104–106, as well as Andrej Angrick, *Besatzungspolitik und Massenmord: Die Einsatzgruppe D in der südlichen Sowjetunion 1941–1943* (Hamburg: Hamburger Edition, 2003), 648–651. For further examples of the patient killings by *Einsatzgruppe D*, see 644–646.

24. From the sources at our disposal, we have compiled a table with the institutions, the killing units and the number of victims, see Ulrike Winkler and Gerrit Hohendorf, "'Nun ist Mogiljew frei von Verrückten': Die Ermordung der PsychiatriepatientInnen in Mogilew 1941/42," in *Krieg und Psychiatrie 1914–1950*, ed. Babette Quinkert, Philipp Rauh, and Ulrike Winkler (Göttingen: Wallstein, 2010), 75–103, table: 81–83.

25. Der Bundesbeauftragte für die Unterlagen des Staatssicherheitsdienstes der ehemaligen Deutschen Demokratischen Republik, Berlin (hereafter BStU), MfS, HA IX/11, ZUV 9, Bd. 1–32. Regarding the prosecution of National Socialist criminals, the participation of the Ministry of State Security (MfS) and the formation of Department IX/11 on August 6, 1965, see the summary by Günther Wieland, "Die Ahndung von NS-Verbrechen in Ostdeutschland 1945–1990," in *DDR-Justiz und NS-Verbrechen: Sammlung ostdeutscher Strafurteile wegen nationalsozialistischer Tötungsverbrechen*, vol. Verfahrensregister (Munich/Amsterdam: De Gruyter Saur, 2002), 12–94, here 73 ff.

26. See the recent: Siegfried Grundmann, *Georg Frentzel: PG und Angehöriger der SS-Einsatzgruppe B in der UdSSR—Genosse und Mitglied der Gesellschaft für Deutsch-Sowjetische Freundschaft* (Berlin: Nora, 2015).

27. Henry Leide, *NS-Verbrecher und Staatssicherheit: Die geheime Vergangenheitspolitik der DDR* (Göttingen: Vandenhoeck & Ruprecht, 2006), 416, from which the following quotations are also taken.

28. See also the findings of Annette Weinke, *Die Verfolgung von NS-Tätern im geteilten Deutschland: Vergangenheitsbewältigungen 1949–1969 oder: Eine deutsch-deutsche Beziehungsgeschichte im Kalten Krieg* (Paderborn: Schöningh, 2002), 323.

29. See indictment of September 8, 1971, BStU, MfS, HA IX/11 ZUV 9, Bd. 16/2, fols. 479–533, and the judgment of December 2, 1971, ibid., Bd. 33, fols. 2–33. Frentzel died in Leipzig prison hospital on June 20, 1979.
30. See Klein, ed., *Einsatzgruppen*.
31. Ultimately, the question of whether and, if so, under what pressure Frentzel made his statements must remain open. See also the source of critical remarks from Christian Dirks, *"Die Verbrechen der anderen": Auschwitz und der Auschwitz-Prozess der DDR: Das Verfahren gegen den KZ-Arzt Dr. Horst Fischer* (Paderborn: Schöningh, 2006), 26–27.
32. Almost exemplary is the hearing of Frentzel on July 23, 1970, BStU, MfS, HA IX/11 ZUV 9, Bd. 4/1, fols. 122–128. However, it can be assumed that the complicity of Frentzel and its severity was certain, since only those cases were heard for which the maximum range of punishments (death penalty or life imprisonment) was guaranteed, see Leide, *NS-Verbrecher*, 124.
33. Antonina Miklashevskaia survived at least the first action in the Mogilev hospital in the autumn of 1941. See the interrogation of Matriona Alekseevna Kovaleva on April 7, 1970, BStU, MfS, IX/11 ZUV 9, Bd. 13/2, fol. 399. The fate of the other female patient is unknown.
34. Israel Gutman, Eberhard Jäckel, Peter Longerich, and Julius H. Schoeps, eds., *Enzyklopädie des Holocaust: Die Verfolgung und Ermordung der europäischen Juden*, vol. II (Berlin: Piper, 1993), 959.
35. Activity report of *Einsatzgruppe B* for the period from June 23, 1941 to July 13, 1941, BStU, MfS, IX/11 ZUV 9, Bd. 26, fols. 107–108.
36. Interrogation reports of Frentzel dated July 28, 1970, BStU, MfS, HA IX/11 ZUV 9, Bd. 4/1, fol. 174, as well as August 12, 1970, BStU, MfS, HA IX/11 ZUV 9, Bd. 14/1, fol. 4.
37. See BStU, MfS, HA IX/11 ZUV 9, Bd. 32.
38. Record of interrogation of Frentzel dated June 9, 1970, BStU, MfS, HA IX/11 ZUV 9, Bd. 2/1, fols. 40–41.
39. Krausnick and Wilhelm, *Truppe des Weltanschauungskrieges*, 158.
40. Record of interrogation of Frentzel dated January 19, 1971, BStU, MfS, HA IX/11 ZUV 9, Bd. 1/1.
41. Record of interrogation of Frentzel dated July 23, 1970, BStU, MfS, HA IX/11 ZUV 9, Bd. 1/1, fol. 123.
42. Record of interrogation of N. A. Pugach dated June 12, 1970, BStU, MfS, HA IX/11 ZUV 9, Bd. 4/2, fol. 331.
43. Record of interrogation of N. A. Pugach dated June 12, 1970, BStU, MfS, HA IX/11 ZUV 9, Bd. 4/2, fol. 331.
44. According to Vera Vikent'evna Levshevich in her hearing on April 9, 1970, BStU, MfS, HA IX/11 ZUV 9, Bd. 4/2, fols. 404–408.
45. Record of interrogation of Starovoitova dated June 10, 1970, BStU, MfS, HA IX/11 ZUV 9, Bd. 13/2, fol. 279.
46. Record of interrogation of A. N. Stepanov dated November 4, 1948, BStU, MfS, HA IX/11 ZUV 9, Bd. 13/2, fol. 312.
47. Record of interrogation of Frentzel dated August 14, 1970, BStU, MfS, HA IX/11 ZUV 9, Bd. 4/2, fol. 278.
48. Record of interrogation of Frentzel dated August 25, 1970, BStU, MfS, HA IX/11 ZUV 9, Bd. 4/2, fol. 279.
49. Record of interrogation of A. N. Stepanov dated November 4, 1948, BStU, MfS, HA IX/11 ZUV 9, Bd. 13/2, fol. 309. Dr. Kliptsan graduated from medical college in 1934 and

started working as chief physician of the City Hospital in Minsk in the same year. Since 1940, he had worked as chief physician at the psychiatric hospital in Mogilev. See "Memoirs of Alla Pavlovna Ulanova," undated, Yad Vashem Archives, Jerusalem (hereafter YVA), 20012/736–738, 739–742.

50. Record of interrogation of A. N. Stepanov dated November 4, 1948, BStU, MfS, HA IX/11, ZUV 9, Bd. 13/2, fol. 309.

51. Record of interrogation of A. N. Stepanov dated November 4, 1948, BStU, MfS, HA IX/11, ZUV 9, Bd. 13/2, fol. 309.

52. Record of interrogation of A. N. Stepanov dated November 4, 1948, BStU, MfS, HA IX/11, ZUV 9, Bd. 13/2, fol. 310. *Alla Pavlovna Ulanova* reported that her mother *Galina Vasil'evna Ulanova*, who worked as a nurse at the Mogilev psychiatric hospital, had told her that Dr. Kliptsan had hidden in the attic of the hospital building. She, Ulanova, and a nurse named Lisa had, she said, supplied Dr. Kliptsan with food. Another employee—*Vasilevskii*—finally denounced the doctor. See "Memoirs of Alla Pavlovna Ulanova," undated, YVA, 20012/736–738, 739–742. Dr. Kliptsan was shot soon after; see the testimony of Sonia Grigor'evna Guselevich, a staff member of the canteen of Mogilev Psychiatric Hospital, undated, *Gosudarstvennyi Arkhiv* Mogilevskoi Oblasti [State Archives of Mogilev Region, hereafter GAMO], f. 306, o. 1, d. 10, fol. 40.

53. Record of interrogation of A. N. Stepanov dated November 4, 1948, BStU, MfS, HA IX/11, ZUV 9, Bd. 13/2, fol. 311.

54. Record of interrogation of A. N. Stepanov dated December 24, 1948, BStU, MfS, HA IX/11, ZUV 9, Bd. 4/2, fol. 315.

55. See Gerlach, *Kalkulierte Morde*, 1069.

56. Gerlach, *Kalkulierte Morde*, 1069.

57. Record of interrogation of A. N. Stepanov dated November 13, 1948, BStU, MfS, HA IX/11, ZUV 9, Bd. 4/1, fol. 236.

58. Record of interrogation of A. N. Stepanov dated December 24, 1948, BStU, MfS, HA IX/11, ZUV 9, Bd. 4/2, fol. 316.

59. Record of interrogation of A. N. Stepanov dated June 1, 1970, BStU, MfS, HA IX/11, ZUV 9, Bd. 4/1, fol. 249. Regarding the figures: record of interrogation of A. N. Stepanov dated December 24, 1948, BStU, MfS, HA IX/11, ZUV 9, Bd. 4/2, fol. 317.

60. Information kindly supplied by his daughter Galina Ivanovna Korso.

61. Record of interrogation of A. N. Stepanov dated December 24, 1948, BStU, MfS, HA IX/11, ZUV 9, Bd. 4/2, fol. 317.

62. Record of interrogation of Levshevich dated April 9, 1970, BstU, MfS, HA IX/11, ZUV 9, Bd. 13/2, fol. 405. Since July 2009, a memorial in front of this building commemorates the victims. The plaque reads: "Those who forget the past are doomed to repeat it." Regarding the origins of the monument see Gerrit Hohendorf, Roswitha Lauter, Ullrich Lochmann, and Maike Rotzoll,"'Den erstickten Seelen zum Gedenken': Ein Mahnmal für die von den deutschen Besatzern ermordeten Patienten des Psychiatrischen Krankenhauses Mogilew," in Stiftung Topographie des Terrors, ed., *Gedenkstätten-Rundbrief* no. 152 (December 2009): 3–10.

63. The film fragment found its way into the film *Die Lehre von Nürnberg* (Nuremberg: Its Lesson for Today), a compilation of the Information Services Division of the Office of Military Government of Germany (U.S.) based on authentic footage for the Nuremberg trials from 1945 to 1949, Bundesarchiv/Filmarchiv Berlin, FBW 0003511. The scenes from Mogilev

can be seen in the thirty-fifth and thirty-sixth minute of the film. See also U.S. Holocaust Memorial Museum, ed., *Deadly Medicine: Creating the Master Race* (Chapel Hill: University of North Carolina Press, 2004), 176–177.

64. Nebe, SS major general since 1941, had contacts with the military resistance and knew of Stauffenberg's assassination attempt against Hitler on July 20, 1944. After the failed coup, he went into hiding, but was betrayed and sentenced to death on March 2, 1945 and executed. See Ronald Rathert, *Verbrechen und Verschwörung: Arthur Nebe, der Kripochef des Dritten Reiches* (Münster: LIT, 2001).

65. Gerlach, *Kalkulierte Morde*, 1068; and Ebbinghaus and Preissler, "Die Ermordung," 83 ff. Himmler's appointments diary confirms a visit by Himmler to the psychiatric colony in Novinki on the afternoon of August 15, 1941 ("visit to the insane asylum"). According to a statement by *Erich von dem Bach-Zelewski (1899–1972)*, Higher SS and Police Leader for Central Russia, Himmler was said to have entrusted Nebe here with the killing of the mentally ill, see Peter Witte, Michael Wildt, Martina Voigt, Dieter Pohl, Peter Klein, Christian Gerlach, Christoph Dieckmann, and Andrej Angrick, eds., *Der Dienstkalender Heinrich Himmlers 1941/42* (Hamburg: Christians, 1999), 195.

66. Gerlach, *Kalkulierte Morde*, 1068.

67. Ebbinghaus and Preissler, "Die Ermordung," 83 ff.

68. Gerlach, *Kalkulierte Morde*, 1070–1071; and Ebbinghaus and Preissler, "Die Ermordung," 88–92.

69. Verdict against Dr. Albert Widmann of September 15, 1967, printed in C. F. Rüter and D. W. de Mildt, eds., *Justiz und NS-Verbrechen: Sammlung der Strafurteile wegen nationalsozialistischer Tötungsverbrechen 1945–1999*, vol. 26 (Amsterdam: Amsterdam University Press, 2001), 562.

70. Verdict against Dr. Albert Widmann of September 15, 1967, printed in C. F. Rüter and D. W. de Mildt, eds., *Justiz und NS-Verbrechen*, vol. 26, 562–563.

71. Verdict against Dr. Albert Widmann of September 15, 1967, printed in Rüter and de Mildt, eds., *Justiz und NS-Verbrechen*, vol. 26, 562.

72. Verdict against Dr. Albert Widmann of September 15, 1967, printed in Rüter and de Mildt, eds., *Justiz und NS-Verbrechen*, vol. 26, 563.

73. Record of interrogation of Frentzel dated July 28, 1970, BStU, MfS, HA IX/11 ZUV 9, Bd. 4/1, fol. 173. For the following description, see Record of interrogation of Frentzel dated July 28, 1970, BStU, MfS, HA IX/11 ZUV 9, Bd. 4/1, fol. 173.

74. Record of interrogation of Frentzel dated July 28, 1970, BStU, MfS, HA IX/11 ZUV 9, Bd. 4/1, fol. 174.

75. Record of interrogation of A. N. Stepanov dated December 24, 1948, BStU, MfS, HA IX/11 ZUV 9, Bd. 4/2, fol. 318.

76. Ibid., in July 1944 Stepanov had claimed that both the mayor and the head of the medical and sanitary department of Mogilev had requested the rescue of the "psychologically sick." Record of interrogation of A. N. Stepanov dated July 20, 1944, BStU, MfS, HA IX/11 ZUV 9, Bd. 13/2, fol. 302.

77. Record of interrogation of Frentzel dated July 28, 1970, BStU, MfS, HA IX/11 ZUV 9, Bd. 4/1, fol. 176.

78. On September 25, 1941, "Order No. 51 of the city council of the city of Mogilev" was issued, which decreed the formation of ghettos; transcript of this order in BStU, MfS, HA IX/11 ZUV 9, Bd. 2/2, fols. 323–324.

79. Record of interrogation of Frentzel dated July 28, 1970, BStU, MfS, HA IX/11 ZUV 9, Bd. 4/1, fol. 177.

80. Record of interrogation of Frentzel dated July 28, 1970, BStU, MfS, HA IX/11 ZUV 9, Bd. 4/1, fol. 177.

81. Record of interrogation of Frentzel dated July 29, 1970, BStU, MfS, HA IX/11 ZUV 9, Bd. 4/1, fol. 182.

82. Record of interrogation of Frentzel dated August 4, 1970, BStU, MfS, HA IX/11 ZUV 9, Bd. 13/2, fol. 224.

83. Record of interrogation of N. A. Pugach dated July 13, 1944, BStU, MfS, HA IX/11 ZUV 9, Bd. 4/1, fol. 253.

84. Record of interrogation of Frentzel dated July 24, 1970, BStU, MfS, HA IX/11 ZUV 9, Bd. 13/2, fol. 220.

85. According to Bradfisch on the occasion of his hearing on June 26, 1958 in Munich, StA München I 22 Ks 1/61, fol. 185, quoted in Gerlach, *Kalkulierte Morde*, 1069.

86. Record of interrogation of Frentzel dated August 24, 1970, BStU, MfS, HA IX/11 ZUV 9, Bd. 4/2, fol. 282.

87. Witness report of Natal'ia Nikitichna Kosakova, undated, *GAMO*, f. 306, o. 1, d. 10, fols. 44–45.

88. Record of interrogation of Frentzel dated August 27, 1970, BStU, MfS, HA IX/11 ZUV 9, Bd. 4/1, fol. 198.

89. Record of interrogation of A. N. Stepanov dated November 13, 1948, BStU, MfS, HA IX/11 ZUV 9, Bd. 4/1, fol. 238. Stepanov could not say whether these comments were really entered. At any rate, he said, he had not checked. See also record of interrogation of A. N. Stepanov dated December 24, 1948, BStU, MfS, HA IX/11 ZUV 9, Bd. 4/2, fol. 320.

90. Record of interrogation of A. N. Stepanov dated December 24, 1948, BStU, MfS, HA IX/11 ZUV 9, Bd. 4/2, fol. 319.

91. Record of interrogation of A. N. Stepanov dated November 13, 1948, BStU, MfS, HA IX/11 ZUV 9, Bd. 4/2, fol. 236.

92. Record of interrogation of A. N. Stepanov dated June 1, 1970, BStU, MfS, HA IX/11 ZUV 9, Bd. 4/2, fol. 250.

93. Record of interrogation of A. N. Stepanov dated December 24, 1948, BStU, MfS, HA IX/11 ZUV 9, Bd. 4/2, fol. 320.

94. List of A. N. Stepanov regarding the number of patients in the Mogilev hospital for the mentally ill as per September 3, 1941, copy, BStU, MfS, HA IX/11 ZUV 9, Bd. 13/2, fol. 293.

95. List of A. N. Stepanov regarding the number of patients in the Mogilev hospital for the mentally ill as per September 3, 1941, copy, BStU, MfS, HA IX/11 ZUV 9, Bd. 13/2, fol. 293.

96. "In Minsk, 632 mentally ill people were shot, and in Mogilev 836"; Operational Situation Report No. 6 of the *Einsatzgruppen* of the Security Police and SD in the USSR for the period October 1, 1941 to October 31, 1941, printed in Klein, ed., *Einsatzgruppen*, 222–241, here 229.

97. Record of interrogation of Frentzel dated August 27, 1970, BStU, MfS, HA IX/11 ZUV 9, Bd. 4/1, fol. 208.

98. Record of interrogation of Frentzel dated August 27, 1970, BStU, MfS, HA IX/11 ZUV 9, Bd. 4/1, fol. 208.

99. Final report dated June 16, 1971, BStU, MfS, HA IX/11 ZUV 9, Bd. 21, fol. 80.

100. Record of interrogation of A. N. Stepanov dated June 1, 1970, BStU, MfS, HA IX/11 ZUV 9, Bd. 4/1, fol. 250.
101. Record of interrogation of A. N. Stepanov dated November 4, 1948, BStU, MfS, HA IX/11 ZUV 9, Bd. 13/2, fol. 313.
102. Record of interrogation of N. A. Pugach dated July 13, 1944, BStU, MfS, HA IX/11 ZUV 9, Bd. 4/1, fol. 254.
103. Record of interrogation of A. N. Stepanov dated November 13, 1948, BStU, MfS, HA IX/11 ZUV 9, Bd. 4/1, fol. 238.
104. Memories of Elizaveta Nikolaevna Laktsiutko, undated, Gosudarstvennyi Arkhiv Obshchestvennykh Ob'edinenii Mogilevskoi Oblasti (State Archives of Public Organizations of Mogilev Region), f. 6115, o. 1, d. 145.
105. Record of interrogation of Frentzel dated August 12, 1970, BStU, MfS, HA IX/11 ZUV 9, Bd. 4/2, fol. 270.
106. Record of interrogation of Frentzel dated August 12, 1970, BStU, MfS, HA IX/11 ZUV 9, Bd. 4/2, fol. 270.
107. Record of interrogation of Frentzel dated August 24, 1970, BStU, MfS, HA IX/11 ZUV 9, Bd. 4/2, fol. 279.
108. Record of interrogation of Frentzel dated August 17, 1970, BStU, MfS, HA IX/11 ZUV 9, Bd. 4/2, fol. 287.
109. Record of interrogation of Frentzel dated August 17, 1970, BStU, MfS, HA IX/11 ZUV 9, Bd. 4/2, fol. 285.
110. Record of interrogation of Frentzel dated August 18, 1970, BStU, MfS, HA IX/11 ZUV 9, Bd. 4/2, fol. 291.
111. Record of interrogation of Frentzel dated August 27, 1970, BStU, MfS, HA IX/11 ZUV 9, Bd. 4/1, fol. 209; see also record of interrogation of Frentzel dated August 14, 1970, BStU, MfS, HA IX/11 ZUV 9, Bd. 4/2, fol. 276.
112. Record of interrogation of Frentzel dated August 14, 1970, BStU, MfS, HA IX/11 ZUV 9, Bd. 4/2, fol. 291.
113. Record of interrogation of Frentzel dated August 14, 1970, BStU, MfS, HA IX/11 ZUV 9, Bd. 4/2, fol. 278.
114. Record of interrogation of Frentzel dated August 27, 1970, BStU, MfS, HA IX/11 ZUV 9, Bd. 4/1, fol. 209.
115. Record of interrogation of Frentzel dated August 27, 1970, BStU, MfS, HA IX/11 ZUV 9, Bd. 4/1, fol. 209.
116. Report of Frentzel dated July 7, 1971, BStU, MfS, HA IX/11 ZUV 9, Bd. 6, fol. 225.
117. Record of interrogation of Frentzel dated August 12, 1970, BStU, MfS, HA IX/11 ZUV 9, Bd. 4/2, fol. 269. For the following quotations, BStU, MfS, HA IX/11 ZUV 9, Bd. 4/2, fols. 269–270.
118. Record of interrogation of Frentzel dated August 14, 1970, BStU, MfS, HA IX/11 ZUV 9, Bd. 4/2, fol. 276.
119. At least, this was the procedure at the shootings in November 1941, record of interrogation of Frentzel dated August 18, 1970, BStU, MfS, HA IX/11 ZUV 9, Bd. 4/2, fol. 292.
120. Dennis Dybsky and Katia Iurgeva from the State University of Mogilev recorded the memoir of *Tatiana Sergeevna Tishina*. We thank them both for their kind support.
121. Record of interrogation of Frentzel dated August 24, 1970, BStU, MfS, HA IX/11 ZUV 9, Bd. 4/2, fol. 280.

122. Record of interrogation of Frentzel dated August 14, 1970, BStU, MfS, HA IX/11 ZUV 9, fol. 276.

123. The resources of Belarus were supposed to benefit the eastern army and the German population in the Reich. These goals were subordinated to the German occupation policy that left behind veritable defoliation zones. In early May 1941, it was clear to the planning staffs that: "The war can only be continued if the entire Wehrmacht is fed from Russia in the third year of the war. If we take what we need out of the country, there can be no doubt that tens of millions of people will die of starvation." Note on a meeting of permanent secretaries and members of the Economic Staff East with representatives of the Economic Command Staff East regarding the planned economic plundering of Soviet territories dated May 2, 1941, doc. PS-2718, IMT, vol. 31, 84, reprinted in Gerd R. Ueberschär and Wolfram Wette, eds., *Der deutsche Überfall auf die Sowjetunion: "Unternehmen Barbarossa" 1941* (Frankfurt am Main: Fischer, 1991), 323.

124. Record of interrogation of Frentzel dated August 14, 1970, BStU, MfS, HA IX/11 ZUV 9, Bd. 4/2, fol. 276.

125. Record of interrogation of A. N. Stepanov dated July 20, 1944, BStU, MfS, HA IX/11 ZUV 9, Bd. 13/2, fol. 301.

126. The following is according to an chapter by V. Iushkevich published in the Mogilev newspaper *Mogilevskie Vedomosti*, March 17, 2001, 6. The title of the chapter translates as "In hell we sang 'Stenka Razin': Account of the eyewitness Stepan Pilunov." Stepan Razin, known as Stenka Razin, was a seventeenth-century Cossack leader and is the subject of the well-known folk song "Ponizovaia Volnitsa."

Part IV. Wehrmacht

8 Reconceiving Criminality in the German Army on the Eastern Front, 1941–1942

Alex J. Kay and David Stahel

THE ADVANCES MADE over the last two decades in our understanding of German occupation policies in the Soviet Union and the crimes committed there by the Wehrmacht, the *Schutzstaffel* (SS), police forces, the civil administration, agricultural authorities, and NSDAP agencies have been immense, yet the discussion in serious scholarship regarding the extent of Wehrmacht participation in atrocities on both an individual and a collective level could not be more divided. Christian Hartmann reopened the discussion with his recent study of five German divisions on the eastern front in 1941 and 1942, which concluded that criminal conduct was largely a feature of rear area security formations and not the frontline units, which made up the greater part of the troops deployed in the east. Hartmann even wonders whether the Wehrmacht can be regarded as a perpetrator organization of the National Socialist regime at all.[1] Although Hartmann certainly deserves credit for devising the kind of scheme that helps make sense of the different structural and situational factors that could help determine a particular unit's propensity for criminal behavior, his conclusions contrast starkly with those reached by Dieter Pohl in his analysis of Wehrmacht policies in the Soviet Union during the entire three-year occupation. Pohl found that the number of divisions deployed on the eastern front in which no war crimes were committed was "low" and added that members of the Wehrmacht may have constituted the majority of those responsible for mass crimes carried out on the part of the German Reich.[2]

Of the up to 18 million men who served in the Wehrmacht during World War II, 10 million were deployed at one time or another between 1941 and 1944 in the conflict against the Soviet Union.[3] It was in the eastern theater of war that the military struggle was most brutally fought and in which more of Nazi Germany's mass crimes were committed than on any other front. The total number of Soviet dead comes to a staggering 27 million people.[4] As around 8.5 million of these were members of the Red Army, the majority of the dead—more than 18 million noncombatants—comprised civilians and unarmed, captured soldiers.⁵ What can we say, then, about the proportion of Wehrmacht soldiers fighting on the eastern front involved in war crimes? Rolf-Dieter Müller concludes that the percentage of German soldiers stationed on the eastern front involved in war crimes was "if anything smaller still" (*eher noch geringer*) than the estimated 5 percent of German soldiers involved in war crimes in occupied Italy.⁶ The contrast between this figure and the estimate subsequently attributed to Hannes Heer could scarcely be greater. According to Heer, "60 to 80 percent" of German soldiers who fought on the eastern front participated in war crimes.⁷ Although Hartmann neglects to cite a specific figure himself, he makes it clear that he shares Müller's view.⁸ In his recent study *Ostkrieg: Hitler's War of Extermination in the East*, the American historian Stephen G. Fritz has favorably repeated the figure of 5 percent.⁹ How credible is a figure of 5 percent or less? In his review of Fritz's book for the journal *German History*, Jeff Rutherford responded: "Such a low estimate is simply untenable, as numerous studies have demonstrated front line troops' involvement in enforcing the starvation policy, rounding up slave laborers, waging a ruthless war against alleged partisans and, as [Fritz] himself points out, carrying out scorched earth retreats."¹⁰

Rutherford cites some important contexts here, in which German troops committed war crimes. The ruthless antipartisan war and scorched earth retreats are two of the five major complexes of crimes examined by Hartmann in his aforementioned study *Wehrmacht im Ostkrieg* and frequently cited in discussions of Wehrmacht criminality.¹¹ Rutherford's remaining two examples, on the other hand, are rarely addressed: the enforcement of the starvation policy and the rounding up of slave laborers. Both tasks—the systematic starvation of civilians and prisoners of war, and the abduction of men and women for deployment as forced laborers—constitute by any standard war crimes.¹²

This brings us to a key argument overlooked in the current literature: the sheer brutality of the German conduct of war and occupation in the Soviet Union has overshadowed many activities that would otherwise be (rightly) held up as criminal acts. In identifying what might be categorized as secondary crimes, our understanding of what constituted criminal behavior is enhanced, while the number of perpetrators is significantly expanded. As many of the examples below will reflect, such crimes often constituted a less overt breach of the international laws of war and, in some cases, exhibited a less direct relationship between the perpetrator's action and the victim's suffering, but these considerations do not ameliorate the criminal responsibility of the German soldiers involved. The examples draw in part on recent advancements in scholarship, providing fresh insights into new areas of criminality, but are largely based on a reconceptualization of the day-to-day reality of life for the average *Landser* on the eastern front.

Sexual Violence

As recently as 2005, the social psychologist Harald Welzer noted that from the available sources we know relatively little about "the exploitation of sexual opportunities by the powerful occupying soldiers."[13] The historian Waitman Beorn concluded for the eastern front: "The power dynamics alone suggest that any relationship between a Jewish woman and an occupying soldier was at least partially exploitative."[14] While exploitative is not the same as criminal, some of these relationships most certainly *were* criminal, and included rape and sexual slavery. Even the divisive exhibition War of Annihilation: Crimes of the Wehrmacht, 1941 to 1944 (*Vernichtungskrieg: Verbrechen der Wehrmacht 1941 bis 1944*) organized by the Hamburg Institute of Social Research, which has been criticized for presenting the Wehrmacht as a "criminal organization,"[15] did not address the subject of rapes perpetrated by German soldiers due to a lack of written sources.[16] It is unclear how widespread this phenomenon was because the Nazi authorities prosecuted Germans for "racial mixing," while victims and witnesses were frequently killed.[17] In order to protect privacy and honor, female survivors were reluctant to speak about this type of assault.[18] As a result of more recent research carried out by Regina Mühlhäuser, however, we now have a much clearer idea of the nature and extent of acts of sexual violence committed by German soldiers in the Soviet Union.[19] Sexual violence against Soviet women was no exception. In some occupied localities, *all* the women were raped by German soldiers. In several cases, entire units participated in extreme acts of sexual violence.[20] The command of the German Ninth Army noted in early August 1941, the distinct increase in "plundering," "rape and so on," even in the combat zone.[21]

As in most military codes of law, rape in the Wehrmacht was officially a crime under the classification of crimes and offences against morality. Yet in the years between 1939 and 1944 only 5,300 members of the Wehrmacht were charged with sexual crimes. In fact, the number of convictions peaked in 1940, and then went into decline until 1943. By removing the compulsion to prosecute lawlessness, the notorious Jurisdiction Decree Barbarossa of May 1941 effectively prevented the punishment of most sexual violations in the war against the Soviet Union, even though the decree nominally categorized "grave actions that are caused by a lack of sexual restraint" as punishable offenses.[22] In fact, in the words of Christian Hartmann, nothing had such an enduring influence on "the conduct of the *Ostheer* and in particular its troops at the front" as the Jurisdiction Decree Barbarossa.[23] Felix Römer notes that the decree provided "the pseudo-legal basis for German policies of violence on the eastern front,"[24] and adds that "the creation of a lawless region through the abolition of obligatory criminal prosecution" as a result of the Jurisdiction Decree Barbarossa made this "a deeply radical order that was to form the basis of German tyranny in the occupied Soviet Union."[25]

In practice then, the main criterion that prompted criminal prosecution in the Wehrmacht, rather than respect for any legal framework, was the perceived threat to *Manneszucht* (military discipline), which was the most important edict of German military life and was especially important for Nazi Germany given its preoccupation with the autumn of 1918 and the breakdown of military discipline leading to mutiny. In 1941, sexual crimes were officially prohibited, but the regulation was seldom enforced and many officers viewed the conduct of their soldiers as a "natural" outcome of privations of deployment in the war and the absence of brothels (at that time) in the east.[26] Beginning in 1942, Wehrmacht brothels soon became a fixed feature of larger towns and cities in the occupied hinterland. It was hoped that they would lead to a reduction in instances of sexually transmitted diseases and, according to the Wehrmacht High Command, prevent "unwanted bastards," in which "Germany [had] no interest."[27]

Not all forms of sexual contact involved violence or even the threat of coercive behavior, since the desperate conditions created by the German occupation forced countless Soviet women to solicit themselves for food. Furthermore, many women—especially young women—opted to work in military brothels rather than be subjected to deportation to the Reich and the feared labor deployment there. For example, around 85 percent of the women who were solicited for the Wehrmacht brothel in the central Ukrainian city of Poltava were still virgins according to a medical examination.[28] The result allowed German soldiers to believe that their actions were consensual and therefore freed them of any guilt. Yet, as one German solider observed of the women who sold themselves for sex: "Some of them had babies, but they did not have enough food to feed themselves or their young. So, for a loaf of bread, one could have a good night with them. Some of my comrades took advantage of the women's plight; they had their good night."[29] Another soldier, William Lubbeck, noted that the same process was common in his regiment. "Putting a loaf of bread under their arm, these men would head for a certain area a couple of miles behind the front where there were hungry Russian women or girls who would willingly exchange sexual favours for food.... I knew of no one who was reprimanded or punished for engaging in this type of act."[30] In March 1942, the Army High Command noted: "In larger towns, a clandestine, completely uncontrolled brothel trade has developed in many places."[31]

Theft and Starvation

Beyond sexual criminality and exploitation, the question of soldiers' guilt must extend to include actions that were deemed to be of military necessity during the Barbarossa campaign and which later became standard practice throughout the German *Ostheer* (eastern army). Included in the May 1941 army administrative regulations for the occupation of Soviet territories was a directive entitled Guidelines for Booty, Confiscation and Exacting of Services (*Richtlinien für*

Beute, Beschlagnahmung und Inanspruchnahme von Dienstleistungen), which translated into the open exploitation of the occupied areas for the army's benefit. In recognition of the enormous burden carried by the motorized transport columns, the Army Quartermaster-General *Generalmajor* Eduard Wagner, issued his own Order for the Securing of Booty during Operations (*Befehl für Erfassung der Beute bei Operationen*). This was intended for army and corps commands and aimed at keeping the operations moving by utilizing captured stocks of vital resources and materials such as foodstuffs, motor vehicles, fuel, horses, wagons, and ammunition.[32]

The great need to supplement the existing supply system was not limited to the utilization of captured Red Army equipment, but extended to the plunder of the local populace. German soldiers ruthlessly looted the impoverished countryside, sometimes out of need, but also out of a desire for personal enrichment. The process also involved countless acts of wanton destruction, especially if nothing of value could be located. Importantly, even before the war, many Soviet peasants had lived at subsistence level and the consequence of the rampant German looting was for many an eventual death sentence. Konrad Jarausch tellingly wrote home: "Everyone is constantly looking for 'booty'." He then noted that even in such a poor country it was still possible to get honey and kilos of butter.[33] Likewise, after observing a collapse of the supply system in his area of operations, Franz Frisch remarked, "we were on our own. Whatever little there was to be taken, we took."[34] Helmut Pabst wrote about how he and his comrades looted onions and turnips from people's gardens and took milk from their churns. "Most of them part with it amiably," he wrote home in a letter, but he also made clear his indifference to the suffering of the local people: "Willingly or unwillingly, the country feeds us."[35]

Soviet peasants naturally sought to protect their precious winter food stocks by hiding them and claiming they had nothing left to give, which in some cases was also the truth, but to many German soldiers this constituted resistance and forestalled any feelings of sympathy for their plight. As Willy Peter Reese wrote: "We saw the hunger and the misery, and under the compulsion of war, we added to it."[36] He then continued:

> The cooks slaughtered cattle and pigs on the way and requisitioned peas, beans, and cucumbers everywhere. But the midday soup wasn't enough to get us through our exertions. So we started taking the last piece of bread from women and children, had chickens and geese prepared for us, pocketed their small supplies of butter and lard, weighed down our vehicles with flitches of bacon and flour from the larders, drank the over rich milk, and cooked and roasted on their stoves, stole honey from their collective farms, came upon stashes of eggs, and weren't bothered by tears, hand wringing and curses. We were the victors. War excused our thefts, encouraged cruelty, and the need to survive didn't go around getting permission from conscience.[37]

Yet for Soviet civilians the need to survive at the margins of subsistence living was a question of life and death, which was not the case for the Wehrmacht. German soldiers did not want to experience hunger, while the civilian population was confronted with starvation. As one man wrote after German soldiers looted his home: "We had saved a few scraps of food—a little butter, a small amount of meat and some white bread. Naturally, everything has now been stolen from us."[38]

The looting of peasant homes held very real consequences in the long winter months when food stocks were depleted and people starved, but German soldiers typically took no responsibility for this and in fact continued to supplement their own rations with whatever remained to be plundered.[39] Many Soviet peasants, especially those in Ukraine, had already seen or experienced the torments of hunger in their own lifetime and knew that starvation was only the most direct consequence of their diminished food stocks. Malnutrition greatly increased the danger of life-threatening illnesses and disease, particularly for the old, weak, and very young. Whether death resulted from starvation or complications brought on by undernourishment, the cause was the same and the role played by everyday German soldiers, even if at times unwittingly, cannot be ignored. Even soldiers who did not participate in the looting benefited from their comrades' actions, thus reinforcing the legitimacy and indeed desirability of the acts themselves and, in turn, functioning as a further incentive to their officially sanctioned theft.

The burden of guilt for the perpetrators was often largely avoided because the suffering and high mortality rate among Soviet civilians was neither the intended result of their actions, nor something that German soldiers remained to witness. A rationalization of their actions was not difficult to achieve: Soviet peasants had always been poor and were used to dealing with scarcity; it was war and beyond their control; retreating Soviet troops were to blame. While their actions led to mass starvation and also, frequently, to death, the role played by German soldiers was less immediate than, for example, in the execution of real or imagined partisans or massacres of Jews, which is why secondary crimes have largely been ignored in discussions of Wehrmacht criminality in the east. The end result, however, was very often the same. The difference was a subjective one: unlike other criminal activities, the vast majority of German soldiers in the east, including many nonparticipants in the looting, partook of eating stolen foodstuffs and therefore circuitously contributed to the Soviet loss of life without incurring any sense of guilt or wrongdoing. Tellingly, Ivan Ivanovich Steblin-Kamenskii, a Russian interpreter serving with the German 206th Infantry Division, noted in his diary in March 1942: "All in all, it is very hard for me to see this new, unknown face of the German soldier, without any human feeling. Having more than is needed for nutrition, he then takes away the last [food] from women and children. I'm completely overwhelmed, shocked, insulted, and yet I can do nothing and have to serve with them."[40]

With the practice of looting food from the local populace well established, German soldiers had no compunction about plundering other essential items as the campaign extended into the colder months. By October 1941, with the temperature dropping below freezing at night, Russian homes were again raided for winter clothing, which the army could not supply to its troops. Franz Frisch recalled: "The winter conditions drove German soldiers to ransack peasant homes looking for anything to supplement their uniform. We used bed covers, tablecloths, curtains, anything at all to provide a layer of warmth."[41] The process of dispossessing Soviet civilians was both ubiquitous and ruthless. Helmut Günther noted: "The time of the large-scale 'procurement' had started ... every unit's main concern was to maintain its own stock of material, even if not by the most ethical means."[42] More to the point, Willy Peter Reese wrote in his journal: "Any woollen garments we found became ours. Blankets, scarves, pullovers, shirts, and especially gloves we made off with at any opportunity. We pulled the boots off the old men and women on the street if ours were wanting."[43] Soldiers rationalized their actions because, while they were fighting in the bitter cold, Soviet civilians could, in theory, remain in their warm homes. However, German forces destroyed thousands of homes and, indeed, entire villages (more than 600 in Belarus alone),[44] forcing countless civilians to become refugees. Dire food shortages resulting from German requisitioning had the same effect, with untold numbers dying as a result of weakness, fatigue, and exposure to the elements. Even at this point civilians were exploited by soldiers who stole their valuable sleighs, leaving them unable to transport their last, most valued possessions. As Walter Tilemann recalled from the winter of 1941–1942: "No one was interested that the sleighs were also essential for the Russian people. In this terrible winter all pity had literally turned to ice."[45]

As temperatures continued to drop in November 1941, and the German advance came to a halt in many places, peasants near the front, who had earlier been stripped of their food and winter clothing, were now forced out of their homes, often with no place else to go. Henry Metelmann, a soldier in Army Group South, wrote of how his unit acquired shelter in the freezing conditions:

> Our orders were to occupy one cottage per crew, and to throw the peasants out. When we entered "ours," a woman and her three young children were sitting around the table by the window, obviously having just finished a meal. She was clearly frightened of us, and I could see that her hands were shaking, while the kids stayed in their seats and looked at us with large, non-understanding eyes. Our Sergeant came straight to the point: "*Raus!*" [Out!] and pointed to the door. When the mother started to remonstrate and her children to cry, he repeated "*Raus!*," opened the door and waved his hand towards the outside in a manner which could not be mistaken anywhere.... Outside it was bitterly cold ... I watched them through the small window standing by their

bundles in the snow, looking helplessly in all directions, not knowing what to do.... When I looked back a little later, they were gone; I did not want to think about it anymore.[46]

Metelmann may have expressed unease about the practice, but there were many German soldiers for whom the bitter cold and extreme fatigue extinguished any sensitivity toward the people they rendered homeless. Other soldiers felt no compassion at the best of times and denounced Slavic peoples as backward and even dangerous enemies. Wilhelm Prüller's diary relates the ruthlessness of the expulsion process. "You should see the act the civilians put on when we make it clear to them that we intend to use their sties to sleep in. A weeping and yelling begins, as if their throats were being cut, until we chuck them out. Whether young or old, man or wife, they stand in their rags and tatters on the doorstep and can't be persuaded to go.... When we finally threaten them at pistol point, they disappear."[47] No doubt many Soviet peasants could well guess at the fate that awaited them and their families without shelter during the coldest months of the year, with temperatures dropping as low as minus forty degrees.

Even in American captivity after the war in Europe had already ended, far away from the cold and privations of the eastern front, the pitilessness of some German soldiers was still in evidence, as the following conversation between Corporal Karl Huber and Private Walter Gumlich illustrates:

> H: Someone came and stole the cow from a Russian, and the Russian defended himself. And then the Germans hanged fifty or a hundred men and women, and they remained hanging there for three or four days. Or they had to dig their own graves, and then stand at the edge of the grave, and then they were shot and fell in, backwards. Fifty to a hundred men and even more. That was "retribution." But it didn't do any good. Or set fire to the villages.... Partisans were, of course, dangerous, we of course had to defend ourselves against them, but that was something completely different....
>
> G: Oh, please, these were wartime operations. They're not really criminals.
>
> H: When entire families are exterminated and children shot, and so on, the family literally wiped out? We're guilty when the military seizes a peasant's last piece of bread, steals it, without any right whatsoever or any kind of order.
>
> G: Skip it!
>
> H: Hey, don't defend them![48]

While Soviet peasants were certainly the most numerous victims of such German behavior, they were not even the most vulnerable. Columns of captured Soviet POWs were deprived of boots, coats, and anything of value, which greatly reduced their chances of survival in the dreadful conditions of German POW camps. While numerous German letters make reference to German troops looting enemy soldiers, few say anything about what their defenseless captives were left with to protect themselves against the cold. For many the only limit to such activity was concern for their own well-being, as Siegfried Knappe noted, "we did not dare wear the heavier quilted jackets for fear of being shot as a Russian."[49]

Coerced and Forced Labor

German soldiers worked closely with employment offices and General Plenipotentiary for Labor Deployment Fritz Sauckel in the systematic recruitment of millions of Soviet civilians to work in German industry and agriculture, often by employing methods of extreme brutality. Civilians were also put to work in the towns and the countryside of the occupied Soviet Union itself or sent to one of the many forced labor camps set up by local army commands throughout the area of operations.[50] By May 1944, Army Group Center's zone of operations, which contained some 1.9 million Soviet civilians, had no less than three hundred thousand performing directly military tasks.[51] The Wehrmacht was furthermore responsible for the illegal forced labor of captured Soviet prisoners of war. Over a million were transported to the Reich for this purpose but Soviet POWs were also deployed in the occupied eastern territories, for example, clearing the battlefield or in road construction.[52] Here average German soldiers saved themselves heavy labor and menial domestic tasks by putting POWs and civilians to work for them. In a letter home from late 1943, Georg Scharnik explained how, before a retreat, any Soviet men of military age were seized and put to work in the rear building roads. This, he explained, saved German soldiers work and prevented the men from being conscripted by the Red Army.[53]

Other soldiers expressed delight when Soviet civilians were located near to their camp so they could serve as a workforce. "Sometimes we have luck. There are still civilians. They must sew my buttons, warm water, wash ... they do it willingly."[54] Not surprisingly, such enthusiasm was absent from the account of Anna Nosova, who spoke of having to wash hundreds of German uniforms covered in blood and lice.[55] Even more exploitative was the forced recruitment of Soviet women for labor in Germany, which Birgit Beck's research suggests could sometimes be avoided if the women consented to work as Wehrmacht prostitutes.[56] German institutions in the east became so reliant on Soviet slave labor that, as late as July 1944, Army Group Center felt able to request a workforce of one hundred thousand complete with equipment for the construction of redoubts. Work was to begin in a mere two days.[57]

Exploitative behavior extended to almost every aspect of the Wehrmacht's advance through the Soviet Union, with profound implications for the survival of anyone in the area of German occupation. Moreover, these conditions were created by the average rank and file German soldiers of the *Ostheer*, not a select few. Their behavior adversely impacted on untold numbers of Soviet civilians, reducing them to the barest means of subsistence and often resulting in their deaths. The mortality rate is impossible to calculate, but the demands made by average German soldiers on the Soviet population were staggering. In addition to the aspects already discussed, German soldiers requisitioned local medical facilities and medicines, plundered factories for equipment and tools, seized vital farming machinery for the army's use, burned any settlements thought useful to partisans and typically showed little or no regard for the well-being of civilians caught up in the fighting.[58] Such actions may not have immediately resulted in the deaths of the victims, nor might their deaths have even been the intention of the soldiers, but the result nevertheless stemmed from the actions of German troops in the east. The point here is not to equate these deaths with the much discussed direct criminality of the Wehrmacht—involving acts of outright murder and execution—but rather to acknowledge that a deadly, indirect criminality involving a much larger percentage of the *Ostheer* also existed. Indeed, if we take into account all forms of criminality—from the plundering of Soviet homes and the exploitation of local resources to rape and sexual slavery—it would be reasonable to conclude that a substantial *majority* of the 10 million Wehrmacht soldiers deployed at one time or another in the German-Soviet War were involved or complicit in criminal conduct.

Environmental and Institutional Factors

In order to understand the indirect criminality of the *Ostheer*, it is important not only to take account of what the soldiers did but also how it was possible for them to do it. Hannes Heer has described it as a process of how "amorality became normality."[59] Warfare on the eastern front constituted a process of brutalization, which resulted from a transformative event in which men experienced first shock and then a process of renormalization. Importantly, German soldiers on the eastern front were not simply engaging in warfare but in a systematic war of extermination in which not only the rules of civil society were being repudiated but also the basic codex of armed conflict. The brutalizing effect of their experiences, and often their own actions, initially induced a sense of shock, brought on by a loss of orientation, the duration of which varied from soldier to soldier. Men wrote home of becoming "a different person," of being forced to "completely readjust" and of experiencing "inner change." Another wrote that he had been forced to "throw overboard several principles held in the past," while others spoke of a new "split consciousness." The shock, however, soon passed, as the daily exposure to unparalleled violence became, out of necessity, normalized.[60]

In identifying this process, Heer was able to point to German soldiers' descriptions of themselves as having become "hard," "indifferent," and "heartless."[61] One soldier wrote: "It's like growing a shell around you that's almost impenetrable. But what happens inside this shell? You become part of a mass, a component of a relentless whole which sucks you up and squeezes you into a mould. You become gross and insensible. You cease to be yourself." Another man simply reflected: "I have forgotten myself."[62] William Lubbeck observed: "Over time, war hardens your heart and leads you to do brutal things that you could never have imagined yourself doing in civilian life."[63] Likewise, Willy Peter Reese wrote of developing an "armour of apathy" that he used to protect himself "against terror, horror, fear, and madness, which saved me from suffering and screaming." Yet Reese noted that this same apathy "crushed any tender stirring within me, snapped off the shoots of hope, faith, and love of my fellow men, and turned my heart to stone."[64] Accordingly, the renormalization process was a coping mechanism aimed at dealing with the shocking brutality of the war in the east, yet the price was a radical desensitization toward violence, allowing for indirect actions of blatant criminality to pass for normality.

Whatever the extent of the Wehrmacht's culture of violence and the acceptance of amorality within its ranks, there were of course those who considered the behavior of the majority as, at the very least, problematic and perhaps even criminal. How are we to understand their position and why did they not act on their good conscience? Thomas Kühne's work on comradeship within the German army suggested that shame culture dominated the Wehrmacht. According to Kühne, in shame culture the adoptive norms of a soldier's community takes on the highest form of moral authority, surpassing any others that may have preceded it. Shame culture is grounded in the fear of exclusion, exposure, and disgrace, which the community imposes on any individual who does not submit to its rules. The controlling gaze of the majority reaffirms and rewards positive behavior toward the community and its social mores, but its shaming culture is what defines it, ensuring a negative consequence for any member who departs from its norms. It teaches one to conform, to be inconspicuous, to participate, and to be content in doing so. The reward for German soldiers on the eastern front was the safety and acceptance of the unit, which was a vital and irreplaceable form of emotional support.[65] Comradeship was as sacrosanct as family, protecting its members as fiercely as it opposed outsiders,[66] but this also created a daunting barrier to anyone seeking to oppose the amoral behavior that the majority endorsed and practiced.

While there was an internal pressure to conform within the soldiers' units, there was also a dominant perception of an external environment characterized as lawless territories in which harsh measures were not only regarded as permissible, but indeed as an absolute necessity. In establishing "law" according to their own system of "order," however, the soldiers often ignored their own role as aggressor in precipitating this anarchic state of affairs.[67] The organized and disciplined staging of executions of partisans, offering a feeble guise of legality to what were often nothing other than summary reprisals,[68] contrasted starkly with the stories of chaos and disorder in the occupied areas that circulated among the soldiers at the front. Beyond any racial prejudice against Slavs, horror stories of partisans (real and imagined) quickly led to a siege mentality that fed a profound distrust of the Soviet population and transformed the soldier-civilian relationship. German troops in every instance became enforcers of law and order—whatever they decided that to be and however much that differed between individual soldiers. It was a system open to flagrant abuse, and, while the murderous consequences of this autonomy have formed the basis of most studies, it must also be acknowledged that such an environment also fostered a ubiquitous culture of secondary criminality, supporting all manner of nonlethal, but no less criminal, corruption and abuse of power by the soldiers.

If internal and environmental pressures helped facilitate this behavior, one must also acknowledge institutional power, which, although diminishing individual agency to some extent, forms an important framework for how soldiers understood and experienced the war in the east. The German army was overwhelmingly conscripted; volunteers are estimated at numbering only about 10 percent, meaning that the army's induction and training programs had to transform "average men" into battle-ready soldiers.[69] The advantage the German army enjoyed was that their recruits had already spent years in paramilitary organizations such as the Hitler Youth or the Reich Labor Service. Yet even these could not always prepare the men for the fearsome demands of German military training, which built a first-rate fighting force but, as Stephan Fritz has observed, "aimed ultimately at control and motivation on the battlefield."[70] Likewise, British historian Richard Holmes has argued: "There is a direct link between the harshness of basic training and the cohesiveness of the group which emerges from it."[71] The German army exhibited powerful cohesion, high levels of motivation and strict control, which was forged in battle even before the invasion of the Soviet Union. Such strong institutional culture proved extremely resilient, especially when confronted with a land and people that were perceived as foreign, dangerous, and inferior. As German historian Wolfram Wette has noted, the brutalization of the German military institution led among the men, "to the dramatic loss of a feeling of individual responsibility and personal guilt, as well as the deformation of their sense of humanity and justice."[72]

If the army's institutional culture perverted individual responsibility in the east, it was reinforced by Nazi racial ideology, but also impacted by what Jeff Rutherford has termed "military necessity." In essence, Rutherford's study has shown that the German army was willing to do whatever was necessary to preserve its combat efficiency and emerge victorious on the battlefield. This is the first theory to explain the otherwise contradictory behavior in German army policy, where the same unit could initially act with relative benevolence toward an occupied population and later display utter ruthlessness. The essential ingredient, according to Rutherford, could not simply be ideology, but rather the perceived needs of the unit or the men themselves.[73] Accordingly, military necessity is not a rigid concept, any more than indirect criminality is. In both cases there are gray areas, degrees of complicity, and blurred lines. Yet the troops were clearly capable of enacting whatever was necessary to ensure their own needs came first and, in the process, any concern for the local population was often absent.

Spectators as Perpetrators

Not only was there a willingness on the part of German soldiers on the eastern front to perpetrate acts that indirectly led to enormous suffering and high mortality rates, there was also a clear enthusiasm for lending their support to more immediate acts of murder, namely as spectators at massacres (and other atrocities). This passive acceptance of the killing process among the soldiers gave legitimacy to the murders, while providing another forum for soldiers to participate indirectly in the war of annihilation. Christian Hartmann has correctly concluded that the number of "members of the Wehrmacht, who articulated their disquiet about the Holocaust, or even resisted it," was "even smaller" than the size of the group directly involved in implementing the genocide of Jews. He adds, however: "This means that we are dealing here with a broad, apparently indifferent middle section."[74] Yet to what extent was the broad middle section really indifferent? There is a legitimate school of thought that regards those who photographed and filmed the mistreatment, degradation, and murder of Jews as *active* participants in those atrocities, and the act of taking photographs and making films as "a distinct form of violence," in the words of Gerhard Paul.[75] The perpetrators engaged in an interaction with the photographers and cameramen "by presenting them the humiliated and naked victims like trophies." They orchestrated executions, beatings, and other abuse not just in front of the camera but also *for* the camera.[76]

This conception of culpability has been extended to include bystanders, thus encompassing a vastly greater proportion of regular German troops than the inclusion of photographers and cameramen already does. As Harald Welzer notes in respect to massacres carried out in the German-occupied east, "spectators are not passive: their presence and obvious interest constitute a framework of social confirmation surrounding the shooting operations. And even the individual spectator can reassure himself, through the simple presence of other spectators, of the legitimacy of his curiosity."[77] Thus, what we have here is a case of mutual reinforcement, for shooter and observer alike, to the effect that what each of them does is acceptable.

To the average observer, however, the onus of moral responsibility (to the extent that such a concept was even considered) lay exclusively with the shooters and even decades after the war few appear to have accepted any degree of personal accountability in spite of acknowledging having been present at executions carried out by the Wehrmacht.[78] Once again, in the mind of the average German soldier, his own role in the crime, and the passive support he lent to it, passed guilt free. Accordingly, attendance at executions was typically high and was treated as a form of officially sanctioned entertainment; a spectacle at which to marvel as well as relish the feeling that justice was being served. Indeed, the photographic evidence suggests that numerous observers enjoyed themselves enough to pose smiling for their comrades' photos.[79] Such "execution tourism"—resulting in a "pornography of death"[80]—not only made the *Landser* an accessory to the crimes he witnessed, but provided an unmistakable lesson in the German disregard for the value of Soviet life and the widely accepted consequences for actions deemed to constitute resistance to the German occupation.

Criminality for German soldiers on the eastern front was thus a series of gradations, not a black and white distinction between onerous guilt and virtuous innocence. The culpability of the soldiers varied from direct complicity in acts of mass murder to a more qualified—but often no less deadly—set of actions, which indirectly led to widespread death throughout the occupied Soviet territories. Most German soldiers already fell into these categories, but of the remaining men there was typically a passive acceptance—and thus condoning—of their comrades and their criminal behavior, which offered support and reinforcement to the whole system of violence. A photograph found on the body of a dead German soldier showed a group of company commanders sitting behind a large sign that read: "The Russian must die, so that we [can] live" (*Der Russe muß sterben, damit wir leben*).[81] While not every member of the *Ostheer* can be condemned as a war criminal, it is at the same time unlikely that many could claim to be entirely innocent.

* * *

If the majority of German soldiers serving on the eastern front were involved in some form of criminal behavior, does this mean that the mass were also Nazis? In his exceptional study *Kameraden*, Felix Römer presents his evaluation of the interrogation reports, morale questionnaires, and bugged room conversations of several thousand Wehrmacht soldiers in US captivity at Fort Hunt, Virginia—the largest and most substantial collection of personal testimonials of German soldiers in World War II yet known.[82] The more than three thousand prisoners were predominantly ordinary German and Austrian soldiers: more than one in two of them was an enlisted man; almost every third was an NCO; and approximately every sixth an officer, although generally only from the subaltern ranks up to captain.[83] They thus constituted a representative segment of the Wehrmacht. Römer convincingly demonstrates how ideology played at most a subordinated role *in the consciousness* of most members of the Wehrmacht.[84] This does not mean that political ideas and National Socialist beliefs did not have any influence on the soldiers. Römer's analysis reveals that nationalism, militarism, and loyalty to Hitler were part of the basic mental configuration of the majority of the ordinary soldiers, and the virtues and interpretative models by which they were guided were in part impregnated by National Socialism. Beyond such basic convictions, however, most of them thought in political terms in less complex categories, without deeper theoretical foundations. For the mass of them, it was above all success and failure that ultimately counted in the assessment of politics and the actions of the state.[85] Ideological convictions counted among the basic certainties that were commonly taken for granted by the soldiers. The largely internalized nationalism and militarism of the vast majority of the soldiers established a fundamental loyalty to the state that was more deep-rooted than the frequently superficial political opinions. In contrast to the oft vague ideas that the soldiers had of National Socialist ideology, these elementary convictions were deeply grounded, long-term cultivated mentalities that were so self-evident as to be scarcely pondered or questioned, least of all when at the front.[86]

This absence of *overt* ideology in the transcripts led Sönke Neitzel and Harald Welzer, in their bestselling book Soldiers: *Soldaten: Protokolle vom Kämpfen, Töten und Sterben* (On Fighting, Killing and Dying) to excessively play down or even dismiss the potency of convictions and ideas in accounting for the enormity of German deeds and the nonchalance of so many perpetrators and witnesses documented in the transcripts, and to prematurely conclude: "These soldiers are no 'ideological warriors,' but rather in most cases wholly unpolitical."[87] Although Neitzel and Welzer deserve credit for bringing to the debate a range of additional factors more common to soldiers and military culture generally, Johannes Hürter is right to warn against generalizations: "If the same soldierly patterns of behaviour really always manifest themselves in the specific area of war, even in the perpetration of crimes, then the war of the Wehrmacht loses its special character, even in its worst excesses on the eastern front."[88]

Illustrative of Felix Römer's findings, on the other hand, are the results of the US opinion polls conducted over the course of 1944 among the Wehrmacht soldiers held captive at Fort Hunt. There was approval for the person of Adolf Hitler among almost 64 percent of those interrogated by the Americans. Among the soldiers born in or after 1923, that is, those who were ten years or younger at the time of the Nazi takeover of power, the rate of approval for Hitler was more than 74 percent. Thus, three out of four members of the youngest generation—who were aged between seventeen and twenty-two in the final year of World War II—continued to hold faith with Hitler, even at this late stage of the war.[89] These findings complement the results of a survey of 1,400 Austrian former members of the Wehrmacht conducted after the war.[90] Asked to name the four most important aims of the Wehrmacht, 78.4 percent of those surveyed said "more living space," 62.1 percent the "struggle against Bolshevism," 41.6 percent the "struggle against world Jewry," and 36.3 percent "racial purity." These percentages—citing not just a selection but the *four main objectives* of the Wehrmacht in the eyes of those surveyed—demonstrate that its members by no means perceived the Wehrmacht as a purely military apparatus free of ideology. On the contrary, the Wehrmacht was for its troops an instrument of the National Socialist regime that not only strove to accomplish its military but also its ideological and political objectives, such as the "struggle against world Jewry" and "racial purity." Asked for their personal opinion, 26.4 percent of the former soldiers surveyed stated that "the Jews" had been the main culprits of the outbreak of World War II. As the political scientist Walter Manoschek rightly points out, given that antisemitic attitudes were something of a taboo in the postwar period, also in Austria, it seems plausible that this percentage might have been considerably higher at the time when those surveyed were still members of the Wehrmacht.[91]

The fact that it was possible even for soldiers who were critical of National Socialism to commit war crimes and other atrocities is demonstrated by the example of the aforementioned Willy Peter Reese. The following excerpt is from a poem he composed in 1942:

> *Murdered the Jews,*
> *marched to Russia*
> *as a roaring horde,*
> *oppressed the people,*
> *fought in blood,*
> *led by a clown,*
> *we are the envoys*
> *of what's known everywhere*
> *and wade in blood.*
> *We carry the flags*
> *of the Aryan ancestors:*
> *they suit us.*[92]

At the same time, however, he describes how his unit shot Soviet prisoners of war, murdered civilians, burned down villages, looted homes, and forced captive Russian women to dance naked. In September 1943, after his unit had laid waste to villages and killed people on the retreat, he wrote: "I crack under this guilt—and hit the sauce!"[93]

In seeking to achieve a fuller understanding of the nature of the war Nazi Germany waged against the Soviet Union and its peoples, we would be better served by not confining our conception of criminal conduct to a small selection of the most heinous crimes. Widening our gaze should not lead us to draw the conclusion, however, that the majority of regular soldiers fighting on the eastern front were die-hard Nazis. Nor should we conclude that the majority of these men committed criminal acts *eagerly*, or even willingly. What a broader gaze will reveal, however, is that the war of annihilation in the East was not just Hitler's war or that of the Wehrmacht High Command, but also of the ordinary German and Austrian soldiers.

ALEX J. KAY is Visiting Lecturer at the University of Potsdam and Fellow of the Royal Historical Society. From 2014 to 2016, he was Senior Academic Project Coordinator at the Institute of Contemporary History Munich–Berlin. Dr. Kay is the author of *Exploitation, Resettlement, Mass Murder: Political and Economic Planning for German Occupation Policy in the Soviet Union, 1940–1941* (2006) and *The Making of an SS Killer: The Life of Colonel Alfred Filbert, 1905–1990* (2016, German ed. 2017), and co-editor of *Nazi Policy on the Eastern Front, 1941: Total War, Genocide, and Radicalization* (2012).

DAVID STAHEL is Senior Lecturer at the University of New South Wales, Canberra, Australia. His publications include *Operation Barbarossa and Germany's Defeat in the East* (2009), *Kiev 1941* (2012), *Operation Typhoon* (2013), and *The Battle for Moscow* (2015). His most recent book was shortlisted for the British Army Military Book of the Year (2016).

Notes

1. Christian Hartmann, *Wehrmacht im Ostkrieg. Front und militärisches Hinterland 1941/42* (Munich: Oldenbourg, 2009), 802.
2. Dieter Pohl, *Die Herrschaft der Wehrmacht. Deutsche Militärbesatzung und einheimische Bevölkerung in der Sowjetunion 1941–1944* (Munich: Oldenbourg, 2008), 348–349.
3. Hartmann, *Wehrmacht im Ostkrieg*, 12–13 and 16n29.
4. John Barber and Mark Harrison, *The Soviet Home Front 1941–1945: A Social and Economic History of the USSR in World War II* (London: Longman, 1991), 40–41; Hartmann, *Wehrmacht im Ostkrieg*, 790.
5. Alex J. Kay, "Ausbeutung, Umsiedlung, Massenmord. NS-Zukunftspläne für den Osten: Hungerplan und Generalplan Ost," in *Ökumenische Friedensdekade 2012. Predigthilfe und Materialien für die Gemeinde*, ed. Aktion Sühnezeichen Friedensdienste (September 2012), 44–50, here 44.
6. "Gegen Kritik immun," Interview by Gerhard Spörl and Klaus Wiegrefe in *Der Spiegel*, 23/1999 (June 1999), 60 and 62, here 62.
7. Klaus Wiegrefe, "Abrechnung mit Hitlers Generälen," *Spiegel Online*, November 27, 2001.
8. Christian Hartmann, "Verbrecherischer Krieg—verbrecherische Wehrmacht? Überlegungen zur Struktur des deutschen Ostheeres 1941–1944," *Vierteljahrshefte für Zeitgeschichte* 52, no. 1 (January 2004): 1–76, here 71; Hartmann, *Wehrmacht im Ostkrieg*, 12–13.

9. Stephen G. Fritz, *Ostkrieg: Hitler's War of Extermination in the East* (Lexington: University Press of Kentucky, 2011), 482.
10. Jeff Rutherford, Review of Stephen G. Fritz, *Ostkrieg: Hitler's War of Extermination in the East*, in *German History* 30, no. 3 (September 2012): 476–478.
11. See Hartmann, *Wehrmacht im Ostkrieg*. The other complexes examined by Hartmann are the treatment of Soviet prisoners of war, the genocide against Soviet Jews and the implementation of the Commissar Order. See also his earlier "Verbrecherischer Krieg—verbrecherische Wehrmacht?."
12. See the relevant provisions in the Hague Convention (II) on the Laws and Customs of War on Land, 1899, and the Hague Convention (IV) on War on Land and its Annexed Regulations, 1907: James Brown Scott, ed., *The Hague Conventions and Declarations of 1899 and 1907* (New York: Oxford University Press, 1915).
13. Harald Welzer, *Täter. Wie aus ganz normalen Menschen Massenmörder werden* (Frankfurt am Main: S. Fischer, 2005), 199.
14. Waitman Wade Beorn, *Marching into Darkness: The Wehrmacht and the Holocaust in Belarus* (Cambridge, MA: Harvard University Press, 2014), 167.
15. See, for example, "Gegen Kritik immun," interview by Gerhard Spörl and Klaus Wiegrefe in *Der Spiegel*, 23/1999 (June 1999), 60 and 62, here 62.
16. On this see the interview with the historian Hannes Heer and the social psychologist Harald Welzer. "Ein Erlebnis absoluter Macht," *DIE ZEIT Geschichte* no. 2 (2011): 88–94, here 94.
17. Pohl, *Die Herrschaft der Wehrmacht*, 132; examples in Hans-Heinrich Nolte, "Vergewaltigungen durch Deutsche im Rußlandfeldzug," *Zeitschrift für Weltgeschichte* 10, no. 1 (spring 2009): 113–133.
18. Wendy Lower, *Hitler's Furies: German Women in the Nazi Killing Fields* (Boston: Houghton Mifflin Harcourt, 2013), 232, n. 104.
19. See Regina Mühlhäuser, *Eroberungen. Sexuelle Gewalttaten und intime Beziehungen deutscher Soldaten in der Sowjetunion, 1941–1945* (Hamburg: Hamburger Edition, 2010). See also the discussion in Beorn, *Marching into Darkness*, 164–173, and Chapter 9 in this volume.
20. Mühlhäuser, *Eroberungen*, esp. 74 and 144. See also Alex J. Kay, Review of Regina Mühlhäuser, *Eroberungen. Sexuelle Gewalttaten und intime Beziehungen deutscher Soldaten in der Sowjetunion, 1941–1945*, in *sehepunkte. Rezensionsjournal für die Geschichtswissenschaften* 11, no. 11 (November 15, 2011), http://www.sehepunkte.de/2011/11/19814.html (last accessed on May 8, 2017).
21. See Felix Römer, "'Im alten Deutschland wäre solcher Befehl nicht möglich gewesen.' Rezeption, Adaption und Umsetzung des Kriegsgerichtsbarkeitserlasses im Ostheer 1941/42," *Vierteljahrshefte für Zeitgeschichte* 56, no. 1 (January 2008): 53–99, here 86.
22. For the text of the so-called Jurisdiction Decree Barbarossa, see Bundesarchiv-Militärarchiv, Freiburg im Breisgau, RW 4/v. 577, fols. 72–75, "Erlass über die Ausübung der Kriegsgerichtsbarkeit im Gebiet 'Barbarossa' und über besondere Massnahmen der Truppe," May 13, 1941, here fol. 75: *"schwere Taten, die auf geschlechtlicher Hemmungslosigkeit beruhen."* The decree was reproduced as Nuremberg document 050-C in: International Military Tribunal, ed., *Der Prozess gegen die Hauptkriegsverbrecher vor dem Internationalen Militärgerichtshof, Nürnberg, 14. November 1945—1. Oktober 1946*, vol. 34 (Nuremberg: Sekretariat des Gerichtshofs, 1949), 252–255.
23. Hartmann, "Verbrecherischer Krieg—verbrecherische Wehrmacht?," 54.
24. Römer, "'Im alten Deutschland'," 54.

25. Felix Römer, "The Wehrmacht in the War of Ideologies: The Army and Hiter's Criminal Orders on the Eastern Front," in *Nazi Policy on the Eastern Front, 1941: Total War, Genocide, and Radicalization*, ed. Alex J. Kay, Jeff Rutherford, and David Stahel (Rochester, NY: University of Rochester Press, 2012), 73–100, here 76.

26. Birgit Beck, "Sexual Violence and its Prosecution by Courts Martial of the Wehrmacht," in *A World at Total War: Global Conflict and the Politics of Destruction, 1937-1945*, ed. Roger Chickering, Stig Förster, and Bernd Greiner (Cambridge: Cambridge University Press, 2005), 320–322 and 326–327.

27. Mühlhäuser, *Eroberungen*, 214–239 (quotes: 214).

28. Mühlhäuser, *Eroberungen*, 224–225.

29. Werner Adamczyk, *Feuer! An Artilleryman's Life on the Eastern Front* (Wilmington, NC: Broadfoot, 1992), 199–200.

30. William Lubbeck with David B. Hurt, *At Leningrad's Gates: The Story of a Soldier with Army Group North* (Philadelphia, PA: Casemate, 2006), 113.

31. Quoted in Theo J. Schulte, "The German Army and National Socialist Occupation Policies in the Occupied Areas of the Soviet Union 1941–1943" (unpublished PhD thesis, University of Warwick, 1987), 182: "*In größeren Orten hat sich an vielen Stellen ein heimlicher, völlig unkontrollierter Bordellbetrieb entwickelt.*"

32. Ernst Klink, "Die militärische Konzeption des Krieges gegen die Sowjetunion," in *Das Deutsche Reich und der Zweite Weltkrieg*, ed. Militärgeschichtliches Forschungsamt, vol. 4: *Der Angriff auf die Sowjetunion* (Stuttgart: Deutsche Verlags-Anstalt, 1983), 257–258.

33. Konrad H. Jarausch and Klaus Jochen Arnold, eds., *"Das stille Sterben" Feldpostbriefe von Konrad Jarausch aus Polen und Russland 1939-1942* (Paderborn: Schöningh, 2008), 311 (entry for September 16, 1941).

34. Franz A. P. Frisch, in association with Wilbur D. Jones, Jr., *Condemned to Live: A Panzer Artilleryman's Five-Front War* (Shippensburg, PA: White Mane, 2000), 95.

35. Helmut Pabst, *The Outermost Frontier: A German Soldier in the Russian Campaign* (London: William Kimber, 1957), 18–19 and 39.

36. Willy Peter Reese, *Mir selber seltsam fremd: Die Unmenschlichkeit des Krieges. Russland 1941-1944*, ed. Stefan Schmitz (Munich: Claasen, 2003), 57.

37. Reese, *Mir selber seltsam fremd*, 62.

38. As cited in: Michael Jones, *The Retreat: Hitler's First Defeat* (London: John Murray, 2009), 76–77.

39. See examples in: Jeff Rutherford, *Combat and Genocide on the Eastern Front: The German Infantry's War, 1941-1944* (Cambridge: Cambridge University Press, 2014); Jeff Rutherford, "The Radicalization of German Occupation Policies: *Wirtschaftsstab Ost* and the 121st Infantry Division in Pavlovsk, 1941," in *Nazi Policy on the Eastern Front, 1941: Total War, Genocide, and Radicalization*, ed. Alex J. Kay, Jeff Rutherford, and David Stahel (Rochester, NY: University of Rochester Press, 2012), 130–154; Norbert Kunz, "Das Beispiel Charkow: Eine Stadtbevölkerung als Opfer der deutschen Hungerstrategie 1941/42," in *Verbrechen der Wehrmacht. Bilanz einer Debatte*, ed. Christian Hartmann, Johannes Hürter, and Ulrike Jureit (Munich: C. H. Beck, 2005), 136–144.

40. Diary entry recorded on March 30, 1942 in the village of Burtsevo. The diary remains unpublished and was made available by the family to Oleg Beyda. We are grateful to Oleg for passing on this excerpt to us.

41. Frisch, in association with Jones, Jr., *Condemned to Live*, 94.

42. Helmut Günther, *Hot Motors, Cold Feet: A Memoir of Service with the Motorcycle Battalion of SS-Division "Reich" 1940–1941* (Winnipeg: J. J. Fedorowicz, 2004), 189.
43. Reese, *Mir selber seltsam fremd*, 63–64.
44. Christian Gerlach, *Kalkulierte Morde. Die deutsche Wirtschafts- und Vernichtungspoltik in Weißrußland 1941 bis 1944* (Hamburg: Hamburger Edition, 1999), 955.
45. Walter Tilemann, *Ich, das Soldatenkind* (Munich: Knaur TB, 2005), 152.
46. Henry Metelmann, *Through Hell for Hitler* (Havertown: Casemate, 2005), 35.
47. H. C. Robbins Landon and Sebastian Leitner, eds., *Diary of a German Soldier* (London: Coward McCann, 1963), 108 (entry for September 26, 1941).
48. Quoted in Felix Römer, *Kameraden. Die Wehrmacht von innen* (Munich: Piper, 2012), 427.
49. Siegfried Knappe with Ted Brusaw, *Soldat: Reflections of a German Soldier, 1936–1949* (New York: Dell Publishing, 1992), 230.
50. Pohl, *Die Herrschaft der Wehrmacht*, 305–319; Gerlach, *Kalkulierte Morde*, 449–501.
51. Nicholas Terry, "'Do not burden one's own army and its hinterland with unneeded mouths!' The Fate of the Soviet Civilian Population Behind the 'Panther Line' in Eastern Belorussia, October 1943–June 1944," in *Kriegführung und Hunger 1939–1945. Zum Verhältnis von militärischen, wirtschaftlichen und politischen Interessen*, ed. Christoph Dieckmann and Babette Quinkert (Göttingen: Wallstein, 2015), 185–209, here 190.
52. Reinhard Otto, Rolf Keller, and Jens Nagel, "Sowjetische Kriegsgefangene in deutschem Gewahrsam 1941–1945. Zahlen und Dimensionen," *Vierteljahrshefte für Zeitgeschichte* 56, no. 4 (October 2008), 557–602, here 562; Pohl, *Die Herrschaft der Wehrmacht*, 212–215.
53. Martin Humburg, *Das Gesicht des Krieges. Feldpostbriefe von Wehrmachtssoldaten aus der Sowjetunion 1941–1944* (Wiesbaden: Westdeutscher Verlag, 1998), 143 (entry for November 22, 1943).
54. Humburg, *Das Gesicht des Krieges*, 165 (entry for November 22, 1941).
55. Laurie R. Cohen, *Smolensk under the Nazis: Everyday life in Occupied Russia* (Rochester, NY: Rochester University Press, 2013), 73.
56. Birgit Beck, "Rape. The Military Trails of Sexual Crimes Committed by Soldiers in the Wehrmacht, 1939–1944," in *Home/Front: The Military, War and Gender in Twentieth-Century Germany*, ed. Karen Hageman and Stefanie Schüler-Springorum (Oxford: Berg, 2002), 267.
57. Norbert Müller, ed., *Okkupation, Raub, Vernichtung. Dokumente zur Besatzungspolitik der faschistischen Wehrmacht auf sowjetischem Territorium 1941 bis 1944* ([East] Berlin: Militärverlag der Deutschen Demokratischen Republik, 1980), 321–322, "Anforderung von 100 000 Arbeitskräften zum Stellungsbau durch das Oberkommando der Heeresgruppe Mitte" (Doc. 133), dated July 8, 1944.
58. On the treatment of Soviet civilians in combat see: Adrian E. Wettstein, "Urban Warfare Doctrine on the Eastern Front," in *Nazi Policy on the Eastern Front, 1941: Total War, Genocide, and Radicalization*, ed. Alex J. Kay, Jeff Rutherford, and David Stahel (Rochester, NY: University of Rochester Press, 2012), 45–72, here 56 and 64.
59. Hannes Heer, "How Amorality Became Normality: Reflections on the Mentality of German Soldiers on the Eastern Front," in *War of Extermination: The German Military in World War II 1941–1944*, ed. Hannes Heer and Klaus Naumann (New York/Oxford: Berghahn Books, 2006), 329–344.
60. All above quotations taken from: Heer, "How Amorality Became Normality," 331–332.
61. Heer, "How Amorality Became Normality," 331–332. See also Klaus Latzel, *Deutsche Soldaten—nationalsozialistischer Kreig? Kriegserlebnis—Kriegserfahrung 1939–1945* (Paderborn: Schöningh, 1996), 315–316.

62. Heer, "How Amorality Became Normality," 332.
63. Lubbeck with Hurt, *At Leningrad's Gates*, 112.
64. Reese, *Mir selber seltsam fremd*, 182: "*Der Panzer der Fühllosigkeit, mit dem ich mich gegen Schrecken, Grauen, Angst und Wahnsinn gewappnet, der mich nicht mehr leiden und aufschreien ließ, erdrückte die zarten Regungen im Innern, knickte die Keime von Hoffnung, Glauben und Menschenliebe und verwandelte das Herz in Stein.*"
65. Thomas Kühne, "Male Bonding and Shame Culture: Hitler's Soldiers and the Moral Basis of Genocidal Warfare," in *Ordinary People as Mass Murderers: Perpetrators in Comparative Perspectives*, ed. Olaf Jensen and Claus-Christian W. Szejnmann (New York: Palgrave Macmillan, 2008), 55–77, here 62; Thomas Kühne, *Belonging and Genocide: Hitler's Community, 1918–1945* (New Haven, CT: Yale University Press, 2010), 29. For similar findings regarding Reserve Police Battalion 101 see Christopher R. Browning, *Ordinary Men: Reserve Police Battalion 101 and the Final Solution in Poland* (London: Penguin Books, 2001 [1992]).
66. Thomas Kühne, "Comradeship: Gender Confusion and Gender Order in the German Military, 1918–1945," in *Home/Front: The Military, War and Gender in Twentieth-Century Germany*, ed. Karen Hagemann and Stefanie Schüler-Springorum (Oxford: Bloomsbury, 2002), 233–254, here 245.
67. Historians Jörg Baberowski and Klaus Jochen Arnold have both presented this as an explanation for German crimes in the east and erroneously suggested that external factors supposedly beyond individual soldiers' control account for the Wehrmacht's war of annihilation. See Jörg Baberowski, "Kriege in staatsfernen Räumen: Rußland und die Sowjetunion 1905–1950," in *Formen des Krieges. Von der Antike bis zur Gegenwart*, ed. Dietrich Beyrau, Michael Hochgeschwender, and Dieter Langewiesche (Paderborn: Schöningh, 2007), 291–309; Klaus Jochen Arnold, *Die Wehrmacht und die Besatzungspolitik in den besetzten Gebieten der Sowjetunion. Kriegführung und Radikalisierung im "Unternehmen Barbarossa"* (Berlin: Duncker & Humblot, 2005). In response to this see Alex J. Kay, "A 'War in a Region beyond State Control'? The German-Soviet War, 1941–1944," *War in History* 18, no. 1 (January 2011): 109–122.
68. Theo J. Schulte, "The German Soldier in Occupied Russia," in *A Time to Kill: The Soldier's Experience of War in the West 1939–1945*, ed. Paul Addison and Angus Calder (London: Pimlico, 1997), 274–283, here 278.
69. Wolfram Wette, *Die Wehrmacht. Feindbilder, Vernichtungskrieg, Legenden* (Frankfurt am Main: S. Fischer, 2002), 158.
70. Stephen G. Fritz, *Frontsoldaten: The German Soldier in World War II* (Lexington: The University Press of Kentucky), 13.
71. Richard Holmes, *Firing Line* (London: Jonathan Cape, 1985), 47.
72. Wette, *Die Wehrmacht*, 158–159.
73. Rutherford, *Combat and Genocide on the Eastern Front*, 7.
74. Hartmann, *Wehrmacht im Ostkrieg*, 661.
75. Gerhard Paul, "Lemberg '41. Bilder der Gewalt—Bilder als Gewalt—Gewalt an Bildern," in *Naziverbrechen. Täter, Taten, Bewältigungsversuche*, ed. Martin Cüppers, Jürgen Matthäus, and Andrej Angrick (Darmstadt: Wissenschaftliche Buchgesellschaft, 2013), 191–212, here 205–208 (quote: 205). See also Petra Bopp, "Images of Violence in Wehrmacht Soldiers' Private Photo Albums," in *Violence and Visibility in Modern History*, ed. Jürgen Martschukat and Silvan Niedermeier (New York: Palgrave Macmillan, 2013), 181–197; Bernd Hüppauf, "Emptying the Gaze: Framing Violence through the Viewfinder," in *War of*

Extermination: The German Military in World War II 1941–1944, ed. Hannes Heer and Klaus Naumann (New York/Oxford: Berghahn Books, 2006), 345–377.

76. Paul, "Lemberg '41," 207.

77. Welzer, *Täter*, 205–206. See also Paul, "Lemberg '41," 205–206, citing the example of sexual voyeurism as a form of approval of what is taking place.

78. See the many personal testimonies in the documentary film directed by Ruth Beckermann, *Jenseits des Krieges* (Austria: Josef Aichholzer Filmproduktion, 1996).

79. Hannes Heer, ed., *Vernichtungskrieg, Verbrechen der Wehrmacht, 1941–1944. Ausstellungskatalog* (Hamburg: Hamburger Edition, 1996). See also the discussion in Michael Verhoeven's documentary film *Der unbekannte Soldat* (Germany: Studiocanal, 2007).

80. Schulte, "The German Soldier in Occupied Russia," 275. On "execution tourism" see also Römer, *Kameraden*, 399–402.

81. As cited in Karel C. Berkhoff, *Motherland in Danger. Soviet Propaganda during World War II* (Cambridge, MA: Harvard University Press, 2012), 123.

82. See Römer, *Kameraden*, 21–25.

83. Römer, *Kameraden*, 41–42.

84. On this see Römer, *Kameraden*, Chapter III, "Ideologie" (60–110), esp. 64, 70, 73–74, and 110.

85. Such a pragmatic rationale is also highlighted in Rutherford, *Combat and Genocide on the Eastern Front*.

86. See Römer, *Kameraden*, Chapter III, "Ideologie" (60–110), esp. 64, 70, 73–74, and 110. See also the discussion of ideological indoctrination in Browning, *Ordinary Men*, 176–184.

87. Sönke Neitzel and Harald Welzer, *Soldaten. Protokolle vom Kämpfen, Töten und Sterben* (Frankfurt am Main: S. Fischer, 2011), esp. 14–15, 17, and 393: *"Diese Soldaten sind keine "Weltanschauungskrieger", sondern meist völlig unpolitisch"* (393).

88. Johannes Hürter, "Vorwort," in Felix Römer, *Kameraden. Die Wehrmacht von innen* (Munich: Piper, 2012), 9–15, here 12–13. See also the points made in MacGregor Knox, Review of Sönke Neitzel and Harald Welzer, *Soldaten. Protokolle vom Kämpfen, Töten und Sterben*, in *sehepunkte. Rezensionsjournal für die Geschichtswissenschaften* 12, no. 3 (March 15, 2012), http://www.sehepunkte.de/2012/03/19936.html (last accessed on May 8, 2017).

89. See Römer, *Kameraden*, 81–82.

90. On this and the following see Walter Manoschek, "'Wo der Partisan ist, ist der Jude, und wo der Jude ist, ist der Partisan.' Die Wehrmacht und die Shoah," in *Täter der Shoah. Fanatische Nationalsozialisten oder ganz normale Deutsche?*, ed. Gerhard Paul (Göttingen: Wallstein, 2002), 167–185, here 177–178. The results of the survey can be found in Josef Schwarz, Christian W. Haerpfer, Peter Malina, and Gustav Spann, "Österreicher im Zweiten Weltkrieg. Bewußtseinsstand von österreichischen Soldaten in der deutschen Wehrmacht 1938–1945" (unpublished final report for the Austrian Federal Ministry of Science and Research, Vienna, 1993).

91. Manoschek, "'Wo der Partisan ist, ist der Jude'," 178.

92. Reese, *Mir selber seltsam fremd*, 242–243: *"Die Juden ermordet, / als brüllende Horde / nach Rußland marschiert, / die Menschen geknebelt, / im Blute gesäbelt, / vom Clowne geführt, / sind wir die Gesandten / des allwärts Bekannten / und waten in Blut. / Wir tragen die Fahnen / der arischen Ahnen: / sie stehen uns gut."*

93. Ibid., 9: *"Ich breche unter dieser Schuld zusammen—und saufe!"*

9 Bodily Conquest: Sexual Violence in the Nazi East

Waitman Wade Beorn

> We sang over claret and liqueurs, vodka, and rum, plunged into intoxication like doomed men, talked drunkenly about sex and science, reeled by the railroad cars, sat outside over campfires, were made ill by the cheap spirits and the sudden rich diet, and carried on anyway, made grotesque speeches about war and peace, grew melancholy, talked about our lovelornness and homesickness, started laughing again, and went on drinking, whooped and skipped over the rails, danced in the cars, and fired into the air, made a Russian woman prisoner dance naked for us, greased her tits with shoe polish, got her as drunk as we were, and sobered up only when we reached Gomel after five days.
>
> —*Wehrmacht* soldier Willi Reese, killed 1944[1]

> [SS Sturmmann] Blum beat and tortured the men who worked in the laundry and killed many with his own hand, likewise the women who he also sexually abused, in spite of the "Nurnberg Laws"; this was generally known by all.
>
> —Zeev Porath, survivor, Janowska Camp, 1960[2]

Introduction

In May 1960, a fifty-one-year-old coal miner, Xavier H., appeared at the court building in Schwabmünchen, Germany. State attorneys deposed the former Army medic regarding the murder of ten thousand Jews in the eastern Polish town of Slonim in 1941, an action in which his Army unit had participated deeply. In the course of questioning, Xavier made the offhand comment that, on the morning of the massacre, he had left the company barracks and entered the Jewish ghetto because he was afraid that his Jewish "girlfriend" Ida had been caught up in the *Aktion*.[3] Prosecutors, clearly not interested in this aspect of his testimony, refocused him on the killing events themselves, leaving us to wonder about this extraordinary statement and the nature of Xavier's relationship with this Jewish woman.

This short vignette is in many ways indicative of the history (or lack thereof) of the sexual nature of Nazi criminality in the context of both the Holocaust and the war, particularly in the east. The story of sexual violence carried out by the Germans and their allies is often, like Xavier's, hinted at and rarely pursued. At a scholarly level, these events have remained obscured or hidden and are only beginning to come to light thanks to the courageous work of a group of historians and scholars, some of whose work will be highlighted in this essay.[4]

Thus, I will attempt to sketch here the varied ways in which Nazi criminality, particularity in the east, delved into the realm of sexual and sexualized violence. Examining Nazi sexual crimes in the east against both Jews and non-Jews reflects a growing trend in Holocaust scholarship, which recognizes the centrality of Eastern Europe as the epicenter of the Nazi genocidal project: the home of the vast majority of its victims, and the site of its most ambitious (and lethal) projects of demographic engineering. This essay adds to this scholarship by examining in some detail the various kinds of nonconsensual sexual interactions that took place on the ground between individuals, for it is only in this way that one can truly begin to understand the complexity of Nazi policy and behavior during the Holocaust.

The forms of sexual abuse endemic to the Nazi east demand some definition. Relying solely on the concept of rape, which is very much conditioned by our contemporary understanding of the term, limits our ability to clearly view the landscape on which sexual exploitation took place. It creates a false dichotomy between consent and nonconsent in an environment in which unfettered consent was impossible, for the perpetrator almost always had complete power and the option to simply murder the victim. In discussing this topic, I will rely on several terms that add nuance to this discussion. First, I will distinguish between sexual violence and sexualized violence. I define sexual violence to mean any nonconsensual interaction that involves an actual sexual act. This is to be meaningfully distinguished from sexualized violence, which may be equally traumatic and brutal without sexual intercourse of any kind but that does have a clearly sexual component. As Brigitte Halbmayr rightfully notes, "The term sexualized violence makes it clear that male violence against females is not about sexuality but is a show of power on the part of the perpetrator and includes many forms of violence with sexual connotations, including humiliation, intimidation, and destruction."[5] Rape itself, then, generally falls under the former category and one could distinguish perhaps between violent physical rape and coerced rape.

I will also use the term "instrumental sex" to distinguish a specific form of behavior from rape, an act in which I consider the victim to be utterly powerless.[6] I must preface this important distinction with the recognition that in almost all instances, the victim was powerless to grant consent; specifically, if they could not refuse consent, then they also could not give consent. However, in what are classic examples of "choiceless choices," some victims may have had the ability to dictate in some way the manner of their own subjugation such that they were able to derive material benefits and, in this manner, survive.[7] The literature on sexual exploitation under slavery can be helpful in this regard. For example, one historian has argued that while "no law or moral scruple prevented white men from forcing themselves on black females ... some women negotiated this predicament by subjecting themselves to patrons, yielding to some white men who could protect them from the rest."[8] Such a description seems equally apt in the context of the Holocaust.

Much of the excellent scholarship on sexual violence during the Holocaust has focused on the experience of Jewish women being raped by men, particularly in camps and ghettos. This was an important part of the Holocaust experience given the special place that Jews held in the Nazi racist worldview. However, to obtain a full picture of sexual violence as a Nazi complex of crimes, we must also explore the rape of non-Jewish women by the Nazis and their auxiliaries.[9] It is likewise essential that sexual and sexualized violence should not be viewed solely in a heteronormative context. Same-sex assaults occurred, although they are far more poorly documented.[10] Taken together, all these permutations represent the Nazi complex of sexual criminality.

Holocaust scholarship has only recently begun to focus more directly on sexual violence for several important reasons. The first is that there is not a large body of survivors who can or will testify to sexual violence during the Holocaust. Many who survived the experience perished in the gas chambers or at a later period. In addition, perpetrators often murdered their victims immediately after the assault to hide the crime itself. Dual survivors of sexual violence and the Holocaust naturally have been reticent to discuss topics that would be considered taboo by most members of their generation. In addition to this general societal silence, many survivors may feel a sense of shame or guilt for their behavior if, for example, they engaged in instrumental sex in an effort to survive. One survivor recalled after the war seeing her fellow Jews question how she survived: "And in their eyes, a glimmer of suspicion: Kapo? Prostitute?"[11] Nechama Tec noted sadly that "judging by the hesitation I encountered among interviewees to recount these coercive sexual experiences, I have to assume that most of these stories will die with the victims."[12] Scholars such as Christopher Browning have also suggested that many survivors carry repressed memories of traumatic events such as rape; this was as much a coping mechanism for survival as an intentional act of forgetting. Even in cases where survivors remember such particularly painful experiences, such memories often remain privately held or only shared among a small survivor community.[13] Only recently has some of this information come to light likely as a combination of scholarly willingness to engage a once taboo topic and aging survivors' willingness to part with some of their most painful memories. As oral historian Michael Nutkiewicz concludes, "there are memories that remain private, iconic incidents during the Holocaust that are banished into the territory of forbidden knowledge."[14] Scholars can assume with a good deal of certainty that the testimonies that exist represent only the tip of the iceberg in a much more widespread phenomenon, as even today rape and sexual assault go substantially unreported.

Likewise, for Germans and other potential perpetrators, few are willing to admit to committing acts of sexual violence or extortion due to similar issues of shame but also to avoid legal troubles if their statements were taken when prosecution was still a possibility. Even after legal punishment for sexual violence was impossible, almost all perpetrators were reluctant to discuss this behavior as they likely recognized it to be degenerate and socially unacceptable in a way that "simply" murdering was not. Much of what we know of sexual violence against Jews and others during the Holocaust comes from survivor testimony itself. Recent discoveries of candid recordings of soldiers and Nazi prisoners after the war have brought to light some of these actions as has, again, a scholarly focus on them.[15] Still, there is much we do not know and scholars are only now beginning to treat this delicate topic with more openness and dedication. Ironically (or perhaps not so ironically) the best-documented and studied example of sexual violence in the east remains the very real mass rape of German women by Soviet soldiers in which Germans are the unquestioned victims.[16]

Sexual Violence and War

All historical evidence suggests that war and sexual violence have been interconnected likely from the earliest days of state-sanctioned violence. Historically, there have been many reasons for this breach of accepted morality; the vulnerability of a defeated people, the lapse in social norms that accompanies sanctioned killing, and the promise of sexual gratification (along with looting) as a reward for military service are all explanations for this phenomenon. As Rhonda Copelon points out: "War tends to intensify the brutality, repetitiveness, public spectacle, and likelihood of rape. War diminishes sensitivity to human suffering and intensifies men's sense of entitlement, superiority, avidity, and social license to rape."[17]

After the modern genocides in the Balkans and in Rwanda, however, sexual violence in the context of war and genocide has taken on a new importance in the realm of international law.[18] In these two instances, international criminal tribunals found rape and sexual violence to be an integral and intentional part of the genocidal and military strategies of the perpetrators. In this way, rape came to be seen in these contexts as a weapon of war rather than simply a criminal consequence so often associated with war itself. In this line of reasoning, the enemy's women become another target for conquest and, in some cases, the means to biologically eradicate the enemy through unwanted pregnancy as a result of rape. In more modern genocides such as those in Rwanda and the Balkans, rape and the resulting pregnancy were often intended by the perpetrators to facilitate ethnic cleansing by forcing the victim to bear a child of the opposing ethnicity.

Such discussions have led scholars to question whether this reasoning applies to the Holocaust. We must then ask two related questions of the evidence. First, how prevalent was sexual violence and, second, was the sexual victimization of civilians, particularly in the east, an intentional weapon of Nazi policy wielded against the local population? There has been recent debate about the frequency of sexual violence, particularly against Jewish women during the Holocaust. Na'ama Shik concisely summarizes the two historiographical approaches to this topic. The first "concludes that there is little evidence of harsh sexual abuse, particularly of incidents of rape, in the various camps. Scholars taking this position argue, correctly, that this is mainly due to strict prohibitions in Nazi ideology, in short, the interdiction against sexual relations, by consent or by force, between members of the 'supreme race' and inferior races [sic], particularly Jews."[19] Auschwitz survivor Kitty Hart went so far as to term "these sexual fantasies of postwar literature and television: 'ridiculous misconceptions'."[20] This position presupposes a strict adherence to lofty Nazi sexual and racial ideals even at the periphery of the Nazi empire. The second approach, Shik continues "has emerged over the last few years and asserts quite an opposing argument: harsh sexual abuse, including many cases of rape, did in fact take place in various Nazi camps."[21] To this, we must also add that sexual and sexualized violence also took place in a variety of other locales such as homes, ghettos, brothels, and so on. The preponderance of the evidence strongly suggests that this second position is closer to the truth, that sexual assault of all kinds was a common occurrence in the east and certainly not limited to exceptional cases.

To the second question of rape as a Nazi weapon of war, there remains a healthy scholarly debate that demands a highly nuanced and precise approach. Elizabeth Wood argues, in general, that "rape is an effective strategy of war" and Regina Mühlhäuser concludes that "far from destabilizing Nazi power or disrupting the pursuit of the war of annihilation, the ambiguities and flexibility of the system served precisely to facilitate its maintenance."[22] Mühlhäuser in particular seems to lean toward the position that the Nazis used rape as a conscious weapon in the war in the east. Yet, it can be difficult to find solid evidence of this from a Nazi policy standpoint. Birgit Beck suggests a middle ground as well as a path to perhaps answering this question of the intentional use of rape by the military (but really this applies to the regime as a whole.) She contends that "in order to find clear proof, it is necessary to examine the question of whether sexual violence was ordered by the military leadership, whether silent toleration constituted giving the soldiers permission to commit such acts, or whether there were any attempts to prevent such crimes by prohibiting and punishing them."[23] In short, we can find no orders or explicit policies directing German soldiers, *Schutzstaffel* (SS) men, and other authorities to utilize sexual violence as a tool of military conquest, though, particularly in the camps, it did become a tool of humiliation, torture, and repression. Indeed, Nazi ideology by definition precluded any possibility of "breeding out" the Jews by its very nature. So, at this moment in the scholarship, we simply cannot prove that the Nazi war machine intentionally sought to coordinate sexual violence into its campaigns of ethnic cleansing and murder.

On the other hand, it seems clear that while the Nazi authorities did not order or openly condone sexual assaults, they did create an environment in which such behavior was ignored and rarely or lightly punished. One can trace the origins of this environment to the racist Nazi image of eastern peoples generally and to the Criminal Orders specifically, which explicitly created a permissive culture in the east that tolerated criminality. The most important of these, the so-called Jurisdiction Decree, clearly stated: "Punishable offenses committed against enemy civilians do not, until further notice, come any more under the jurisdiction of the courts-martial and the summary courts-martial."[24] The only limitation was that any prosecution of crimes was to be considered only if "necessary for the maintenance of discipline or the security of the troops." This decree effectively removed enemy civilians from the protection of military law, giving German soldiers legal impunity in their treatment of civilians. Some effects of this order can be seen in the prevalence of rape and its relatively lenient punishments, which were rarely meted out. Indeed, these punishments, when given, were usually based on damage done to the reputation of the *Wehrmacht* or to discipline and were often weaker than punishments for the same crimes given on the western front.[25] Thus, behavior often punished harshly in Western Europe was almost explicitly condoned in the east.

A final argument made against the widespread nature of sexual assault on the eastern front, in ghettos, and in camps is the Nazi's own obsession with racial purity and the accompanying laws against *Rassenschande*, or race defilement. These laws, dating back to the Nuremberg Laws of 1935, prohibited sexual relationships between Germans and "ethnically inferior peoples," particularly Jews but also Slavs. Nazi ideology and official party propaganda threatened dire consequences for the race and the individual if such activities were to take place. Yet, as more and more historians study the behavior of actual individuals on the ground, we find that *Rassenschande* did not act as a meaningful deterrent to sexual activity, consensual or otherwise. Mühlhäuser has argued that *Wehrmacht* and SS members took the prohibition on sexual relationships "less seriously in the east than within the borders of the Reich."[26] Another scholar has noted that "it is clear that what took place on the ground during the Holocaust did not always match the directed racial policy."[27] On February 25, 1942, eight months after the invasion of the Soviet Union, the Security Service Reichsführer-SS (*Sicherheitsdienst Reichsführer-SS*; SD) noted that Wehrmacht orders "to ban any kind of sexual intercourse with Russian women and girls have up to now been without any noteworthy effect."²⁸ In June 1942, the Army High Command was forced to publish a bulletin reiterating that "sexual relations with Jews violated the racial laws and would lead to judicial penalties."²⁹ At a conference of SS and Police Judges in 1943, one participant estimated that "50 percent of all members of the SS and the police violated the 'ban on undesirable sexual intercourse with ethnically alien women.'"³⁰ Indeed, even those not directly associated with the regime appear to have violated these prohibitions. For example, one survivor of the Janowska camp accused the wife of the German commandant, Fritz Gebauer, of the *Deutsche Ausrüstungswerke*, of having an affair with his Jewish chauffeur while Gebauer himself slept with a Jewish prisoner.³¹ One should not conclude that Nazi racial theory and its prohibitions against miscegenation did not prevent some Germans from engaging in sexual activity with "inferior races." Indeed, knowledge of such behavior could be used as a weapon in larger disputes between German personnel and as a way to settle scores. However, the bulk of the evidence strongly suggests that *Rassenschande* or the threat of punishment for it had very little influence on the decisions of men to rape in towns, ghettos, and camps. On the other hand, *Rassenschande* and the worst-case scenario of a pregnant Jewish victim did likely lead to the increased likelihood of the victim's murder.³²

In short, while Nazi authorities did not actively or explicitly encourage sexual assaults, they did create a permissive environment in the east, which allowed moral transgressions of all kinds from torture to theft, murder, and rape. Combined with more primal associations of the right to conquer women's bodies by soldiers, the setting of the wild east also became an area where sexual crimes could become commonplace. Yet, in attempting to understand how these sexual crimes manifested themselves, we must distinguish between the spaces in which they took place, for these spaces often helped to determine the purpose and kinds of acts that occurred. One can generally divide these eastern spaces into the following: (1) a general category that includes towns and villages, the front, open-air shooting sites and areas in which Jews and non-Jews were relatively free, (2) ghettos, and (3) camps of all kinds, from extermination to factory to labor. These spaces represent areas of increasing control by the Nazis and increasingly circumscribed freedoms of the victims.

The Eastern Territories in General

German men exercised sexual violence not only in the combat zone. Rape was a form of aggression that structured the everyday life of occupation in the military rear.³³

Beginning in 1939, the Nazis became masters of eastern territory that formed a crucial part of their larger fantasies of a German Empire in the east.³⁴ Immediately after the defeat of Poland, they began a program of murder and demographic engineering that would be exported further east in 1941. With the war against the Soviet Union, Hitler took even more drastic actions to realize his dream of a German eastern colony. The Führer himself stated that he would treat the people of the east "like a colonial people."[35] The Nazi desire to subjugate the east was not empty rhetoric but was accompanied by plans for lethal demographic engineering described in the "Hunger Plan" and its subsection, the "Green Folder."[36] The Nazi leadership openly estimated that "without a doubt umpteen millions of people will starve when we extract all our necessities from the land."[37] Some administrators predicted death tolls of up to 30 million.[38] These figures represented non-Jews. The *Einsatzgruppen* began targeting the entire Jewish population of the western Soviet Union by the late summer of 1941.

In this region where human life counted for little, sexual violence and the license to commit it seem to have been widespread. Moreover, given that many men of military age had either been drafted into the Red Army or had fled, the Germans encountered in many places a population that consisted mainly of women, children, and the elderly. During the June–July pogroms in Lvov, instigated by Germans and carried out mostly by Ukrainians, sexual violence seems to have been a major component, as evidenced not least in the shocking photos from the event. The Soviet Union reported as early as January 6, 1942, that "thirty-two workers of the local clothes factory were raped and then killed by the German storm troopers" and that "the drunk German soldiers pulled Lvov girls and young women into Kostiuszko Park and brutally raped them."[39] During these pogroms, Germans also looked on with an approving gaze. A survivor reported the following to the Jewish Historical Institute in Warsaw in 1945: "And while the greedy killers [Ukrainians] took all the clothes of one of the women and were mercilessly beating her naked body with a stick, the German soldiers who were passing by and who we asked to get involved, answered: '*Das ist die Rache der Ukrainer*' (This is the revenge of the Ukrainians), in a tone full of approval of their actions. They were passing by with a look of masters and taking pictures of the naked women who were raped and violently beaten."[40] Here it seems that the Germans openly sanctioned sexual and sexualized violence, which, given their own transgressions, is not surprising.

Accounts of sexual violence by German forces in the east are numerous.[41] A survivor from Novogrudok in Belarus recalled a German doctor passing through who had been a "specialist" in entering (presumably Jewish) homes and raping the women.[42] German sentries in Poland took two Jewish teenagers from their home at gunpoint and raped one of them in the Jewish cemetery.[43] A German soldier in Slonim, Belarus remembered a Nazi functionary who would "pretend to be a friend to the Jews, win their trust and get different information out of them. He would lure young Jewish girls into his apartment where he would prey upon them sadistically. Afterward, any trace of them would disappear behind them."[44]

The connection between sexual violence and murder is also made clear in the east. Quite often Jewish women were raped at the site of mass executions.

Historian Stephen Katz sees in the Final Solution a "license to kill."[45] A witness at the Babi Yar massacre recounted that "[A]t the opposite side of the ravine, seven or so Germans brought two young Jewish women. They went down lower to the ravine, chose an even place and began to rape these women by turns. When they became satisfied, they stabbed the women with daggers, so that they even did not cry out. And they left the bodies like this, naked, with their legs open."[46] Some victims were not killed immediately but kept for a short period of time as sexual slaves, as Father Desbois discovered in his research in Ukraine. One witness told him that "the Germans kept 30 or so very pretty Jewish women that they put to work in the offices of the Gestapo but whom they also used as 'sex objects' for the police and the Germans."[47]

This seemingly common sexual violence against Jews can, perhaps, be described as taking place in the context of the conquest period of the war in the east. It certainly was both a frontline and rear area phenomenon as soldiers and Nazi civilians took what they wanted from a conquered population, caring little for the racial characteristics of their victims, who they would kill anyway. The prevalent use of alcohol at these killing sites also likely contributed to the general depravity of these operations. For other German military personnel, sexual violence and torture became a method for interrogating female prisoners. One female prisoner who was caught in a failed escape attempt was led to the commanding officer "who tortured her with a whip and brutally raped her."[48] Captured female partisans were often forced to strip and then photographed naked by German authorities—a form of sexualized violence in its own right; male partisans did not suffer this.[49]

Another form of more systematic sexual violence was the forced prostitution of eastern women by the Army and the SS. The research on military brothels is growing ever more complete and gives a clear picture of the ways in which most of the women working in them were forced to do so. In Kovno, Lithuania, a female doctor noted in her diary that young women were scared to leave their houses in the evenings for fear of being abducted and forced to work in a brothel. There, she wrote, "women who come down with venereal diseases are not treated but are simply shot; after all, they belong to 'inferior races'—Jews, Poles, and Russians."[50] These military brothels were set up officially by the Army and Armed Forces High Commands (OKH and OKW) ostensibly "in order to ensure military discipline, prevent sexually transmitted diseases, and reduce sexual violence as well as homosexual activity."[51] Scholars estimate that at least 500 of these brothels were set up both in the east and west and that "it is safe to assume from the evidence available that the Germans enslaved at least fifty thousand women into sexual slavery during World War II, but it is likely that the number is far higher."[52]

A third form of sexual violence carried out in the east in general can be termed that of instrumental sex. Here, women, facing the all too common choiceless choices of the Holocaust, sought to gain the means for survival (food, shelter, protection) by offering sex to their victimizers. This, also, appears to have not been an uncommon phenomenon. Soldier Xavier H., mentioned at the beginning, as well as other members of his unit testified that they had kept Jewish women as "girlfriends" during their stay in Slonim.[53] While these relationships seem to have offered protection and survival for a while, the fates of these women rarely differed from others in the area. As Anatoly Podolsky rightly notes, "We can only conjecture that the 'household service' sometimes included sexual slavery, yet almost all of these women were murdered during the second and the third actions of mass executions, which took place during 1942."[54]

One of the most neglected aspects of Nazi sexual criminality in the east is homosexual rape. As homosexual behavior *was* punished with far more frequency than heterosexual rape, those who perpetrated sexual assaults on men were likely to be far more secretive and far more likely to murder their victims to conceal the act. Ironically, we know more about homosexual assaults on and relationships between fellow German soldiers than we do about such assaults on Jews or non-Germans.[55] As one Jewish survivor of homosexual rape noted, "I heard many terrible stories but not like what had happened to me."[56] The Nazi state had many reasons to object to particularly male homosexuality in terms of masculinity and procreation; yet, punishments for homosexual behavior in Nazi organizations, even the SS, often appear quite lenient. Geoffrey Giles has shown both the somewhat surprising frequency of homosexual activity within the SS as well as the judicial results in his work.[57] Given that there certainly were homosexual men serving in the east, we must assume that homosexual assault of the vulnerable population also occurred there, though the evidence is scant. Giles has, however, uncovered at least two instances in court records. In the first, "the twenty-three-year-old Lieutenant Rudolf T., who had forced a fifteen-year-old Russian youth, Alexander L., to perform oral sex on him in a farm building, was subjected to a court martial at the front, and sent to prison for nine months."[58] In another, a German soldier had "slept almost daily under a blanket with the sixteen-year-old Russian kitchen help, Baraschkow, causing him to ejaculate on at least three occasions."[59] Thus, we must add homosexual violence to the pantheon of Nazi crimes in the east, but far more research is needed on this subject for a variety of reasons. In these situations, more than perhaps any other, the victim was likely to be murdered as a matter of course by the perpetrator in an attempt to cover up the crime itself, for homosexual behavior was *not* tacitly accepted by Nazi authorities in the way that heterosexual violence was. Moreover, we face the same dilemma with victims of homosexual violence as we do with the others. Male victims, even more than women, would be far less likely to either report these attacks at the time or to discuss them in any form of postwar testimony.

The east, a larger space consisting of villages, cities, and the front with little oversight, was characterized by a proliferation of sexual crimes, many of which fell within the realm of military occupation and behavior. Also, from an historical standpoint, many of these crimes may be lost to history when they occurred out of the sight of witnesses and/or in the context of mass shootings where the victims of rape were also murdered. However, as ghettoization policy followed the *Wehrmacht* into the east, it created a new space for victimization, this time primarily a space of Jewish suffering but also one which impacted the nature of the assaults that took place.

In the Ghettos

As Nazi control over Eastern Europe was solidified, so too was the system of ghettos designed to confine Jews while their final fate was debated. The move toward ghettoization further isolated the Jewish population and placed them in an increasingly vulnerable position vis-à-vis sexual assault. First, Germans were free to enter the ghetto and attack the inhabitants. One of the more infamous of these rapists was Hans Biebow, administrator of the Lodz ghetto who frequently assaulted women and, in one instance, had the victim's family deported, presumably to cover up his crime or as a further demonstration of his power.[60] This phenomenon of the ghetto as the scene of sexual violence appears in both large ghettos and the very small. In the Piortkow Tribunalski ghetto, the Nazi mayor demanded that the *Judenrat* (Jewish Council) supply him with women for his sexual needs.[61]

The captive existence of ghetto Jews made the forced abduction of Jewish women yet another sexual threat and an agonizing choice for the councils. The German mayor or *Oberbürgermeister* Hans Drexel appeared at a Jewish Council meeting in the Polish town of Piotrkow Tybunalski in 1940. It was Rosh Hashanah. He demanded that the council supply what he referred to as "hostesses." When he was rebuffed, Drexel left with some ominous words of advice for the *Judenrat*: "'You Jews had better realize what's good for you. After all, we're here to stay and you must serve our needs.'"[62] Clearly this man and many others viewed the ghettos as a ready supply of young women for sexual exploitation.

While there do not seem to have been brothels located within ghettos, some survivor testimony suggests that women were taken from ghettos to serve in German brothels. Girls were taken from the Tulchin ghetto to serve as sex slaves for Italian and Hungarian divisions stationed 15 km away.[63] In another similar example, "German gendarmes in Grabowiec, Poland ... were supplied by the *Judenrat* with housekeepers, cooks and servants who had to be young and attractive women. They were treated like slaves. Rape by two or three men was the order of the day."[64]

The ghettos also served as the scene for what seem to be relatively frequent incursions by SS, military, and civilian officials (usually under the influence of alcohol) bent on the violent rape of any young women present. A rabbi from Pinsk remembered that three policemen broke into an apartment and raped the daughter of the family living there. When they were finished, they threatened the family that if they told anyone, the police would return in the morning and kill them all.[65] As elsewhere, these assaults were not always heterosexual. A sixteen-year-old German Jewish boy deported to the Riga ghetto recalled being pulled from his home and raped by two SS men. Different SS men thereafter repeatedly raped him.[66]

The imprisoned population in Jewish ghettos faced increasingly dire circumstances that often coerced women into sexual exploitation. These overcrowded living spaces lacked sufficient food, sanitation, and medical supplies. In order to procure the basic necessities needed for survival, some women found themselves in the impossible situation of offering sexual favors to their captors in return for life. In some instances, this would have been food, but in others it often meant a valid work permit indicating that a critical German firm employed the holder and protecting them from ever more frequent deportations to extermination centers. In the Lviv ghetto, we have what appears to be an instance of a Jewish woman becoming the mistress of the German head of the *Arbeitsamt*, Heinz Weber.[67] Some evidence suggests that she then abused her own position of power with regard to her fellow ghetto inhabitants seeking permits. The burden of instrumental sex for work cards fell almost exclusively on women as men were more likely to be forced to pay bribes in cash or valuables.

With a confined population and an often bored and cruel German administration, sexualized violence seems to have been more prevalent. Regina Mühlhäuser notes that supervisors of ghettos or work columns would often force women to swim, dance, sing, or play sports naked.[68] In another instance, survivors testified that Jewish women were forced to undergo "gynecological examinations" as part of the search for valuables.[69] This sexualized violence seems aimed at humiliating the female inhabitants of the ghetto in particularly sexual ways. Many survivor testimonies speak of women afraid to leave their houses for fear of being accosted on the street by Germans or their non-German allies and sexually assaulted.

The ghettoization of Eastern European Jews created a captive population from which the Nazi authorities and their collaborators could choose victims. Jews were now physically confined within a geographic space where their movement and behavior was circumscribed. As such, they often provided a pool of victims for sexually criminal practices that had already begun prior to ghettoization, such as sexual slave labor. Conversely, it also allowed for more survivor witnesses of these events while limiting access to a smaller cross-section of the Nazi apparatus. One can, then, perhaps view the camps system as the final step in both confinement and sexual victimization.

In the Camps

A multitude of camps grew in the Nazi east, from extermination centers like Auschwitz to factory camps like those in Starachowice. These locations also became sites for both sexual and sexualized violence. Of course, there were important quantitative and qualitative differences between the dizzying varieties of forms that camps took. However, some generalizations can be made with regard to sexual and sexualized violence. In the camps, women (and boys) were also vulnerable to other prisoners. This is not the subject of this chapter, but has become an additional sexual threat to be recognized within the camp system.[70] The camps were the most constrained of the settings discussed here, places where victims' attempts to hide or avoid targeting were the most circumscribed. They were at the mercy of the guard force and camp administration in ways not experienced before. In many camps, attacks on women seem to have been commonplace and not condemned.

Survivor Felicja Karay describes in detail some of the sexual violence that took place in the Skarzysko-Kamienna labor camp. She characterized the camp as a place where "the 'rites of manhood' were expressed in orgies of drunkenness and gang rapes of Jewish girls."[71] As happened often in the east, many of these girls were murdered afterward. Indeed, in the intimate space of the camp, sexual transgressions like those of a German SS man raping a Jewish woman could not be secret and therefore necessitated the elimination of the victim. In the Janowska camp outside of Lvov, survivor Leon Wells recalled a blond Jewish woman named Hilda who "was known to have affairs with SS men." He went on to note that "Hilda has something on them and because of it she must be silenced." She was murdered shortly thereafter.[72] Wells also wrote of a party in the camp where the SS had brought (presumably Jewish) girls. "In the morning," he remembered, "to rid themselves of any witnesses, the SS men brought them to the 'sands' [the execution site at Janowska]."[73] Even at Auschwitz, the centerpiece model of the Nazi camp universe, some SS men raped Jewish inmates. Na'ama Shik relates the story of one survivor who recalled: "And all of a sudden, the door opened and three Nazis came and they dragged us on the floor, they violated us, sexually violated us. They smelled like beer, you know. They raped us."[74] It is important to remember that not all of this sexual violence was heterosexual, though, as we have seen, the evidence of homosexual assaults is *very* sparse. Perhaps the most famous example is Irma Grese, a female guard at a variety of camps including Auschwitz, who was bisexual and allegedly took sexual pleasure from her abuse of prisoners.[75] However, other cases of homosexual victimization likely occurred. An anonymous memoirist survivor recalled a "[camp] commander was panting with excitement, and masturbated wildly in his trousers until he came" as he ordered a guard to whip a homosexual prisoner.[76] Certainly, these and other instances of homosexual exploitation occurred and remain mostly absent from the historical record.

A phenomenon that appears to have been more widespread in the camp system than elsewhere was that of public rape. An Auschwitz survivor recalled a "show" in which the Germans raped twenty Jewish women prisoners in public and ordered the men to applaud. A German administrator in the Starachowice factory publicly raped a young woman. Christopher Browning characterizes this rape as "a ritual of humiliation aimed at degrading the entire camp population, which was forced to stand by and witness helplessly."[77] This form of sexual violence is an indication of the level of impunity with which the SS and Nazi officials were able to operate within the closed camp setting, an impunity that exceeded that of the ghettos and certainly of the eastern landscape in general. These public displays also demonstrated the complete power of the SS over the prisoners under their control and sometimes was expressed in proxy via sexualized violence. Samuel Drix, a survivor from the Janowska camp, recalls the SS forcing a married couple to have sex while the "the SS men were beside themselves with laughter. Fantastic fun." He continued, "for some moments they enjoyed this funny view. Finally, the game became boring for them, and with shots in the necks of both spouses the entertainment was finished."[78] In the Skaryosko-Kamienna camp, a prisoner couple caught having sex in secret was forced to "perform" again in front of the entire camp.[79] Beyond the sadistic nature of this humiliation, one could perhaps see here the SS choosing this form of torture because they could not carry out the rapes themselves, at least not in a public arena. These public sexual violations served the purpose of both humiliation and physical abuse while reinforcing the god-like power of the camp authorities. As Stephen Katz rightly concludes, "the rape of Jewish girls and women was perceived, within the totality of the Shoah, not only as a discrete, individual, localized sexual performance, but as an assault on the collective body, the communal being, of the Jewish People."[80] Moreover, in the hidden world of the camp, where most of the prisoners were never expected to leave, such performances seem to have been more common than elsewhere.

As in the other spaces already discussed, brothels also appeared in the camp settings. Current research indicates that the most official of these brothels were established in camps within Germany, though Auschwitz established two in 1943. As in other places, selection was mostly forced and at best coerced. As Robert Sommer notes, "during roll calls, SS officers would walk down the columns of the lined-up prisoners and pick out women they found 'suitable' for a brothel Kommando." Contrary to some popular belief, these brothels were intended to be used by privileged, non-Jewish prisoners, though there is at least circumstantial evidence that occasionally Germans and their non-German collaborators partook. Typically, non-Jews were forced into this sexual slavery and their "clients" tended to be mostly non-Jews. It is also likely that more informal such arrangements existed in other smaller camps in the east (and included Jews). Regardless, the camp brothels constituted another form of sexual assault on the subjected people of the east. And while the sexual acts concerned most often occurred between non-Germans and non-Jewish prisoners, SS men did take advantage of the camp brothel system to further humiliate and antagonize their victims. As Sommer notes,

> Not only was control one of the SS men's preferred expressions of power, but they never missed an opportunity to humiliate the prisoners in the *Sonderbau*. Voyeurism especially seems to have been one of the favourite games of the camp officers. A survivor of Auschwitz-Monowitz, Hermann Leonhardt, who was the block elder of the camp infirmary, stated that at the opening of the Monowitz *Sonderbau* at the end of October 1943, he saw how a group of SS officers appeared in the barrack to watch what was happening inside the single brothel rooms. It was obvious to Leonhardt that they were enjoying it because they continuously made dirty comments.[81]

These brothels were sometimes used as a way to "correct" homosexuals. This kind of behavior follows a general pattern in which Nazi officials degraded and terrorized their victims in sexual ways. A homosexual survivor recalled being forced to visit the camp brothel as part of his "rehabilitation."[82] This, of course, was also a form of sexual humiliation specific to homosexuals who already were singled out for additional abuse in the camps.

Sexualized violence, that is violence of a sexual nature that did not include actual sexual relations, also appears to have been endemic to the camp experience. Camp authorities at all levels and in all categories of camps often consciously or unconsciously gravitated toward forms of sexualized violence as a further tactic to abuse the prisoners. The most obvious form of this was the enforced nudity, both for those selected for death and for forced labor. The shaving of all body hair including pubic hair was a humiliating event remembered by many new arrivals in the camps and can certainly be seen as a form of sexual humiliation, particularly for female prisoners. Many survivors speak of being leered at by German personnel (and male prisoners) as well having to endure sexual comments. Often, this sexual humiliation turned violent. As Mühlhäuser notes, "the practice of beating women on the breasts and genital area seems to have been used more often as a form of intimidation or torture."[83] For men, too, the genitals were a frequent target of abuse. In the Janowska camp, this physical abuse turned fatal. One guard, Friedrich Heinen, forced two attractive female Jewish prisoners to undress and then shot one of them in the vagina. After watching her writhe in pain for a bit, he then shot her in the mouth. Heinen then shot the other woman and left the bodies lying there.[84] There could be multiple explanations for such a brutal and sadistic display, but clearly it was intended as an act of sexualized violence. This is but one of many examples in the literature of specifically sexualized assault and perhaps is a performance of the ultimate in sexual degradation or an expression of frustration that these women were unavailable as sexual "partners." Here might be a case where Nazi prohibitions against sexual contact with Jews impacted the attitude of the guards, particularly in an environment where such taboo activities would be more difficult to conceal.

Camps seem to be a space where sadism, boredom, and absolute control combined to create an environment in which all kinds of sexual and sexualized violence could escalate. As the purpose of confinement changed from simple concentration to forced labor to places where death was a welcome if not desired outcome, it seems that sexual assaults and violence increased in magnitude and perhaps frequency. In addition, the camp environment, controlled as it was primarily by the SS establishment, paradoxically offered both total control over prisoners and a high degree of surveillance even over those same SS men. This may account for the argument that some of the sexualized violence resulted from a frustration on the part of guards at not being able to fully exploit their victims without exposing themselves to self-serving condemnation from their peers. On the other hand, in some camps, sexual violence including intercourse seems to have been a phenomenon that was tacitly approved by the authorities concerned.

Questions and Conclusions

As this relatively short chapter has attempted to show, the issue of Nazi criminality in the form of sexual and sexualized violence in the east remains a complex topic that demands nuanced and in-depth research. We have seen that, from the outset, the very historical source material necessary for such a study is sparse or underexplored. In addition, homosexual violence and sexual violence against children is almost completely absent from the literature, particularly when we are looking at Germans committing these acts against non-Germans.[85] It is vital to recognize that sexual violence was not solely the result of heterosexual encounters but also likely encompassed other forms that are even more difficult to uncover based on the dearth of sources, as has been discussed above. In addition, more work must be done on non-German sexual criminals who were allies of the Nazi state. Finally, while we are beginning to better understand the frequency and circumstances of German/Nazi sexual violence, it remains difficult to parse out potential motivations for this behavior by the perpetrators based primarily on their own reluctance to admit to let alone explain these actions. This is also true of responses and resistance by victims and potential victims. Yet, it seems that we *can* draw some important preliminary conclusions about the nature of these phenomena.

First, we must conclude that the sexual and sexualized abuse of both Jewish and non-Jewish inhabitants of the east was far more widespread than previously imagined. The (relatively) numerous accounts of these atrocities suggest the tip of an historical iceberg remaining to be uncovered. Second, it seems relatively clear that the Nazis did not use sexual violence, in particular rape, officially or consciously as a weapon of war in the manner seen in more recent genocides in the Balkans and Rwanda. This does not negate what appears to have been a Nazi culture that accepted and even condoned such behavior; it is merely to recognize that we have yet to find the kinds of orders and policies that would support such a conclusion. Third, evidence from survivors and German sources themselves indicates that the ideologically strict prohibitions against sexual interaction with "inferior" races (*Rassenschande*), particularly with Jews, may have figured prominently in Nazi propaganda but had little effect on the actual behavior of individuals on the ground in the world of sexual interaction. Such a conclusion importantly demonstrates the not uncommon disconnect between ideology and human behavior on the ground. Finally, I have sought to suggest a new perspective from which to analyze sexual violence against subject peoples in the east. I examine this deviant behavior in the context of the physical spaces in which it occurred and ask how these spaces themselves mediated the frequency, nature, and motivation for sexual assault in the Nazi east. Such a methodology draws heavily on some of the newest analytical approaches that seek to incorporate geographical theory and approaches in our study of the Holocaust.[86]

The study of sexual violence during the Holocaust adds a vital component to our understanding of this event, particularly because it was never an explicit dictate of the Nazi regime itself in the way that the physical extermination of Jews and other "inferior" races was. Therefore, from the outset, sexual assault and exploitation was a voluntary act. Exploring this choice by perpetrators, then, is an important step in understanding the sexual violence that continues to this day in the context of war and genocide.

WAITMAN WADE BEORN is Lecturer in the Corcoran Department of History at the University of Virginia. He is the author of *Marching into Darkness: The Wehrmacht and the Holocaust in Belarus*, which received the Thomas J. Wilson Memorial Prize from Harvard Press and the Honorable Mention for the Sybil Milton Prize from the German Studies Association. His second book, *The Holocaust in Eastern Europe: At the Epicentre of the Final Solution*, was published by Bloomsbury Press in 2018.

Notes

1. Willy Peter Reese and Stefan Schmitz, *A Stranger to Myself: The Inhumanity of War: Russia, 1941–1944*, trans. Michael Hoffmann (New York: Farrar, Straus and Giroux, 2005), 149.
2. Porath Letter, November 30, 1960, (StAL: EL 317 III, Bü 1505), fol. 505.
3. H., Xavier Statement, May 30, 1960 (BA-ZS: B162/5102), fol. 194. It should be noted here and throughout that while the term *Freundin* in German can mean both female friend and

girlfriend, in almost all cases we should assume that the relationship was at a minimum less than consensual unless facts show otherwise.

4. See Jeffrey Burds, "Sexual Violence in Europe in World War II, 1939–1945," *Politics & Society* 37, no. 1 (2009): 35–73; David Raub Snyder, *Sex Crimes under the Wehrmacht* (Lincoln: University of Nebraska Press, 2007), 200; Regina Mühlhäuser, "Rasse, Blut und Männlichkeit: Politiken sexueller Regulierung in den besetzten Gebieten der Sowjetunion (1941–1945)," *Feministische Studien* 25, no. 1 (2007): 55–69; Regina Mühlhäuser, *Eroberungen: sexuelle Gewalttaten und intime Beziehungen deutscher Soldaten in der Sowjetunion 1941–1945* (Hamburg: Hamburger Edition, 2010); Sonja M. Hedgepeth and Rochelle G. Saidel, eds., *Sexual Violence against Jewish Women During the Holocaust* (Waltham, MA: Brandeis University Press, 2010); Anatoly Podolsky, "The Tragic Fate of Ukrainian Jewish Women under Nazi Occupation, 1941–1944," in *Sexual Violence against Jewish Women During the Holocaust*, ed. Sonja M. Hedgepeth and Rochelle G. Saidel (Waltham, MA: Brandeis University Press, 2010), 94–107; Anna Hájková, "Sexual Barter in Times of Genocide: Negotiating the Sexual Economy of the Theresienstadt Ghetto," *Signs* 38, no. 3 (2013): 503–533.

5. Brigitte Halbmayr, "Sexualized Violence against Women During Nazi 'Racial' Persecution," in *Sexual Violence against Jewish Women During the Holocaust*, ed. Sonja M. Hedgepeth and Rochelle G. Saidel (Waltham, MA: Brandeis University Press, 2010), 30.

6. Historian Anna Hájková has called this instead "sex for barter." I choose the term "instrumental sex" here as I believe that barter indicates too much parity between victim and victimizer.

7. For the term "choiceless choices," see Lawrence L. Langer, *Versions of Survival: The Holocaust and the Human Spirit* (Albany: State University of New York Press, 1982).

8. Vincent Brown, *The Reaper's Garden: Death and Power in the World of Atlantic Slavery* (Cambridge, MA: Harvard University Press, 2008), 107.

9. More recently, some scholars have also begun to examine the rape of Jews by other Jews but, as this chapter is aimed at illuminating Nazi crimes, those experiences will not be explored here.

10. At the moment, historian Geoffrey Giles seems to be the only one who touches on the homosexual rape of non-Germans in the east.

11. Na'ama Shik, "Sexual Abuse of Jewish Women in Auschwitz-Birkenau," in *Brutality and Desire: War and Sexuality in Europe's Twentieth Century*, ed. Dagmar Herzog (New York: Palgrave Macmillan, 2009), 238.

12. Helene Sinnreich, "The Rape of Jewish Women During the Holocaust," in *Sexual Violence against Jewish Women During the Holocaust*, ed. Sonja M. Hedgepeth and Rochelle G. Saidel (Waltham, MA: Brandeis University Press, 2010), 108.

13. See Christopher R. Browning, *Remembering Survival: Inside a Nazi Slave-Labor Camp* (New York: W.W. Norton & Company, 2010), 9–11.

14. Michael Nutkiewicz, "Shame, Guilt, and Anguish in Holocaust Survivor Testimony," *The Oral History Review* 30, no. 1 (2003): 21.

15. For recent discoveries of secret recordings of German soldiers, see Sönke Neitzel and Harald Welzer, *Soldaten: The Secret World of Transcripts of German Pows*, trans. Jefferson Chase (New York: Alfred A. Knopf, 2012); Felix Römer, *Kameraden: Die Wehrmacht von innen* (Munich: Piper, 2012).

16. See Helke Sander and Barbara Johr, eds., *Befreier und Befreite: Krieg, Vergewaltigungen, Kinder* (Munich: A. Kunstmann, 1992); Andrea Peto, "Stimmen

des Schweigens. Erinnerungen an Vergewaltigungen in den Hauptstädten des 'ersten Opfers' (Wien) und des 'letzten Verbundeten' Hitlers (Budapest) 1945," *Zeitschrift für Geschichtswissenschaft* 47 (1999).

17. Anne Llewellyn Barstow, *War's Dirty Secret: Rape, Prostitution, and Other Crimes against Women* (Cleveland, OH: Pilgrim, 2000), 8.

18. See "Security Council Resolution 1820 (2008)" (New York: United Nations Security Council, June 19, 2008).

19. Shik, "Sexual Abuse of Jewish Women in Auschwitz-Birkenau," 225.

20. Shik, "Sexual Abuse of Jewish Women in Auschwitz-Birkenau," 225.

21. Shik, "Sexual Abuse of Jewish Women in Auschwitz-Birkenau," 226.

22. Regina Mühlhäuser, "Between 'Racial Awareness' and Fantasies of Potency: Nazi Sexual Politics in the Occupied Territories of the Soviet Union, 1942–1945," in *Brutality and Desire: War and Sexuality in Europe's Twentieth Century*, ed. Dagmar Herzog (New York: Palgrave Macmillan, 2009), 197–220, here 213; Elisabeth Jean Wood, "Armed Groups and Sexual Violence: When Is Wartime Rape Rare?," *Politics & Society* 37, no. 1 (2009): 132.

23. Birgit Beck, "Rape: The Military Trials of Sexual Crimes Committed by Soldiers in the Wehrmacht, 1939–1944," in *Home/Front: The Military, War, and Gender in Twentieth-Century Germany*, ed. Karen Hagemann and Stefanie Schüler-Springorum (Oxford: Berg, 2002), 255–273, here 255.

24. "Decree for the Conduct of Courts-Martial in the District 'Barbarossa' and for Special Measures for the Troops, May 13, 1941" (Nazi Conspiracy and Aggression, Washington, DC, US G.P.O., vol. III, 1946: Document 886-PS).

25. Beck, "Rape: The Military Trials of Sexual Crimes Committed by Soldiers in the Wehrmacht, 1939–1944," 268. In this, Beck differs greatly with David Snyder, who claims that sentencing was not significantly less strict in the east than the west and did not encourage criminal behavior. Snyder, unfortunately, is working with an extremely limited data set, which, along with the obviously large number of unreported assaults, makes Beck's position more compelling. For more see, Birgit Beck, *Wehrmacht und sexuelle Gewalt: Sexualverbrechen vor deutschen Militärgerichten 1939–1945* (Paderborn: Schöningh, 2004); Snyder, *Sex Crimes under the Wehrmacht*.

26. Mühlhäuser, *Eroberungen*, 88.

27. Sinnreich, "The Rape of Jewish Women During the Holocaust," 109.

28. Mühlhäuser, "Between 'Racial Awareness' and Fantasies of Potency," 198.

29. Mühlhäuser, *Eroberungen*, 125–126.

30. Mühlhäuser, "Between 'Racial Awareness' and Fantasies of Potency," 88.

31. Leon Weliczker Wells, *The Janowska Road* (New York: MacMillan Company, 1963), 88.

32. See Steven T. Katz, "Thoughts on the Intersection of Rape and *Rassenschande* during the Holocaust," *Modern Judaism* 32, no. 3 (2012): 293–322, here 303.

33. Mühlhäuser, "Between 'Racial Awareness' and Fantasies of Potency," 201.

34. For more on Nazi fantasies of and plans for the East see Michael Burleigh, *Germany Turns Eastwards: A Study of Ostforschung in the Third Reich* (Cambridge: Cambridge University Press, 1988).

35. David Olusoga and Casper W. Erichsen, *The Kaiser's Holocaust: Germany's Forgotten Genocide and the Colonial Roots of Nazism* (London: Faber and Faber, 2010), 13.

36. See Alex J. Kay, "'The Purpose of the Russian Campaign Is the Decimation of the Slavic Population by Thirty Million': The Radicalization of German Food Policy in Early 1941," in *Nazi*

Policy on the Eastern Front, 1941: Total War, Genocide, and Radicalization, ed. Alex J. Kay, Jeff Rutherford, and David Stahel (Rochester, NY: University of Rochester Press, 2012), 101–129; Alex J. Kay, *Exploitation, Resettlement, Mass Murder: Political and Economic Planning for German Occupation Policy in the Soviet Union, 1940–1941* (New York/Oxford: Berghahn Books, 2006).

37. Christian Gerlach, *Kalkulierte Morde: die deutsche Wirtschafts- und Vernichtungspolitik in Weissrussland 1941 bis 1944* (Hamburg: Hamburger Edition, 1999), 66.

38. Dieter Pohl, *Die Herrschaft der Wehrmacht: Deutsche Militärbesatzung und einheimische Bevölkerung in der Sowjetunion 1941–1944* (Munich: Oldenbourg, 2008), 66.

39. A. F. Vysotsky et al., eds., *Nazi Crimes in Ukraine, 1941–1944: Documents and Materials* (Kiev: Naukova Dumka Publishers, 1987), 33–34.

40. Podolsky, "The Tragic Fate," 102.

41. Survivor and perpetrator testimony as well as the fragmentary court records of those few prosecuted make this clear.

42. "Kagan, Jack Interview, July 4, 2009" (Author's Personal Archive).

43. Helene Sinnreich, "'And It Was Something We Didn't Talk About': Rape of Jewish Women During the Holocaust," *Holocaust Studies: A Journal of Culture and History* 14, no. 2 (2008): 8.

44. "H., Johann Statement, October 13, 1965," (BA-ZS: B162/5092), fol. 5663.

45. Katz, "Thoughts," 311.

46. Podolsky, "The Tragic Fate," 99.

47. Patrick Desbois, *The Holocaust by Bullets: A Priest's Journey to Uncover the Truth Behind the Murder of 1.5 Million Jews* (New York: Palgrave Macmillan, 2008), 167.

48. Mühlhäuser, "Between 'Racial Awareness' and Fantasies of Potency."

49. Mühlhäuser, *Eroberungen*, 119.

50. Wendy Jo Gertjejanssen, "Victims, Heroes, Survivors: Sexual Violence on the Eastern Front during World War II" (Doctoral Thesis, University of Minnesota, 2004), 213.

51. Mühlhäuser, "Between 'Racial Awareness' and Fantasies of Potency," 207.

52. Beck, "Rape: The Military Trials of Sexual Crimes Committed by Soldiers in the Wehrmacht, 1939–1944"; Gertjejanssen, "Victims, Heroes, Survivors."

53. For more see Waitman Wade Beorn, *Marching into Darkness: The Wehrmacht and the Holocaust in Belarus* (Cambridge, MA: Harvard University Press, 2014), chapter 6.

54. Podolsky, "The Tragic Fate," 99.

55. Judicial records, while fragmentary, are available but focus almost exclusively on relationships between and assaults on German soldiers, not any potential assaults on subject populations. Records for homosexual violence against other groups, including Jews, appear to be almost nonexistent.

56. Nutkiewicz, "Shame, Guilt, and Anguish in Holocaust Survivor Testimony," 6.

57. See Geoffrey J. Giles, "The Denial of Homosexuality: Same-Sex Incidents in Himmler's SS and Police," in *Sexuality and German Fascism*, ed. Dagmar Herzog (New York: Berghahn Books, 2005), 256–290.

58. Geoffrey J. Giles, unpublished manuscript.

59. Geoffrey J. Giles, "Good Comrades or Gay Degenerates? Homosexual Offenses in Military Courts During the Third Reich," in *German Studies Association Annual Conference* (Denver, Colorado, 2013).

60. Sinnreich, "'And It Was Something We Didn't Talk About': Rape of Jewish Women During the Holocaust," 8.

Part V. Memorialization

10 The Holocaust in the Occupied USSR and Its Memorialization in Contemporary Russia

Il'ya Al'tman

In the west, the subject of the Holocaust is shaped by a collective memory of World War II and an aversion to violence and intolerance. In Russia, by contrast, it is the memory of heroism and victimization in the war that shapes views of the Holocaust. One cannot deny that the Russian population is very well aware of the war between Nazi Germany and the Soviet Union, which is called the Great Patriotic War in Russia. Indeed, the victory over Nazi Germany is much propagandized in Russia. Huge placards hang on the walls of houses, war monuments adorn—or disfigure—many Russian cities, newspapers report, and people discuss the events and personalities of the Great Patriotic War.

But this memory culture of World War II is rather superficial because it leaves out one essential aspect that is intrinsically linked with the war: the Holocaust. As a result, the collective memory of Jewish victims is presented in Russia in a rather fragmented manner. There are both objective and subjective reasons for this. In the occupied Soviet territories, more than seven million civilians were killed by the Nazis and their collaborators.[1] Another 20 million died in battles and on the home front, during the occupation and in the siege of Leningrad. The majority of them were non-Jews.

The subject of the Holocaust is still painful in Russia, as in other post-Soviet states. There are several reasons for this. In contrast to Germany and many countries occupied by the Germans, here Jews were killed in the open, and millions of people witnessed it. Local collaborators were actively involved in persecuting and murdering Jews. The property of Jews was given to their neighbors. Nevertheless, with a minor exception, Soviet propaganda, history, and literature stubbornly defended the position that all Soviet people, and above all Slavs, were equally victimized by the Nazis. As Prof. Zvi Gitelman has noted, what was denied in the USSR was not that the Holocaust was an historical fact, but that it was exceptional.[2] This approach is shared by many in Russia today.

Only in recent years has Russian society begun to understand the Holocaust. This long, complicated process can be explained in several ways. First, during the war, Soviet propaganda emphasized that the Nazis targeted Slavic peoples. This pragmatic approach by the Kremlin ensured enthusiasm and self-sacrifice on the part of those who were fighting against Germany. Second, antisemitism was state ideology from the late 1940s until the beginning of Mikhail Gorbachev's perestroika. The suffering of Jewish victims did not fit with the ideology of a struggle against world Zionism. Third, there were few studies on the fate of Soviet people living in the occupied territories or on collaboration. Writing on the occupation was subject to particularly rigid censorship.

The fate of the *Black Book* is characteristic for this silencing of the Holocaust. This is a collection of essays and documents on the destruction of the Soviet Jews by the Nazis and their collaborators, which was prepared under this name in the years 1943–1947 in the USSR and the United States. The preparation of the book in the USSR was conducted by the Jewish Antifascist Committee, and the Literary Commission was headed first by Il'ya Ehrenburg, and then by Vasily Grossman. The idea of publishing the *Black Book* belonged to the outstanding scientist Albert Einstein and the American Committee of Jewish Writers, Scholars, and Artists. The *Black Book* is the first joint Soviet-American historical documentary project, but its origins have not yet been sufficiently uncovered. It addressed the entire occupied territory of the USSR and included various aspects of the Holocaust: destruction, salvation, spiritual and physical resistance. In the foreword of Vasily Grossman, written in 1946, a general picture of the Holocaust in the USSR was given and its scale was indicated, perhaps for the first time. The book was prepared on a strictly documentary basis, using the numerous collected sources. In the first edition, any mention of collaborators was cut out, and in the penultimate version, everything that pertained to Jewish self-consciousness was excluded. This volume was presented at the Nuremberg trials but in 1947, its publication was forbidden in the Soviet Union. Later, the initiative and involvement in creating this book figured in the 1952 indictment of the Jewish Anti-Fascist Committee.

These documents have since appeared in several publications. In 1993, the first complete edition of the *Black Book* was prepared by Il'ya Al'tman. It included almost sixty pages that the book's editors had expunged from the 1945–1947 manuscript.[3] Also in 1993, the Moscow publishing house Text issued a collection of documents entitled *The Unknown Black Book*.[4] It included material that the editors of the *Black Book* had rejected for fear of the censors. In 2008, this volume was published in English by the US Holocaust Memorial Museum.[5] In 2014–2015 the Moscow publishing house Corpus issued a revised text of these publications with our detailed comments.[6] The publication was financed by crowdfunding, collected in the internet on the initiative of the publishing house. Around 500 notes were written for the new editions of the *Black Book* and the

Unknown Black Book, many of them biographical. Unlike previous editions, this book appeared in bookshops in all major Russian cities from Arkhangelsk to Vladivostok. This publication caused a public response in the form of reviews, radio programs, and interviews. Several presentations took place both in Russia and in other countries.

At the beginning of the 1990s the renowned American Holocaust historian Raul Hilberg noted that the opening of previously unknown Soviet archives would influence Holocaust research. Symptomatically, his last book was devoted to sources available for use in Holocaust research.[7] Among the important collections of archival documents from former Soviet archives that have not been the subject of special analysis, we shall emphasize here the "Statements (*akty*) about the atrocities of fascist aggressors." They are stored in the collection of the Main Political Administration of the Red Army (GlavPUR RKKA), in the Central Archives of the Ministry of Defense of the Russian Federation (TsAMO RF).[8] The stamp "confidential" was removed from most of these documents only in 2010–2011, owing to the preparation of a documentary collection entitled *The Red Army and the Holocaust*, which will be produced by the Russian Research and Educational Holocaust Center together with the Yad Vashem Research Institute. Altogether, we revealed approximately one hundred files numbering more than 4,000 pages of documents on the subject.

These documents can be divided into some lexical sets, according to origin, and by types of sources. Among them there are enemy documents and testimonies of prisoners of war (military personnel of the Wehrmacht and the Romanian army); reports by political departments of the Red Army of atrocities committed by the invaders both on the territory of the USSR and in Nazi-occupied Europe; propaganda materials of the Red Army, including information on the Holocaust and the analysis of the reasons for Germany's antisemitism; personal collections (letters and diaries of Jews from the occupied territories) found after the liberation; testimonies of escaped Soviet prisoners of war about the execution of their Jewish comrades; photographs taken by German military personnel.

Letters and diaries of German soldiers and officers often abound with openly antisemitic motives.[9] They write publicly about mass executions of Jews and their personal participation in them. Testimonies of captured German prisoners of war provide similar information, but from an eyewitness's point of view. In many cases, specific names of executioners are mentioned. However, these testimonies were provided two to three years after the events and they are very short and abrupt.

The largest type of sources preserved in TsAMO includes statements about German atrocities. They were recorded already in the first months after the beginning of the war. They are particularly valuable as they appeared eighteen months before similar statements collected by the Extraordinary State Commission (ChGK). This enabled the army's political staff and lawyers to interrogate those eyewitnesses who no longer lived in the given settlements in 1943–1944 when the ChGK statements were made.

Written in the most complicated of conditions, immediately after or prior to the fighting, these documents are striking in their details. They specify precise sites of execution; make reference to the names of witnesses and eyewitnesses; contain detailed citations from their testimonies. Of special interest are statements made in connection with the liberation of prisoners from the main factories of death, Auschwitz and Majdanek. Angry reactions on the part of Soviet military personnel to Nazi crimes are reflected even in otherwise emotionless Soviet documentation.

It is natural that the Holocaust was not unique and not even the main object of these documents. The fate of POWs and violence against women were central in the statements made since summer 1941. But they nonetheless served as a basis for the Holocaust to be reflected in military newspapers and special propaganda volumes published from the first months of the war onward.

The special bulletin issued by the section of information of the Seventh Department of GlavPUR dated September 20, 1944, contained a letter by a Jewish woman, Salomea Oks. In the foreword, it was stated that it "was kept by the inhabitant of Ternopol, and after the liberation of the city by the Red Army, it was sent by her to the addressee, in Tel Aviv. The letter was written in Polish, the publication has only insignificant stylistic changes." The letter was written in Ternopol on April 7, 1943, and completed in two sittings—on April 23 and 26, 1943. It was addressed to the Lichtblau family in Tel Aviv. The author describes the destruction of her family and all prisoners of a ghetto from July 1941. Here are some passages from this farewell letter:

> My dear,
>
> Departing from life, I wish to leave to you, my loved ones, some lines.... I wish to tell you so much! But what language can one use to describe tortures ... It is impossible.... Alas, we shall not survive to take revenge; it will be left to you! ... I cannot write further. I cannot! It is possible to fill in lots of pages and all the same, you won't understand!
>
> It is not easy to say goodbye forever, but we expect the future and we shall face death with proud laughter. Be happy, farewell. Do not forget about revenge and if you can—avenge us! Musia[10]

Analysis of the documents in the published collection *The Red Army and the Holocaust* allows us to make a number of important conclusions about their value as a historical source. First, they testify that military personnel of the Red Army involved in fighting against German and Romanian invaders, as well as in liberating European states and death camps, knew a great deal about the crimes committed by the Nazis against Jews, including Soviet prisoners of war.

Second, from the first weeks of the war, these crimes by the Nazis and their collaborators became the subject of special monitoring in statements and political reports, including collection, translation, and analysis of captured German and Romanian documents (letters, diaries, photos). Political departments of the Red Army were the first in Europe to regularly collect and publish data about the Holocaust and other crimes committed by the invaders. They began this work almost eighteen months before the ChGK began its activity. This experience was later used and developed by the ChGK, whose bodies only started to produce similar statements and to collect the testimony of eyewitnesses and victims from March 1943.

After the ChGK commenced its work, the army's political departments at all levels continued to monitor the crimes of the invaders from the first hours after the liberation of Soviet territories. The ChGK came to work several months later when a number of witnesses, especially enlistable men, were no longer present. ChGK statements were largely based on the reports and statements made by the Red Army. Of special value was a thorough reporting on execution sites, the location of tombs, and identifying marks close by. In all instances, these documents passed from a regiment to the Main Political Administration of the RKKA. They were then duplicated, included in military surveys and propaganda materials, and reproduced in army publications and special chapters about Nazi atrocities.

Statements about Nazi atrocities were not only of huge academic value, as they disclose unknown facts, names of victims and perpetrators, and dates of executions, but also constitute the major proof against Holocaust deniers. Of special significance are the diaries written during the war and narrative sources (both Soviet and German), which reflect the psychological conditions of perpetrators and victims, as well as the fighting spirit of Red Army soldiers.

* * *

Among other groups of sources actively explored in contemporary Russia and in the post-Soviet states, we shall highlight here the press in the occupied territories. More than 400 newspapers, each of which paid special attention to antisemitic propaganda, were published under Nazi control. These press publications shaped an image of the Jew as the enemy of all other peoples of the USSR, responsible for the crimes of the Bolshevik regime. The press also published important statistical data about the national composition of the population in the occupied territories, anti-Jewish activities taking place all over the world, including the creation of a ghetto in Shanghai and even the information on the suppression of the revolt in the Warsaw Ghetto. Thus, the reader in the occupied territories received indirect information on Jewish resistance across Europe.

In recent years, revealing new facts have been made available about Jewish refugees and émigrés, connected with the Soviet Union, and, in particular, about the proposal Germany made to the USSR to admit "all Reich Jews," made at the beginning of 1940 and rejected by the Soviet government.[11]

Of great interest is the data on the transport of several thousand refugees from Lithuania via the USSR to Japan in late 1940, and early 1941. As is known, visas were given to refugees by the Japanese Consul in Kaunas, Chiune Sugihara. But only recently did we learn from declassified documents from the Archives of Foreign Policy of the Russian Federation about the role played by the Soviet authorities in this episode and the problems the refugees faced when entering Japan.[12]

It turned out that the transit of refugees through the USSR to Japan was the result of complex political maneuvering. For almost a year, Soviet authorities were involved in solving the problem of the departure from the USSR of Polish Jews in possession of foreign visas and living on Soviet territory. The initiative for the travel of Jewish refugees through the USSR in 1939 came from the Lithuanian Ministry of Foreign Affairs. The government of Lithuania inquired about transit through Odessa to Haifa for several thousand Polish Jews who had received their visas before World War II and appeared in Vilna (under the Soviet-German pact this city and the Vilna district had been given to Lithuania). The Lithuanian side suggested that if any kind of difficultly should arise because some Jews had former Polish passports, then the Lithuanian government would be prepared to give them documents for passage under its own authority.

The Soviet ambassador in London, Ivan Mayski, was approached by the chief rabbi of Palestine, who requested assistance in the transit of students from the Jewish Ecclesiastical Seminary near Vilna. The chief rabbi declared he would be ready to offset all the costs related to the passage of the seminary students and teachers and indicated that the British government would support this action. Mayski not only promised assistance but also expressed the readiness of the Soviet side to cover the expenses incurred by their travel. It was planned to carry out the transportation of 5,000 passengers through the Kaunas branch of *Intourist*. Japanese visas were not needed for such a transit. However, this proposal of the Ministry of Lithuanian Foreign Affairs, like numerous other proposals made by Lithuanian diplomats in Moscow, was rejected until the spring of 1940 by People's Commissar of Foreign Affairs Vyacheslav Molotov.

The situation fundamentally changed when on April 21, 1940, Molotov was approached by his deputy, Vladimir Dekanozov, who had only recently been appointed to the positions of Deputy People's Commissar of Internal Affairs and Head of External Investigation, and was also the Kremlin's future envoy to Soviet-occupied Lithuania. Referring to the consent of the powerful People's Commissariat of Internal Affairs and the initiative of the *Inturist* agency, responsible for arranging visits to the USSR by tourists from other countries, Dekanozov developed a very interesting economic argument: "The total number of Jews wishing to pass by transit through the USSR amounts to around 3,000–5,000 from Lithuania and a few thousand Jews from Latvia. 'Inturist' indicated that by organizing this transit, it would receive nine hundred thousand rubles in hard currency." Dekanozov mentioned twice in his letter that the People's Commissariat of Internal Affairs offered no opposition to the transit of the aforementioned Jews through the USSR to Palestine, since they would be dispatched through Soviet territory in special groups accompanied by guards.

He also noted that transit through the USSR could only be permitted by persons having the necessary visa for entry into Palestine. The majority of Jews who hoped to leave for Palestine had these visas. They all had in their possession either former Polish passports (with Palestinian visas), or statements given to them by British consulates and possibly also documents issued by local authorities in the Baltic countries.

The letter concluded with the words that under existing circumstances transit through the USSR was not only the shortest but also the safest way of moving these Jews to Palestine. It is possible that *Inturist* was authorized to organize the transport itself of Jews to Palestine through the USSR, and to reach agreements directly with the People's Commissariat for Internal Affairs (*Narodnyy Komissariat Vnutrennikh Del*, or NKVD), the People's Commissariat of Railways and the People's Commissar of the Maritime Fleet about the logistical details of this undertaking.

The fate of these Jews was positively resolved some months later when Dekanozov appeared in Lithuania, which in the meantime had become part of the Soviet Union. The refugees were no longer to be transported southward into the Middle East, but rather they would head to the Far East as foreign tourists and refugees. The journey would take them through Moscow by railroad and then all the way to Vladivostok with a symbolic stop in the capital of the Jewish Autonomous Region of Birobidzhan.

* * *

The last decade has seen several new trends in Holocaust studies in Russia. First, there are more scholarly works and memoirs. Some of them have been published in the Russian provinces, including in cities that were not occupied by the Germans (St. Petersburg, Vologda, Yaroslavl, and Chelyabinsk). In recent years, Jewish communities in Orel and Rostov-on-Don, and local researchers in Taganrog, Pyatigorsk, Nevel, and Pskov have become involved in preparing books and chapters on the Holocaust. Only two doctoral theses (*kandidatskie*) were defended on the Holocaust in the North Caucasus (Elena Voitenko) and Nazi persecution policies toward German Jews (Elena Andreeva). There are several reasons for this: the funding problems for students, the lack of academics to supervise these PhDs, underestimation of the topic of Holocaust history itself, and so on. These works are largely descriptive rather than analytical. Also noteworthy are works by Prof. Boris Kovalev from the University of Novgorod dealing with collaboration; he studies anti-Jewish propaganda in the German-controlled press, theater, and radio in the occupied areas. Here we can also mention the works of Dmitry Zhukov and Ivan Kovtun.[13]

Second, works by foreign researchers have been translated into Russian. In contrast to Ukraine, Latvia, and Lithuania, few readers in Russia are aware of works by some of the most prominent Holocaust researchers writing in English and not translated into Russian (for example, Hilberg, Berenbaum, Michman). In 2005, one of the most prestigious Russian publishers ROSSPEN issued the book *Holocaust* edited by Walter Laqueur (originally published by Yale University Press in 2001), but this has proven to be the exception rather than the rule.

In 2009, with support from the Russian State Scientific Fund and other organizations, ROSSPEN published the *Encyclopedia of the Holocaust on the Territory of the Soviet Union*.[14] This was the biggest project of the Russian Holocaust Center. It brought together almost a hundred scholars from fifteen Russian universities to write more than 2,000 chapters on specific localities. There are also more than 300 thematic chapters dealing with literature, poetry, theater, cinema, and so on. All of them relate to the Holocaust of Soviet Jews or the fates of the citizens of other countries (victims and perpetrators) on Soviet territory. Many of these chapters are entirely original contributions, because at the time when they appeared, nothing else had been written on these topics.

The *Encyclopedia* summarizes Holocaust research by Russian scholars and their colleagues in the post-Soviet states. It was particularly important for general Holocaust statistics to establish the number of Holocaust victims on Soviet territory. Thanks to the studies of Russian scholars (Mark Kupovetsky and myself) and an Israeli scholar (Yitzhak Arad), it was ascertained that more than 2.8 million Jews were killed on the territory of the former Soviet Union or deported to death camps between 1941 and 1945. Another three hundred thousand Jews were deported from Germany and German-occupied Europe to this region and then murdered. These numbers make up nearly 50 percent of the total number of killed Jews during World War II. Moreover, in this region there were 800 ghettos, in which about 2 million Jews had to live. About 1,000 ghettos and camps were set up on Soviet territory,[15] a higher number than in any other country occupied by the Nazis and their allies.

These numbers were determined through the comprehensive analysis and juxtaposition of German and official Soviet data about the number of victims. These statistics are also important in order to assess the number of Holocaust victims in Poland, Romania, and Lithuania. Many works by Israeli and Western historians overlook the fact that by June 1941, Jews who had previously lived in eastern Poland, Bukovina, and Bessarabia already had Soviet citizenship.

The (partial) opening of Soviet archives, and the work done by Russian and foreign researchers made it possible to prove that the total annihilation of Jews (including children, women, and old men, the eradication of entire communities) began on the territory of the Soviet Union. A contrasting version is the claim that the Holocaust had already begun much earlier, at the beginning of World War II or even as early as the pogroms of November 1938. Holocaust victims constitute over 40 percent of all peaceful Soviet citizens killed by the Nazis and their collaborators. Up to the end of 1941, the vast majority of the Germans' victims were Jews and Soviet prisoners of war.

In 1942–1944, when the partisan movement intensified, Nazis and their helpers used the experiences gained from the anti-Jewish operations in their reprisal measures. The universality of the Holocaust is usually demonstrated by pointing to the late twentieth-century genocides. Meanwhile, methods and forms of destruction of the civilian population, used against Jews and, in part, Roma (without the propagandistic component), were applied on the occupied territory of the Soviet Union against the civilians of other nationalities: shooting of hostages, incorporation into antiguerrilla operations, and so on.

It seems self-evident that the Holocaust is an integral component of the history of World War II on Soviet territory. However, the Holocaust is dealt with only cursorily in Russian academic journals. Indeed, many authors' approach to the subject of Jewish victims has changed only formally. Jews are not placed in a separate category of victims (only "especially cruel persecutions of them" are mentioned); and the number of victims of the Holocaust—and this term is not always used in the scholarly and educational literature—in the USSR is significantly diminished. It is connected with the Soviet (now Russian) tradition of considering the total number of victims; in this case, 27 million Soviet people are hardly compared with the 6 million Jews in public consciousness. The only exceptions are studies by Gennady Kostyrchenko and Pavel Polian,[16] which deal with important aspects of the Kremlin's policy toward the Holocaust and Holocaust memory in the USSR during and after the war. Polian also investigated the fate of the Soviet Jewish prisoners of war, payments to Holocaust survivors, and Holocaust denial.[17] Maria Al'tman's book about Holocaust denial in Russia was also devoted to the same problem.[18] The book demonstrates that at the turn of the century Russia became the center of Holocaust denial by virtue of publications of both individual titles and translated editions. The book examines the main arguments of the deniers and provides counterevidence by actively using facts from the trial of David Irving.

The history of the Holocaust on the territory of the Russian Federation is the least studied in the post-Soviet and Western historiography. This is the only Soviet republic on which there is no special, separate research. Currently underway is the publication in English of Kiril Feferman's doctoral thesis on the history of the Holocaust in Crimea and the North Caucasus,[19] and Vadim Dubson's chapter concerning the history of ghettos in Central Russia.[20] The only chapter that previously handled the subject was published by myself in English in 2005.[21]

Nazis and their collaborators killed Jews in all of Russia's twenty-three occupied districts, territories, and republics (within the contemporary Russian borders). The total number of victims (including evacuees) was about 145,000 (excluding the Crimea and the Kaliningrad districts). But till now, Western and Israeli scholarship cite figures ranging from "several dozen thousands" to one hundred thousand persons for the number of victims.[22]

The Russian Soviet Federative Socialist Republic (RSFSR) was the biggest Soviet republic—in terms of the length of its borders, from the Gulf of Finland to the Black Sea—occupied by the Germans. The RSFSR was the only republic occupied only partially by the Nazis. Its largest centers with the biggest Jewish population (first of all, Moscow and Leningrad) were not occupied by the Germans. Two hundred thousand Jews lived on the territory of the RSFSR (including the Crimea) before the Nazi occupation.

Russia was the last Soviet republic to be occupied by the Germans (with the exception of several eastern Ukrainian districts). As a result, its Jewish population was better informed about the Holocaust and had more chance to survive by escaping eastward. At the same time, many Jews from Ukraine, Belarus, Moldova, as well as Leningrad, Moscow, and other Russian cities were evacuated to areas of Russia later occupied, notably the North Caucasus. From mid-October to December 1941, 300,653 Jews were transported there. Tens of thousands of them did not manage to evacuate in 1942. Only the central areas of Russia could be reached by refugees from Belarus, the Baltic republics, Ukraine, and Moldova in 1941. All in all, no less than 155,000–160,000 Jews found themselves under the German occupation in Russia.

All occupied Russian territory—and herein lies its main peculiarity—was in a zone of military, not civilian control, in immediate proximity to the front line. Various groups of armies and SS Einsatzgruppen operated here, and this affected Jewish policies and the ways Jews were eliminated. On the occupied Russian territory, Nazi theorists and experts had to solve the problem of Jewishness of Karaites, Mountain Jews (tats), and Krymchaks. The last group was recognized as Jews and killed. But Karaites professing Judaism, as well as a proportion of the Mountain Jews, were not targeted by the Germans.

Jewish children from mixed marriages were usually viewed as Jews if their father was the Jew. But often all Jewish children from such marriages were regarded as Jews. During resettlement to a ghetto or the first executions, exemptions were sometimes made for women with children whose husbands were non-Jews (e.g., in Stavropol). All these exceptional cases were handled by local police bodies.

The number of Holocaust victims in Russia (without Crimea) amounts to not less than 145,000 people.[23] In this respect, more Jews were destroyed in four other Soviet republics: Ukraine, Belarus, Moldova, and Lithuania. But the figure for Russia exceeds the Holocaust death toll in many European countries, including France, the Netherlands, and Greece. Unlike the Baltic republics, Moldova, Ukraine, and western Belarus, in Russia the local population did not initiate Jewish pogroms. At the same time, members of police formations were actively involved in the implementation of the persecution and destruction of Jews.

The Holocaust on Russian territory cannot be understood and assessed outside of the general context of Nazi population and occupation policies in the USSR. In the central and western regions of Russia, these policies were especially severe, unlike in the North Caucasus in 1942–1943.

Thus, the peculiarities of the Holocaust in Russia are:

1. The Nazi occupation regime was far harsher here than the norm.
   The destruction of the non-Jewish civilian population began in earnest with the retreat of the Wehrmacht troops following their defeat in the Battle of Moscow in winter 1941–1942 (in Ukraine and Belarus, "reprisals" against civilians commenced from mid-1942, as a result of increasing partisan activity and as a response to evasion from deportations for forced labor deployment in Germany).
2. At the same time, in Russia (apart from several regions in the North Caucasus and the Crimea) it was useless for the Nazis to play the anti-Russian card in order to win over the local population. Unlike other regions of the RSFSR, only in the Caucasus and Crimea were there large national minority communities, which could be tempted by this idea. Therefore, the notion of "Judeo-Bolshevism" was especially salient and a clear-cut feature of Nazi propaganda. This propaganda tool affected the recruitment of local collaborators and was publicized widely.
3. An absence of pogroms arranged by the Germans can be explained by the more advanced phase of the occupation of Russian territory, as compared to other republics. In Russia, unlike western regions of the USSR and the Baltic States occupied earlier, the Germans had become well aware not only of the positive impact of their propaganda, but also the negative effects, which highlighted the inefficiency of the pogroms.
4. The relative proximity to the front line provided Jews (not only those previously living there, but also refugees who found themselves there) with a unique possibility of rescue by escape, because by this time they had already learned about the annihilation of Jews under the Nazi regime.
5. Of special importance is the analysis of evacuees fleeing Russia's western and central regions, as well as those fleeing other Soviet areas, who found themselves on Russian territory later occupied, largely in the North

Caucasus. This problem has not been studied yet in terms of sources and historiography.

6. The first successes by the Red Army in liberating Russian territory in 1941–1942 enabled Soviet propaganda to become aware of the unique dimensions of the Holocaust; yet, this did not affect its priorities. Furthermore, information about Nazi antisemitism led to a growth of antisemitism among certain elements of the Communist Party apparatus.[24] The evacuation and flight of Jews to the eastern regions of the USSR and familiarity with antisemitic leaflets of those wounded Red Army soldiers and officers who were in the rear led to a surge of antisemitism (see further research by G. Kostyrchenko). The Soviet authorities tried to react preventively. In August 1942, a high-ranking Party official Grigory Aleksandrov offered to remove all the Jews from the Moscow and Leningrad conservatories, drawing attention to a significant percentage of Jews in cultural institutions.[25]

7. The relatively small number of Righteous Among the Nations in Russia does not reflect the dimensions of rescue and support in this region. Rather, it results from the small number of survivors, the unavailability of information required for identifying Righteous people, and a lack of awareness of the distinction by the Russian state and public.

8. Memorialization of the Holocaust on Russian territory was impacted by the total annihilation of Jewish communities, on the one hand, and a relatively high number of Jews conscripted into the army who returned home and were often the first to launch memorialization, on the other. The support of churches, most specifically of the Russian Orthodox Church but also Russian Protestants, made it possible for Jewish religious organizations to obtain recognition in memorializing the Holocaust.

Thus, the USSR was consistent and persistent in granting the opportunity to several thousand Jews to leave the territory of the Soviet Union, while, at the same time, refusing to admit their emigration from Nazi Germany. But this help to the Jewish refugees was local, allowing them to remain on Soviet territory, but not to enter it. The Soviet government (along with the western democracies) bears full responsibility for their indifferent attitude to the fate of the Jews of Germany and countries occupied by her in 1940.[26]

Holocaust researchers in Russia face numerous problems. Many collections of documents from departmental archives (the Ministry of Foreign Affairs, special services, the Presidential Archives) are only partially available to historians. As noted above, Russian academics often overlook the Holocaust, including works that concern Nazi ideology, policy, and practice. Furthermore, in those cases where the destruction of the Jews is mentioned, the number of victims is considerably diminished. This was the case, for example, regarding a book published in 2010 and edited by one of the most well-known Russian historians of World War II, Oleg

Rzheshevski. He spoke of about seven hundred thousand Jewish victims on the territory of the USSR.[27]

Holocaust denial has become a separate feature of the historiography in Russia. Dozens of Russian-language internet sites maintain that the Holocaust is a myth. "Our contemporary" (*Nash sovremennik*)[28] and some other popular sites express the view that the subject of the Holocaust is not important in modern Russia and that any reference to it belittles the exploits of the Red Army and all other Soviet victims of the Great Patriotic War. Popular newspapers publish opinion pieces written by professional historians and teachers to the effect that "Russia has nothing to do with the Holocaust,"[29] and that it is not necessary to teach this subject at Russian schools and universities. Holocaust denial in modern Russia is one of the worst forms of antisemitism. The book *The Holocaust Scam*, written by the Swiss teacher, Jürgen Graf, who is assumed to be currently living in Moscow, was published in Russia.[30] Its circulation so far is about two hundred thousand copies and it is found on many nationalist internet sites.

The arguments of Holocaust deniers penetrate the popular as well as scholarly presses, appearing in such well-known Russian publishing houses as Eksmo and Yauza. Their authors maintain that they do not deny the Holocaust, but only that it did not take place on the territory of the USSR and beyond that on a much smaller scale than other historians have argued. The destruction of the Soviet Jews, they maintain, was a myth organized by Zionists to intimidate Jews of other countries. Soviet Jews were not killed, they say, but instead left for Palestine and the United States. Consequently, there were no death camps or gas chambers.[31]

Holocaust remembrance is rarely a feature of the Russian public discourse. Hushing up the Jewish tragedy for almost fifty years had an impact on Russian society, its educational structures, historical institutions, and intellectual environment. This reactionary and revisionist impact is stronger than elsewhere in the post-Soviet European space. It is small wonder that Russia still has no Holocaust Remembrance Day, although it was the Red Army that liberated Auschwitz. Indeed, far from memorializing the Jewish tragedy, government officials in Rostov decided to take down a memorial plaque that was erected in 2004, identifying most of the 27,000 victims of the Zmievskaya Balka massacre as Jews. The replacement plaque does not mention Jews, but rather peaceful citizens of Rostov-on-Don and Soviet prisoners of war. One of the major, although not the most important, motives behind this decision was the reluctance to mention the term Holocaust on the plaque, while Jews here were not gassed but shot.

Unfortunately, Russia is not a member of the International Holocaust Remembrance Alliance (IHRA). The Russian Holocaust Center's international cooperation network is an essential component of the connections forged by this organization with Russia. Further international cooperation in studying, teaching, and memorializing the Holocaust is necessary.

To sum up, national Holocaust Remembrance Day still does not exist in Russia despite all the attempts of the Russian Holocaust Center and Jewish organizations to implement it based on the fact that Russia has ratified the United Nations General Assembly resolution 60/7 on November 1, 2005 about commemorating the tragedy of the Holocaust. Meanwhile, since 2015 the Government of Moscow, the Russian Jewish Congress, and the Russian Holocaust Center have organized the annual Week of Remembrance. This is a series of memorial and educational events marking the anniversary of the liberation of Auschwitz and International Holocaust Remembrance Day. The highlight of this series of cultural and educational events is the evening requiem held in the prestigious halls of Moscow. Guests of these events include representatives from the political, social, and religious spheres, ambassadors and diplomats from more than twenty-five countries, as well as World War II veterans and former ghetto prisoners, teachers, and students. The official part includes welcome speeches by government representatives of the Russian Federation. The Week of Remembrance is widely covered in the media.

Since 2015, some aspects of the Holocaust have become relevant in the political discourse. The Holocaust assumed its place in the state struggle against the rehabilitation of Nazism. The topic of the Holocaust appeared in state educational programs. For example, International Holocaust Remembrance Day was integrated for the first time into the calendar for educational institutions' measures. By 2017, the number of regions and cities that officially commemorated International Holocaust Remembrance Day throughout Russia had risen to 143 and included sixty-three out of eighty-five Russian regions. Moreover, a program for commemorating Holocaust victims began in the framework of the project "Return Dignity," which resulted in the installation of fifty monuments at the sites of mass killings of Jews, covering a distance of more than 1,600 kilometers.

Comprehension of the Holocaust commemoration experience is in demand for the commemoration of other tragedies, such as the Armenian genocide and the tragedy in Beslan. In 2015, the International Forum "Holocaust: 70 Years Later" was held, and different problems of the Holocaust, genocides, and terror were discussed in the context of historical memory. This provided a basis for the creation in 2016 of the first International Educational and Research Center of the Holocaust and Genocides at the Russian State University for the Humanities. Problems of studying and teaching the history of antisemitism, the Holocaust and genocides of the twentieth century are among the issues explored by the Center.

IL'YA AL'TMAN is Professor at the Russian State University for the Humanities, as well as founder and co-chairman of the Russian Research and Educational Holocaust Center. His many books on the Holocaust in the USSR include *Zhertvy nenavisti: Kholokost v SSSR 1941–1945 gg.* (2002, German ed. 2008), *Kholokost i evreiskoe soprotivlenie na okkupirovannoi territorii SSSR* (2002), *The Unknown Black Book* (ed. with Joshua Rubenstein, 2008), and, as editor-in-chief, *Kholokost na territorii SSSR: Entsiklopediia* (2009).

Notes

1. This data was first published in 1991 in the book by B. V. Sokolov, *Tsena pobedy. Velikaia Otechestvennaia: neizvestnoe ob izvestnom* (Moscow: Moskovskiy rabochii, 1991), 7, 13–15, and 19. In 1998 it was repeated in volume 4 of the multivolume history "Great Patriotic War" prepared by several institutions of the Russian Academy of Science. Usually these figures are mentioned in general calculations of Soviet human losses during the war, including textbooks, ranging from 12 to 15 million peaceful Soviet citizens.

2. Zvi Gitelman, "Soviet reactions to the Holocaust, 1945–1991," in *The Holocaust in the Soviet Union: Studies and Sources on the Destruction of the Jews in the Nazi Occupied Territories of the USSR, 1941–1945*, ed. Lucian Dobroszycki and Jeffrey S. Gurok (New York: M. E. Sharpe, 1993), 4.

3. Il'ya Ehrenburg and Vasiliy Grossman, eds., *Chernaya kniga* (Vilnius: Yad, 1993); reprinted in Germany, the United States, and other countries.

4. Il'ya Al'tman, Shmuel Krakowski, Yitzhak Arad, and Tatyana Pavlova, eds., *Neizvestnaya chernaya kniga* (Moscow: GARF, 1993).

5. Joshua Rubinstein and Il'ya Al'tman, eds., *The Unknown Black Book* (Bloomington: Indiana University Press, 2008).

6. Il'ya Ehrenburg and Vasiliy Grossman, eds., *Chernaya kniga* (Moscow: CORPUS, 2015); Il'ya Al'tman, ed., *Neizvestnaya "Chernaya kniga." Materialy k "Chernoy knige" pod redaktsiyey Vasiliya Grossmana i Il'ya Erenburga* (Moscow: AST Corpus, 2015).

7. Raul Hilberg, *Sources of Holocaust Research: An Analysis* (Chicago: I. R. Dee, 2001), 196.

8. Central Archives of the Russian Ministry of Defense (hereafter TsAMO RF), f. 32 (GlavPUR), inv. 11302.

9. Examples are provided in Saul Friedländer, *The Years of Extermination: Nazi Germany and the Jews, 1939–1945* (New York: HarperCollins, 2007), 107–108, 159, and 211–212; Thomas Kühne, *Belonging and Genocide: Hitler's Community, 1918–1945* (New Haven/London: Yale University Press, 2010), 105–107, 131–132, and 156–157.

10. TsAMO RF, f. 32, inv. 11306, case 544, L. 361–366. See also "Maariv," April 18, 2012, 1 (Hebrew).

11. Dr. Gennady Kostyrchenko was the first to use these documents.

12. For further reading on this see I. A. Al'tman, "The Issuance of Visas to War Refugees by Chiune Sugihara as Reflected in the Documents Stored in Russian Archives," in *Casablanca of the North: Refugees and Rescuers in Kaunas, 1939–1940*, ed. I. A. Al'tman (Kaunas: Versus Aureus, 2017), 133–139.

13. D. A. Zhukov and I. I. Kovtun, *29-ya Grenaderskaya Diviziya SS "Kaminskii"* (Moscow: Veche, 2009); D. A. Zhukov and I. I. Kovtun, *Russkaya politsiya* (Moscow: Veche, 2010); D. A. Zhukov and I. I. Kovtun, *Russkie esesovtsy* (Moscow: Veche, 2013).

14. Il'ya Al'tman, ed., *Kholokost na territorii SSSR: Entsiklopediia*, 2nd rev. ed. (Moscow: ROSSPEN, 2011 [2009]).

15. See Il'ya Al'tman, *Zhertvy nenavisti. Kholokost v SSSR 1941–1945 gg.* (Moscow: Fond Kovcheg, 2002).

16. G. V. Kostyrchenko, *Stalinskii Sovetskii Souz I Kholokost // Kholokost: istoriya I pamyati*, in *Proceedings of the international academic conference at Budapest University*, December 2–3, 2005, ed. T. Kraus (Budapest: Maguar Ruszisztikai Intézet, 2006), 145–153; Pavel Polian, *Zhertvy dvukh diktatur. Ostarbeitery i voennoplennye v Tretyem Reikhe i ikh repatriatsia*, 2nd rev. and exp. ed. (Moscow: ROSSPEN, 2002 [1996]).

17. Alfred Koch and Pavel Polian, *Otritsanie otritsaniya, ili Bitva pod Aushvitsem Debaty o demografii i geopolitike Kholokosta* (Moscow: Tri kvadrata, 2008).

18. M. M. Al'tman, *Otritsanie Kholokosta v Rossii: istoriya I sovremennie tendentsii* (Moscow: Fond "Kholokost"/Journalistic and Publishing Agency "JAG-VM," 2001).

19. Kiril Feferman "The Holocaust in the Crimea and the North Caucasus" (PhD thesis, Hebrew University of Jerusalem, 2008).

20. Vadim Dubson, "Getto na okkupirovannoi territorii Rossiiskoi Federatsii (1941–1942)," *Vestnik evreiskogo universiteta v Moskve* 21, 3 (2000): 157–184.

21. Il'ya Al'tman, "Holocaust in the Territory of the Russian Federation," in *Facing the Nazi Genocide: Non-Jews and Jews in Europe*, ed. Beate Kosmala and Feliks Tych (Berlin: Metropol, 2005), 169–203.

22. Sara Bender and Pearl Weiss, ed., *The Encyclopedia of the Righteous Among the Nations: Rescuers of Jews during the Holocaust, Europe (Part II)* (Jerusalem: Yad Vashem, 2011), LXXIV.

23. Al'tman, *Zhertvy nenavisti*; Al'tman, ed., *Kholokost na territorii SSSR*.

24. Gennady Kostyrchenko, *Out of the Red Shadows: Anti-Semitism in Stalin's Russia* (Amherst, MA: Prometheus Books, 1995).

25. For further reading on this see Mordechai Altshuler, Yitzhak Arad, and Shmuel Krakowski, eds., *Sovetskiye yevrei pishut Ilye Ehrenburgu, 1943–1966* (Jerusalem: Yad Vashem, 1993).

26. Il'ya Al'tman, *Kholokost i evreiskoe soprotivlenie na okkupirovannoi territorii SSSR* (Moscow: Kaleidoskop, 2002).

27. O. A. Rzheshevsky and Y.A. Nikiforov, *Velikaya Otechestvennaya voina*, anniversary edition (Moscow: Olma Media Group, 2010).

28. Chronologically, the most recent works in this genre were the chapters by Stanislav Kunyayev, "Zhretsy i zhertvy Kholokosta," *Nash sovremennik* 1–10 (2010). In 2012, they were published in book format by Algorithm, Moscow.

29. *Komsomolskaya Pravda*, May 7, 2009.

30. Jürgen Graf, *Mif o Kholokoste* (Moscow: "Russkiy vestnik," 1996).

31. This trend appeared first in the USSR after the Six-Day War in the so-called anti-Zionist literature.

11 The Baltic Movement to Obfuscate the Holocaust

Dovid Katz

THE THREE BALTIC States, Lithuania, Latvia, and Estonia (in descending order of population, land mass, and size of prewar Jewish minorities) share a painful statistic.[1] Their percentages of Jews murdered in the Holocaust are the highest in Europe, hovering around 95 percent. But the numbers of Jews actually on site, when the Nazis arrived in the last week of June 1941 (the point of departure for derivative figures) varied significantly. Estimates range from 210,000 to 220,000 in Lithuania; 70,000 to 75,000 in Latvia; and 1,000 to 1,500 in Estonia.[2] In a number of localities, the murder, humiliation, and pillage of Jewish civilians, by local nationalists, was underway shortly after war broke out and the occupying Soviet Army was rapidly fleeing eastward, before the Germans arrived or had set up administrative control.[3] Once the invading Nazi forces had taken over, they swiftly found large numbers of enthusiastic volunteer killers. These operations were so productive for the Nazis that they would go on to deport Jews from various parts of Europe (as far away as France) to these states for murder, and to export local murderers and accessories to other parts of occupied Europe. It has been noted more than once that the courage and determination of the local rescuers—the Righteous Among the Nations, *Khsídey úmes ho-óylem* in Yiddish—in the Baltics was an extraordinary and inspiring chapter in the annals of humanism. Rescuers were treated as traitors against their own nationals rather than resisters against an occupying power.[4]

There is, moreover, a range of historic circumstances before and after the war that the three states—and they alone—have in common beyond the gruesome Holocaust statistics. During the interwar period they were largely successful, independent states with records of nonviolence toward Jews and other minorities, and levels of interethnic coexistence impressive for Eastern Europe of the day.[5] The three states were forcibly incorporated into the Soviet Union as republics via rigged elections in the summer of 1940, followed by nearly a year of occupation that was characterized by loss of liberty, deportations, and forced communization. Their peoples suffered considerably. With the Soviet rout of German forces in 1944 and until the Soviet Union's collapse in 1991, they remained actual USSR republics, not merely Warsaw Pact satellite states. On de facto independence in 1991, all three rapidly became successful democracies. Since 2004, they have been members of the European Union and NATO. In our own time, they share a justified fear of Putinist revanchism and mischief.

That is part of the backdrop for a need felt by some Baltic (ultra)nationalists, like their brethren elsewhere in Eastern Europe, underpinned by elites in politics, academia, media, and the arts, to somehow fix the Holocaust. Straight Holocaust Denial would not play in a part of the world where the Jewish population was mostly shot and buried in seemingly innumerable mass grave sites that lurk in perpetuity not far from many a town. The climate was conducive to the evolution of a convoluted politics that included a need to "satisfy" both domestic far-right nationalist establishments and the opposite pressures emanating from Western and Jewish circles.[6]

One common denominator is the desire to have a national history of pure victimhood without stains (no nation-state has that). In the matter at hand, it has led some to embark on an inversion exercise that would sully the victims while salvaging the local perpetrators as some kind of heroes. Another is a lingering specific antisemitism that accuses *local* (not Western or other) Jews of communism. Most local Jews do indeed carry (an, objectively speaking, accurate) collective memory, first of massive local Baltic collaboration with the Nazis, and second, of the survival of the few being ultimately thanks to the Soviet Union of the years 1941–1944 (in no way a stamp of approval, even remotely, of twenty-first century Putinism, a charge increasingly hurled at those who take issue with the Holocaust revisionism underway). That supernarrative includes a number of individual survivor histories including most often an escape eastward to uninvaded parts of the USSR in the days following June 22, 1941, and, in other cases, escape from ghettos to join up with the Soviet anti-Nazi partisans, or rescue by local Righteous followed (when successful) by liberation by the Soviets in 1944.

The special relationship of post-Soviet Holocaust revisionism with East European antisemitism has been demonstrated.[7] There is, moreover, a line after which nationalist positions on history cannot be disentangled from unseemly bias. This line is the point at which states use taxpayers' money to heap honors, commemoration, and glorification on Holocaust collaborators or the actual local murderers. As the Lithuanian philosopher Leonidas Donskis has put it: "We cannot sympathize with both victims and perpetrators."[8] The fact of the matter is that the vast majority of the many Eastern European killers were anti-Soviet and yearned for Hitler's victory. If that makes them heroes, then virtually all who carried out the Holocaust in Eastern Europe would ipso facto be heroes. That is a sample of the absurdity to which the debate is liable to sink.

Holocaust Obfuscation

Holocaust Obfuscation refers to a specifically post-Soviet, East European brand of revisionism that seeks to downgrade the Holocaust internationally, not just locally, by means of a number of mutually interacting mechanisms.[9] Variants of the model have included claims of overwhelming Jewish complicity in communism; claims that the murder of the Jewish populations in Eastern Europe was a reaction to alleged Jewish communist atrocities; claims that the miniscule percentage of Jews who survived by escaping to Soviet-supported partisan groups in the forests are a priori guilty of "war crimes" (hence they may be defamed by prosecutors, for their lifetimes and for posterity, with neither evidence nor charges as, after all, the partisans in the forests verily did not adhere to the Geneva Conventions).[10] But these elements on their own are details. It is their metamorphosis into components of a coherent and sophisticated new historical model, underwritten by state budgets, and at times by the European Union, that has brought about a significant twenty-first century Holocaust revisionism that continues to be passed over largely in silence by major Jewish organizations, western governments, and the academic world.[11]

Various of the individual elements reemerge as supposedly logical components of the revisionism underway, including: (1) inflation of the word genocide to include such Soviet crimes as deportation; (2) the demand for a declared equality of Nazi and Soviet regimes and crimes; (3) the leveling of perpetrators and victims; (4) the notion that European unity depends on having a common history agreed on by all (or else), in this case the revisionist easterners' history. Finally, there is an untoward state-sponsored element that is kept far from public events and publications in the field: (5) suspension or reversal of democratic guarantees of free speech on these matters by criminalizing the opinion that the classic narrative (recognizing but one genocide in the Baltics) is correct, and by criminalizing criticism of Nazi collaborators whom the state has declared to be national heroes.

There are, moreover, numerous smaller details of history that are repeatedly challenged in the same spirit. They include downward revision of percentages of victims (sometimes just far enough to be in the around-90-percent range of other countries);[12] (usually major) revisions downward of massive local voluntary enthusiastic collaboration;[13] and Holocaust history downplaying smaller towns and emphasizing the Nazi ghettos in larger cities where German cruelty was much more visible for much longer, and where attempts are made to deflect guilt to the Jewish police or the Jewish Council (*Judenrat*).[14]

In the more than a quarter century that has elapsed since the collapse of the Soviet Union, the new paradigm has acquired a host of names including post-Soviet historiography, symmetry, equivalence, and, in that Brussels style of European Union discourse known as Eurospeak: the equal evaluation of totalitarian regimes. The name that has gained predominance is Double Genocide, of which Holocaust Obfuscation is a pronounced and ubiquitous element.

Redefinition of Genocide

To make it stick, the vernacular definition of genocide had to undergo modification. But truth to tell, the standard UN definition, adopted in Resolution 260 (III), Chapter 2, on December 9, 1948 itself opened potential floodgates for the future: "In the present Convention, genocide means any of the following acts committed with intent to destroy, in whole or in part, a national, ethnical, racial or religious group, as such, followed by the acts so considered: (a) Killing members of the group; (b) Causing serious bodily or mental harm to members of the group; (c) Deliberately inflicting on the group conditions of life calculated to bring about its physical destruction in whole or in part; (d) Imposing measures intended to prevent births within the group; (e) Forcibly transferring children of the group to another group."[15]

The basis was the coinage by Raphael Lemkin in the preface to his 1944 book *Axis Rule* (the preface is itself dated November 15, 1943). In his section "Genocide—A New Term and New Conception for Destruction of Nations" there is, to start with, a succinct and precise formulation: "New conceptions require new terms. By 'genocide' we mean the destruction of a nation or of an ethnic group," a definition that is clear as daylight. In subsequent passages, however, lesser bars come into an increasingly casual discussion, for example: "Generally speaking, genocide does not necessarily mean the immediate destruction of a nation, except when accomplished by mass killings of all members of a nation. It is intended rather to signify a coordinated plan of different actions aiming at the destruction of essential foundations of the life of national groups."[16]

Fast forward to the collapse of the Soviet Union. The three Baltic States lost little time in setting the stage for Holocaust Obfuscation within the Double Genocide paradigm via legally redefining genocide to ensure it includes, by law, Soviet crimes against the Baltic countries. Lithuania's 1992 law has the language: "The killing and torturing and deportation of Lithuanian inhabitants committed during the occupation and annexation of Lithuania by Nazi Germany and the USSR correspond to the crime of genocide as contemplated by international law."[17]

The critical additives here are torturing, deportation, occupation, and annexation, which are declared to correspond to the crime of genocide by international law by virtue of it being so stipulated. The Soviet deportation of a minority of the Lithuanian population is equated with the Nazi-led massacre of virtually the entirety of the country's Jewish population. When the Soviet Union collapsed, there were more Baltic citizens than when it first came. Dovilė Budrytė is among the scholars who suggest that this use of the word genocide originates not in Lithuania, but from the (nationalist) diaspora, particularly in the United States, and came into vogue in the home country during the years of glasnost, rebellion against Soviet rule and early independence (1986–1992, corresponding to the Lithuanian *Atgimimas* or "Revival" or national rebirth). She traces the rise of the phenomenon of "remembering two genocides."[18]

Analogously, Latvian law likewise further adapted the United Nations' Genocide Convention:

> For a person who commits genocide, that is, commits intentional acts for purposes of the destruction in whole or in part of any group of persons identifiable as such by nationality, ethnic origin, race, social class or a defined collective belief or faith, by killing members of the group, inflicting upon them physical injuries hazardous to life or health or causing them to become mentally ill, intentionally causing conditions of life for such people as result in their physical destruction in whole or in part, utilizing measures the purpose of which is to prevent the birth of children in such group, or transferring children on a compulsory basis from one group of persons into another.[19]

The critical phrases here include "social class or a defined collective belief or faith," "causing them to become mentally ill," "physical destruction in whole or in part." In other words, if the Soviet Union set about to bring an end to the class of religious leaders or capitalists or dissidents by a variety of means, this automatically becomes genocide. Spiritual anguish (mental illness) and destruction of even a small percentage of the population (physical destruction in part) is joined here to the genocide family.

With respect to Estonia, Doyle Stevick has outlined the parallel efforts to expand genocide and to equalize the Holocaust with Soviet crimes. He traces the typical Baltic trajectory from reluctance to institute a day to commemorate the Holocaust at all, to doing so under US and western pressure, to then combining Nazi and Soviet crimes in a single category.[20] Stevick cites Estonian responses that effectively reject a supposed uniqueness of the Holocaust. Among them is the claim by David Nersessian that the grievous damage caused by Soviet policies, including resettlement, deportation, russification, and more, is indeed cultural genocide. Nersessian is not happy with applying a physical condition to the notion of genocide: "By limiting genocide to its physical and biological manifestations, a group can be kept physically and biologically intact even as its collective identity suffers in a fundamental and irremediable manner. Put another way, the present understanding of genocide preserves the body of the group but allows its very soul to be destroyed."[21]

The wording of the Estonian law, dating from 1994, follows its Baltic neighbors in the discrete expansion of the notion genocide to include deprivation of political rights, among others.

> Perpetration of crimes against humanity, including genocide as defined by the norms of international law, entailing deliberate actions whose aim was fully or partly to destroy ethnic, national, racial, religious, resisters to occupation or other social groups or their members by killing or causing major injury or

causing mental illness or other punishment, for taking of children by force, for armed attack, in the case of occupation or annexation or deporting of civilians, or depriving them of economic, political or social rights or restricting these essential rights, will be punishable by prison for eight to fifteen years or lifetime imprisonment.[22]

The late Leonidas Donskis's essay, "The Inflation of Genocide" remains a potent rejoinder, not least because of the author's status as a proudly patriotic Lithuanian citizen himself. Among its arguments:

> In recent decades, the concept of genocide has undergone a perilous devaluation.... A genocide is the annihilation en bloc of a people or of a race, irrespective of class divisions, dominant ideology and internal social and cultural differences.... Genocide is annihilation without pre-selection, where the victims are utterly unable to save themselves—in theory or in practice—by an ideological change of heart, by religious apostasy or, ultimately, by betraying the group and going over to the other side.... You are guilty at birth, and this fatal error of having been born—this original sin—can be corrected only by your extermination. Such is the metaphysics of genocide and absolute hatred. The only way of resolving the "problem" is by the complete and utter annihilation of bodies, lives, blood and skin pigment.[23]

Research Centers and Museums

In the immediate wake of independence from Soviet rule, the three Baltic States set up research institutes to deal with both Soviet and Nazi crimes, each controlling one or more major state museums. Lithuania's Genocide and Resistance Research Center of Lithuania (LGGRIC), known as the Genocide Center, in Vilnius, was formally established in 1992. Its associated Museum of Genocide Victims was set up the same year. It also provided the historical texts for the popular (now privatized) tourist site featuring the nationally collected statues of Lenin and other Soviet leaders at Gruto Park (Grūto parkas, colloquially known as The Lenin Park), near Druskininkai in southeastern Lithuania. Latvia's Center for Documentation of the Consequences of Totalitarianism was set up in 1992. The associated museum, which recently underwent a major overhaul, is the Museum of the Occupation of Latvia 1940–1991. Estonia's national research center is named in a different spirit, openly as part of the ongoing memory wars in Europe. It is the Estonian Institute of Historical Memory. In a spirit analogous to the naming of Latvia's museum, it is called the Museum of Occupations.

The three research institutes, with their elite state-remunerated scholars, often figures of high academic, political, and societal stature, are in a sense the engines of the Baltic movement for a revision of World War II and Holocaust history to a narrative of two equal totalitarian regimes. The museums play their role too, being on the tourist lists of large numbers of Western visitors. Until 2011, the word "Holocaust" could not be found in Vilnius's Museum of Genocide Victims.²⁴ In other words, the one genocide that actually occurred in Lithuania was omitted, while the series of odious crimes that nevertheless left a vibrant and successful country with an increased population, ready, after the collapse of the USSR, for near-term EU and NATO accession, were here being defined as "the genocide."²⁵

An entire hall was (and as of writing, still is) devoted to the Lithuanian Activist Front (LAF) fascists who carried out the early murders before German occupation in the week of June 22, 1941, treating them as national heroes with no mention of their part in the genocide of Lithuanian Jewry. Another room, dedicated to the postwar Forest Brothers contained until 2015 three antisemitic images implying that Stalinist rule was carried out by Jews portrayed in the caricatures; one had Lenin, Stalin and "the Jew Yánkele" (in the original: Jenkelkė) driving an ominous Soviet jeep. After repeated protests, these caricatures were removed, at least temporarily, in 2015.²⁶ The Lenin Park historical texts provided by the Genocide Center go rather further, including a description of the anti-Nazi partisan resistance: "Soviet activists, Red Army men, escaped prisoners of war and some inhabitants of Lithuania (mostly of Jewish nationality) formed groups of saboteurs." One of the placards dedicated to the prewar communists has this about a certain Icikas Meskupas-Adomas: "After LCP [Lithuanian Communist Party] became the support [sic] of occupational regime during the occupation of Lithuania, he worked as the Second Secretary of LCP CC. In 1940–1941 he guided the cleansing of Lithuanian officials, sought to keep the traditional Jewish communists' influence upon LCP."²⁷

For years, the Genocide Center in Vilnius had on its website a statement that is a classic example of the strange phenomenon of Holocaust Envy: "One may cut off all four of a person's limbs and he or she will still be alive, but it is enough to cut off the one and only head to send him or her to another dimension. The Jewish example clearly indicates that this is also true about genocide. Although an impressive percentage of the Jews were killed by the Nazis, their ethnic group survived, established its own extremely national state and continuously grew stronger."²⁸

Like other Baltic research institutions on Nazi and Soviet crimes, the Genocide Center contained practical researchers interested in uncovering evidence for prosecutable crimes (from the Soviet side only, to be sure), and hosts actual parts of the state's prosecutorial apparatus including a Special Investigation Department, a name unceremoniously taken from the American agency responsible for hunting Nazi war criminals.²⁹ The dismal record of Lithuanian prosecutors in taking seriously suspected Nazi war criminals, including some fifteen deported from the United States, has been repeatedly documented by Efraim

Zuroff of the Simon Wiesenthal Center, who has stressed repeatedly that early fair trials before local judges, in the local language and under the national flag, would have been to the nation's great benefit.[30]

National Days of Remembrance

The major effort to codify a commemoration day that is at least in the direction of Double Genocide is the joint day of commemoration of Nazi and Soviet crimes, August 23, commemorating the Molotov-Ribbentrop Pact of 1939. The Baltics have been regarded as the primary engine of the movement, but its genesis is to be found in the 1980s in the North American diaspora communities of the Baltics, Ukraine, and other East European nations. Packaged in the west as Black Ribbon Day, it gained currency particularly in 1986 when the proposal, initiated by these East European diaspora communities, led to observances in twenty-one North American cities. The idea was rapidly exported back home and culminated in the famous 1989 Baltic Way demonstration that was a potent, peaceful, and effective democratic demonstration against brutal Soviet domination and occupation.

As a choice of day to demonstrate against Soviet repression, domination, and occupation, August 23 is a priori unassailable. Stalin had divided Poland and other countries with Hitler, and had proceeded within weeks to take "his" eastern part of the divided Eastern Europe. The Soviet Union incorporated some of these lands in 1939 and the remainder in 1940, robbing them all of their freedom. The domination was to resume after the defeat of Hitler, mostly in 1944 on the Eastern Front, right up until the collapse of the Soviet Union in 1991. The movement of the 1980s, the Baltic Way of 1989, and the subsequent years of celebration of the day started out and could have remained as an honest, straightforward day of commemoration of the individual and national victims of Soviet communism and its many crimes.

But over the course of the past quarter century, the observance of August 23 grew into a symbol of the new Double Genocide inspired revised history of World War II, in which Nazism and Communism are to be equally commemorated on a single day. A monograph would be needed to establish the evolution in each country. But it is clear that by the time the Baltic States joined NATO and the European Union in 2004, the day had somehow shifted to symbolize a radical reassignment of the elements of history in the post-Soviet East European and, particularly, in the Baltic spirit. But it was in 2009, as the Double Genocide movement was at its peak following the Prague Declaration (see Export), that the three Baltic States re-legislated the day. On June 18, 2009, the Estonian parliament adopted August 23 as the Day of Remembrance for Victims of Stalinism and Nazism while naming the statute itself "23 August: The Europe-Wide Remembrance Day for the Victims of All Totalitarian and Authoritarian Regimes." On July 17, 2009, Latvia named the day the Day of Remembrance for Victims of Stalinism and Nazism.

Lithuania followed on July 22 with a wider scope, renaming Black Ribbon Day as the European Day of Remembrance for Victims of Stalinism and Nazism, and Day of the Baltic Way. Lithuania alone added in the name a reference to its actual anti-Soviet origin within Eastern Europe.

State "Red Brown" Commissions

Under pressure from the West, and particularly the United States, as well as Holocaust survivors' groups, the three Baltic States had been warned through much of the 1990s that they would need to confront their Holocaust histories at a state level if they were to win acceptance to the European Union, NATO, and other western institutions. That pressure was a grave error. Bold indigenous individuals and NGOs from a variety of walks of life were rising to tell the painful truth in all three Baltic countries and were making visible progress. The Jewish organizations and western grant-giving bodies should have identified and supported them. By pressuring the state authorities of these proud nations, a Pandora's box of mirrors and ruses was inadvertently opened. The Baltic States naturally colluded, and all came up with "red-brown commissions," as they have become informally known. These are state-sponsored commissions set up in 1998 to provide research and education on *both* Nazi and Soviet crimes. They have at the same time been at a high level politically and close to each nation's leaders. They all sought to involve western (and Jewish) scholars who would add legitimacy. All had access to plentiful state funding for staging well-organized and enjoyable events.

In the case of Latvia and Estonia, the commissions in point of fact had limited life spans devoted to producing a series of books on the crimes of both totalitarian regimes. Latvia's History Commission was established, it explains, on the initiative of the president, Guntis Ulmanis in November 1998. Listed under the government's Ministry of Foreign Affairs, it was divided into four sub-commissions and produced a number of volumes.[31] The president's website explains that "the main task of the Commission during its initial working period was to study the issue 'Crimes against Humanity Committed in the Territory of Latvia under Two Occupations, 1940–1956,' as well as to organize the production of the final report on the theme."[32] The National Director of the Anti-Defamation League, Abraham H. Foxman, famously resigned from the Latvian Commission in 1999. In a letter to the President of Latvia, Vaira Vike-Freiberga, Foxman explained that his decision was due to the "intermingling and confusion of the Holocaust and the Soviet occupation of Latvia."

"While I acknowledge the suffering of many Latvians at the hands of the Soviets and Latvia's desire to investigate this history, as a Jew and a Holocaust survivor, I am deeply offended by the intermingling and confusion of these two very different experiences," said Mr. Foxman. "Therefore, I am resigning from the Latvian Commission of Historians. I am deeply concerned that Latvia is not yet ready to truly examine and confront the experience of Latvian Jews during the Holocaust."[33]

Analogously, the Estonian International Commission for Investigation of Crimes Against Humanity was founded in October 1998, and announced by the president himself. In the spirit of many "tasked commissions," it published a number of reports and books before putting itself to bed in December 2008.[34] Anton Weiss-Wendt's critique of the Estonian Commission's record merits being cited at length precisely because it can in principle shed light on all the East European "red-brown commissions."

> The larger question is whether the Commission has achieved its objectives and if its work has furthered Holocaust awareness among the Estonian population. The main goal has definitely been attained—to show the Western European and American political establishment that the Baltic governments are ready to submit even the most complex aspects of recent history to critical examination. Ironically, the Reports were published after Estonia officially joined the NATO and the EU. After all, setting the historical record straight was not the most important criterion for admission.... The way the Commission treated the Holocaust does not open new vistas but rather reinforces old misconceptions. Estonian scholars compartmentalized the history of the Holocaust by dealing separately with the Estonian, Czech/German, Polish/Lithuanian and French Jews. As we know all too well, the Nazis were exterminating the Jewish people not as Estonian, Lithuanian, French, etc. nationals but as Jews. Finally there is a question of accessibility: how many Estonian readers would be willing to spend 750 Estonian crowns (around one-fifth of the [monthly] minimum wage) for an encyclopaedic volume in English that contains information on both Soviet and Nazi occupations?[35]

When the Lithuanian commission was announced in 1998, it drew protests from the association of Lithuanian Holocaust survivors in Israel and the Simon Wiesenthal Center, precisely because of its equal—and mixed—dedication to Nazi and Soviet crimes.[36] The survivors' letter, signed by Holocaust survivor Joseph Melamed, then chairman of the Association of Lithuanian Jews in Israel, included the text: "The linking of the histories of the Nazi and Soviet occupations is the heart of the problem. More than any other factor, this false symmetry has been a major obstacle to any serious soul-searching by Lithuanian society in regard to the extensive collaboration of Lithuanians with the Nazis in the murder of Lithuanian Jewry. Even worse, false accusations and patent exaggerations regarding Jewish participation in Communist crimes against Lithuanians have been adduced time and again to explain, and in some cases even justify, the participation of Lithuanians in the murder of Jews during the Holocaust."[37]

Melamed's words would come to be seen as uncannily prophetic, as fate would have it, not only about the wider mood in the Baltics, but in an international sensation about the commission itself. Given the Lithuanian state investment in legitimizing Holocaust revisionism via participation of prominent Jewish personalities, it was perhaps natural that Lithuania's new commission, which bears an unwieldy name, The International Commission for the Evaluation of the Crimes of the Nazi and Soviet Occupation Regimes in Lithuania, would seek legitimacy by foreign Jewish participation. Lithuanian leaders persuaded Dr. Yitzhak Arad, a Holocaust survivor from Lithuania and scholar who had been the director of Yad Vashem for over two decades, to join the commission. He did, and participated successfully in deliberations leading to a number of publications.

But then in 2006, a period during which Dr. Arad was assisting the American government on a certain Lithuanian Nazi war criminal, the daily newspaper *Respublika* published a broadside against him, accusing him—a member of the same state's official historical "red-brown" commission—of himself being a war criminal.[38] The basis of the accusation was an out-of-context passage from Arad's own memoir published in English over a quarter of a century earlier and widely known.[39] A then leading figure at the Genocide Center (who has since been named a member of Lithuania's red-brown commission), is quoted in the chapter as lamenting that "There is no statute of limitation for the Jewish genocide, because this is approved at the international level. The genocide of Lithuanians has no such status, and for the physical extermination of our nation essentially nobody is accountable."[40] In September 2007, the Prosecution Service of the Republic of Lithuania issued a comprehensive statement confirming that a pretrial investigation of Dr. Arad on suspicion of crimes against humanity had begun in May 2006, and that a request had been sent to Israeli authorities for his appearance for questioning.[41] In the wake of an international uproar, the investigations against Arad were partly discontinued in September 2008, but with a defamatory statement from prosecutors calling on the public to come forward with more evidence.[42]

The macabre plotline, of a NATO-EU state pursuing a Holocaust survivor for war crimes without any charges, on the basis of survivors' (in his case his own) memoirs, repeated itself in 2008. A January 29 newspaper chapter called on prosecutors to pursue two Holocaust survivors, women who had also been Soviet partisans, Fania Yocheles Brantsovsky (Brancovskaja, b. 1922) and Rachel Margolis (1921–2015), on the basis of a passage in Margolis's memoirs.[43] Dr. Margolis, one of the creators of Vilnius's modest post-Soviet Holocaust museum, popularly known as The Green House, was long despised by the ultranationalist establishment for having rediscovered, deciphered, and published, in the 1990s, the eyewitness diary of a Christian Polish journalist who had seen tens of thousands of killings by local volunteer shooters at the mass murder site Ponár (Polish Ponary, now Paneriai, outside Vilnius).[44] On May 5, 2008, two armed plainclothes police came looking for the two women.[45] For the first time since the demise of the Soviet Union, Western ambassadors found themselves honoring people being criminally pursued by prosecutors. The Irish ambassador Dónal Denham took the initiative, and was rapidly followed by the ambassadors of Austria, Britain, Norway, and the United States, among others.[46] Among the figures who provided rapid responses to the first state campaign against Jewish heroes of the anti-Nazi resistance was then UK MP Denis MacShane in his book *Globalizing Hatred*:

> The rise of nationalist antisemitic politics can be seen in Lithuania. Jews who escaped to join the anti-Nazi partisans in Lithuania in the Second World War are now being accused by Lithuanian antisemites of taking part in war crimes. Ninety-five percent of Lithuania's 200,000 Jews ... were killed by Germans and their Lithuanian collaborators. Lithuanian Jews who survived the Holocaust are now in their eighties, but such is the antisemitism coming back to life in some quarters of nationalist politics in the Baltic state, it has been possible to open investigations that put Jews on the same level as their executioners.[47]

The joint formal letter of protest from the Jewish Community of Lithuania and the Union of Former Ghetto and Concentration Camp Prisoners noted with some irony in 2008 that "the Prosecution Service's claims that 'hundreds of witnesses are being questioned' are belied by the fact that only Jewish names are being heard in the media."[48]

Of the remaining instances, the best known is of a former partisan wanted for questioning not for alleged war crimes while in the partisans but for allegedly defaming Lithuanian heroes. It came as a shock to Holocaust survivor communities that Interpol was sent to interview Joseph Melamed in Tel Aviv in August 2011, over his book of a dozen years earlier, *Crime and Punishment*, which listed potential Holocaust perpetrators whom he had asked Lithuanian prosecutors to investigate.[49] The situation elicited an Early Day Motion in the British Parliament on September 8, 2011:

> That this House condemns attempts by the Lithuanian government to investigate 86 year-old Kovno Ghetto Holocaust survivor Joseph Melamed for slander; welcomes attempts by Mr. Melamed to bring his document listing eyewitness accounts of thousands of wartime Lithuanian Nazi collaborators to the attention of the Lithuanian prosecutor general in 1999; notes that of the nine Lithuanians executed by the Soviet government for Nazi collaboration, whom Mr. Melamed is accused of slandering, one ... in 1941 used his sword to saw off the head of Rabbi Zalman Osovsky and then put it on public display; further condemns repeated attempts of the Lithuanian government to extradite Holocaust survivors such as 90 year-old Lithuanian war hero, Rachel Margolis, from their homes to face war crimes charges.[50]

Earlier, in 2009, the Lithuanian media stormed against the Association of Lithuanian Jews' website for containing a list of local perpetrators. Then, and during the 2011 Interpol saga, Melamed received no support from the Israeli Foreign Ministry or other state authorities, who in fact pressured him to remove the list from the website. With the exception of one remarkable Israeli ambassador, Chen Ivri Apter (1958–2012),[51] Israel's legendary support for its citizens was largely suspended in the case of its three Holocaust-survivor citizens who were persecuted by a foreign state: Yitzhak Arad, Rachel Margolis, and Joseph Melamed.[52] One of the most academically creative results of the saga is Arad's 2012 paper, "The Holocaust in Lithuania, and Its Obfuscation in Lithuanian Sources," which goes a long way toward unraveling and making clear the nationalistic, political, and historical motivations of a state commission of which he was for many years a member.[53]

State Glorification of Nazi Collaborators and Perpetrators

As noted near the outset, making heroes of the local killers or their collaborators is not compatible with sincere Holocaust commemoration or sincere regret over the fate of the annihilated minority. This topic has in recent times attracted much attention in Hungary, Ukraine, and elsewhere.[54]

Latvia and Estonia differ markedly from Lithuania, ultimately going back to differences in the wartime history per se. They have invested a lot of political capital to honor their respective Waffen-SS legions, which were set up in Estonia in 1942 and Latvia in 1943, in both cases after nearly all those countries' Jews had been killed. The legions themselves were not directly involved in the killing, though views vary on the numbers in each who were, or may have been recycled killers of 1941. There is less mystery about what their role would have been in instances when a Jew in hiding was encountered, about their allegiance to Hitler to whom each swore an oath, and about their wartime activities having served to delay the liberation of the camps further west by the approaching Soviet Army. In Estonia, a long series of events, either financed by the state or supported by major political features, has honored the Waffen-SS.[55] Over the years, there have been numerous Estonia-specific incidents, including celebrations in 2011 of the seventieth anniversary of Hitler's invasion, which drew a pained response from the nation's small Jewish community.[56] In 2014, the last Estonian SS veteran to have been awarded the Nazis' Knight's Cross, received a funeral with full state military honors.[57] In the case of Latvia, the recurring issue has been the allocation of the center of the nation's capital, Riga, for a parade and ceremony glorifying the Waffen-SS on March 16 each year and frequently supported and attended by some mainstream politicians.[58]

Lithuania had no Waffen-SS division, and its militias served the Nazis via other categories of units.[59] For reasons that need to be studied, parts of the academic, political, and intellectual elite of nationalist circles are determined to have as national heroes the leaders, members, and allies of the Lithuanian Activist Front (LAF) and the short-lived Provisional Government (PG), which was active for under two months, from June 23, 1941, a day after Operation Barbarossa was launched, until early August of that year. Before the invasion, when the LAF was based in Berlin, it issued leaflets that expressed the need for ethnic cleansing of the nation's Jewish minority.⁶⁰ In the days from June 23 onward, before the arrival of German forces or before their establishment of control, the LAF and other nationalist groups were responsible for thousands of murders of civilian Jews.

Still, much of modern Lithuanian historiography regards the Lithuanian Activist Front as rebels who drove out the Soviets. That is an ahistorical contention. The Soviet army's retreat and flight eastward on June 22 and 23, 1941, was obviously a result of the Nazis' invasion and more than 3 million German soldiers—the largest invasion in human history—driving eastward. They were not running from the white-arm-banded LAF nationalists who were busy killing local Jews. It is therefore an issue of pain for many, and indeed many Lithuanians, that there are street names, statues, school names, and plaques both for LAF leaders of the early days of the war, many of whom morphed into parts of the Germans' killing machine once it was set up in July 1941.⁶¹ In 2011, on the seventieth anniversary of the events of June and July 1941, a series of events was organized by state-funded bodies to commemorate the LAF and the Provisional Government.⁶² The small but vibrant Jewish community protested.⁶³ For some months, the Lithuanian Parliament's website listed it as a year of remembrance for victims of the Holocaust on its English website, while stating, on its Lithuanian website, that the same year was one of remembrance for the "freedom fighters" of the LAF.⁶⁴

A modest international uproar ensued in 2012 when it was announced that the state was financing the repatriation of the remains of the provisional government's Nazi-puppet Prime Minister, Juozas Ambrazevičius (later Brazaitis) from Putnam, Connecticut for reburial with full honors in Lithuania.⁶⁵ Hard as it may be to fathom, the politics of the day kept the event out of mainstream western media. During his brief tenure as prime minister, Ambrazevičius signed orders confirming German demands, inter alia, for Jews to be sent to a concentration camp (it was actually the Seventh Fort murder site outside Kaunas), and for the remainder to be incarcerated in a ghetto within one month.⁶⁶ The reburial led to a passionate debate in which a number of Lithuanians protested their government's decision. The most dramatic confrontation was on the floor of the Lithuanian parliament, where MP Vytenis Povilas Andriukaitis challenged the prime minister and foreign minister on May 17, 2012.

> I do not know whether all MPs got it, but I found a booklet that is being distributed for the Brazaitis commemoration. The information published in the booklet has very serious omissions. I have in my hands the protocols of the [1941] Provisional Government of Lithuania relating to the establishment of a concentration camp for Jews, to the nationalization of Jewish property, and to organizing a Jewish ghetto in Kaunas. Unfortunately, this information is not contained in the booklet. Do tell us, is it true that the government financed it and allocated 30,000 litas for the commemoration and moving the mortal remains and for organizing the events?⁶⁷

In 2016, a British-born member of the Vilnius city council initiated an attempt to change the name of a central Vilnius street named for a vocal supporter of ethnic cleansing and expulsion of Lithuanian Jews in 1941. The proposal was for the street to be renamed to honor rescuers. By mid-2017 the issue had died down with no changes.[68]

Legislation of Historic "Truth" and Criminalization of Dissent

The three Baltic States (among others in Eastern Europe) have passed de facto legislation of historical truth of the Baltic nationalist narrative via laws that criminalize the western (and Jewish) narratives, generally speaking indirectly. In the case of Estonia, the Valentine's Day Law (so dubbed by its critics) of February 14, 2012, enshrines in a parliamentary declaration the heroic status of the Estonian Waffen-SS, thereby in effect criminalizing those who might dare to disagree and consider them Nazi collaborators of which the nation should not be particularly proud.[69] As in other regional laws on the subject, there is enough vagueness (and local complexity) to avert serious European Union scrutiny, but enough force to deter any young historian from compromising his or her career prospects by standing up against this supposed national consensus. The law was sponsored by the defense minister, underlying the ongoing effort to hitch revisionism of the past to current national security.

The Latvian and Lithuanian laws follow a model of a law passed in Hungary in 2010, shortly after the right-wing Fidesz party came to power, where the strategy is to criminalize a trivialization of either genocidal regime by holding to the view that only one was genocidal. Latvia was the last of the Baltics to legislate in this vein. On May 15, 2014, the Latvian parliament (*Saeima*) passed legislation that includes the crime of gross derogation of genocide. Its text includes "genocide" among the crimes "perpetrated by the Soviet Union or Nazi Germany."[70] Two months later, the Constitutional Court turned down challenges to the law put forward by the "Harmony Centre," a largely Russian-speaking party.[71] The maximum sentence for violating the law is five years' imprisonment.

The major and most widely illustrative paradigm emanates from Lithuania. For years there had been talk in parliamentary circles about a law to criminalize the diminution of—as it is seen in these circles—either of the two genocides. The bill's originators made no attempt to hide the intended legislation's purpose: "Meanwhile, in the Lithuanian legal system, acts regarding the crimes of Soviet genocide, i.e., their denial or justification, are not criminalized, and, experts say, this is an obstacle in attempting to equate the crimes of Soviet genocide with the Nazi genocide."[72]

However, the law's wording was eventually made more ambiguous by phraseology such as "anyone who publicly approves of aggression carried out by the USSR or Nazi Germany against the Republic of Lithuania, the crime of genocide or other crimes against humanity or war crimes committed by the USSR or Nazi Germany against Lithuanian residents or on Lithuanian territory ... is punishable by limitation of freedom, arrest or loss of freedom for up to two years."[73]

Analyzing the law's dismal performance after its first few years, legal scholar Justinas Žilinskas concedes as point of fact its purpose: "The EU Member States with different historic experience (including Lithuania) availed of this opportunity for another step in the desired equal legal treatment of totalitarian regime crimes, by including crimes committed by the USSR in the scope of the crime of denial."[74]

What was outside the scope of Žilinskas's inquiry is the lurking intimidation of budding scholars, researchers, and human rights activists. Anyone thinking of disagreeing with Double Genocide would think again, particularly if they were interested in an academic, political, or media career in Lithuania.

Serious objections to the law were put forward by Milan Chersonski, then editor of the Lithuanian Jewish Community's quadrilingual publication, who was among the very few to openly challenge it. He began an extended signed editorial, called "Criminal Code Now as History Guide," as follows: "Why did the debates about Lithuania's history suddenly, as if by agreement, stop? Can it be that once again, as in Soviet times, one cannot freely discuss questions of history or express one's own opinion? Why? For fear of the historical truth? A wish to ignore failures and defeats? A declared taboo to research them? Can it be that time in Lithuania has reverted to when only one opinion—the official one—was permitted? In those days any other opinion was 'false' and punishable: 'the disobedient ones' were accused of slander against Soviet authority, and imprisoned."[75]

But something else was changing in Lithuania around the time of the rise, passage, and implementation of this "red-brown law." Police and prosecutors began harassing a handful of intellectuals who disagreed with the official Holocaust narrative, in all cases with no charges that ever led to any convictions, and without using even the threat of *this* particular law. The law that was most often invoked was that against slandering heroes of the state, the one that had been used against Joseph Melamed.[76] In 2014, police disturbed the Lithuanian documentary filmmaker (and acclaimed Holocaust truth-teller) Saulius Beržinis with a demand for facts about certain alleged Nazi war criminals he or his circle had presumably berated.[77] But the primary victim of repeated frivolous cases has been Evaldas Balčiūnas for his series of chapters calling on his country to just stop glorifying Holocaust murderers, perpetrators, and collaborators. There has never been a substantive charge against him, and in July 2016 he was found not guilty in the most recent frivolous case, after a dozen 450 kilometer round trips from his home to attend hearings in Vilnius.[78] Such cases seem to be a message to others to avoid disagreeing with state-sponsored commemorations for Holocaust collaborators.

Export

The successor states of Nazi-occupied Europe are littered with local forms of Holocaust obfuscation. It is not comfortable for communities to have in their collective heritage the notion that in living or near-living memory, local people, much less family, and church members, dignitaries or presumed heroes collaborated with an occupying power in the deportation or murder of most or all of their own neighbors of a certain ethnicity or religion, with no opportunity even for those neighbors to change or recant any of their beliefs to save themselves.

What is singularly significant about the case of the Baltics is, first, that collaboration often entailed massive participation in the actual nearby massacres (not deportation), exponentially impacting on the desire for history-repair; and second, that the attempted repair has taken the form of an intricately sophisticated, state-financed, fellow-traveler mobilizing model of revisionism that is linked to supposed current patriotism. It has been the purpose of this paper to outline that model and some aspects of its goals, its mechanics, and its progress.

Third, and outside the scope of this paper, has been the massive campaign to export Double Genocide to the West, most famously by the Prague Declaration of 2008. It is a document that boasts the word "same" five times in referring to Nazi and Soviet crimes, and one that includes the rather Orwellian demand that "all European minds" agree to the text proposed.[79] The export campaign has included a substantial investment in conferences internationally, and in awards and medals for acquiescent western personalities.[80] In 2012, Prof. Danny Ben-Moshe and the present author partnered to produce the Euro-parliamentary rejoinder, the Seventy Years Declaration.[81] These matters are explored elsewhere.[82]

The rapid growth and international dissemination of the Double Genocide movement has been significantly enabled by the geopolitical environment of our century's second decade. In the more than a quarter century that has elapsed since the collapse of the USSR there has been a seismic shift in the status of Russia, from friendly new democracy in the 1990s to a contemporary Putinist, authoritarian, revanchist, unpredictable behemoth. Its policies encompass gross mistreatment of citizens as well as the posing of threats to neighboring states.[83]

Strangely enough, the US State Department's response has included a policy shift toward unmitigated acceptance of Holocaust revisionism, as if negating the history of the Anglo-American-Soviet alliance of 1941–1945 is a current geopolitical issue because some of our eastern New Europe allies say so. Checked for some years by the emergence of a second opinion, centered around the Seventy Years Declaration in the European Parliament and beyond, these policies have taken on dramatic new life following the Maidan revolution in Ukraine in 2014. At the same time, Western leaders largely continue to fail to express significant opposition to Ukraine enacting Europe's harshest Holocaust-obfuscating free-speech-stifling law yet. This law places dissenters at risk of ten years' imprisonment (in 2015), while a boulevard in the capital was renamed (in 2016) for the fascist leader Stepan Bandera, whose loyal organization butchered hundreds of thousands of Jews and Poles.[84] This was followed in 2017 by the naming of another thoroughfare in the Ukrainian capital for Roman Shukhevych, a fascist wartime leader likewise responsible for the mass murder of civilians.[85]

During the same years, Israeli foreign policy has shifted radically toward indulging the Baltic and other regional states on matters of Holocaust history.[86] The late Barry Rubin was among those advocating accommodations on history issues in Eastern European countries whose votes in the EU, UN, and other international bodies are important to Israel.[87] There has been spirited debate on the subject.[88] Moreover, Israeli foreign policy has so far abandoned to permanent defamation in history three Israeli citizens, all wartime heroes (as anti-Nazi partisans, participants in Israel's 1948 War of Independence, or both). In the absence of written state apologies, they remain defamed for posterity as a result of a Baltic state policy of looking for equal war criminals on both sides.

Hopefully, Western—and Israeli—policymakers will come to see that saying No to gross distortions of history, distortions that incidentally belittle the Allied war effort that brought down Nazism in Europe, is in no way a contradiction to building permanent new ties of friendship with allies and supporting NATO members against aggression. Genuine friendship entails license to disagree on such matters as the last century's history.

It would be a regrettable and tragic irony if the last century's classic Holocaust Denial, defeated in the west by concerted efforts of states, and of scholars, writers, activists, and diverse people of goodwill, would find itself reincarnated by a cunning new paradigm claiming academic status. The discourse, and the growing willingness of the West—and the Jews—to acquiesce, just when the last witnesses are leaving this world is progressing with a momentum that is cause for concern. Lurking in the debate are such timeless issues as racism, antisemitism, equal rights, and free speech (which includes discourse on history). By glorifying those who strove for ethnic purity via mass murder, and protecting them posthumously, by law, from contemporary criticism and historical scrutiny, certain states send a worrying message in our own times about essential values.

DOVID KATZ is editor of the web journal *DefendingHistory.com*, which he founded in 2009. He established and led Yiddish studies at Oxford (1978–1997). After a stint at Yale (1998–1999), he took up a professorship in Yiddish studies at Vilnius University (1999–2010) and since 2016 is Professor at Vilnius Gediminas Technical University. He is the author of numerous books and studies, and has conducted thousands of hours of interviews with Holocaust survivors.

Notes

1. Sincere thanks to Alex J. Kay and David Stahel for their invitation to contribute this paper, their generosity of spirit in assisting at each stage, and their important suggestions and improvements. They are of course not responsible for the views or faults herein.

2. See, for example, Yitzhak Arad, *The Holocaust in the Soviet Union* (Lincoln, NE: University of Nebraska Press, 2009), 521–522; Dina Porat, "The Holocaust in Lithuania. Some Unique Aspects," in *The Final Solution: Origins and Implementation*, ed. David Cesarani (London/New York: Routledge, 1994, 159–174), 160; Bernhard Press, *The Murder of the Jews in Latvia, 1941–1945* (Evanston, IL: Northwestern University Press, 2000), x; Gertrude Schneider, "The Two Ghettos in Riga, Latvia, 1941–1943," in *The Holocaust in the Soviet Union. Studies and Sources on the Destruction of the Jews in the Nazi-Occupied Territories of the USSR, 1941–1945*, ed. Lucjan Dobroszycki and Jeffrey S. Gurock (Armonk, NY: M. E. Sharpe, 1993), 181–193, here 183; Efraim Zuroff, *Operation Last Chance. One Man's Quest to Bring Nazi Criminals to Justice* (New York: Palgrave Macmillan, 2009), 113–122.

3. On Lithuania see Dov Levin, "Lithuania," in *Encyclopedia of the Holocaust*, vol. 3, ed. Israel Gutman (New York: Macmillan, 1990), 895–899, here 898. On Latvia see Meir Meller [Mejers Melers], interview (2011), https://youtu.be/17AatLsaDFQ (last accessed on April 23, 2018).

4. Efraim Zuroff, "The Memory of Murder and the Murder of Memory," in *Atminties dienos: The Days of Memory*, ed. Emanuelis Zingeris (Vilnius: Baltos lankos, 1995), 391–405, here 396.

5. See Ezra Mendelsohn, *The Jews of East Central Europe Between the World Wars* (Bloomington: Indiana University Press, 1983), 212–254.

6. One of the first to formulate this political double game was N. N. Shneidman in his *Jerusalem of Lithuania: The Rise and Fall of Jewish Vilnius* (Oakville: Mosaic Press, 1998), 168.

7. Papers on the subject include Efraim Zuroff, "Eastern Europe: Antisemitism in the Wake of Holocaust Related Issues," *Jewish Political Studies Review* 17, nos. 1–2 (spring 2005): 63–79; Leonidas Donskis, "Another Word for Uncertainty: Antisemitism in Modern Lithuania," in *NORDEUROPAForum* 1 (2006): 7–26, http://edoc.hu-berlin.de/nordeuropaforum/2006-1/donskis-leonidas-7/PDF/donskis.pdf (last accessed on January 22, 2018); the late Robert Wistrich's chapter "Lying about the Holocaust," in his *A Lethal Obsession: Antisemitism from Antiquity to the Global Jihad* (New York: Random House, 2010), 631–661 and 1065–1070.

8. Leonidas Donskis, "Text of the Letter from MEP Leonidas Donskis on the Ambrazevičius-Brazaitis Festivities," in *Defending History*, May 15, 2012, http://defendinghistory.com/text-of-the-letter-from-mep-leonidas-donskis-on-the-ambrazevicius-brazaitis-festivities/35485 (last accessed on January 22, 2018). See also his "A Heroic Narrative in Violation of Good Conscience," in *Defending History*, June 12, 2012, http://defendinghistory.com/a-heroic-narrative-in-violation-of-good-conscience/36789 (last accessed on January 22, 2018).

9. The term Holocaust Obfuscation was formally proposed by the author in "On Three Definitions: Genocide; Holocaust Denial; Holocaust Obfuscation," in *A Litmus Test Case of Modernity: Examining Modern Sensibilities and the Public Domain in the Baltic States at the Turn of the Century*, ed. Leonidas Donskis (Bern: Peter Lang, 2009), 259–277. It was first introduced in the author's February 28, 2008 presentation at the Rothschild Foundation Europe Talk Series in London. On the subsequent fate of the term and concept for Eastern

Europe more widely, see Michael Shafir, "Conceptualizing Hungarian Negationism in Comparative Perspective: Deflection and Obfuscation," in *L'Europe à contre-pied: idéologie populiste et extrémisme de droite en Europe centrale et orientale*, ed. Traian Sandu (dir.) and Judit Maár (*Cahiers d'Études Hongroises et Finlandaises*, 2014), 265–310, 266, http://defendinghistory.com/wp-content/uploads/2015/05/MICHAEL-SHAFIR-ON-NEGATIONISM-IN-HUNGARY3.pdf (last accessed on January 22, 2018).

10. For a chronological monitoring of events to date see the page "Blaming the Victims," in *Defending History*, http://defendinghistory.com/blaming-the-victims (last accessed on January 22, 2018).

11. While the actual, organized, political, and academic movements for Double Genocide and Holocaust Obfuscation remain understudied, there have been many significant studies on the issues surrounding post-Soviet states' policies on the Holocaust. Among the important academic collections: Jay Hančil and Michael Chase, eds., *Anti-semitism in Post-Totalitarian Europe* (Prague: Franz Kafka Publishers, 1993); Randolph L. Braham, *Anti-Semitism and the Treatment of the Holocaust in Post-Communist Eastern Europe* (New York: Columbia University Press and the Rosenthal Institute for Holocaust Studies, 1994); John-Paul Himka and Joanna Beata Michlic, eds., *Bringing the Dark Past to Light: The Reception of the Holocaust in Postcommunist Europe* (Lincoln: University of Nebraska Press, 2013), where, however, the write-up for one state, Lithuania, is by two members of the very state-sponsored commission that is the heart of the problem (see below). See also Michael Shafir's important review of the last-cited volume in *Yad Vashem Studies* 42, no. 2 (2015).

12. The Lithuanian media, for example, regularly uses around 90 percent instead of 95 percent, for example, "About 90% of Lithuania's prewar Jewish population of over 200,000 perished during the Holocaust" (a formulation that also avoids mention of massive local collaboration) in Baltic News Service (hereafter BNS), "Lithuania to Mark Jewish Genocide Day," September 22, 2014, http://en.delfi.lt/lithuania/society/lithuania-to-mark-jewish-genocide-memorial-day.d?id=65911048 (last accessed on January 22, 2018).

13. For example, "Efraim Zuroff Critiques Vilnius Genocide Centre's Latest Attempt to Massage Figures (and Ethics) of Local Holocaust Perpetrators," *Defending History*'s October 30, 2013 report, http://defendinghistory.com/60277/60277 (last accessed on January 22, 2018).

14. See, for example, Dovid Katz, "Vilnius Genocide Centre Releases a New Graywash on the Vilna Ghetto" (review of A. Bubnys, *Vilniaus Ghetto 1941–1943*), in *Defending History*, November 19, 2013, http://defendinghistory.com/genocide-center-releases-a-new-graywash-on-the-vilna-ghetto/60925 (last accessed on January 22, 2018).

15. United Nations' 1948 Genocide Convention. Chapter 3 proceeds to enumerate the punishable crimes under Chapter 2: "(a) Genocide; (b) Conspiracy to commit genocide; (c) Direct and public incitement to commit genocide; (d) Attempt to commit genocide; (e) Complicity in genocide." In *Convention on the Prevention and Punishment of the Crime of Genocide. Adopted by Resolution 260 (III) A of the United Nations General Assembly*, December 9, 1948, http://www.hrweb.org/legal/genocide.html; http://www.un.org/millennium/law/iv-1.htm (last accessed on January 22, 2018).

16. Raphael Lemkin, *Axis Rule in Occupied Europe: Laws of Occupation. Analysis of Government. Proposals for Redress* (Washington, DC: Carnegie Endowment for International Peace, 1944), 79.

17. Parliament of Lithuania. *Įstatymas: Dėl atsakomybės už Lietuvos gyventojų genocidą* (*Law on Responsibility for the Genocide of Lithuanian Inhabitants*), *Valstybės žinios* (Official

Gazette) 1992, no. 13–342 (1992). See discussion in Justinas Žilinskas, "Broadening the Concept of Genocide in Lithuania's Criminal Law and the Principle of *Nullum crimen sine lege*," *Jurisprudencija / Jurisprudence* 4, no. 118 (2009): 333–348, which is rich in facts, but concludes with a nationalist defense of de facto Holocaust revisionism.

18. Dovilė Budrytė, "We Call it Genocide: Soviet Deportations and Repression in the Memory of Lithuanians," in *The Genocidal Temptation: Auschwitz, Hiroshima, Rwanda, and Beyond*, ed. Robert S. Frey (Lanham, MD: University Press of America, 2004), 79–101, here 83 and 86.

19. Parliament of Latvia, "Chapter IX. Crimes against Humanity and Peace, War Crimes and Genocide. Section 71. Genocide," in *The Criminal Law. Special Part*, 1998, http://unpan1.un.org/intradoc/groups/public/documents/untc/unpan018405.pdf (last accessed on January 22, 2018).

20. Doyle Stevick, "The Politics of the Holocaust in Estonia: Historical Memory and Social Divisions in Estonian Education," in *Reimagining Civic Education: How Diverse Societies Form Democratic Citizens*, ed. E. Doyle Stevick and Bradley A. U. Levinson (Lanham, MD: Rowman and Littlefield, 2007), 223–230.

21. David Nersessian, "Rethinking Cultural Genocide Under International Law," in *Carnegie Council on Ethics and International Affairs*, http://www.carnegiecouncil.org/publications/archive/dialogue/2_12/section_1/5139.html (last accessed on January 22, 2018).

22. Parliament of Estonia, "Specific Part PP11. Crimes Against Humanity and War Crimes," in *The Criminal Code. Chapter 611*, 1994, http://www.preventgenocide.org/law/domestic/estonia.htm (last accessed on January 22, 2018). Thanks to Reiu Tűűr (Vilnius) for translation of Estonian text.

23. Leonidas Donskis, "The Inflation of Genocide," in *EuropeanVoice.com*, 2009, http://www.donskis.lt/p/en/1/1_/39 (last accessed January 22, 2018).

24. See Defending History, "The Museum of Genocide Victims," August 1, 2010, http://defendinghistory.com/genocide-museum-in-vilnius/45534 (last accessed on January 22, 2018).

25. Over the years, many visitors have noticed something wrong, for example, journalist Jonathan Steele: "In the Jerusalem of the North, the Jewish Story is Forgotten," *The Guardian*, June 20, 2008.

26. Details and images of these features of the museum see Steele: "In the Jerusalem of the North, the Jewish Story is Forgotten." After years of protest, a Holocaust exhibit cubicle was added in the basement in October 2011, and in late winter or early spring 2015 the three offending images were removed. On the basement cubicle added, see Defending History, "The New Holocaust Room in the Basement of the Genocide Museum in Vilnius," November 21, 2011, http://defendinghistory.com/genocide-museum-new-holocaust-room-in-the-basement (last accessed on January 22, 2018).

27. Images of these and related placards at Gruto Park are in Defending History, "Gruto Parkas, the Fun Park near Druskininkai" (2010). English has been corrected in the citation.

28. Genocide and Resistance Research Center of Lithuania, "Lithuanian Experience of the Soviet Genocide Investigation," January 13, 2005, http://www.genocid.lt/Spec/gailius.htm; removed sometime before June 2015 and preserved by Defending History, http://defendinghistory.com/wp-content/uploads/2015/05/Holocaust-Envy-page-from-Genocide-Centers-website.pdf (last accessed on January 22, 2018).

29. Genocide and Resistance Research Centre of Lithuania, "Organization Chart," 2015, http://genocid.lt/centras/en/296/c/ (last accessed on January 22, 2018).

30. For example, Zuroff, *Operation Last Chance*, 95–111. See also the "Lithuania" section of the Operation Last Chance website: http://www.operationlastchance.org/LITHUANIA_Holocaust.htm (last accessed on January 22, 2018).

31. See Ministry of Foreign Affairs of the Republic of Latvia, "Latvia's History Commission (update of 2002)," http://www.mfa.gov.lv/en/policy/society-integration/history/latvia-s-history-commission (last accessed on January 22, 2018).

32. President of Latvia. "Commission of Historians" established November 13, 1998, http://www.president.lv/pk/content/?cat_id=7&lng=en (last accessed on January 22, 2018).

33. Anti-Defamation League, "ADL National Director Resigns from Latvian Commission of Historians Due to Latvia's Treatment of the Holocaust," press release of October 29, 1999, http://archive.adl.org/presrele/holna_52/3498_52.html (last accessed on January 22, 2018).

34. Estonian International Commission for Investigation of Crimes Against Humanity. (Undated statement at conclusion of commission's work), http://historycommission.ee/ (last accessed on January 22, 2018).

35. Anton Weiss-Wendt, "Why the Holocaust Does Not Matter to Estonians," *Journal of Baltic Studies* 39, no. 4 (December 2008), 475–497, here 481.

36. Letter from Joseph Melamed, chairman of the Association of Lithuanian Jews, November 6, 1999, to Valdas Adamkus, president of Lithuania, in Joseph Melamed, ed., *Crime and Punishment* (no. 6, Tel Aviv: Association of Lithuanian Jews, 1999), 5, http://www.defendinghistory.com/1998Nov6ALJ.pdf (last accessed on January 22, 2018). See also letter from Dr. Efraim Zuroff to President Adamkus, in Simon Wiesenthal Center, Israel Office, press release of November 19, 1998, http://defendinghistory.com/SWC%20statement%20on%20the%20Commission%20%281998%29.jpg (last accessed on January 22, 2018).

37. Melamed, *Crime and Punishment*.

38. Julius Girdvainis, "The Expert with Blood on his Hands," *Respublika*, April 22, 2006 (original in Lithuanian), English translation: http://defendinghistory.com/wp-content/uploads/2014/04/Original-attack-on-Arad-April-2006-inc.-ANUSAUSKAS.pdf (last accessed on January 22, 2018).

39. Yitzhak Arad, *The Partisan: From the Valley of Death to Mount Zion* (New York: Holocaust Library, 1979).

40. Girdvainis, "The Expert with Blood on his Hands."

41. Prosecution Service of the Republic of Lithuania. Prosecution Service of the Republic of Lithuania, "Information on Suspicions Against Yizthak [sic] Arad," September 10, 2007, http://www.prokuraturos.lt/News/YizthakArad/tabid/252/Default.aspx (last accessed on January 22, 2018).

42. Prosecution Service of the Republic of Lithuania, "Part of the pre-trial investigation in respect of crimes committed by the Soviet partisan squad during the WWII and related to Yizthak [sic] Arad was closed," September 25, 2008, http://www.prokuraturos.lt/News/YizthakArad2/tabid/290/Default.aspx (last accessed on January 22, 2018). Also as PDF: http://defendinghistory.com/wp-content/uploads/2014/12/Prosecutors-2008-further-defamation-of-Yitzhak-Arad.pdf (last accessed on January 22, 2018).

43. Irena Tumavičiūtė, "A Boy from the Warsaw Ghetto and the Lithuanian Attitude" [in Lithuanian], *Lietuvos aidas*, January 29, 2008, 8, English translation, http://www.defendinghistory.com/29January2008Englishtranslation.pdf (last accessed on January 22, 2018).

44. In addition to her own edition in the original Polish (in 1999), Dr. Margolis's discovery of the diary of Kazimierz Sakowicz eventually led to the publication of an English edition: Kazimierz Sakowicz, *Ponary Diary 1941–1942: A Bystander's Account of a Mass Murder*, ed. Yitzhak Arad, with a foreword by Rachel Margolis (New Haven, CT: Yale University Press, 2005).

45. Among the press reports: Danielle Singer, "Lithuania Accuses Holocaust Survivors of War Crimes," in *Jerusalem Post*, May 28, 2008, 7; Dana Gloger, "The Holocaust Survivors Facing War-Crimes Trials," *Jewish Chronicle*, June 6, 2008, 21.

46. Defending History, "Ireland's Ambassador Dónal Denham Hosts a Reception for Fania Yocheles Brantsovsky at his Residence in Vilnius," in *Defending History*, June 3, 2008, http://defendinghistory.com/irelands-ambassador-donal-denham-hosts-a-reception-for-fania-yocheles-brantsovsky-at-his-residence-in-vilnius/2620 (last accessed on January 22, 2018). A list of additional responses, from the local diplomatic corps, the international media and foreign political figures was published by *Defending History*, "Responses to a State Campaign against Holocaust Survivors who Joined the Anti-Nazi Resistance, 2008–2015," http://defendinghistory.com/blaming-the-victims/responses (last accessed on January 22, 2018).

47. Denis MacShane, *Globalizing Hatred: The New Antisemitism* (London: Weidenfeld & Nicolson, 2008), 33.

48. Simonas Alperavičius (Shimon Alperovich) and Tobijas Jafetas (Tuvia Jafet), "Open Letter," in *Defending History*, "Jewish Community and Union of Ghetto Survivors Speak Out on Harassment of Holocaust Survivors who Joined the Resistance," June 19, 2008, http://defendinghistory.com/jewish-community-and-union-of-ghetto-survivors-speak-out-on-harassment-of-holocaust-survivors-who-joined-the-resistance/38731 (last accessed on January 22, 2018).

49. Melamed, *Crime and Punishment*. The 2011 Interpol incident was widely reported, inter alia in Yossi Melman "Expelling the Ambassador," *Haaretz*, September 7, 2011; Aron Heller, "Israel Shuns Lithuanians over Holocaust probe," in *YahooNews* (Associated Press report), September 15, 2011, http://news.yahoo.com/israel-shuns-lithuanians-over-holocaust-probe-144309941.html (last accessed on January 22, 2018); "Yad Vashem Disinvited Lithuanian officials in Protest Against Treatment of Holocaust Survivor" by World Jewish Congress, September 16, 2011, http://www.worldjewishcongress.org/en/news/yad-vashem-disinvites-lithuanian-officials-in-protest-against-treatment-of-holocaust-survivor (last accessed on January 22, 2018).

50. John Mann, Peter Bottomley, and Bob Russell, "Lithuania and Holocaust Survivors," UK Parliament House of Commons Early Day Motion 2161, September 8, 2011, http://www.parliament.uk/edm/2010-12/2161 (last accessed on January 22, 2018). The text contains an apparent mix-up between the perpetrator alleged to have beheaded Rabbi Osovsky and the perpetrator alleged to have participated prominently in the Lietukis Garage Massacre, though the status of alleged Holocaust perpetrator glorified by a Baltic state government and contested by the Association of Lithuanian Jews, is common to both.

51. Ambassador Chen Ivri Apter's Tel Aviv speech honoring Dr. Rachel Margolis in 2009 is available in the original Hebrew: https://www.youtube.com/watch?v=mzqymUZ-JrA (last accessed on January 22, 2018). Background and partial translation at: http://defendinghistory.com/tel-avivs-leivick-house-releases-2009-video-of-ambassador-chen-ivri-apter/44176 (last accessed on January 22, 2018).

52. More references to the Israeli aspects are provided at: http://defendinghistory.com/israel-debates/43340 (last accessed on January 22, 2018).

53. Yitzhak Arad, "The Holocaust in Lithuania, and Its Obfuscation, in Lithuanian Sources," in *Defending History*, December 1, 2012, http://defendinghistory.com/yitzhak-arad-on-the-holocaust-in-lithuania-and-its-obfuscation-in-lithuanian-sources/46252 (last accessed on January 22, 2018).

54. See Defending History's source pages for Hungary, http://defendinghistory.com/defense-of-history-in-hungary-items-from-early-2014/63167 (last accessed on January 22, 2018), and Ukraine, http://defendinghistory.com/ukraine-issues-in-early-2014/63714 (last accessed on January 22, 2018), and the "Collaborators Glorified" section, http://defendinghistory.com/category/collaborators-glorified (last accessed on January 22, 2018).

55. See Per Anders Rudling, "The Waffen-SS as Freedom Fighters" in *Defending History*, January 24, 2012, http://defendinghistory.com/the-waffen-ss-as-freedom-fighters-by-per-anders-rudling/29648 (last accessed on January 22, 2018); the series of chapters, 2012 to 2014, by Leena Hietanin, http://defendinghistory.com/category/hietanen-leena (last accessed on January 22, 2018).

56. BNS, "Estonian Jewish Community Unhappy with Plans to Commemorate 70th Anniversary of the Arrival of Hitler's Army," July 7, 2001, English translation, http://defendinghistory.com/wp-content/uploads/2011/07/Estonian-celebration-of-Nazi-arrival-70-years-ag.pdf (last accessed on January 22, 2018).

57. Leena Hietanen and Petri Krohn, "Estonia's Last Knight's Cross Waffen SS Man Gets Full-Honors Military Funeral," in *Defending History*, January 13, 2014, http://defendinghistory.com/last-knights-cross-waffen-ss-veteran-buried-in-estonia/62614 (last accessed on January 22, 2018).

58. The central address for international protest is (Londoner) Monica Lowenberg's site (http://stop16marchinriga.blogspot.co.uk/; last accessed on January 22, 2018). Annual eyewitness reports for recent years, with links to world media coverage, can be found in the "Latvia" section of *Defending History*, http://defendinghistory.com/category/latvia (last accessed on January 22, 2018).

59. See Karen Sutton, *The Massacre of the Jews of Lithuania: Lithuanian Collaboration in the Final Solution, 1941–1944* (Jerusalem: Gefen, 2008), 157–208.

60. English translations of some of these Lithuanian texts are available in Joseph Levinson, *The Shoah (Holocaust) in Lithuania* (Vilnius: Vilna Gaon Jewish State Museum, 2006), 166–169.

61. See Defending History, "Memorials to Holocaust Collaborators," http://defendinghistory.com/memorials-to-holocaust-collaborators-in-public-spaces-and-state-sponsored-institutions-in-lithuania (last accessed on January 22, 2018). Evaldas Balčiūnas has documented numerous memorials to perpetrators in different parts of Lithuania in a series of online chapters, http://defendinghistory.com/category/balciunas-evaldas (last accessed on January 22, 2018).

62. See the links provided on the *Defending History* page "Glorification of Local Holocaust Perpetrators in Lithuania," http://defendinghistory.com/glorification-of-local-holocaust-perpetrators-in-lithuania/33745 (last accessed on January 22, 2018).

63. Jewish Community of Lithuania, "Activities of the 1941 Provisional Lithuanian Government with Regard to Jewish Lithuanian Citizens" in the Jewish community's official newspaper, *Jerusalem of Lithuania*, http://holocaustinthebaltics.com/wp-content/uploads

/2010/11/2010JewComStatementOnRehabilitatingLAF.pdf (last accessed on January 22, 2018); also the Jewish community's statement, "Regarding Judgment of the Lithuanian Provisional Government of 1941 and the LAF" in *Defending History*, September 7, 2010, http://defendinghistory.com/2010Sept8LJCstatementOnLAFandPG.pdf (last accessed on January 22, 2018).

64. Defending History, "Lithuanian Parliament's 'Dualism' Strikes Again," October 12, 2010, http://defendinghistory.com/lithuanian-parliaments-dualism-strikes-again/3609 (last accessed on January 22, 2018).

65. Links to the extensive debate around the reburial of a Nazi puppet prime minister by an EU/NATO member state: "Shock of 2012: 1941 Nazi Puppet Prime Minister Reburied with Full Honors," in *Defending History*, December 31, 2012, http://defendinghistory.com/new/34584 (last accessed on January 22, 2018).

66. Juozas Ambrazevičius [later: Brazaitis], "Protocol No. 6" [in Lithuanian] of the 1941 Provisional Government, June 30, 1941, http://defendinghistory.com/wp-content/uploads/2012/05/Brazaitis-Ambrazevicius-chief-signatory-on-30-June-1941-order-for-Jews-to-be-put-in-a-concentration-camp.pdf (last accessed on January 22, 2018); "Protocol No. 12" of the 1941 Provisional Government, July 7, 1941, http://defendinghistory.com/35322-2 (last accessed on January 22, 2018).

67. Vytenis Andriukaitis, "Question to the Foreign Minister and Prime Minister," Lithuanian parliament, May 17, 2012, English translation, http://defendinghistory.com/dramatic-confrontation-on-the-floor-of-the-lithuanian-parliament/35827 (last accessed on January 22, 2018).

68. For a summary of the debate with links to the documents, see "'Surreal' Nov. 29th Vilnius Public Debate on Street Named for Nazi Collaborator," in *Defending History*, December 8, 2016, http://defendinghistory.com/85364-2/85364 (last accessed on January 22, 2018).

69. See Leena Hietanen and Petri Krohn, "Estonia's 2012 'Valentine's Day Law'," in *Defending History*, May 26, 2012, http://defendinghistory.com/estonias-2012-valentines-day-law/36263 (last accessed on January 22, 2018).

70. Baltic Course, "Latvian Seima Approves Criminal Liability for Gross Derogation of Crimes Perpetrated by Soviet Union or Nazi Germany," May 15, 2014, http://www.baltic-course.com/eng/legislation/?doc=91593 (last accessed on January 22, 2018).

71. Baltic Course, "Latvian Court Rejects Claim in Regard to Gross Derogation of Crimes Perpetrated by USSR and Nazi Germany," July 15, 2014, http://www.baltic-course.com/eng/legislation/?doc=94053 (last accessed on January 22, 2018).

72. Baltic News Service (BNS), "Placing the Equals Sign between Nazism and Communism," in *Delfi.lt*, March 19, 2009, Lithuanian original, http://www.delfi.lt/news/daily/lithuania/nori-lygybes-zenklo-tarp-komunizmo-ir-nacizmo.d?id=21075147 (last accessed on January 22, 2018); English translation, http://www.defendinghistory.com/2009March19RedEqualsBrownRationaleForCriminalization.pdf (last accessed on January 22, 2018).

73. Parliament of Lithuania, "Amendment to Criminal Code, Chapter 95, Addition of Chapter 170(2) and Addition to Code Appendix," June 15, 2010, Lithuanian original, http://www3.lrs.lt/pls/inter3/dokpaieska.showdoc_l?p_id=375951 (last accessed on January 22, 2018); English translation, http://www.defendinghistory.com/2010June29Red-BrownLawPassedBy%20Seimas.pdf (last accessed on January 22, 2018).

74. Justinas Žilinskas, "Introduction of 'Crime of Denial' in the Lithuanian Criminal Law and First Instances of Its Application," *Jurisprudence* 19, no. 1 (2012): 315–329, here 326.

75. Milan Chersonski, "History: Education or Modern Politics?" *Jerusalem of Lithuania*, nos. 155–156 (April–June 2010): 2 and 6, here 2, http://defendinghistory.com/wp-content/uploads/2010/11/2010ChersonskiOnCriminalizationOfUniqueHolocaust.pdf (last accessed on January 22, 2018).

76. See note 49.

77. Brief background, a facsimile of the letter Mr. Beržinis received from the police and translation into English are available in "Is the Vilnius Police Criminal Division Harassing a Veteran Holocaust Researcher?," in *Defending History*, March 31, 2014, http://defendinghistory.com/vilnius-polices-criminal-division-harassing-veteran-holocaust-researcher/65215 (last accessed on January 22, 2018). In this case a derivative law was used, and is cited in the letter: "Based on chapter 97 of the Lithuanian Republic's Criminal Code (hereafter LR CC), 'Demanding items and documents with a bearing on the investigation and analysis of criminal action' for additional information."

78. A selection of Balčiūnas's chapters in English translation, and chronicle of his legal ordeals, is available in the Evaldas Balčiūnas section of *Defending History*, http://defendinghistory.com/category/balciunas-evaldas (last accessed on January 22, 2018).

79. "Prague Declaration on European Conscience and Communism," June 3, 2008 in the Senate of the Parliament of the Czech Republic, http://www.praguedeclaration.eu/ (last accessed on January 22, 2018); Defending History, "Critiques of the 2008 Prague Declaration," http://defendinghistory.com/prague-declaration/opposition (last accessed on January 22, 2018).

80. Defending History, "Double Genocide" section, http://defendinghistory.com/category/double-genocide (last accessed on January 22, 2018); Defending History, "When Government Honors are Part of a Plan to Rewrite History," http://defendinghistory.com/when-a-picture-tells-a-story (last accessed on January 22, 2018).

81. "Seventy Years Declaration," http://www.seventyyearsdeclaration.org/ (last accessed on January 22, 2018); Defending History's section on its history, http://defendinghistory.com/category/the-seventy-years-declaration (last accessed on January 22, 2018); the text in European languages, http://defendinghistory.com/the-seventy-years-declaration-in-various-languages (last accessed on January 22, 2018). On the "Battle of the Declarations" see Dan Stone, *Goodbye to All That? A History of Europe Since 1945* (Oxford: Oxford University Press, 2014), 281.

82. Katz, "On Three Definitions" (see note 9); Dovid Katz, "Is Eastern European 'Double Genocide' Revisionism Reaching Museums?," *Dapim: Studies on the Holocaust* 30, no. 3 (2016): 1–30; Dovid Katz, "Free Trade Awry? The Westward Export of Double Genocide," in *Mélanges offerts à Jeff Richards par ses amis à l'occasion de son 65e anniversaire*, ed. Danielle Buschinger et al. (Amiens: Centre d'Etudes Médiévales de la Picardie, 2017), http://defendinghistory.com/wp-content/uploads/2017/04/Dovid-Katzs-paper-in-Earl-Jeffrey-Richards-festschrift-2017.pdf (last accessed on January 22, 2018).

83. On frequent intersection of east-west geopolitics and Holocaust issues, see, for example three 2010 chapters by the present author in the *Guardian*, https://www.theguardian.com/profile/dovid-katz (last accessed on January 22, 2018); Dovid Katz, "The Neocons and Holocaust Revisionism in Eastern Europe," *Jewish Currents*, July 22 and

26, 2014, http://jewishcurrents.org/neocons-holocaust-revisionism-eastern-europe/ (last accessed on January 22, 2018).

84. "Select Bibliography: Media on Ukraine Holocaust Issues (2014–2015)," in *Defending History*, http://defendinghistory.com/63714/63714 (last accessed on January 22, 2018); Lev Golinkin, "You Want to Name Streets after the Murderers of Ukraine's Jews?," in *Forward*, August 2, 2016, http://forward.com/opinion/345738/you-want-to-name-streets-after-the-murderers-of-ukraines-jews/ (last accessed on January 22, 2018).

85. See report in *Strana.ua*, June 1, 2017, https://strana.ua/news/73921--den-nacionalnogo-pozora-kak-socseti-otreagirovali-na-poyavlenie-prospekta-shuhevicha-v-kieve.html (last accessed on January 22, 2018).

86. Israel-related debates are listed on the "Israel" page, *Defending History*, http://defendinghistory.com/israel-debates/43340 (last accessed on January 22, 2018).

87. See Barry Rubin, "Unfinished Business and Unexplained Opportunities: Central and Eastern Europe, Jews and the Jewish State," *Israel Journal of Foreign Affairs* 4, no. 2 (2010): 37–47.

88. See the discussion hosted by *Israel Journal of Foreign Affairs*, with participation by Jan Grabowski, Juliana Geran Pilon, Dovid Katz, and John S. Micgiel 4, no. 3 (2010): 187–194, http://holocaustinthebaltics.com/wp-content/uploads/2010/10/2010IsraelJournalofForeignAffairs.pdf (last accessed on January 22, 2018).

Part VI. History as Comparison

12 Comparing Soviet and Nazi Mass Crimes

Hans-Heinrich Nolte

Memories and Political Debates

A German historian of my generation (I was born in 1938), when asked to submit a contribution to *Mass Violence in Nazi-Occupied Europe*, has to start with memories. Discussing Nazi criminality was for me part of growing up. The question as to whether my father—in his last Wehrmacht function chief of the General Staff of the German *Afrika Korps*—had been involved in any crimes, has accompanied my life. But even earlier than that I had experience with Soviet crimes (mass rape), when the attempt of my mother to escape the Soviet Army in April / May 1945 failed.[1] Only a few years ago, reading the memoirs of a Jew from Riga I learned that during this escape we passed by a forced labor camp, where starving slave workers were waiting desperately for that same Soviet Army, as it was their last chance to survive.[2]

The debate on mass crimes in the Soviet system had already been the subject of public debate during the Weimar Republic. My grandfather, a Protestant pastor (who later became a member of the Confessing Church and was openly attacked by the *Schutzstaffel* [SS])[3] owned a book about the persecution of religions in the Soviet Union, which I inherited.[4] In the early 1930s, Communist publishers pushed books defending Stalinism, contrasting the 6 million people out of work in Germany in 1931 with pictures of happy workers during the first years of the Five-Year Plan.[5] On the other side, Nazi propaganda—the Nibelungen-Verlag in a special series called anti-Bolshevik writings (*antibolschewistisches Schrifttum*)—published memoirs of a former Communist, who had worked as a forest engineer in the Soviet Union and wrote about forced labor and prisons there, with photos from the Gulag, including images from Solovki Prison and the Belomorski Canal. By June 1939, this memoir had sold eighty thousand copies.[6]

During World War II, anti-Soviet propaganda was common in Germany. For instance, mass graves of victims of the OGPU (Joint State Political Directorate) were opened and made public, as far as that suited German interests, such as in Katyn to foster the Polish dispute between the Allies and in Vinnitsa to support

Ukrainian collaboration. However, they did not open Kurapaty near Minsk, although Soviet citizens of course told German officers about that particular killing site.

Differing perhaps from some left-wing milieus in France or England,[7] Germany heard a lot about Soviet mass crimes after the war. Many students my age had been victims of the ethnic cleansing of the territories assigned to Poland in Potsdam, and / or had taken part in westward flights in 1944–1945.[8] During the Cold War, all young Germans (myself included) in the Federal Republic grew up with images of the Berlin Wall and with stories of escapes. Following the Hungarian Uprising, we had refugees from that country, and the first book on Russian history I bought for myself in 1962 had a chapter on Stalinism.[9]

In the late 1930s in Western Europe the theory of totalitarianism was originally proposed, which claimed to reveal structural equalities between communism and fascism.[10] As long as Great Britain and the United States were allied with the Soviet Union that theory was put aside, but it gained new importance as ideology in the period of the Cold War.[11] Hannah Arendt's *The Origins of Totalitarianism* was published in 1951 and in German translation in 1955.[12] Although in considerable parts of the global academic community, totalitarianism as a concept was criticized from the 1970s,[13] the concept remained quite popular in Germany.[14] In 1996 Russian and German historians together edited a collection of chapters on different totalitarian systems of the twentieth century.[15]

The public debate on Soviet mass crimes in West Germany after 1945 was intertwined with the question as to whether Soviet mass crimes were one of the reasons for the German ones. Ernst Nolte (no relation) started one of the last debates on the topic in the *Frankfurter Allgemeine Zeitung* of June 6, 1986. He argued that the "class murder" of the Bolsheviks was the logical and actual "precursor" to the "race murder" of the National Socialists.[16] There was an uproar, which is understandable, since the Holocaust in Germany in fact had been kept out of public discussion until the 1960s, and there was reason to fear that a new intellectual obfuscation was intended.

To my mind, there were two historical arguments against Ernst Nolte, the first chronological and the second comparative:[17]

1. Hitler had written *Mein Kampf* in 1923 and this chronology simply meant that Stalinist crimes cannot have been the "precursor" of National Socialism. Moreover, Hitler did not use his image of the terrors during revolution and civil war in Russia to legitimate any use of violence by fascists and did not side with the murdered enemies of Bolshevism. Rather, he saw it as "a hint of fate" that the "race-core of Germanic organizers and leaders" in Russia "may today be considered as almost without a remainder eradicated and extinguished." Hitler wrote that a Russian state led by Jews (as he imagined)

would be easy prey, and considered this mass murder as a chance to pursue the "politics of soil" in Eastern Europe, which would finally create the precondition for Germany to become a world power.[18]

2. Hitler's knowledge of the Bolshevik terror relied on novels and reminiscences of white counterrevolutionaries, including the German Free Corps, who dwelled on Communist mass crimes. That was a very tarnished source. Certainly, this civil war (like others) was terrible.[19] Documents on both, or rather all sides, have been published in Russian, and the military losses are estimated at 2.5 million people. The Cheka claimed that the "Red Terror" officially ordered by the Party on November 1, 1918 was a response to white terror—the attempt on Lenin's life and the shootings of more then 10,000 "reds" by white organizations in the summer of that same year.[20]

New Research

The only university course on National Socialism I attended in Göttingen was at the end of my studies; we discussed Bracher, Sauer, and Schulz.[21] Privately we consulted the blue series of the Nuremberg Trials in the library. We also discussed Nazi crimes with Reinhard Wittram, who had been a member of the Nazi Party.[22] In 1959, I visited Mauthausen, and in 1960–1961 in the context of student politics I took part in the *Verjährungsdebatte*; in prewar German law, the statute of limitations for murder was twenty years, which would have led to the end of trials in 1965. In a series of debates after 1960, however, the German parliament altered the time limit and in 1979 finally ended all restrictions on the prosecution of murder. I also met Reinhard Strecker and learnt about the pitfalls of using materials from Eastern European archives.[23] I did not engage in contemporary history, following the doubts of my academic mentors about whether objective research would be possible in that field, and consciously chose for my PhD an early modern Russian topic on the history of Eastern Europe, and for my post-doctoral thesis (*Habilitation*) I chose historiography. Only after I started teaching in Hanover in 1970 did I learn from colleagues about the ubiquity of slave labor in the town I was then living in[24] and was introduced to research on National Socialism. I offered university courses on Operation Barbarossa.[25] For the Soviet side I used printed sources as writings, memoirs, the Smolensk Archives,[26] Khrushchev's "secret speech" and, of course very cautiously, Soviet editions[27] and oral history collections.[28]

Comparison was difficult, as long as knowledge from sources was on different levels. The political scientists and sociologists used information of different qualities about both National Socialism and the Soviet Union as quarries for their constructions. For historians, however, these constructions were not very convincing, not only because we had not learned that approach, but also because we had to take into account the different situation of the archives. Most German records had been captured by the Americans, brought to the United States and opened for research. Yet the Americans ensured that they were microfilmed before returning them to Germany. There was little possibility for cover-ups.

Soviet records (except for the Smolensk ones captured by the Germans in 1941 and, luckily for historians, shipped to the United States right under the nose of their Soviet ally) were opened only in 1991. Now research in archives supported the concept of force as a fundamental instrument and dictatorship as a political form in the Soviet Union, but new editions on the camps and the killing fields, the factories and the kolkhozes were now added to the many reports from victims, some of which had been known before. By opening the archives (not quite without exceptions[29] and mainly to those who brought along some money) the source base of knowledge was multiplied.[30] German historians published important sources on the period in Russian,[31] and following independent research and voluminous new Russian editions Bernd Bonwetsch edited a selection of sources in a relatively cheap sourcebook in German translation.[32] New histories of the period were written,[33] and old ones rewritten.[34] Obviously, as the archives had been in the control of the government for more than seventy years, there had been opportunities for cover-ups, but fundamental comparison was now possible.[35] In my judgment, the best methodological approach for such comparisons was made by Stein Rokkan: one must be able to transition back and forth between the phenomena one is comparing.

Together with Pavel Polian I published a short general comparison of Nazi and Soviet mass crimes in 2001.[36] Using the unity of a region as a concept, I compared the murders in the Bolshevik killing field Kurapaty near Minsk and the Nazi killings of Jews near Slonim, both in Belarus. I found them similar in many regards, but also with important differences—the Cheka killed by shooting adults in the head, the SS and Security Service (*Sicherheitsdienst*, or SD) killed Jews at pits by gunning them down, children and adults together. I interpret the difference by concluding that in the Soviet killings social and political control over the killers was tighter, while the German killings at the pits offered more possibilities for individual sadism.[37] More comparative research followed. Fine examples are found in the comparisons of camps, slave labor, expulsion, and deportation edited by Dittmar Dahlmann and Gerhard Hirschfeld[38] and of POWs edited by Klaus-Dieter Müller and others.[39] Detlef Schmiechen-Ackermann showed in 2006 the different reach of the two concepts in comparing "totalitarianisms" or "dictatorships."[40]

Michael Geyer and Sheila Fitzpatrick organized a series of conferences in which comparisons were made and carefully controlled by some of the best-known specialists in their fields, published in 2009 with the title *Beyond Totalitarianism*.[41] The editors of this volume successfully managed their comparative approaches by inviting specialists, asking them for papers and encouraging them, more than once, to rethink the comparisons they had made. To my mind, that volume demonstrated, with regard to research, that totalitarianism is not the most adequate tool for this particular comparison. Without doubt, however, and by their own definitions, both governments were dictatorships, therefore my proposal is to use this term for starting comparisons.[42]

A specific point was the systematic mass killings of Jews. In the tradition of the pogroms committed in the late years of the Russian Empire, whites and Ukrainian nationalists transgressed the border between pogrom and genocide of Jews in the south in 1919, murdering whole Yiddish populations of *Shtetl*, including women and children.[43] Heinz-Dietrich Löwe showed that the thesis that capitalism as well as socialism had the same source, namely the Jewish people, originated in Russia following 1890.[44] Mostly antisemites argued in religious terms, yet in 1905 Michail O. Menshikov published the thesis that the Jews constituted a "race."[45] This kind of antisemitism was welcomed by Adolf Hitler and the German Nazis.

During World War II, the Allies kept the reports on the Holocaust low-key—the Anglo-Saxons, who knew about it from the very beginning,[46] because they wanted to stop Jewish emigration to Palestine and decide on the course of the war without political pressures, and the Soviets, since the Party was afraid of the slogan that Communism was "Jewish," propagated by Nazi propaganda in the Soviet Union not without success.[47] Holocaust studies started relatively late, led first and foremost by Raul Hilberg in the United States.[48] In Germany, as noted above, the Holocaust was hardly a subject of research in the 1950s,[49] although the Poliakov and Wulf collection was published by the government.[50] Mainly the Auschwitz trial of 1963–1965, with Fritz Bauer as chief public prosecutor, brought the Holocaust back into German consciousness,[51] changed criminal procedures,[52] and gave a boost to research in Germany.[53] Today there are comprehensive monographs on the genocide against the Jews using the available databases.[54] Adding to a relatively small collection of published sources by Peter Longerich,[55] a new and more comprehensive edition is currently being edited.[56]

In Eastern Europe, Holocaust studies were placed on a new footing only following the breakup of the Soviet Union. Yitzhak Arad[57] and R. A. Chernoglazova edited collections of sources.[58] I may point to Pavel Polian[59] and Il'ya Al'tman[60] as leading Russian scholars, but most of all I want to point to the encyclopedia of the Holocaust on the territory of the former USSR, which makes it easy to access the collected knowledge of the Russian-language community on certain places or certain persons in the genocide against the Jews in Eastern Europe.[61] It is surprising that Russian-language research[62] and research in other languages of the countries victimized by the German attack were and are hardly noted in the west.

It is convincing to constitute relations between the different mass crimes of the twentieth century. But whatever is proven by being a precursor (by being earlier)—for example, gunning down Native people at Wounded Knee and Asian Indians in Jallianwalla Bag, forcing the Herero nation to starve in the desert, the pogrom at Kishinev in 1905, and, last but not least, the genocide of Armenians by Turks in 1915 were committed long before the first Cheka murders were.[63] It was most important that Michael Mann extended this research on genocide by asking for the connections not only to dictatorships, but also to democracies.[64]

It seemed obvious that the murders during the Civil War in Russia 1918–1921 and the Stalinist murders accompanying Soviet industrialization may be researched in that context. But in the 1990s a dispute was started as to whether or not it was adequate to carry out comparative research on the Holocaust, since some researchers considered it to have been unique.[65] As far as every historical event is unique, this of course is true, but if the slogan meant that the Holocaust was not comparable, it is not convincing. And, as in the question of totalitarianism, one has to keep in mind still that comparing is not the same as equating.[66]

It is even difficult to separate the German genocide against the Roma from the Holocaust in research, or putting it another way: if you read sources on the German Holocaust in the Soviet Union, you cannot help but read about the genocide against the Roma, too, committed by the same troops as part of the same "campaign."[67] The question is unavoidable as to whether German occupation politics in partisan regions of Belarus, committed in those regions where Jewish partisans were active and Jewish family camps were trying to survive, were not genocidal in character, too.[68] This means, also from the perspective of German occupation politics, that the contexts "call" for cooperation between Holocaust and genocide studies,[69] extending that to the study of massacres.

In the German public following 1945 the war against the Soviet Union was for a long time pictured as a defensive measure against Bolshevism or an attempt to defeat Great Britain by defeating its Soviet ally, the *Festlanddegen*. However, since the 1960s the history of the German campaign against the Soviet Union has been rewritten—mostly using the German archival material that had been the booty of the United States and was safeguarded by them for the use of historians. It was Andreas Hillgruber who first demonstrated that the war in the east really was "Hitler's true and proper war,"[70] planned as an instrument for Germany's ascendance as a world power. In the following decades the rapacious and murderous character of the expansion in the east was elaborated by many historians—Heinz Höhne published on the SS,[71] Helmut Krausnick and Hans-Heinrich Wilhelm on the Einsatzgruppen in Poland and the USSR,[72] and Christian Streit showed that the Wehrmacht had more than 3 million Soviet POWs starved to death.[73] Gerd R. Ueberschär and Wolfram Wette put the new view into a short, comprehensive, and successful book,[74] and it was my turn to add some sources translated from Russian to the broad picture.⁷⁵ In 1991, Omer Bartov published his research on the brutalization of the war in the east.⁷⁶

Meanwhile, research in related areas was broadly established.⁷⁷ Christopher Browning's *Ordinary Men* could be singled out, since he showed that the policemen killing Jewish people in Poland were not fanatically National Socialist, but rather an average cross section of the German police.⁷⁸ "Research on perpetrators" (*Täterforschung*) opened up a new field,⁷⁹ and research on institutions and persons has brought impressive results.⁸⁰ Among new biographies, Wolfram Wette on Karl Jäger,⁸¹ Wigbert Benz on Hans-Joachim Riecke,⁸² and Alex Kay on Alfred Filbert⁸³ should be noted. There have been and are fierce debates of course, the best known maybe on the "Wehrmacht exhibition" (*Wehrmachtsausstellung*) of 1995, that—despite legitimate criticism of the naiveté with which photographs were used in that exhibition—established the term "war of annihilation" (*Vernichtungskrieg*), which does seem fitting.⁸⁴

Of the ongoing research during the last fifteen years perhaps the question might be singled out as to whether the starvation of the Soviet people envisaged by German experts in May 1941 as a result of planned occupation politics was a fleshed out "plan" or more a mere "intention" and how many people were actually starved to death.⁸⁵ Detailed studies have appeared on regions—like Christian Gerlach's outstanding book on Belarus⁸⁶—and on cities and towns like Leningrad⁸⁷ or Smolensk.⁸⁸

As one special group of victims, forced laborers (*Zwangsarbeiter*), citizens of occupied territories in Eastern Europe forced to toil for the "Reich," have been researched—both comprehensively⁸⁹ and in the villages or factories in which they worked.⁹⁰ Soviet concentration camp inmates have been questioned, in the case of Bergen-Belsen, as far as they had survived, till 1997–1999.⁹¹ To my mind, marginal groups of victims such as Roma or the mentally ill remain underresearched.⁹²

New overviews have been published, which use Russian sources.⁹³ Babette Quinkert and Jörg Morré have published a collection of chapters on German occupation politics, which offer an informative view of recent research from mostly young researchers in Germany, Russia, and Ukraine.⁹⁴ Alex Kay, Jeff Rutherford, and David Stahel published a collection on 1941, which offers a similarly informative view on English-language and further German-language research.⁹⁵ Frank Bajohr and Andrea Löw have edited an up-to-date collection on the latest research on the Holocaust in German and English, with a fine leading chapter from Ulrich Herbert,⁹⁶ but they do not include Russian research.

The Revival of East-Central Europe

In addition to new Russian archival possibilities as well as historiography, an important change resulted from historical scholarship in the nations between Germany and Russia, which after the end of the officially ordered friendship of the Warsaw Pact countries took a sharp turn against Russia. In 1984, Milan Kundera saw these countries as the "kidnapped West."[97] In a cultural respect, that turn led to the revival of older concepts of "*Ostmitteleuropa*" (East-Central Europe)—seen as a region in its own right between Germany and Russia.[98] But was it part of the West, was it an independent (semiperipheral or peripheral) region of Europe[99] or was it just a collection of separate national states with heavy prejudices and deep border problems between one another?[100] Most of these countries entered the European Union after 1991,[101] but the question as to whether their elites followed national aims or European ones has not yet definitively been answered. The reconstruction of the concept of East-Central Europe also fueled debates in the historiographies, the two most popular cases being Polish writing on Katyn and Ukrainian writing on the so-called Holodomor. Reconstructing East-Central Europe as a historical region was a precondition for writing a history of this region for the first half of the short nineteenth century.

The first one to do that was Dietrich Beyrau with his "battlefield of dictators" published in 2000.[102] Beyrau writes about the similarities between National Socialism and Stalinism and adds to the features known from the concept of totalitarianism—"uniform ideology, existence of a one-party state, control of media and instruments of violence ... ideological fanaticising of strategically important parts of the population, focussing all social and political activity on a few goals, the capacity of the leadership to acquire and use all instruments—economy, administration, media, apparatus of violence—for strategic aims."[103] Imagined enemies provided dynamism as a precondition for ending moral restraints on the part of the perpetrators and the total deprivation of victims' rights.

But Beyrau also states the differences—the intellectual roots of Bolshevism were embedded in the European Enlightenment, those of Nazism were anti-Enlightenment and postrevolutionary conservatism, and not only the marking of the victims put those roots into action. Attempts to exclude Nazism or Communism from the European tradition are not acceptable for Beyrau—"the so-called falling back into barbarism is neither a monopoly of certain civilisations nor one of national traditions, but a continuous present danger, which in the age of technical civilisation may almost unavoidably end up in million-fold murder."[104]

Beyrau gives a reason for choosing Eastern Europe as the scene of his study: many mass crimes of the two regimes were committed in this region. He also divides the topic following the provenience of his sources—drawing on Alexander Solzhenitsyn, whose role in the late-Soviet intelligentsia he had previously researched—into the following categories:[105] (1) The Soviet circle: socialist purgatory, and (2) The German circle: National Socialist hell.

While Beyrau published in 2000 a well-balanced book for the German reading public, in 2010 Timothy Snyder published a popular book aimed at a global and European public. It is well written, convincingly researched, and well propagated by the media. Also, the author had a broad intellectual background of well-informed discussants in Yale and Vienna.[106] The effect is a very successful book, which spurred discussions.[107] Which decisions in regard to his material did he take, and in what direction does he influence the view of Stalinism and Nazism? Snyder brings both closer together and regionalizes them. Since he is not using a common scientific term but creating his own, he can also skip the discussion on regionalizing Europe from Halecki to Szüs sketched above. His subtitle—Europe between Hitler and Stalin—might be misinterpreted to mean that neither one of these two was situated within the boundaries of Europe.

Snyder's *Bloodlands* stretch from Germany's eastern border in 1937 to Smolensk and from the Baltic to the Black Sea, including East Prussia. This is—and I guess, not by chance—also the territory of the kingdom of Poland (including the then Duchy of Prussia and the Grand Duchy of Lithuania) following the standstill with Moscow of 1618, plus the khanate of the Crimea, then a dependency of the Ottoman Empire, and Livonia, Estonia, and Ingermanland, then provinces of Sweden. Snyder repeats this map a couple of times, although Czechoslovakia, Hungary, and Romania are not included. This is also the space that is disputed today between Russia and NATO. It follows from this creation of a space that in the west and the south major sites of Nazi mass crimes are omitted—from Berlin to Bergen-Belsen, from Paris to Theresienstadt. Important places of the Holocaust are left out, like those in Slovakia and Hungary, but also the many Serbian and Greek villages, burnt down in German operations during the antipartisan war.

What is left out from Stalinism? Its mass crimes were committed all over the Soviet Union; therefore, this is the space that lends itself to the discussion, in case one chooses to write about them starting from the sources. Khrushchev in his secret speech of February 25, 1956, defended Stalin's crimes against Russian peasants from 1928 onward as a struggle against the Kulaks, but criticized his politics against the Communist Party in the years 1935–1938, as well as Stalin's originating the concept "enemy of the people."[108] Since the protocol of the meeting of the presidium before that speech has been published, we know of the debate beforehand, but we do not know what other mass crimes were known in this circle.[109] For instance, Robert Payne followed the focus on mass crimes against communists.[110]

This view of Stalinist terror was definitely wrong and misleading. As noted above, in Germany knowledge about the Soviet system of camps was existent and for instance reiterated in anticommunist literature following the war.[111] The camps were a topic in academic teaching.[112] This view was insufficient and indeed it was fundamentally enlarged following the collapse of the Soviet Union.[113] The regional focus on all of the Soviet Union was not questioned in this new research. The main regions of the Gulag were the north of Russia and Siberia. Mass terror was mostly applied against "normal" citizens, also in Kurapaty near Minsk in Belarus, where very many victims have been buried.[114] But, terrible as it is,

Kurapaty was in no way unique, rather the mass shootings of 1937 were planned and enacted as a process for the whole Union from the Far East to Kiev.[115] Relevant documents have been edited by Bernd Bonwetsch in a popular collection.[116]

The fact that there is no focus on the "bloodlands" is true also for Soviet deportations. In Germany, it was impossible to forget that deportations were an instrument of Soviet power, because there were enough relatives of the Russian Germans living in the west to keep the memory alive that the Volga Germans had been deported to Siberia. It was Pavel Polian who first showed that many ethnic or social groups were deported—from Cossacks on the River Terek in order to make peace with the Muslims of the North Caucasus in 1920 to Finns, Poles, and Germans living close to the borders in 1935–1936—but also for Koreans, when the confrontation with Japan loomed.[117] These deportation politics were carried out in all border regions, including the western borders, but as noted above also for the kulaks from all over the country, and they constituted the biggest number, estimated at up to 2.5 million.[118] We have a fine edition of sources on the topic.[119]

In terms of the numbers of people killed, the biggest Stalinist mass crime was the famine of 1932–1933, in which more than 7 million Soviet citizens died, more than half of them in Ukraine.[120] It was a man-made famine, not in the sense that the Bolshevik leadership had organized it to kill people, but in the sense that the agrarian politics of the Communist Party interrupted and deregulated the inherited form of production in such a form and to such a degree, that a poor harvest in all wheat-growing regions of the Soviet Union in the following year was to be expected. The livestock was forcibly collected from the well-to-do peasants (kulaks) and was not cared for adequately in the new kolkhozes. Many cattle and horses died. There were no tractors and no artificial fertilizer yet, and the loss of livestock led to a deficit in traction during the harvest and to a loss of manure for the next season. The government tried to cover up its blunder by changing statistics—harvests were now assessed on the basis of the stalk instead of the grain collected in the farm or kolkhoz, as before. Such statistics "showed" that forced collectivization had even increased the harvest from 73.3 million tons in 1928 to 89.8 million tons in 1933, while following the old statistical procedure it had in fact decreased to 68.4 million tons.[121] This statistical self-deception also allowed the peasants to be blamed for not harvesting correctly or even for concealing grain. On top of that, the government insisted on delivery quotas for export, although the collapsing world market for grain caused a sharp downturn anyway.[122] But this inhuman policy was not enforced only in Ukraine, but across the country.

Many Ukrainians today speak of this famine as Holodomor and give the impression of a similarity with the Holocaust committed in these very same regions less than ten years later. But while on the one hand there is no doubt that the famine was man-made, on the other hand there are no documents that prove an intent or even a plan to murder by famine.[123] But, while the interpretation that "Russia" (identifying it with the Georgian Stalin) attempted to extinguish the Ukrainian nation by starvation is difficult to maintain, the starvation without doubt profoundly changed Ukraine: "Similar to the Irish Great Famine between 1846 and 1851, which cost about one million victims, the Holodomor has changed the country irreversibly."[124] Even if there is no proof for the planning of genocide—the economy of the Soviet Union was definitely governed from the center, which therefore gives responsibility for the famine, and for the fact that no help was provided, to the Soviet leadership. But a historian has to follow the sources, which again tell us that the agrarian policy of the Communist Party was directed against all peasants, and not only the Ukrainian ones.[125]

The (Western) Bug River as Border Running Through the "Bloodlands"

The region that Snyder calls the "bloodlands" in fact constitutes not only the territory of six nations—Estonia, Latvia, Lithuania, Poland, Belarus, and Ukraine—but also historically is connected to the growth and expansion of empires and states bordering it in the east and west. During the period of Arab economic influence up to the Baltic Sea,[126] Poland was founded and Kievan Rus was the birthplace of the Russian state(s). But during the twelfth and thirteenth centuries what Snyder has called the "bloodlands" were constituted as a semiperipheral region to the east of northern France and the Rhineland, which at that time belonged to the center of the European world system. The elites of the region had two political options: becoming internal, colonial peripheries of center countries like eastern Germany or Bohemia, or starting their own developments as autonomous states like Poland or Russia. Prussia and Pomerania were conquered by German powers in the Middle Ages and Silesia was annexed by Bohemia—and in these different ways territories settled mostly by Slavs at that time became parts of the Holy Roman Empire or of the Teutonic Order, which also occupied the Baltic states of today's Latvia and Estonia.

Poland was able to remain outside the Mongol Empire and to fence off the Teutonic Order. In the fifteenth century it attained a kingdom, which for all but the title might have been an empire—in the context of the merger with Lithuania it expanded as far as Smolensk and the Black Sea. But while the Orthodox nobility of that space was won over for a union with Catholicism, peasants and Cossacks east of the (Western) Bug River remained Orthodox, which in the seventeenth century led to the partition of Ukraine between Warsaw and Moscow. The Tsar had collected those Russian territories where Orthodox princes had weathered the Mongol storm. In the seventeenth century Sweden cut off Russia from the Baltic Sea, but in the eighteenth century Russia in alliance with the two German powers Austria and Prussia annexed east Poland. Following 1815 the Bug—as the eastern border of the Polish kingdom united with Russia—retained its religious and ethnic importance, and that convinced the British Foreign Minister George Curzon in 1919 that this river should delineate Poland in the east.

From 1918 to 1921, East-Central Europe was reconstituted as a series of independent states, but in 1938 the West allowed Germany to occupy Czechoslovakia and in 1939 Nazi Germany and the Soviet Union divided the rest of the region between themselves. Germany murdered the Jews of the region, as far as German troops went. In 1945 the region was divided yet again and all Germans east of the River Oder and south of Austria were expelled. In this way, over the course of the twentieth century some of these territories changed hands almost every decade. Following the defeat of the German powers in World War I, it looked for a moment as if communists might march right through to Berlin, and, in the next moment, as if Russia's success in the eighteenth century was being called into question by Poland's expansion to the east; but in 1921 at the Peace of Riga the border was drawn right between the Dnjepr and Bug Rivers.

From Snyder's point of view, contemporary history is not how the medieval and modern history of the region may perhaps be explained, but what use the elites of the region made of that history. The Germans highlighted medieval expansion to the east as *Ostsiedlung* (settling the East) and used it quite openly for legitimating German expansionism in the twentieth century.[127] For considerable parts of the German elites the East was a space to be conquered, or as Hitler put it in 1923: "if you want new ground and soil in Europe, generally this can only be done at the expense of Russia. And then the new Empire must again march on the road of the knights of the Teutonic Order, to conquer with the German sword soil for the German plough and daily bread for the German nation."[128] The elites of the new Polish republic used similar, if opposite historical arguments for claiming either Silesia and Pomerania as ethnically and historically Polish from the period of the Piast kings or Ukraine and Belarus as historical parts of the Polish noble commonwealth up to the divisions in the years 1772–1815. For both German and Polish elites, national history played a central role in their argumentation.

For the Communist elites, though, economic and social history played the central role. Industry and raw materials, good harbors and also strategic territories were important for them, but not national histories. In the late 1930s some ingredients of national Russian history were added[129] but a massive and systematic return to topics of the imperial historiography was only enforced when German tanks reached the outskirts of Moscow in 1941.[130] For the Communist elites in the early 1930s, the space where the Holodomor took place, Ukraine, had no special historical meaning. It had economic meaning as a granary, and many members of the Communist leadership may have had experiences with Nestor Makhno, the anarchist leader—first as an ally, later as an enemy. Ukraine was peasant country; the rate of urbanization among Ukrainians was on average half that among Russians,[131] a quarter of that among Armenians, and about a tenth of that among Jews in the Soviet Union. In a state governed by townspeople,[132] Ukraine was an internal periphery.[133] The very east of Ukraine, where a very large percentage of the population spoke Russian, not Ukrainian, did have importance for the economic thinking of the Bolsheviks as a center of heavy industry: the Donbass. Indeed, in the debates of the Communist Party regarding whether a second center of heavy industry should be planned, the argument was made that the Donbass in case of an attack from Germany was not strategically safe; Germans and Austrians had reached it in 1918.

Mass murder to the east of the Bug River differed substantially from that to the west of it. East of the border of the German Reich, according to its own claims, from 1941 to 1945,[134] genocide against Jews and Roma was committed mainly by mass shootings and starvation, and only in relatively few cases by asphyxiation of the victims (using gas vans). The difference meant that to the east of the (Western) Bug River genocide was committed face to face, in a way often considered as "archaic" and without extermination camps like Treblinka or Auschwitz designed to kill by gas without direct contact to the victims.[135] For the victims themselves, the difference meant that to the east of the border of the German Reich of 1941 there was extremely little chance of survival. If a Jew had not escaped to Soviet-held territories before the advancing German troops, only joining the Soviet partisans offered any hope of survival.[136] Maybe this hopelessness was one of the reasons for the fact that in almost every ghetto east of the Bug River we find armed resistance.[137] To the west of the Bug River (even from Grodno, which belonged to southeast Prussia)[138] there was a, if very small, chance to survive the concentration and even some extermination camps.[139] This border, though, runs right through the middle of the "bloodlands" and this rather is an argument to place the history of the Holocaust in the context of the history of German expansion and occupation, as Tatjana Tönsmeyer argues.[140] The internal borders of German expansion had more importance for the fates of the occupied than the old border of the Polish republic following the Peace of Riga[141] or the new borders of Ukraine.[142]

The Holocaust in the sense of an (almost) complete and systematic genocide started on June 22, 1941. Western research is predominantly occupied with the Holocaust to the west of the Bug River, but it should be kept in mind that chronologically that was the second one. Since almost half of the victims were murdered to the east of the Bug River, this constituted about half of the Shoah. Obviously, research on the other half of the Holocaust is not possible without knowledge of the region and of the languages spoken there, and of Yiddish (which is now almost extinguished there).[143] Translations should be offered.[144] Of course, research in the region, like that fostered by the Holocaust-Fond in Moscow, should be encouraged. Emphasizing the special role of East-Central Europe in German mass crimes fits to my concept of the world system, in which this region is interpreted as internal periphery, as long as it is governed from a capital outside of the region such as Vienna, St. Petersburg, or Berlin.[145] The whole of Eastern

Europe (east of the German borders) is interpreted as semiperiphery for the twentieth century.[146]

In political, social, and economic terms, the difference between Russia and Germany was striking: Germany had successfully reached the status of a fully industrialized center country during the long nineteenth century, with an effective government, public spending in infrastructure, and so on, while the Soviet Union in the tradition of the Russian Empire was a big power on the basis of its semiperipheral resources.[147] Russia was also culturally a "member of the family," but economically just a producer of raw materials. As Stalin put it in 1913, arguing against the Bund, who wanted special Jewish institutions: "Russia is a half Asiatic country, and therefore the politics of 'blows' not rarely turns to its most barbarous form, that of pogroms... Germany—that already is Europe with more or less freedom. No wonder that a politics of 'blows' there never turns into a pogrom. In France, of course, you have more 'guarantees,' since France is more democratic than Germany."[148] As we know from hindsight, Stalin was wrong in his judgment of Germany, but the point here is that he put the country into another category, using the continents as signatures for political progress. The Soviet Union in the process of industrialization—despite its enormous costs[149]—succeeded in building enough heavy industry overnight by June 22, 1941, to win the battle of Moscow in the winter of that year and remain a resourceful ally of Great Britain and the United States up to the common victories against Germany and Japan.

Comparing Again

The simplest way of comparing was and is that "Hitler killed foreign people and Stalin his own." This comparison is imprecise—the Nazis killed their own Communists (not to mention the question as to whether German Jews were even foreign) and the Stalinists killed Polish prisoners of war. In any case, this difference does make an important distinction—Nazism was about nationality (in the guise of natural science seen as race), Communism was about equality (in the guise of social and economic sciences seen as class). These definitions are quite general, but provide us with a starting point for diversifying the question.

Doris Bergen has proposed six historical places and intellectual contexts discussed in recent historiography for the Holocaust, which include: (1) modernity, (2) bloodlands, (3) ending empires, (4) genocide, (5) colonialism, and (6) occupation politics.

I propose to use these as categories for discussing our topic—not only the genocide against the Jews, but also the other German and Soviet mass crimes of the years 1918 and 1945, and to start with Germany:

1. Modernity in the common sense of progress toward more technical means and of dividing human actions into small divisions of labor,

which make it difficult to assume personal responsibility has explanatory capacity especially for the Western part of the Holocaust. But this definition of modernity is not exhaustive, as follows from Zygmunt Baumann's arguments and also from Shmul Eisenstadt's concept of a multiplicity of modernities.
2. The term "bloodlands" gives a vivid impression of the German-occupied territory in Eastern Europe, but leaves out other places like Serbia or Greece and overrides the internal difference between the western and the eastern halves of the Holocaust.
3. That the end of empire was one of the starting points of National Socialism is certain; even if they themselves thought that now a new empire, a third one, would be founded, which would last for a thousand years.
4. At least three genocides were committed by Germans—against the Jews, the Roma, and against Soviet POWs. To my mind, the arguments that German politics against the partisans at least in Belarus had genocidal traits is also convincing.
5. Colonialism, not so much in the sense of continuity with the Herero murders, as Zimmer argues, but in the more general sense of a coinage of European culture by the colonial experience, helps to explain the mass crimes.
6. Occupation politics played a role—practically and ideologically. Imitating a common image of the American West, the occupied territories for Germans were to be regions without many rules, where space for later settlement might be created (by expelling or killing inhabitants).

Do these six concepts explain traits of the Soviet mass crimes?

1. Modernity—the idea behind Soviet agrarian politics, the reason for the mass starvation, was to modernize the Soviet agrarian structure. This was quite a different kind of modernity though to that common in Western Europe.
2. Bloodlands—as argued above, this term does not really represent the Soviet mass killings of the period, which were mostly committed in the north and the east of the Soviet Union.
3. Ends of empires—the downfall of the Russian Empire with the terrible civil war and the expulsion, if not the killing of the old elites, deeply destabilized Russia and Ukraine.
4. Genocide—as argued above, the Holodomor was no genocide. The murders of Katyn were genocidal, since belonging to the Polish nation was a criterion for singling out the victims. Not all Polish POWs in the Soviet Union were murdered though.
5. Colonialism—part of the Bolshevik leading group was thinking in colonial terms, for instance Stalin. But Ukraine was not a colony of Moscow at the time.
6. Occupation—Ukraine was not occupied during the Holodomor.

How to conceive the criminality of Nazism and of Stalinism? There are different views on guilt—Protestant or Catholic, Jewish or Atheist, French or Polish, upper or lower class, academics or peasants, religious and secular. From a feminist point of view, mass rape may take first place, from a view on civilizing, it might be area bombing. But to come to an inclusive position a historian has to look for positions built on a political consensus on right or wrong. This consensus in our cases has to be global. Therefore, I propose the Genocide Convention, as adopted December 9, 1948, by the General Assembly of the UN, as a step in global judgments founded on written international law created by the international community.[150]

There is no reason to skip over its shortcomings. The signature of the Soviet Union was only attained because the convention did not categorize mass murder of the domestic population as an international crime, since the Soviet camps and mass shootings were known. And the signature of the United States and Great Britain was only attained because ethnic cleansing was not explicitly forbidden and rather some strange formulas on psychological hardship in forced migration were introduced, since they just had consented in Potsdam to the biggest population transfer of the period. The Genocide Convention is a compromise, no doubt, but what else can a law enacted by a community be than a compromise?

In this sense, the international community in the years from 1947 onward decided that genocide in the global context is more dangerous than other crimes against humanity. The reason for that had been noted by Albert Einstein in 1946, when he argued against the principle of nonintervention in the context of the publication of the Black Book about the genocide of Soviet Jews: "that an international organisation for safeguarding our existence only then may reach its aim, when it does not limit herself to protecting states against military assault, but also extends its actions to protecting national minorities within single states."[151] As long as our global order is resting on nations, it would rock the foundations if one member were to be allowed to destroy another one—also a potential subject of the global order, one that may still be in the making. It might follow that there would be no order and no instrument to prevent a global war.

Thus, despite obvious similarities between Soviet and German crimes, the differences should be kept in mind. Genocide is the crime that the nations of the world have condemned most vehemently. From Wounded Knee to Srbrenica, from Katyn to Guatemala there are, terribly enough, many actions with genocidal traits in the world.[152] But the genocides against the Jews and Roma committed by Germans in the years 1941–1945 stand out in terms of their ruthlessness and thoroughness. Of course, they should be compared. But because of their global importance they should also be remembered (and researched) in their own right.

HANS-HEINRICH NOLTE was Professor for the History of Eastern Europe in Hanover, 1980–2003, and Guest Professor for Global History in Vienna, 2003–2014. His most recent books include *Weltgeschichte des 20. Jahrhunderts* (2009), *Russische Geschichte* (2012), and *Religions in World and Global History* (2015). He was editor-in-chief of the *Zeitschrift für Weltgeschichte* from 2000 to 2018.

Notes

1. Hans-Heinrich Nolte, "Kindheit und Jugend in Deutschland," in *Kindheit und Nachkriegsjugend in zwei Welten. Deutsche und Russen blicken zurück*, ed. Bernd Bonwetsch (Essen: Klartext, 2009), 83–98; Hans-Heinrich Nolte, "Kaukesselchen," *Wo denken wir hin? Lebensthemen, Zivilisationsprozesse, demokratische Verantwortung*, ed. in Hans-Peter Waldhoff, Christine Morgenroth, Angela Moré, and Michael Kopel (Giessen: Psychosozial-Verlag, 2015), 237–246 [Russian translation by Igor Smirnov in: Ju. M. Osipov and L. I. Rostovceva, eds., *My pomnim. Srazu posle vojny* (Tula: Grif i K, 2017), 552–564].

2. Meir Levenshtejn, *U kraja Bezdny, Vospominanija* (Moscow: Gamma, 2012), 168–173.

3. H. Krieger, "Nicht alle wollen Noltes sein," *Das Schwarze Korps*, July 15, 1937. See also "Eine schwarze Seele enthüllt sich," *Das Schwarze Korps*, June 24, 1937.

4. N. N. Glubowsky, ed., *Das Notbuch der russischen Christenheit* (Berlin: Eckart, 1930).

5. Ernst Glaeser and F. C. Weiskopf, eds., *Der Staat ohne Arbeitslose* (Berlin: Universum-Bücherei für alle, 1931).

6. K. I. Albrecht, *Der verratene Sozialismus* (Berlin: Nibelungen-Verlag, 1939).

7. See the criticism of Robert Conquest, *The Harvest of Sorrow* (Oxford: Oxford University Press, 1986), 308–321.

8. Bernd Bonwetsch, ed., *Kindheit und Nachkriegsjugend in zwei Welten. Deutsche und Russen blicken zurück* (Essen: Klartext, 2009). Most German contributors came from east of the borders of 1937, the others from Berlin or Leipzig.

9. Günther Stökl, *Russische Geschichte* (Stuttgart: Kröner, 1962), 712–736.

10. Vadim Damiers, "Frühe linke Kritik des Totalitarismus," in *Auseinandersetzungen mit den Diktaturen*, ed. Hans-Heinrich Nolte (Gleichen: Musterschmift, 2005), 65–72.

11. For example see Hans Buchheim, *Totalitäre Herrschaft* (Munich: Kösel, 1962).

12. Hannah Arendt, *Elemente und Ursprünge totaler Herrschaft* (Munich: Piper, 1986).

13. Chalmers Johnson, ed., *Change in Communist Systems* (Stanford, CA: Stanford University Press, 1970); Roger E. Kanet, ed., *The Behavioral Revolution and Communist Studies* (New York: Free Press, 1971).

14. Bruno Seidel and Siegfried Jenkner, eds., *Wege der Totalitarismusforschung* (Darmstadt: Wissenschaftliche Buchgesellschaft, 1968); Eckhard Jesse, ed., *Totalitarismus im 20. Jahrhundert. Eine Bilanz der internationalen Forschung* (Bonn: Bundeszentrale für politische Bildung, 1996).

15. Aleksandr Chubarjan, Jakov Samojlovich Drabkin, and Adolf Jakobsen, eds., *Totalitarizm v Evrope XX veka*, (Moscow: Pamjatniki istoricheskoj mysli 1996); Marianna Kortschagina, "Die russische Diskussion über Totalitarismus," in *Auseinandersetzungen mit den Diktaturen*, ed. Hans-Heinrich Nolte (Gleichen: Musterschmift, 2005), 51–64.

16. The text in Ernst Nolte, *Das Vergehen der Vergangenheit* (Frankfurt: Ullstein, 1987), 171–179.

17. Hans-Heinrich Nolte, "Inwieweit sind russisch-sowjetische und deutsche Massenmorde vergleichbar?," in *Von der Verdrängung zur Bagatellisierung?*, ed. Niedersächsische Landeszentrale für politische Bildung (Hanover: Niedersächsiche Landeszentrale für politische Bildung, 1988), 49–58.

18. Adolf Hitler, *Mein Kampf* (Munich: Zentralverlag der NSDAP, 1938), 742–743. This second part of *Mein Kampf* was first published in 1927—also before the Stalinist crimes of the industrialization period were known in Germany or had even been committed in the Soviet Union. This copy was donated to me by my mother-in-law, who had (of course) been a member of the *Bund Deutscher Mädel* (League of German Girls).

19. M. E. Glavackij, ed., *Istorija Rossii 1917–1940* (Ekaterinburg: Ural'skii Gosudarstvennyi Universitet, 1993), 4–138; G. F. Krivosheev, *Rossija I SSSR v vojnakh XX. Veka* (Moscow: OLMA-Press, 2001), 110–151.

20. A. S. Velidova, ed., *Krasnaja kniga VCHk*, 2nd ed. (Moscow: Politizdat, 1989 [1920]), 6.

21. Karl Dietrich Bracher, Wolfgang Sauer, and Gerhard Schulz, *Die nationalsozialistische Machtergreifung. Studien zur Errichtung des totalitären Herrschaftssystems* (Opladen: Leske & Budrich, 1962).

22. Compare Błażej Białkowski, *Utopie einer Tyrannis. Deutsche Historiker an der Reichsuniversität Posen (1941–1945)* (Paderborn: Schöningh, 2011).

23. See Gottfried Oy and Christoph Schneider, *Die Schärfe der Konkretion. Reinhard Strecker, 1968 und der Nationalsozialismus in der bundesdeutschen Historiographie* (Münster: Westfälisches Dampfboot, 2014).

24. The result of many of years of research and local exhibitions was: Rainer Fröbe, Claus Füllberg-Stolberg, Christoph Gutmann, Rolf Keller, Herbert Obenaus, and Hans Hermann Schröder, *Konzentrationslager in Hannover*, parts 1 & 2 (Hildesheim: Lax, 1985).

25. For German language publications and literature of that time see the bibliography in Hans-Heinrich Nolte, *Der deutsche Überfall auf die Sowjetunion 1941* (Hanover: Landeszentrale, 1991), 185–191.

26. See National Archives and Record Service, *Guide to the Records of the Smolensk Oblast of the All-Union Communist Party of the Soviet Union 1917–1941* (Washington, DC: General Services Administration, 1980).

27. A. A. Grechko, ed., *Istorija Vtoroj Mirovoj Vojny*, vols. 1–12 (Moscow: Voennoe izdatel'stvo, 1973–1982); Central'noe Statisticheskoe Upravlenie SSSR, *Narodnoe Khozjajstvo* (Moscow: CSU, 1972).

28. Ales' Adamovich, Janka Bryl' and Vladimir Kolesnik, eds., *Ja iz ognennoj derevni* (Minsk: Mastackaja literatura, 1977); Ales Adamovich and Daniil Granin, *Blokadnaja kniga* (Moscow: Sovetskij Pisatel, 1982). Compare Ales' Adamovich, "Kennen wir uns selbst?," and Ales' Adamovich, "Zusammen mit dem Volk geschrieben," German translation in, *Der Mensch gegen den Menschen*, ed. Hans-Heinrich Nolte (Hannover: Fackelträger, 1991), 13–24 and 48–65.

29. Michail Gefter, "Wenn wie sie vertrieben haben," German translation in, *Der Mensch gegen den Menschen*, ed. Hans-Heinrich Nolte (Hannover: Fackelträger, 1991), 28–47; Pavel Poljan, "Die russische Auseinandersetzung mit der Schuld," in *Auseinandersetzungen mit den Diktaturen*, ed. Hans-Heinrich Nolte (Gleichen: Musterschmift, 2005), 27–44.

30. See the bibliography in Jörg Baberowski, *Verbrannte Erde. Stalins Herrschaft der Gewalt* (Frankfurt: Fischer, 2014), 565–571.

31. Mark Junge and Rolf Binner, *Kak terror stal "bol'shim." Sekretnyj prikaz No. 00447* (Moscow: AIRO-XX, 2003).

32. Bernd Bonwetsch, "Sowjetmacht und Gewalt," in *Quellen zur Geschichte Russlands*, ed. Hans-Heinrich Nolte, Bernhard Schalhorn, and Bernd Bonwetsch (Stuttgart: Reclam, 2014), 285–376; cf. the voluminous edition of sources in German translation in Rolf Binner, Bernd Bonwetsch, and Marc Junge, eds., *Massenmord und Lagerhaft. Die andere Geschichte des Großen Terrors* (Berlin: Akademie, 2009).

33. Sheila Fitzpatrick, ed., *Stalinism: New Directions* (London: Routledge, 2000); Manfred Hildermeier, *Geschichte des Sowjetunion 1917–1991* (Munich: C. H. Beck, 1998).

34. Hans-Heinrich Nolte, *Geschichte Russlands*, (Stuttgart: Reclam, 2014), 204–274. cf. Hans-Heinrich Nolte: "Stalinism as Total War," in *The Shadows of Total War*, ed. Roger Chickering and Stig Förster (Cambridge: Cambridge University Press, 2009), 295–312.

35. Stein Rokkan, *Vergleichende Sozialwissenschaft* (Frankfurt: Ullstein, 1972); see now Hartmut Kaelble: *Der historische Vergleich* (Frankfurt: Campus, 1999).

36. Pavel Poljan and Hans-Heinrich Nolte: "Massenverbrechen in der Sowjetunion und im Nationalsozialistischen Deutschland. Zum Vergleich der Diktaturen," *Zeitschrift für Weltgeschichte* 2, no. 1 (2001): 125–148. Abridged Russian translation: "Gitler i Stalin: s kem zhit' luche, s kem veselej?," *Neprikosvennyj Zapas* 28 no. 2 (2003): 195–211.

37. Hans-Heinrich Nolte, "Töten in Belorussland 1936–1944," in *Massenhaftes Töten. Kriege und Genozide im 20. Jahrhundert*, ed. Peter Gleichmann and Thomas Kühne (Essen: Klartext, 2004), 143–157.

38. Dittmar Dahlmann and Gerhard Hirschfeld, eds., *Lager, Zwangsarbeit, Vertreibung und Deportation* (Essen: Klartext, 1999).

39. Klaus-Dieter Müller, Konstantin Nikischkin, and Günther Wagenlehner, eds., *Die Tragödie der Gefangenschaft in Deutschland und der Sowjetunion* (Cologne: Böhlau, 1998). Compare Vasilis Vourkoutiotis, "Institutionalisierte Schizophrenie. Vergleich der Behandlung von angloamerikanischen und sowjetischen Kriegsgefangenen in deutscher Hand im Zweiten Weltkrieg," *Zeitschrift für Weltgeschichte* 6, no. 2 (2005): 65–82.

40. Detlef Schmiechen-Ackermann, *Diktaturen im Vergleich* (Darmstadt: Wissenschaftliche Buchgesellschaft, 2010 [2006]), especially 78–82.

41. Michael Geyer and Sheila Fitzpatrick, eds., *Beyond Totalitarianism: Stalinism and Nazism Compared* (Cambridge: Cambridge University Press, 2009).

42. Nolte, ed., *Auseinandersetzungen*; Marina Korchagina, ed., *Izuchenie diktatur* (Moscow: Pamjatniki istoricheskoj mysli, 2007).

43. Zvi Gitelman, *A Century of Ambivalence* (New York: Schocken, 1988), 96–108.

44. Heins-Dietrich Löwe, *Antisemitismus als reaktionäre Utopie, Russischer Konservativismus im Kampf gegen den Wandel von Staat und Gesellschaft 1890–1917* (Hamburg: Hoffmann & Campe, 1978).

45. Löwe, *Antisemitismus als reaktionäre Utopie*, 132–134.

46. See already David S. Wyman, *The Abandonment of the Jews* (New York: The New Press, 1984). Great Britain and, following its entry into the war, the United States were informed from the very beginning, since the British had decoded the German Police radio traffic: Richard Breitman, *Official Secrets: What the Nazis Planned, What the British and Americans Knew* (New York: Hill and Wang, 1998). As a case in point see: Hans-Heinrich Nolte, "Partisanenkrieg ohne Partisanen? Ein Konstrukt," in *Auseinandersetzungen mit den Diktaturen*, ed. Hans-Heinrich Nolte (Gleichen: Musterschmift, 2005), 171–176.

47. Il'ya Al'tman, *Zhertvy nenavisti. Kholokost v SSSR 1941–1945 gg.* (Moscow: Fond Kovcheg, 2002) [German translation: *Opfer des Hasses. Der Holocaust in der UdSSR 1941–1945* (Gleichen: Musterschmidt, 2008), 58–76]. It was impossible for religious people, Christians or Jews, to belong to the Communist Party, but those who were Jewish according to their passports from the beginning of the Soviet Union toward the end were represented in the Communist Party more than their percentage in the population was: Gerhard Simon, *Nationalismus und Nationalitätenpolitik in der Sowjetunion* (Baden-Baden: Nomos, 1986) 449–450. Compare Mordechai Altshuler, *Soviet Jewry on the Eve of the Holocaust* (Jerusalem: Yad Vashem, 1998); and Yuri Slezkine, *Das jüdische Jahrhundert* (Göttingen: Vandenhoeck & Ruprecht, 2007).

48. Raul Hilberg: *The Destruction of the European Jews* (New York: Harper & Row, 1983 [1961]).

49. Hans-Adolf Jacobsen, *1939–1945. Der Zweite Weltkrieg in Chronik und Dokumenten* (Darmstadt: Wehr und Wissen, 1959), 409–432 contained a chapter on "Wider die Tradition" featuring the Commissar Order, Backe's "12 Commandments," the order to raze Warsaw, the Morgenthau Plan and others, but nothing on the Holocaust. There followed a chapter on mostly military resistance to Hitler.

50. Leon Poliakov and Josef Wulf, eds., *Das Dritte Reich und die Juden* (Berlin: Bundeszentrale für politische Bildung, 1961).

51. Irmtraud Wojak, "Der erste Frankfurter Auschwitz-Prozess und die 'Bewältigung' der Vergangenheit" in *Auschwitz-Prozess 4 Ks 2/63*, ed. Fritz Bauer-Institut (Cologne: Snoeck, 2004), 53–70.

52. Joachim Perels, "Die Strafsache gegen Mulka," in *Auschwitz-Prozess 4 Ks 2/63*, ed. Fritz Bauer-Institut (Cologne: Snoeck, 2004), 124–147.

53. Wolfgang Benz, ed., *Der Holocaust* (Munich: C. H. Beck, 1999); Omer Bartov, ed., *The Holocaust* (London/New York: Routledge, 2000).

54. Peter Longerich, "Der Russlandfeldzug als rassistischer Vernichtungskrieg" in *Der Mensch gegen den Menschen*, ed. Hans-Heinrich Nolte (Hannover: Fackelträger, 1991), 78–92; Peter Longerich, *Politik der Vernichtung. Eine Gesamtdarstellung der nationalsozialistischen Judenverfolgung* (Munich: Piper, 1998); brief: Philippe Burrin, *Warum die Deutschen? Antisemitismus, Nationalsozialismus, Genozid* (Berlin: Ullstein, 2004).

55. Peter Longerich, ed., *Die Ermordung der europäischen Juden* (Munich: Piper, 1989).

56. See especially volume 7 of the sixteen-volume source edition: *Die Verfolgung und Ermordung der europäischen Juden durch das nationalsozialistische Deutschland*, vol. 7: *Sowjetunion mit annektierten Gebieten*, vol. ed. Bert Hoppe and Hildrun Glass (Munich: Oldenbourg, 2012).

57. Yitzhak Arad, ed., *Unichtozhenie evreev SSSR v gody nemeckoj okkupacii* (Jerusalem/Moscow: Jad Va-Shem/Tekst, 1992).

58. R. A. Chernoglazova, *Tragedija evreev Belorusii v 1941–1944 gg.* (Minsk: Gal'perin, 1997).

59. Pavel Polian, *Obrechennye pogibnut. Sud'ba sovetskikh voennoplennykh-evreev vo Vtoroj mirovoj vojne* (Moscow: Novoe izdatel'stvo, 2006); Pavel Polian, *Mezhdu Aushwvicem i Bab'im Jarom* (Moscow: ROSSPEN, 2010).

60. See Al'tman, *Opfer des Hasses*.

61. I. A. Al'tman, ed., *Kholokost na territorii SSSR: Entsiklopediia* (Moscow: ROSSPEN, 2009).

62. Hans-Heinrich Nolte, "Vom Umgang mit Asymmetrien und Kampf um Zivilisierung," in *Der Mensch gegen den Menschen*, ed. Hans-Heinrich Nolte (Hannover: Fackelträger, 1991), 237–248.

63. Mark Levene and Penny Roberts, eds., *The Massacre in History* (New York: Berghahn, 1999).

64. Michael Mann, *The Dark Side of Democracy: Explaining Ethnic Cleansing* (Cambridge: Cambridge University Press, 2005).

65. Alan S. Rosenbaum, ed., *Is the Holocaust unique? Perspectives on Comparative Genocide* (Boulder, CO: Westview, 1996).

66. Cf. Nancy L. Green, "Forms of Comparison," in *Comparison in History*, ed. Deborah Cohen and Maura O'Connor (New York: Routledge, 2004), 41–56.

67. Christian Gerlach, *Kalkulierte Morde* (Hamburg: Hamburger Edition, 1999), 859–1054; as examples see the "Unternehmen" Hamburg and Altona in 1942: Hans-Heinrich Nolte, "Destruction and Resistance. The Jewish Shtetl Slonim 1941–1944," in *The People's War: Responses to World War II in the Soviet Union*, ed. Bernd Bonwetsch and Robert Thurston (Urbana, IL: Illinois University Press, 2000), 29–53, here 45–46.

68. U. M. Mikhnjuk, *Njamecka-fashycki genacid na Belarusi (1941–1944)* (Minsk: BelNDCDAAS, 1995).

69. See the leading journal *Holocaust and Genocide Studies* 1ff. 1986 ff, and Jürgen Zimmerer, "Intersections: Holocaust Scholarship, Genocide Research and Histories of Mass Violence, 5th Global Conference on Genocide," http://hsozkult.geschichte.hu-berlin.de/termine/id=28868 (last accessed on January 20, 2016).

70. Andreas Hillgruber, *Hitlers Strategie. Politik und Kriegführung 1940–1941* (Frankfurt: Bernard Graefe, 1965).

71. Heinz Höhne, *Der Orden unter dem Totenkopf* (Munich: Piper, 1967).

72. Helmut Krausnick and Hans-Heinrich Wilhelm, *Die Truppe des Weltanschauungskrieges* (Stuttgart: Deutsche Verlags-Anstalt, 1981).

73. Christian Streit, *Keine Kameraden. Die Wehrmacht und die sowjetischen Kriegsgefangenen 1941–1945* (Stuttgart: Deutsche Verlags-Anstalt, 1978). A new edition of sources: Rüdiger Overmans, Andreas Hilger, and Pavel Poljan, eds., *Rotarmisten in deutscher Hand. Dokumente zu Gefangenschaft, Repatriierung und Rehabilitierung sowjetischer Soldaten des Zweiten Weltkrieges* (Paderborn: Schöningh, 2012).

74. Gerd R. Uberschär and Wolfram Wette, eds., *"Unternehmen Barbarossa"* (Paderborn: Schöningh, 1984); many subsequent editions with Fischer Verlag in Frankfurt. See also Gerd Überschär, "'Russland ist unser Indien.' Das Unternehmen Barbarossa als Lebensraumkrieg," in *Der Mensch gegen den Menschen*, ed. Hans-Heinrich Nolte (Hannover: Fackelträger, 1991), 66–77.

75. Nolte, *Überfall*.

76. Omer Bartov, *Hitler's Army: Soldiers, Nazis, and War in the Third Reich* (Oxford: Oxford University Press, 1992).

77. Rolf-Dieter Müller and Gerd R. Ueberschär, *Hitler's War in the East: A Critical Assessment*, 3rd ed. (New York: Berghahn, 2009).

78. Christopher R. Browning, *Ordinary Men: Reserve Police Battalion 101 and the Final Solution in Poland* (New York: HarperCollins, 1992).

79. One of the first was Gerhard Paul and Klaus-Michael Mallmann, eds., *Die Gestapo: Mythos und Realität* (Darmstadt: Wissenschaftliche Buchgesellschaft, 1995); overview in

Hans-Heinrich Nolte, "Nazi-Mörder—'Ganz normale Männer'?," in *Normalität der NS-Täter?*, ed. Rolf Pohl and Joachim Perels (Hanover: Offizin, 2011), 63–82.

80. Gerd Ueberschär, *Hitlers Militärische Elite*, 2 vols. (Darmstadt: Wissenschaftliche Buchgesellschaft, 1998); cf. Gerhard Hirschfeld and Jersak Tobias, eds., *Karrieren im Nationalsozialismus* (Frankfurt: Campus, 2004).

81. Wolfram Wette, *Karl Jäger, Mörder der litauischen Juden* (Frankfurt: Fischer, 2011); with a facsimile of the "Jäger-Report."

82. Wigbert Benz, *Hans-Joachim Riecke, NS-Staatssekretär* (Berlin: Wissenschaftlicher Verlag Berlin, 2014).

83. Alex J. Kay, *The Making of an SS Killer: The Life of Colonel Alfred Filbert, 1905–1990* (Cambridge: Cambridge University Press, 2016).

84. See inter alia Hans-Heinrich Nolte, "Der Krieg im Osten als Vernichtungskrieg," in *Der Landtag debattiert November/Dezember 1998*, ed. Präsident des Niedersächsischen Landtages (Hanover: Niedersächsischer Landtag, 1999), 43–68.

85. Alex J. Kay, *Exploitation, Resettlement, Mass Murder: Political and Economic Planning for German Occupation Policy in the Soviet Union, 1940–1941* (New York/Oxford: Berghahn, 2006), 57–73; Hans-Heinrich Nolte, "Kriegskinder. Zu den Differenzen zwischen Russland und Deutschland," *Zeitgeschichte* 36 (2009): 311–323; Alex J. Kay, "Verhungernlassen als Massenmordstrategie: Das Treffen der deutschen Staatssekretäre am 2. Mai 1941," *Zeitschrift für Weltgeschichte* 11, no. 1 (2010): 81–105; Wigbert Benz, *Der Hungerplan im "Unternehmen Barbarossa"* (Berlin: Wissenschaftlicher Verlag Berlin, 2011); cf. Nolte, *Überfall*, 121–126 and 149–154.

86. Gerlach, *Kalkulierte Morde*.

87. Jörg Ganzenmüller, *Das belagerte Leningrad. Die Stadt in den Strategien von Angreifern und Verteidigern* (Paderborn: Schöningh, 2005); Manfred Sapper and Volker Weichsel, eds., *Die Leningrader Blockade. Der Krieg, die Stadt und der Tod*, special issue of *Osteuropa* 61 no. 8–9 (August–September 2011).

88. Laurie R. Cohen, *Smolensk under the Nazis: Everyday Life in Occupied Russia* (Rochester, NY: University of Rochester Press, 2013).

89. Pavel Polian, *Zhertvy dvukh diktatur*, 2nd ed. (Moscow: ROSSPEN, 2002); Jens Binner, *"Ostarbeiter" und Deutsche im Zweiten Weltkrieg* (Munich: Meidenbauer, 2008). Overview for the Reich: Mark Spoerer, *Zwangsarbeit unter dem Hakenkreuz* (Stuttgart: dva, 2001).

90. Editions of sources for Belarus: V. I. Adamushko, M. I. Bogdan, et al., eds., *Belorusskie ostarbejtery*, vols. 1–3 (Minsk: NARB, 1996–1998). For POWs in a specific region: Rolf Keller and Silke Petry, eds., *Sowjetische Kriegsgefangene im Arbeitseinsatz 1941–1945* (Göttingen: Wallstein, 2013).

91. Hans-Heinrich Nolte, ed., *Häftlinge aus der UdSSR in Bergen-Belsen* (Frankfurt: Peter Lang, 2001). The questioned group consisted of surviving POWs, victims of forced labor, inhabitants of partisan regions, children, and two Jewish women.

92. Hans-Heinrich Nolte, "Vernichtungskrieg: Vergessene Völker. Review neuer Literatur," www.fes.de/cgi-bin/afs.cgi?id=81425 (last accessed on January 20, 2016).

93. Dieter Pohl, *Die Herrschaft der Wehrmacht. Deutsche Militärbesatzung und einheimische Bevölkerung in der Sowjetunion 1941–1944*, new ed. (Frankfurt: Fischer, 2011 [2008]); Christian Hartmann, *Die Wehrmacht im Ostkrieg. Front und militärisches Hinterland 1941/42* (Munich: Oldenbourg, 2010).

94. Babette Quinkert and Jörg Morré, eds., *Deutsche Besatzung in der Sowjetunion 1941–1944* (Paderborn: Schöningh, 2014).

95. Alex J. Kay, Jeff Rutherford, and David Stahel, eds., *Nazi Policy on the Eastern Front, 1941: Total War, Genocide, and Radicalization* (Rochester, NY: University of Rochester Press, 2012).

96. Ulrich Herbert, "Holocaust-Forschung in Deutschland: Geschichte und Perspektiven einer schwierigen Disziplin," in *Der Holocaust, Ergebnisse und neue Fragen der Forschung*, ed. Frank Bajohr and Andrea Löw (Frankfurt: S. Fischer, 2015), 31–79. Doris L. Bergen, "Holocaust und Besatzungsgeschichte," in *Der Holocaust, Ergebnisse und neue Fragen der Forschung*, ed. Frank Bajohr and Andrea Löw (Frankfurt: S. Fischer, 2015), 299–320, only lists one Russian-language researcher (316).

97. Milan Kundera, "Un occident kidnapé," *Kommune* 2 (1984): 43–52.

98. In political history see: Oskar Halecki, *Grenzraum des Abendlandes* (Salzburg: Otto Müller, 1956); Jenö Szüs, *Die drei historischen Regionen Europas* (Frankfurt: Neue Kritik, 1994 [1983]).

99. Ivan T. Berend, *Central and Eastern Europe 1944–1993. Detour from the periphery to the periphery* (Cambridge: Cambridge University Press, 1996); Hans-Heinrich Nolte, "Osteuropa," in *Enzyklopädie der Neuzeit*, vol. 9, ed. Friedrich Jaeger (Stuttgart: Metzler, 2009), columns 662–686; Włodzimierz Borodziej, Stanislav Holoubec, and Joachim von Puttkamer, eds., *Mastery and lost Illusions: Space and Time in the Modernization of Eastern and Central Europe* (Munich: Oldenbourg, 2014).

100. István Bibó, *Die Misere der osteuropäischen Kleinstaaterei* (Frankfurt: Neue Kritik, 1992 [1946]); André Gerrits and Nanci Adler, eds., *Vampires Unstaked. National Images, Stereotypes and Myths in East Central Europe* (Amsterdam: Koninklijke Nederlandes Akademie van Wetenschappen, 1995).

101. Hans-Heinrich Nolte, "Die Osterweiterung der EU—eine historische Perspektive" in *Demokratien in Europa*, ed. Ines Katenhusen and Wolfram Lamping (Opladen: Leske + Budrich, 2003), 45–70; Matthias Chardon, Siegfried Frech, and Martin Große Hüttmann, eds., *EU-Osterweiterung* (Schwalbach: Wochenschau, 2005); Hannes Hofbauer, *Osterweiterung* (Vienna: Promedia, 2003).

102. Dietrich Beyrau, *Schlachtfeld der Diktatoren. Osteuropa im Schatten von Hitler und Stalin* (Göttingen: Vandenhoeck & Ruprecht, 2000).

103. Beyrau, *Schlachtfeld der Diktatoren*, 9.

104. Beyrau, *Schlachtfeld der Diktatoren*, 11.

105. Dietrich Beyrau, *Intelligenz und Dissens. Die russischen Bildungsschichten in der Sowjetunion 1917–1985* (Göttingen: Vandenhoeck & Ruprecht, 1993), 191–208.

106. Not the university, but the "Institut für die Wissenschaften vom Menschen" (Institute for Human Sciences), which has its first focus of six on culture and institutions in Central and Eastern Europe, see http://www.iwm.at (last accessed on September 27, 2015).

107. Timothy Snyder, *Bloodlands: Europe between Hitler and Stalin* (New York: Basic Books, 2010). I used the reviews Jörg Ganzenmüller, "Stalins Völkermord? Zu den Grenzen des Genozidbegriffs und den Chancen eines historischen Vergleichs," in *Holocaust und Völkermorde. Die Reichweite des Vergleichs*, ed. Sybille Steinbacher (Frankfurt: Campus, 2012), 145–166; Jürgen Zarusky, "Timothy Snyders 'Bloodlands.' Kritische Anmerkungen zur Konstruktion einer Geschichtslandschaft," *Vierteljahreshefte für Zeitgeschichte* 60, no. 1 (2012): 1–31.

108. Henry L. Roberts, ed., *The Anti-Stalin Campaign and International Communism* (New York: Columbia University Press, 1956), 10–18.
109. A. A. Fursenko, ed., *Prezidim CK KPSS*, vol. 1 (Moscow: ROSSPEN, 2003), 95–97; German in Hans-Heinrich Nolte, Bernhard Schalhorn, and Bernd Bonwetsch, eds., *Quellen zur Geschichte Russlands* Hans-Heinrich Nolte, Bernhard Schalhorn, and Bernd Bonwetsch (Stuttgart: Reclam, 2014)377–379.
110. Robert Payne, *Stalin* (Stuttgart: Hans E. Günther, 1967 [1965]), 393–492.
111. Hermann L. Brill, *Das sowjetische Herrschaftssystem. Der Weg in die Staatssklaverei* (Cologne: Rote Weißbücher, 1951), 57–78.
112. Georg von Rauch, *Geschichte des bolschewistischen Russland* (Frankfurt: Fischer, 1963), 182–191 and 240–254; numbers of victims on 245.
113. Ralf Stettner, *"Archipel GULag"* (Paderborn: Schöningh, 1996); I. B. Smirnov, *Sistema Ispravitel'no Trudovykh lagerej* (Moscow: Memorial, 1998); Anne Applebaum, *GULAG* (New York: Random House, 2003).
114. To the best of my knowledge, I was the first to publish a German translation of the archaeological report A. V. Iou, M. M. Kryval'cevich, Z. S. Paz'njak, and J. Shmygaleu, *Kurapaty* (Minsk: Tekhnalogija, 1994) translated by H. Pinl, *Kurapaty = Verein für Geschichte des Weltsystems*, Rundbrief Nr. 21, Anlage 1 (Hanover/Barsinghausen, 1997).
115. Rolf Binner, Bernd Bonwetsch, and Marc Jung, eds., *Massenmord und Lagerhaft* (Berlin: Akademie, 2009); Rolf Binner, Bernd Bonwetsch, and Marc Jung, eds., *Stalinismus in der sowjetischen Provinz 1937–1938* (Berlin: Akademie, 2010).
116. Nolte, Schalhorn, and Bonwetsch, eds., *Quellen zur Geschichte Russlands*, 306–325.
117. Pavel Polian, *Ne po svoej vole* (Moscow: Memorial, 2001).
118. Polian, *Ne po svoej vole*, 78–79.
119. N. L. Pobol' and P. M. Polian, eds., *Stalinskie deportacii 1928–1956* (Moscow: Demokratija, 2005) cf. the deportation of the Kalmyks to Siberia and Altaj on 410–434.
120. My own calculation: Nolte, *Geschichte Russlands*, 234–236. Cf. documents in Nolte, Schalhorn, and Bonwetsch, eds., *Quellen zur Geschichte Russlands*, 326–330.
121. Nolte, Schalhorn, and Bonwetsch, eds., *Quellen zur Geschichte Russlands*, 307.
122. The export of grain between 1930 and 1933 dropped from 4.8 million tons to 1.7 million tons, and the income from that commodity from 157.8 million to 31.2 million roubles: MVT SSSR, ed., *Vneshnjaja torgovlja SSSR, Statisticheski sbornik* (Moscow: Mezhdunarodnye otnoshenija, 1967), 21.
123. Andreas Kappeler, *Kleine Geschichte der Ukraine* (Munich: C. H. Beck, 1994), 107–203.
124. Kerstin Jobst, *Geschichte der Ukraine* (Stuttgart: Reclam, 2010), 227.
125. Hans-Heinrich Nolte, "Was waren Bauern? Erinnerungen an einen west-östlichen Diskurs und eine (begriffsgeschichtlich einsetzende) Katastrophe," *Zeitschrift für Weltgeschichte* 8, no. 2 (2007): 33–58; cf. idem, "Stalinism as Total War," in *The Shadows of Total War*, ed. Roger Chickering and Stig Förster (Cambridge: Cambridge University Press, 2009), 295–312.
126. Dariusz Adamczyk, "Friesen, Wikinger Araber," in *Ostsee 700–2000*, ed. Andrea Komlosy and Hans-Heinrich Nolte (Vienna: Pro Media, 2008), 32–48; Dariusz Adamczyk, *Silber und Macht. Fernhandel, Tribute und die piastische Herrschaftsbildung in nordosteuropäischer Perspektive (800–1100)* (Wiesbaden: Harrassowitz, 2014).
127. F. Eberhardt, *Neuer Deutscher Geschichts- und Kulturatlas* (Leipzig: List & von Bressensdorf, 1937), 32–35 and 89–90.

128. Adolf Hitler, *Mein Kampf* (Munich: Zentralverlag der NSDAP, 1938), 154.

129. Erwin Oberländer, *Sowjetpatriotismus und Geschichte* (Cologne: Wissenschaft und Politik, 1967); Hans-Heinrich Nolte, *"Drang nach Osten." Sowjetische Geschichtsschreibung der deutschen Ostexpansion* (Frankfurt: EVA, 1976).

130. Hans-Heinrich Nolte, "Ot sovetskogo patriotizma k rossijskomu nacionalizmu," in *Germanija i Rossija v sud'be istorika (Deutschland und Russland im Schicksal eines Historikers) Festschrift zum 90jährigen Geburtstag von Jakov Samojlovich Drabkin*, ed. M. B. Korchagina and V. V. Ishhenko (Moscow: Sobranie, 2008), 171–182.

131. If we define the average of urbanization as 100, Ukrainians were at 58, Russians at 118, Armenians at 198, and Jews at 458: Gerhard Simon, *Nationalismus und Nationalitätenpolitik in der Sowjetunion* (Baden-Baden: Nomos, 1986), 433.

132. In the year 1927, out of 10,000 of the following nationalities members of the Communist Party numbered on average: 155 Jews, 116 Armenians, 88 Russians, and 39 Ukrainians—and 42 Germans, since the German minority in that year consisted almost completely of peasants. Ibid., 448.

133. Hans-Heinrich Nolte, "Why is Europe's South Poor? A Chain of Internal Peripheries along the Old Muslim-Christian Borders," *Review* XXVI (2003): 49–63; extended version in: Peter Herrmann and Arno Tausch, eds., *Dar al Islam, The Mediterranean, the World System and the Wider Europe* (New York: Nova Science, 2005), 21–35.

134. Including the "General Government" and "South Prussia," but not the "occupied Eastern territories" nor those under the rule of the Wehrmacht as *rückwärtige Heeresgebiete* (army rear areas). Therefore, Jews from Białystok or Grodno were brought to selections in Majdanek or Auschwitz and some, if very few, of them survived, going through several camps, while Jews from the east of this line only had a chance to survive by escaping to the east in time or joining the partisans. One common chance for survival from Paris to Kaunas was hiding, like Tamara Lazerson, see excerpts from her diary in: *Zeitschrift für Weltgeschichte* 13, no. 1 (2012): 99–100; all my translations and editions.

135. Hans-Heinrich Nolte, "Die andere Hälfte des Holocaust," introduction to Il'ya Al'tman, *Opfer des Hasses. Der Holocaust in der UdSSR 1941–1945* (Gleichen: Musterschmidt, 2008), 7–14; Hans-Heinrich Nolte, "Die andere Seite des Holocaust," *DIE ZEIT* (January 24, 2008): 82; Hans-Heinrich Nolte, "Das Gedenken an den Holocaust östlich und westlich des Bug," *Mitteilungen der Stiftung Deutsches Holocaust-Museum*, no. 16 (March 2008): 29–32.

136. Example: Ljuba I. Abramowitsch, *Die faschistische Gehenna am Beispiel des Ghettos der Stadt Slonim* (Hanover: Niedersächsische Landeszentrale, 1995); Ljuba I. Abramowitsch, "Jüdischer Widerstand gegen den Genozid 1941–1944 in Weißrußland," in *Der Fremde im Dorf, Festschrift Rex Rexheuser*, ed. Jürgen Bömelburg and Beate Eschment (Lüneburg: Verlag Nordostdeutsches Kulturwerk, 1998), 353–366.

137. Shalom Cholawsky, *The Jews of Belorussia during World War II* (Amsterdam: Harwood, 1998); Il'ya Al'tman, *Kholokost i evreiskoe soprotivlenie na okkupirovannoi territorii SSSR* (Moscow: Fond Kholokost, 2002).

138. Danil Klovskij, *Doroga iz Grodno* (Samara: Mezhdunarodnyj centr kul'tury VOLGA, 1994).

139. Hans-Heinrich Nolte, "Fira Borisovna Smirnovskaja: Überleben in deutschen Konzentrationslagern," in *Europa und die Welt in der Geschichte*, ed. Raphaela Averkorn, Winfried Eberhard, Raimund Haas, and Bernd Schmies (Bochum: Festschrift Berg, 2004), 1223–1244.

140. Tatjana Tönsmeyer, "Besatzung als europäische Erfahrungs- und Gesellschaftsgeschichte: Der Holocaust im Kontext des Zweiten Weltkriegs," in *Der Holocaust, Ergebnisse und neue Fragen der Forschung*, ed. Frank Bajohr and Andrea Löw (Frankfurt: S. Fischer, 2015), 281–298.

141. Hilberg, *The Destruction of the European Jews*, 670, counts all victims by state in the borders of 1938 and therefore does not differentiate between western and eastern Poland.

142. Patrick Desbois, *Der vergessene Holocaust. Die Ermordung der ukrainischen Juden* (Berlin: Berlin—Verlag, 2009). This, however, sometimes gives the impression that the mass murderers of 1941 cared about the borders of Ukraine today.

143. Hans-Heinrich Nolte, "Zum transnationalen Charakter der Holocaustforschung," *Mitteilungen der Stiftung Deutsches Holocaust-Museum* 18 (2010): 40–43.

144. For instance Jizchak katzenelson, *Dos lied vunem ojsgehargetn jidischn volk*, ed. Arno Lustiger, translation to Russian by Ė. Etkind (Moscow: Jazyki russkoj kul'tury, 2000); Pavel Polian, ed., *Svitiki iz pepla* (Moscow: Feniks, 2013). A Yiddish to Russian translation of the notes from the "*Sonderkommando*" had been buried in the ground at Auschwitz.

145. Hans-Heinrich Nolte, "Eine Kette innerer Peripherien entlang der alten christlich-muslimischen Grenze," *Zeitschrift für Weltgeschichte* 3, no. 1 (2004): 41–58; expanded reprint in: Peter Herrmann and Arno Tausch, eds., *Dar al Islam, The Mediterranean, the World System and the Wider Europe, The Chain of Peripheries and the New Wider Europe* (New York: Nova Science Publishers, 2005), 21–35.

146. Hans-Heinrich Nolte, "Zur Stellung Osteuropas im internationalen System der Frühen Neuzeit. Außenhandel und Sozialgeschichte bei der Bestimmung der Regionen," *Jahrbücher für Geschichte Osteuropas* 28 (1980): 161–197. English translation in *Review* VI/1 (1982): 25–84.

147. Hans-Heinrich Nolte, *Weltgeschichte des 20. Jahrhunderts* (Vienna: Boehlau, 2009). The Russian Finance Minister Witte put it to the Emperor in 1899 clearly: Russia economically is a colony, but politically a big power; see Quellenbuch Nr. 4.5.1. The term "A member of the Family" in Susan P. Mccaffray and Michael Melancon, eds., *Russia in the European Context* (New York, Palgrave, 2005). Research on moral and intellectual contexts of the differences between semiperipheries and centers is multiple, but poorly summarized, see for an introduction H.-H. Nolte: "Überforderung und Pathos: ein Aufriß. Zur politischen Kultur halbperipherer Länder," in *Brücken zwischen den Zivilisationen. Zur Zivilisierung ethnisch-kultureller Differenzen und Machtungleichheiten*, ed. Hans-Peter Waldhoff, Dursun Tan, and Elcin Kürsat-Ahlers (Frankfurt am Main: IKO—Verlag für Interkulturelle Kommunikation, 1997), 63–82.

148. J. W. Stalin, *Marxismus und nationale Frage* [1913], in J. W. Stalin, *Werke*, vol. 2, ed. Marx-Engels-Lenin-Stalin-Institut beim ZK der KPdSU, reprint (Hamburg: Roter Morgen, 1971), 266–333, here 307.

149. Hans-Heinrich Nolte, "Kosten nachholender Entwicklung: der sowjetische Fall," in Andrea Komlosy, ed., "Nachholende Entwicklung," special issue of *Zeitschrift für Weltgeschichte* 13, no. 2 (2012): 95–117.

150. I use the German publication: *Bundesgesetzblatt* 12 no. VIII (1954): 729–739. § 2 (b) forbids "causing serious bodily or mental harm to members of the group"—but not forced expulsion. Compare Stephan Hobe, *Einführung in das Völkerrecht* (Tübingen: Francke, 2008), 640 ff.; Harald Kleinschmidt, *Geschichte des Völkerrechts* (Tübingen: Francke, 2013), 464 ff.

151. Albert Einstein, "Zum Schwarzbuch," in *Das Schwarzbuch. Der Genozid an den sowjetischen Juden*, ed. Arno Lustiger, Wassilij Grossmann, and Ilja Ehrenburg (Reinbek: Rowohlt, 1994), 1013–1014, here 1013; compare 1074–1076. My translation from Einstein's German. See also Joshua Rubenstein and Il'ya Al'tman, eds., *The Unknown Black Book* (Bloomington: Indiana University Press, 2008).

152. An overview of the rich literature is provided by Boris Barth, *Genozid. Völkermord im 20. Jahrhundert: Geschichte, Theorien, Kontroversen* (Munich: C. H. Beck, 2006); compare the cases in Jens Binner and Hans-Heinrich Nolte, eds., "Massenverbrechen im Unterricht," special issue of the *Zeitschrift für Weltgeschichte* 13, no. 1 (2012).

Selected Bibliography

Abitbol, Michel. *Les Juifs d'Afrique du Nord sous Vichy*. Paris: G.-P. Maisonneuve et Larose, 1983.

Altshuler, Mordechai, Yitzhak Arad, and Shmuel Krakowski, eds. *Sovetskiye yevrei pishut Ilye Ehrenburgu, 1943–1966*. Jerusalem: Yad Vashem, 1993.

Al'tman, Il'ya. *Zhertvy nenavisti. Kholokost v SSSR 1941–1945 gg*. Moscow: Fond Kovcheg, 2002.

Al'tman, Il'ya. *Kholokost i evreiskoe soprotivlenie na okkupirovannoi territorii SSSR*. Moscow: Kaleidoskop, 2002.

Al'tman, Il'ya, ed. *Kholokost na territorii SSSR: Entsiklopediia*, 2nd rev. ed. Moscow: ROSSPEN, 2011 [2009].

Angrick, Andrej. *Besatzungspolitik und Massenmord. Die Einsatzgruppe D in der südlichen Sowjetunion 1941–1943*. Hamburg: Hamburger Edition, 2003.

Angrick, Andrej, and Peter Klein. *Die "Endlösung" in Riga. Ausbeutung und Vernichtung 1941–1944*. Darmstadt: Wissenschaftliche Buchgesellschaft, 2006.

Arad, Yitzhak. *The Holocaust in the Soviet Union*. Lincoln, NE: University of Nebraska Press, 2009.

Barth, Boris. *Genozid. Völkermord im 20. Jahrhundert: Geschichte, Theorien, Kontroversen*. Munich: C. H. Beck, 2006.

Bartov, Omer, ed. *The Holocaust*. London/New York: Routledge, 2000.

Bastian, Till. *Sinti und Roma im Dritten Reich. Geschichte einer Verfolgung*. Munich: C. H. Beck, 2001.

Beck, Birgit. *Wehrmacht und sexuelle Gewalt. Sexualverbrechen vor deutschen Militärgerichten 1939–1945*. Paderborn: Schöningh, 2004.

Benz, Wolfgang, ed. *Der Holocaust*. Munich: C. H. Beck, 1999.

Beorn, Waitman Wade. *Marching into Darkness: The Wehrmacht and the Holocaust in Belarus*. Cambridge, MA: Harvard University Press, 2014.

Beyrau, Dietrich. *Schlachtfeld der Diktatoren. Osteuropa im Schatten von Hitler und Stalin*. Göttingen: Vandenhoeck & Ruprecht, 2000.

Böhler, Jochen. *Auftakt zum Vernichtungskrieg. Die Wehrmacht in Polen 1939*. Frankfurt am Main: Fischer, 2006.

Brandon, Ray, and Wendy Lower, eds. *The Shoah in Ukraine: History, Testimony, Memorialization*. Bloomington: Indiana University Press, in association with the United States Holocaust Memorial Museum, 2008.

Browning, Christopher R. *Ordinary Men: Reserve Police Battalion 101 and the Final Solution in Poland*. New York: HarperCollins, 1992.

Browning, Christopher R. *Nazi Policy, Jewish Workers, German Killers*. Cambridge/New York: Cambridge University Press, 2000.

Browning, Christopher R. *Remembering Survival: Inside A Nazi Slave-Labor Camp*. New York: W.W. Norton & Company, 2010.

Browning, Christopher R., with contributions by Jürgen Matthäus. *The Origins of the Final Solution: The Evolution of Nazi Jewish Policy, September 1939–March 1942*. Lincoln, NE/ Jerusalem: University of Nebraska Press and Yad Vashem, 2004.

Budrytė, Dovilė. "We Call it Genocide: Soviet Deportations and Repression in the Memory of Lithuanians." In *The Genocidal Temptation: Auschwitz, Hiroshima, Rwanda, and Beyond*, edited by Robert S. Frey, 79–101. Lanham, MD: University Press of America, 2004.

Burrin, Philippe. *Warum die Deutschen? Antisemitismus, Nationalsozialismus, Genozid*. Berlin: Ullstein, 2004.

Cohen, Laurie R. *Smolensk under the Nazis: Everyday life in Occupied Russia*. Rochester, NY: University of Rochester Press, 2013.

Czech, Danuta. *Kalendarium der Ereignisse im Konzentrationslager Auschwitz-Birkenau 1939–1945*. Reinbek bei Hamburg: Rowohlt, 1989.

Desbois, Patrick. *The Holocaust by Bullets: A Priest's Journey to Uncover the Truth Behind the Murder of 1.5 Million Jews*. New York: Palgrave Macmillan, 2008.

Dieckmann, Christoph. *Deutsche Besatzungspolitik in Litauen 1941–1944*, 2 vols. Göttingen: Wallstein, 2011.

Dieckmann, Christoph, and Babette Quinkert, eds. *Kriegführung und Hunger 1939–1945. Zum Verhältnis von militärischen, wirtschaftlichen und politischen Interessen*. Göttingen: Wallstein, 2015.

Dillon, Christopher. *Dachau and the SS: A Schooling in Violence*. Oxford: Oxford University Press, 2015.

Dobroszycki, Lucjan, and Jeffrey S. Gurock, eds. *The Holocaust in the Soviet Union: Studies and Sources on the Destruction of the Jews in the Nazi-Occupied Territories of the USSR, 1941–1945*. Armonk, NY: M. E. Sharpe, 1993.

Dubson, Vadim. "Getto na okkupirovannoi territorii Rossiiskoi Federatsii (1941–1942)." *Vestnik evreiskogo universiteta v Moskve* 21, no. 3 (2000): 157–184.

Faulstich, Heinz. *Hungersterben in der Psychiatrie 1914–1949. Mit einer Topographie der NS-Psychiatrie*. Freiburg: Lambertus, 1998.

Friedlander, Henry. *The Origins of Nazi Genocide: From Euthanasia to the Final Solution*. Chapel Hill/London: University of North Carolina Press, 1995.

Friedländer, Saul. *The Years of Extermination: Nazi Germany and the Jews, 1939–1945*. New York: HarperCollins, 2007.

Fings, Karola, and Frank Sparing. *Rassismus—Lager—Völkermord: Die nationalsozialistische Zigeunerverfolgung in Köln*. Cologne: Emons, 2005.

Ganzenmüller, Jörg. "Stalins Völkermord? Zu den Grenzen des Genozidbegriffs und den Chancen eines historischen Vergleichs." In *Holocaust und Völkermorde. Die Reichweite des Vergleichs*, edited by Sybille Steinbacher, 145–166. Frankfurt: Campus, 2012.

Gerlach, Christian. *Kalkulierte Morde. Die deutsche Wirtschafts- und Vernichtungspolitik in Weissrussland 1941 bis 1944*. Hamburg: Hamburger Edition, 1999.

Gerlach, Christian. *Extremely Violent Societies: Mass Violence in the Twentieth-Century World*. Cambridge: Cambridge University Press, 2010.

Gerlach, Christian. *The Extermination of the European Jews*. Cambridge: Cambridge University Press, 2016.

Gertjejanssen, Wendy Jo. "Victims, Heroes, Survivors: Sexual Violence on the Eastern Front during World War II." Doctoral thesis, University of Minnesota, 2004.

Geyer, Michael, and Sheila Fitzpatrick, eds. *Beyond Totalitarianism: Stalinism and Nazism Compared*. Cambridge: Cambridge University Press, 2009.

Giles, Geoffrey J. "The Denial of Homosexuality: Same-Sex Incidents in Himmler's SS and Police." In *Sexuality and German Fascism*, edited by Dagmar Herzog, 256–290. New York: Berghahn Books, 2005.

Hartmann, Christian. *Wehrmacht im Ostkrieg. Front und militärisches Hinterland 1941/42*. Munich: Oldenbourg, 2009.

Hedgepeth, Sonja M., and Rochelle G. Saidel, eds. *Sexual Violence against Jewish Women During the Holocaust*. Waltham, MA: Brandeis University Press, 2010.

Hilberg, Raul. *The Destruction of the European Jews*. Chicago: Quadrangle Books, 1961.

Hilberg, Raul. *Sources of Holocaust Research: An Analysis*. Chicago: I. R. Dee, 2001.

Hinz-Wessels, Annette. "Antisemitismus und Krankenmord. Zum Umgang mit jüdischen Anstaltspatienten im Nationalsozialismus." *Vierteljahrshefte für Zeitgeschichte* 61, no. 1 (2013): 65–92.

Hof, Tobias, ed. *Empire, Ideology, Mass Violence: The Long 20th Century in Comparative Perspective*. Munich: Herbert Utz, 2016.

Hohendorf, Gerrit. *Der Tod als Erlösung vom Leiden: Geschichte und Ethik der Sterbehilfe seit dem Ende des 19. Jahrhunderts in Deutschland*. Göttingen: Wallstein, 2013.

Holler, Martin. *Der nationalsozialistische Völkermord an den Roma in der besetzten Sowjetunion (1941–1944)*. Heidelberg: Dokumentations- und Kulturzentrum Deutscher Sinti und Roma, 2009.

Holler, Martin. "Extending the Genocidal Program: Did Otto Ohlendorf Initiate the Systematic Extermination of Soviet 'Gypsies'?." In *Nazi Policy on the Eastern Front, 1941: Total War, Genocide, and Radicalization*, edited by Alex J. Kay, Jeff Rutherford, and David Stahel, 267–288. Rochester, NY: University of Rochester Press, 2012.

Hürter, Johannes. *Hitlers Heerführer. Die deutschen Oberbefehlshaber im Krieg gegen die Sowjetunion 1941/42*. Munich: Oldenbourg, 2006.

Hürter, Johannes. *A German General on the Eastern Front: The Letters and Diaries of Gotthard Heinrici 1941–1942*. Barnsley: Pen and Sword, 2014.

Hürter, Johannes, und Jürgen Zarusky, eds. *Besatzung, Kollaboration und Holocaust. Neue Studien zu Verfolgung und Ermordung der europäischen Juden*. Munich: Oldenbourg, 2008.

Ibel, Johannes, ed. *Einvernehmliche Zusammenarbeit? Wehrmacht, Gestapo, SS und sowjetische Kriegsgefangene*. Berlin: Metropol, 2008.

Ionid, Radu. *The Holocaust in Romania: The Destruction of Jews and Gypsies under the Antonescu Regime, 1940–1944*. Chicago: Ivan R. Dee, 2000.

Jaroszewski, Zdzisław, ed. *Die Ermordung der Geisteskranken in Polen 1939–1945*. Warsaw: Wydawnictwo Naukowe PWN, 1993.

Katz, Steven T. "Thoughts on the Intersection of Rape and *Rassenchande* during the Holocaust." *Modern Judaism* 32, no. 3 (2012): 293–322.

Kay, Alex J. *Exploitation, Resettlement, Mass Murder: Political and Economic Planning for German Occupation Policy in the Soviet Union, 1940–1941*. New York/Oxford: Berghahn Books, 2006.

Kay, Alex J. "A 'War in a Region beyond State Control'? The German-Soviet War, 1941–1944." *War in History* 18, no. 1 (January 2011): 109–122.

Kay, Alex J. "Transition to Genocide, July 1941: Einsatzkommando 9 and the Annihilation of Soviet Jewry." *Holocaust and Genocide Studies* 27, no. 3 (winter 2013): 411–442.
Kay, Alex J. *The Making of an SS Killer: The Life of Colonel Alfred Filbert, 1905–1990*. Cambridge: Cambridge University Press, 2016.
Kay, Alex J., Jeff Rutherford, and David Stahel, eds. *Nazi Policy on the Eastern Front, 1941: Total War, Genocide, and Radicalization*. Rochester, NY: University of Rochester Press, 2012.
Keller, Rolf. *Sowjetische Kriegsgefangene im Deutschen Reich 1941/42. Behandlung und Arbeitseinsatz zwischen Vernichtungspolitik und kriegswirtschaftlichen Zwängen*. Göttingen: Wallstein, 2011.
Keller, Rolf, and Reinhard Otto. "Das Massensterben der sowjetischen Kriegsgefangenen und die Wehrmachtbürokratie. Unterlagen zur Registrierung der sowjetischen Kriegsgefangenen 1941–1945 in deutschen und russischen Institutionen. Ein Forschungsbericht." *Militärgeschichtliche Mitteilungen* 57, no. 1 (1998): 149–180.
Keller, Rolf, and Silke Petry, eds. *Sowjetische Kriegsgefangene im Arbeitseinsatz 1941–1945. Dokumente zu den Lebens- und Arbeitsbedingungen in Norddeutschland*. Göttingen: Wallstein, 2013.
Kenrick, Donald, and Grattan Puxon. *The Destiny of Europe's Gypsies*. London: Sussex University Press, 1972.
Klee, Ernst. *"Euthanasie" im Dritten Reich: Die "Vernichtung lebensunwerten Lebens."* Frankfurt am Main: Fischer, 2010.
Klee, Ernst, and Willy Dressen, eds. *"Gott mit uns." Der deutsche Vernichtungskrieg im Osten 1939–1945*. Frankfurt am Main: Fischer, 1989.
Krausnick, Helmut, and Hans-Heinrich Wilhelm. *Die Truppe des Weltanschauungskrieges. Die Einsatzgruppen der Sicherheitspolizei und des SD 1938–1942*. Stuttgart: Deutsche Verlags-Anstalt, 1981.
Kruglov, Aleksandr. "Genotsid tsygan v Ukraine v 1941–1944 gg.: statistiko-regional'nyi aspekt." *Golokost i Suchasnist'* 2, no. 6 (2009): 83–113.
Kruk, Herman. *The Last Days of the Jerusalem of Lithuania: Chronicles from the Vilna Ghetto and the Camps, 1939–1944*. Edited by Benjamin Harshav. New Haven, CT/London: YIVO Institute for Jewish Research/Yale University Press, 2002.
Kühne, Thomas *Belonging and Genocide: Hitler's Community, 1918–1945*. New Haven, CT: Yale University Press, 2010.
Lewy, Guenter. *The Nazi Persecution of the Gypsies*. New York: Oxford University Press, 2000.
Longerich, Peter. *Politik der Vernichtung. Eine Gesamtdarstellung der nationalsozialistischen Judenverfolgung*. Munich: Piper, 1998.
Longerich, Peter. *Holocaust: The Nazi Persecution and Murder of the Jews*. Oxford: Oxford University Press, 2010.
Lower, Wendy. *Hitler's Furies: German Women in the Nazi Killing Fields*. Boston: Houghton Mifflin Harcourt, 2013.
Luchterhandt, Martin. *Der Weg nach Birkenau. Entstehung und Verlauf der nationalsozialistischen Verfolgung der "Zigeuner."* Lübeck: Schmidt-Römhild, 2000.
MacShane, Denis. *Globalizing Hatred: The New Antisemitism*. London: Weidenfeld & Nicolson, 2008.
Mallmann, Klaus-Michael, Andrej Angrick, Jürgen Matthäus, and Martin Cüppers, eds. *Dokumente der Einsatzgruppen in der Sowjetunion*, vol. 1: *Die "Ereignismeldungen UdSSR" 1941*. Darmstadt: Wissenschaftliche Buchgesellschaft, 2011.

Mann, Michael. *The Dark Side of Democracy: Explaining Ethnic Cleansing*. Cambridge: Cambridge University Press, 2005.

Manoschek, Walter. "'Wo der Partisan ist, ist der Jude, und wo der Jude ist, ist der Partisan.' Die Wehrmacht und die Shoah." In *Täter der Shoah. Fanatische Nationalsozialisten oder ganz normale Deutsche?*, edited by Gerhard Paul, 167–185. Göttingen: Wallstein, 2002.

Megargee, Geoffrey P., ed. *The United States Holocaust Memorial Museum Encyclopedia of Camps and Ghettos, 1933–1945*, vol. 1: *Early Camps, Youth Camps, and Concentration Camps and Subcamps under the SS-Business Administration Main Office (WVHA)*. Bloomington: Indiana University Press in association with the United States Holocaust Memorial Museum, 2009.

Megargee, Geoffrey, and Martin Dean, eds. *The United States Holocaust Memorial Museum Encyclopedia of Camps and Ghettos 1933–1945*, vol. 2: *Ghettos in German-Occupied Eastern Europe*. Bloomington: Indiana University Press in association with the United States Holocaust Memorial Museum, 2012.

Michman, Dan. "The 'Final Solution to the Jewish Question,' its Emergence and Implementation: The State of Research and its Implications for Other Issues in Holocaust Research." In *Holocaust Historiography: A Jewish Perspective— Conceptualizations, Terminology, Approaches and Fundamental Issues*. London: Vallentine Mitchell, 2003, 91–126.

Mühlhäuser, Regina. "Between 'Racial Awareness' and Fantasies of Potency: Nazi Sexual Politics in the Occupied Territories of the Soviet Union, 1942–1945." In *Brutality and Desire: War and Sexuality in Europe's Twentieth Century*, edited by Dagmar Herzog, 197–220. New York: Palgrave Macmillan, 2009.

Mühlhäuser, Regina. *Eroberungen. Sexuelle Gewalttaten und intime Beziehungen deutscher Soldaten in der Sowjetunion, 1941–1945*. Hamburg: Hamburger Edition, 2010.

Müller, Rolf-Dieter, and Gerd R. Ueberschär. *Hitler's War in the East: A Critical Assessment*, 3rd rev. ed. New York: Berghahn, 2009.

Neitzel, Sönke, and Harald Welzer. *Soldaten. Protokolle vom Kämpfen, Töten und Sterben*. Frankfurt am Main: S. Fischer, 2011.

Nolte, Hans-Heinrich. *Der deutsche Überfall auf die Sowjetunion 1941*. Hanover: Landeszentrale, 1991.

Nolte, Hans-Heinrich. "Töten in Belorussland 1936–1944." In *Massenhaftes Töten. Kriege und Genozide im 20. Jahrhundert*, edited by Peter Gleichmann and Thomas Kühne, 143–157. Essen: Klartext, 2004.

Nolte, Hans-Heinrich, ed. *Auseinandersetzungen mit den Diktaturen*. Gleichen: Musterschmift, 2005.

Otto, Reinhard. *Wehrmacht, Gestapo und sowjetische Kriegsgefangene im deutschen Reichsgebiet 1941/42*. Munich: Oldenbourg, 1998.

Otto, Reinhard, Rolf Keller, and Jens Nagel. "Sowjetische Kriegsgefangene in deutschem Gewahrsam 1941–1945. Zahlen und Dimensionen." *Vierteljahrshefte für Zeitgeschichte* 56, no. 4 (October 2008): 557–602.

Overmans, Rüdiger, Andreas Hilger, and Pavel Poljan, eds. *Rotarmisten in deutscher Hand. Dokumente zu Gefangenschaft, Repatriierung und Rehabilitierung sowjetischer Soldaten des Zweiten Weltkrieges*. Paderborn: Schöningh, 2012.

Paul, Gerhard. "Lemberg '41. Bilder der Gewalt—Bilder als Gewalt—Gewalt an Bildern." In *Naziverbrechen. Täter, Taten, Bewältigungsversuche*, edited by Martin Cüppers,

Jürgen Matthäus, and Andrej Angrick, 191–212. Darmstadt: Wissenschaftliche Buchgesellschaft, 2013.

Pohl, Dieter. *Die Herrschaft der Wehrmacht. Deutsche Militärbesatzung und einheimische Bevölkerung in der Sowjetunion 1941–1944*. Munich: Oldenbourg, 2008.

Pohl, Dieter. *Verfolgung und Massenmord in der NS-Zeit 1933–1945*, 3rd rev. ed. Darmstadt: Wissenschaftliche Buchgesellschaft, 2010 [2003].

Polian, Pavel. *Zhertvy dvukh diktatur. Ostarbeitery i voennoplennye v Tretyem Reikhe i ikh repatriatsia*, 2nd rev. and exp. ed. Moscow: ROSSPEN, 2002 [1996].

Press, Bernhard. *The Murder of the Jews in Latvia, 1941–1945*. Evanston, IL: Northwestern University Press, 2000.

Reese, Willy Peter. *Mir selber seltsam fremd. Die Unmenschlichkeit des Krieges: Russland 1941–44*. Edited by Stefan Schmitz. Munich: Claasen, 2003.

Rieß, Volker. *Die Anfänge der Vernichtung "lebensunwerten Lebens" in den Reichsgauen Danzig-Westpreußen und Wartheland 1939/1940*. Frankfurt am Main: Peter Lang, 1995.

Römer, Felix. "'Im alten Deutschland wäre solcher Befehl nicht möglich gewesen.' Rezeption, Adaption und Umsetzung des Kriegsgerichtsbarkeitserlasses im Ostheer 1941/42." *Vierteljahrshefte für Zeitgeschichte* 56, no. 1 (January 2008): 53–99.

Römer, Felix. *Kameraden. Die Wehrmacht von innen*. Munich: Piper, 2012.

Roseman, Mark. *The Villa, the Lake, the Meeting: Wannsee and the Final Solution*. London: Penguin, 2002.

Rubinstein, Joshua, and Il'ya Al'tman, eds. *The Unknown Black Book*. Bloomington: Indiana University Press, 2008.

Rutherford, Jeff. *Combat and Genocide on the Eastern Front: The German Infantry's War, 1941–1944*. Cambridge: Cambridge University Press, 2014.

Sakowicz, Kazimierz. *Ponary Diary 1941–1942: A Bystander's Account of a Mass Murder*. Edited by Yitzhak Arad, with a foreword by Rachel Margolis. New Haven, CT: Yale University Press, 2005.

Snyder, David Raub. *Sex Crimes under the Wehrmacht*. Lincoln, NE: University of Nebraska Press, 2007.

Snyder, Timothy. *Bloodlands: Europe between Hitler and Stalin*. New York: Basic Books, 2010.

Sokolov, B. V. *Tsena pobedy. Velikaia Otechestvennaia: neizvestnoe ob izvestnom*. Moscow: Moskovskiy rabochii, 1991.

Steim, Alfred. *Die Behandlung der sowjetischen Kriegsgefangenen im Fall Barbarossa*. Heidelberg/Karlsruhe: Juristischer Verlag, 1981.

Streit, Christian. *Keine Kameraden. Die Wehrmacht und die sowjetischen Kriegsgefangenen 1941–1945*, 4th rev. ed. Bonn: Dietz, 1997 [1978].

Süß, Winfried. *Der "Volkskörper" im Krieg: Gesundheitspolitik, Gesundheitsverhältnisse und Krankenmord im nationalsozialistischen Deutschland 1939–1945*. Munich: De Gruyter Oldenbourg, 2003.

Sutton, Karen. *The Massacre of the Jews of Lithuania: Lithuanian Collaboration in the Final Solution, 1941–1944*. Jerusalem: Gefen, 2008.

Tory, Avraham. *Surviving the Holocaust: The Kovno Ghetto Diary*. Cambridge, MA: Harvard University Press, 1990.

Ueberschär, Gerd R., and Wolfram Wette, eds. *"Unternehmen Barbarossa." Der deutsche Überfall auf die Sowjetunion 1941: Berichte, Analysen, Dokumente*. Paderborn: Schöningh, 1984.

Wachsmann, Nikolaus. *KL: A History of the Nazi Concentration Camps*. New York: Farrar, Straus & Giroux, 2015.
Weiss-Wendt, Anton. "Why the Holocaust Does Not Matter to Estonians." *Journal of Baltic Studies* 39, no. 4 (December 2008): 475–497.
Welzer, Harald. *Täter. Wie aus ganz normalen Menschen Massenmörder werden*. Frankfurt am Main: S. Fischer, 2005.
Wette, Wolfram. *Die Wehrmacht. Feindbilder, Vernichtungskrieg, Legenden*. Frankfurt am Main: S. Fischer, 2002.
Wippermann, Wolfgang. *Geschichte der Sinti und Roma in Deutschland. Darstellung und Dokumente*. Berlin: Pädagogisches Zentrum, 1993.
Wippermann, Wolfgang. *"Auserwählte Opfer"? Shoah und Porrajmos im Vergleich. Eine Kontroverse*. Berlin: Frank & Timme, 2005.
Wippermann, Wolfgang. *Niemand ist ein Zigeuner. Zur Ächtung eines europäischen Vorurteils*. Hamburg: Körber-Stiftung, 2015.
Witte, Peter et al., eds. *Der Dienstkalender Heinrich Himmlers 1941/42*. Hamburg: Christians, 1999.
Zarusky, Jürgen. "Timothy Snyders 'Bloodlands.' Kritische Anmerkungen zur Konstruktion einer Geschichtslandschaft." *Vierteljahreshefte für Zeitgeschichte* 60, no. 1 (2012): 1–31.
Zimmermann, Michael. *Rassenutopie und Genozid: Die nationalsozialistische "Lösung der Zigeunerfrage."* Hamburg: Christians, 1996.

Index

Albania, 67, 71
Algeria, 62, 65–66, 68, 72
Al-Husseini, Haj Amin, 60
Allenstein, 97
Allies, 17, 88. *See also* Britain; Soviet Union; United States
Arad, Yitzhak, 245, 247, 269
Army Group Center, 28, 33, 181; Ninth Army, 25–26, 175. *See also* Wehrmacht
Army Group North, 151; Eighteenth Army, 151. *See also* Wehrmacht
Army Group South, 31, 179; Eleventh Army, 31; Seventeenth Army, 31; Sixth Army, 30. *See also* Wehrmacht
Arrow Cross, 87
Aruba, 67
Auenrode, 44
Auschwitz. *See* concentration camps; extermination camps
Austria, 7, 64, 71, 90, 246
Azov Sea, 151

Balkans, 34, 198, 211
Baltic Sea, 24, 275
Baltic States, 6, 20, 42, 47, 53, 225, 228–229, 235–252. *See also* Estonia; Latvia; Lithuania
Battista, Hans, 157
Bergen-Belsen. *See* concentration camps
Belarus, 6, 42–43, 53, 156–157, 161, 228–229, 270–271, 273, 275. *See also* Soviet Union
Belaya Tserkov, 30
Belgium, 19, 71
Berger, Ernst, 99
Berlin, 60, 64, 71, 83, 128, 133–134, 137, 148–149, 156, 247, 277
Bessarabia, 71, 226
Białystok, 4, 94–95, 97–103, 105, 107, 110, 150
Biebow, Hans, 205
Black Sea, 24, 228, 275

Blaskowitz, 21
Blobel, Paul, 30
Blume, Walter, 26
Bobruisk, 41, 53–54
Bock, Fedor von, 28, 33
Borisov, 53
Bormann, Martin, 64
Borowensee, 46
Bradfisch, Otto, 155, 157–158
Brande, 44
Breslau, 43–45
Brest-Litovsk, 4, 94–95, 98–107, 110–111. *See also* ghetto, Jewish
Britain, 8, 246, 266, 270, 278, 280. *See also* England
Buchenwald. *See* concentration camps
Budapest, 2
Bukovina, 71, 226
Bulgaria, 71
Bundeswehr, 4
Bunzlau, 45
Burat, Franz, 94, 99–101, 103, 105–106, 110

Carpatho-Ukraine, 72
Catholic Church, 87
Caucasus, 19, 60, 70, 225, 228–230, 274
Central Office for Jewish Emigration, 64–65, 71
Chashniki, 43
Chelyabinsk, 225
Chełm, 148
Chikhachevo, 44–45
concentration camps, 5, 126–127, 136, 139; Auschwitz, 97, 100, 106–109, 111, 128, 133, 138–139, 207, 209, 231; Bergen-Belsen, 271, 273; Buchenwald, 109, 128, 133, 135, 137–141; Dachau, 132–133, 137, 140; Flossenbürg, 125–128, 133, 139; Fort VII, 148; Groß-Rosen, 133, 136; Lublin-Majdanek, 125, 134–135, 137–138; Mauthausen, 54,

125–126, 128–141; Neuengamme, 128, 139; Ravensbrück, 108–109; Riga-Kaiserwald, 47, 52–53; Sachsenhausen, 133, 136, 138–140; Stutthof, 47, 53; Theresienstadt, 273. *See also* extermination camps
Crimea, 18, 70, 85, 228–229
Croatia, 71, 87, 89
Curaçao, 67
Czechoslovakia, 273, 276. *See also* Protectorate of Bohemia and Moravia; Slovakia

Dachau. *See* concentration camps
Danneker, Theodor, 63, 68
Danzig, 45
Danzig-West Prussia, 46–47
Dekanozov, Vladimir, 224–225
Denmark, 71
Dnepropetrovsk, 104–105, 110
Drexel, Hans, 205
Dworzec, 48–49

East India, 67
East Prussia, 95–98, 101–102, 104, 109–110, 149
Egypt, 65, 70, 72
Ehrenburg, Il'ya, 220
Ehrhardt, Sophie, 95, 98
Eichmann, Adolf, 61, 63–70, 73, 87
Eichtal, 44
Eimann, Kurt, 148
Einsatzgruppe A, 151; Sonderkommando 1b, 151. *See also* Einsatzgruppen
Einsatzgruppe B, 28, 48, 156; Einsatzkommando 8, 152–155, 157, 159–160, 162; Sonderkommando 7a, 25–26. *See also* Einsatzgruppen
Einsatzgruppe C: Sonderkommando 4a, 30. *See also* Einsatzgruppen
Einsatzgruppe D, 85, 152. *See also* Einsatzgruppen
Einsatzgruppen, 23–27, 29, 41–42, 54, 60–61, 64, 83, 85, 94, 149–152, 156, 159, 162, 202, 228, 270. *See also* Einsatzgruppe A; Einsatzgruppe B; Einsatzgruppe C; Einsatzgruppe D; SD; Security Police; SS

Einstein, Albert, 280
England, 62, 67, 71. *See also* Britain
Estonia, 8, 41, 52–53, 64, 71, 135, 138, 235, 240, 243, 247, 249, 275. *See also* Baltic States
Ethiopia, 65, 72
EU. *See* European Union
European Union, 8–9, 236–237, 241–242, 244–245, 249–252, 272
"euthanasia". *See* psychiatric patients
extermination camps, 87, 231; Auschwitz-Birkenau, 3–4, 35, 83, 89, 109, 111, 222, 277; Majdanek, 222; Treblinka, 277. *See also* concentration camps

Facebook, 9
Finland, 71
Fleschütz, Eugen, 153, 160
Flossenbürg. *See* concentration camps
Fort VII. *See* concentration camps
France, 7, 19, 62–63, 66–69, 71, 73, 86, 90, 229, 235
Frank, Hans, 83
Frentzel, Georg, 152–154, 157–158, 160–161
Front National, 9

Galen, Clemens August von, 149
General Government. *See* Government General
German Army. *See* High Command of the Army (OKH); Wehrmacht
German Nationalist People's Party, 20
Gersdorff, Rudolf-Christoph von, 28
Gestapo, 5, 48, 123–126, 129, 137–138, 140, 203; Munich Office, 137; Regensburg Office, 137. *See also* Security Police
ghetto, Jewish, 19, 43, 47, 49–50, 237; in Brest-Litovsk, 103, 105, 110; in Grójec, 49; in Kaunas, 46, 52; in Litzmannstadt (Łódź), 46, 205; in L'vov, 206; in Minsk, 48–49; in Mogilev, 157; in Smolensk, 41, 48; in Szczuczyn, 53; in Tulchin, 205; in Vilnius, 46, 52; in Warsaw, 41, 48–49, 53, 223
Głębokie, 43
Globke, Hans, 82
Goebbels, Joseph, 7
Gorbachev, Mikhail, 220

Göring, Hermann, 60, 64
Government General, 34, 71, 83, 104, 129–130, 149. *See also* Poland
Gräditz, 45
Greece, 19, 71, 229, 279
Grodno, 277
Grossman, Vasily, 220
Gross Masselwitz, 43–45
Groß-Rosen. *See* concentration camps
Guderian, Heinz, 35

Haider, Jörg, 7
Halder, Franz, 26, 151
Hamburg Institute of Social Research, 6, 175
Hausner, Gideon, 69
Heinrici, Gotthard, 20–21
Heydrich, Reinhard, 23–25, 27, 33, 60–62, 64–65, 67, 69, 133
High Command of the Army (OKH), 18, 22–23, 26, 31, 127, 131, 135, 176, 201, 203. *See also* Wehrmacht
High Command of the Wehrmacht (OKW). *See* Wehrmacht
Himmler, Heinrich, 2–3, 23, 25–27, 33–35, 43, 60, 68, 81, 83, 85, 89, 133–134, 151, 156, 161
Hindenburg, 108
Hitler, Adolf, 7–9, 17–18, 20–21, 23, 28, 32–35, 59–61, 64–65, 68, 70, 84–85, 101, 129, 149, 187, 202, 236, 242, 247, 266–267, 273, 278
Hitler-Stalin Pact. *See* Nazi-Soviet Pact
Hitler Youth, 184
Hoepner, Erich, 33
Holocaust, 1–4, 9, 18–19, 24, 30, 32–33, 61–65, 90, 185, 195–199, 204, 211, 219–223, 225–232, 235–252, 266, 269–270, 274, 277, 279. *See also* Jews
Holszany, 50
Höß, Rudolf, 108
Hoth, Hermann, 31
Hungary, 2, 41, 72, 87, 89, 108, 247, 249, 273

Idritsa, 44
Institute of Contemporary History Munich–Berlin, 8
Ireland, 71
Iron Guard, 87

Israel, 3, 88, 244, 247, 252
Italy, 67, 71, 86

Jalkh, Jean-François, 9
Japan, 66, 224, 274, 278
Jarausch, Konrad, 177
Jerusalem, 60, 69
Jews, 3–5, 7, 9, 17–23, 27, 29–32, 34–35, 41–47, 53–54, 59–60, 62–71, 73, 82, 84–88, 90–91, 94, 103, 106, 108, 111, 150, 178, 200, 203, 207, 210–211, 221, 223–231, 235–252, 266, 269, 276, 278. *See also* Holocaust
Jodl, Alfred, 17
Johnson, Boris, 8

Kaliningrad, 228. *See also* Königsberg
Kamenets-Podolskiy, 31
Karlsruhe, 88
Katyn, 265, 272, 279–280
Kaunas, 44–45, 129, 203, 224, 248. *See also* ghetto, Jewish
Keitel, Wilhelm, 17, 64
Kharkov, 30
Khotimsk, 42
Khrushchev, Nikita, 267
Kiev, 2, 30, 60, 252, 274
Kluge, Günther von, 33
Kocborowo, 148
Koch, Erich, 149
Königsberg, 44, 95–97, 110. *See also* Kaliningrad
Krasne, 43
Kremenchug, 31
Kube, Wilhelm, 156
Küchler, 21
Kūdupe, 52–53
Kurapaty, 266, 268, 273–274

Lammers, Hans-Heinrich, 64
Lange, Herbert, 148–149
Latvia, 8, 46–47, 52–53, 71, 225–226, 235, 239–240, 242–243, 247, 249, 275. *See also* Baltic States
Lauenburg, 149
Leeb, Wilhelm von, 35
Lemkin, Raphael, 238

Lenin, Vladimir, 240–241, 267
Leningrad, 52, 151, 219, 225, 228, 230, 271, 277
Le Pen, Jean-Marie, 7
Le Pen, Marine, 9
Libya, 65–66, 70
Lida, 43, 53
Lithuania, 8, 45, 47, 50, 71, 224–226, 229, 235, 238, 240–241, 243–250, 275. *See also* Baltic States
Lublin, 54, 130. *See also* concentration camps
Lublin-Majdanek. *See* concentration camps
Luther, Martin, 68
Luxembourg, 71, 88
L'vov, 31–32, 202, 207. *See also* ghetto, Jewish

Majdanek. *See* extermination camps
Manstein, Erich von, 18, 21, 28, 31
Margolis, Rachel, 45, 247
Markstädt, 45
Mauthausen. *See* concentration camps
Mayski, Ivan, 224
Mazirbe, 46
Mein Kampf, 8, 59, 266
Metelmann, Henry, 179–180
Middle East, 4, 225
Ministry of State Security (MfS), 152
Minsk, 2, 41–43, 48–49, 54, 153, 156–157, 161, 266, 268, 273. *See also* ghetto, Jewish
Mogilev, 5, 41, 48–49, 53–54, 152–162. *See also* ghetto, Jewish
Mokrovo, 50–51, 54
Moldova, 228–229. *See also* Soviet Union
Molotov-Ribbentrop Pact. *See* Nazi-Soviet Pact
Molotov, Vyacheslav, 224
Montenegro, 71
Morocco, 62, 65–66, 68, 72
Moscow, 3, 42–43, 224–225, 228–230, 232, 276, 278–279
Munich, 137

NATO, 8, 236, 241–242, 244–245, 252
Nazi Party, 17, 68, 95–96, 148–149, 173
Nazi-Soviet Pact, 9, 150, 242
Naumann, Erich, 48
Nebe, Arthur, 28, 156–157, 161

Netherlands, 3, 64, 67, 71, 90, 229
Neuengamme. *See* concentration camps
Nevel, 225
New York (state), 2
Night of Broken Glass, 20–21
North Africa, 3, 59, 62–63, 65, 67, 69–70, 73
North Bukovina. *See* Bukovina
Norway, 71, 246
Novogrudok, 202
Nowogródek, 43
NSDAP. *See* Nazi Party
Nuremberg Trials, 17, 88, 220, 267

Ohlendorf, Otto, 85
OKH. *See* High Command of the Army (OKH)
OKW. *See* Wehrmacht
Operation Barbarossa, 2, 22, 33, 45, 60, 176, 247, 267
Order Police, 27
Orel, 225
Organisation Todt (OT), 41, 44–47, 53–54
Orsha, 161
Oster, 43
Oszmiana, 50
Ozorków, 45–46

Palemonas, 45–46
Palestine, 65, 70, 225, 231
Pan-German League, 19–20
Pavelić, Ante, 87
Pearl Harbor, 66
PEGIDA, 7–8
Petrovichi, 43
Petschur, 52–53
Pinsk, 206
Plensums, 47
Podolia, 94, 99, 102, 110–111
Podolsk, 2
Poland, 3, 5, 8, 21–22, 34, 42, 48, 60, 83, 90, 147–148, 161, 201, 205, 226, 270–271, 275. *See also* Government General; Warthegau
police. *See* Gestapo; Order Police; Police Battalion 310; Reich Criminal Police Office (RKPA); Reserve Police Battalion 13; Security Police; Urban Police

Police Battalion 310, 103
Polish intelligentsia, 1, 21
Poltava, 176
Pomerania, 149
Ponár, 245
Porajmos, 89–90. *See also* Roma; Sinti
Portugal, 62, 67, 71
Poznań, 35
Praust, 45
Prieb, Adolf, 153–154, 157–159
Protectorate of Bohemia and Moravia, 71, 106, 149. *See also* Czechoslovakia
Pskov, 43, 50, 52–54, 225
psychiatric patients, 1, 4–5, 147–162, 271
Putin, Vladimir, 9, 236, 251
Pyatigorsk, 225

Rademacher, Franz, 63, 68
Radom, 54
Rauff, Walter, 70
Ravensbrück. *See* concentration camps
Red Army, 1, 5, 7, 19, 47, 105, 123–124, 129, 132, 135–138, 141, 153–154, 159, 161, 173, 177, 181, 221, 223, 230–231, 241, 247–248, 265. *See also* Soviet prisoners of war
Reese, Willy Peter, 177, 179, 183, 188, 195
Reich Agricultural League, 20
Reich Association of Jews in Germany, 64–66, 69, 71, 73
Reich Criminal Police Office (RKPA), 95, 156, 161
Reichenau, Walter von, 21, 30–31, 34
Reich Labor Service, 184
Reich Ministry for the Occupied Eastern Territories, 94, 106
Reich Ministry of Foreign Affairs, 63, 68
Reich Ministry of Health, 95
Reich Ministry of the Interior, 81–82
Reich Security Main Office (RSHA), 25–26, 31, 68, 95, 125, 137, 156
Reichstag, 68, 84
Reserve Police Battalion 13, 97
Rhineland, 149
Rhodesia, 66
Riga, 247, 265
Riga-Kaiserwald. *See* concentration camps

Ritter, Robert, 81, 95, 98–99, 110
Rohde, Friedrich Wilhelm, 99–102, 110
Roja, 46
Rolle, Curt, 99
Roma, 1, 4–5, 81–91, 94, 101, 106–109, 111, 270–271, 277. *See also* Porajmos; Sinti
Romania, 8, 67, 71, 87, 89, 148, 226
Rommel, Erwin, 70
Rosenberg, Alfred, 2, 21, 64, 94, 151
Roslavl, 43
Rostov-on-Don, 225, 231
Rundstedt, Gerd von, 31
Russia, 6–7, 41–43, 50, 54, 71, 219, 227–232, 273, 275. *See also* Soviet Union
Rzhev, 43

SA, 20
Sachsenhausen. *See* concentration camps
Sakrau, 44
Sauckel, Fritz, 181
Saunags, 46
Schmidt, Hans, 156
Schwede-Coburg, Franz, 149
SD, 23, 25–26, 105–106, 131, 200, 267. *See also* Einsatzgruppen
Sdroien, 46
Secret Field Police. *See* Wehrmacht
Shoigu, Sergei, 7
Schutzstaffel. *See* SS
Sebezh, 41–45, 54
Security Police, 19, 22–27, 31, 33, 41, 48, 102–103, 105, 111. *See also* Einsatzgruppen; Gestapo
Security Service. *See* SD
Serbia, 4, 19, 71, 84, 279
Shoah. *See* Holocaust
Siedlce, 21
Silesia, 41, 43, 71, 128, 275–276
Sinti, 1, 4–5, 81–83, 88–90, 94–110. *See also* Porajmos; Roma
Sloboda, 42
Slonim, 48, 54, 132, 202, 204, 268
Slovakia, 71–72, 87, 273. *See also* Czechoslovakia
Smolensk, 41–43, 47–50, 53, 271. *See also* ghetto, Jewish

Smorgonie, 50
Snyder, Timothy, 9, 272–273, 275
Sosnowiec, 45
South Africa, 66, 72
South African Union. *See* South Africa
Soviet Extraordinary State Commission (ChGK), 42, 161, 221–223
Soviet prisoners of war, 4–5, 48, 123–141, 180–181, 221–222, 227, 270. *See also* Red Army
Soviet Union, 2, 4–6, 19, 22–24, 31–32, 34–35, 41, 45, 47, 59–60, 64, 67–68, 86, 129, 132, 147, 149–152, 154, 161, 173, 175, 202, 219–221, 223–225, 227, 230–231, 235–239, 241–242, 245, 249–251, 265–266, 268–270, 273–274, 276, 278–280. *See also* Baltic States; Belarus; Estonia; Latvia; Lithuania; Moldova; Russia; Ukraine
Spain, 62, 67, 71
SS, 3–6, 17, 23–29, 32–33, 49–50, 52–54, 60, 68, 97, 108–109, 123–128, 130–131, 136, 139, 148–150, 157, 161, 173, 199–201, 204–210, 268, 270; SS Economics and Administration Main Office (WVHA), 135. *See also* Einsatzgruppen; SD; Waffen SS
Stalin, Joseph, 241–242, 273, 275, 278–279
Stalingrad, 19, 49, 105
Stavropol, 228
St. Petersburg. *See* Leningrad
Stralsund, 149
Strauß, Adolf, 25
Strohammer, Karl, 157
Stuckart, Wilhelm, 82
Stülpnagel, Carl von, 31–34
Sturmabteilung. See SA
Stuttgart, 132
Stutthof. *See* concentration camps
Sugihara, Chiune, 224
Surinam, 67
Sweden, 62, 71
Switzerland, 62, 71
Szálasi, Ferenc, 87

Taganrog, 225
Tangier, 66, 72
Tangiers. *See* Tangier
Tarnopol, 31
Tatars, 85–86
Theresienstadt. *See* concentration camps
Tiegenhof, 148–149
Tiso, Jozef, 87
Transylvania, 72
Treblinka. *See* extermination camps
Tripoli, 70
Trump, Donald, 9
Tunisia, 62–63, 65–66, 68, 70, 72
Turner, Harald, 84
Turkey, 67, 72

Ueckermünde, 149
Ukraine, 6–7, 31, 41, 95, 99, 101, 104–105, 110–111, 178, 226, 228–229, 242, 247, 251, 274–277, 279. *See also* Soviet Union
United Nations, 239, 252, 280
United States, 3, 65, 220, 231, 238–239, 241, 243, 246, 266, 278, 280
United States Holocaust Memorial Museum, 3, 220
Upper Silesia. *See* Silesia
Urban Police, 99, 101–103, 106
USSR. *See* Soviet Union
Ustaša, 87

Vallat, Xavier, 66
Velikie Luki, 44–45
Vienna, 128, 277
Vilnius, 44–45, 50, 71, 224, 240–241, 245, 249, 251. *See also* ghetto, Jewish
Vinnitsa, 151, 265
Vitebsk, 161
Vladivostok, 225
Volhynia, 94, 99, 102, 110–111
Vologda, 225

Waffen SS, 25, 27, 42, 47, 247, 249. *See also* SS
Wagner, Eduard, 24–26, 177
Walther, Gebhardt von, 70
Wannsee Conference, 59–64, 66–70
Warsaw, 42, 202, 275. *See also* ghetto, Jewish
Warsaw Pact, 236, 272
Warthegau, 42, 46–47, 71, 148–149. *See also* Poland

Wartheland. *See* Warthegau
Weber, Heinz, 206
Wehrmacht, 1, 4–6, 17, 19, 21–25, 27–28, 31–33, 35, 43, 45, 49, 51, 53, 83, 85, 98, 105, 108, 111, 124, 126–133, 136–137, 139, 141, 147–151, 155, 161, 173–189, 200, 203, 205, 229, 265, 270; High Command of the Wehrmacht (OKW), 18, 22, 125–127, 129, 131, 136–137, 176, 189, 203; Secret Field Police, 26–27, 150. *See also* Army Group Center; Army Group North; Army Group South; High Command of the Army (OKH)

Weichs, Maximilian von, 21, 34
Weizsäcker, Ernst von, 68
Westphalia, 132, 149
Widmann, Albert, 156–157, 161

Yaroslavl, 225
Yekaterinburg, 6
Young German League, 20
Yugoslavia, 71

Zapp, Paul, 68
Zolochov, 31
Zuroff, Efraim, 241–242

www.ingramcontent.com/pod-product-compliance
Lightning Source LLC
Chambersburg PA
CBHW071402300426
44114CB00016B/2149